Evangelical vs. Liberal

Evangelical vs. Liberal

*The Clash of Christian Cultures
in the Pacific Northwest*

JAMES K. WELLMAN JR.

OXFORD
UNIVERSITY PRESS

2008

OXFORD
UNIVERSITY PRESS

Oxford University Press, Inc., publishes works that further
Oxford University's objective of excellence
in research, scholarship, and education.

Oxford   New York
Auckland   Cape Town   Dar es Salaam   Hong Kong   Karachi
Kuala Lumpur   Madrid   Melbourne   Mexico City   Nairobi
New Delhi   Shanghai   Taipei   Toronto

With offices in
Argentina   Austria   Brazil   Chile   Czech Republic   France   Greece
Guatemala   Hungary   Italy   Japan   Poland   Portugal   Singapore
South Korea   Switzerland   Thailand   Turkey   Ukraine   Vietnam

Published by Oxford University Press, Inc.
198 Madison Avenue, New York, New York 10016

www.oup.com

Oxford is a registered trademark of Oxford University Press

Library of Congress Cataloging-in-Publication Data
Wellman, James K.
Evangelical vs. liberal : the clash of Christian cultures in the Pacific
Northwest / James K. Wellman, Jr.
    p. cm.
Includes bibliographical references and index.
ISBN 978-0-19-530011-6; 978-0-19-530012-3 (pbk.)
  1. Northwest, Pacific—Church history—20th century.   2. Evangelicalism—
Northwest, Pacific—History—20th century.   3. Conservatism—Religious
aspects—Christianity—History—20th century.   4. Liberalism
(Religion)—Northwest, Pacific—History—20th century.   5. Liberalism
(Religion)—Protestant churches—History—20th century.   I. Title:
Evangelical versus liberal.   II. Title.
BR550.W45 2008
280'.409795—dc22   2007034726

9 8 7 6 5 4 3 2 1

Printed in the United States of America
on acid-free paper

For Constance and Georgia, my two bright and shining morning stars

Acknowledgments

It is conventional wisdom for authors to say that their books could not have been completed without others, and this is no doubt true in this case. Many have enabled and made possible the writing of this book. Nonetheless, carrying the vision is something that comes from within and it is by and large a lonely task of showing others why it is important and must be done. I appreciate very much my editor's belief in the project and her guidance along the way. Cynthia Read is a strong and sure hand in this process and without her it would not have happened. Indeed, the staff at Oxford University has been a joy to work with, in particular, Daniel Gonzalez, Gwen Colvin, and my copyeditor, Renee Leath.

In the initial stages of the research, Jim Lewis at the Louisville Institute made the research possible through grants and encouragement. I was also helped by grants from the Religious Research Association as well as the Society for the Scientific Study of Religion, along with a grant from the Lilly Endowment for the "Religion by Region" study, led by Mark Silk at the The Leonard E. Greenberg Center for the Study of Religion in Public Life. In the process I contributed an essay on evangelicalism in the Pacific Northwest to a volume edited by Silk and Patricia Killen (2004). This spurred my interest in the topic and allowed me to begin to develop the data that I needed to produce this book.

Along the way, my graduate students and, in particular, Matthew Keyes were absolutely indispensable in collecting the enormous amount of data needed for the study. His passion, intelligence, and sheer drive made the experience more enjoyable, richer personally and intellectually. Rachael Morris and Charles Richter were also invaluable as research assistants, as was Katie Corcoran who helped me with interviews and with statistical analysis. As always, Heather Burger, the transcriber of my interview transcripts, was both precise and perspicuous in her work and comments. I am fortunate to work, teach, and do research at the University of Washington that offers me support with excellent students and colleagues, like my friend Martin Jaffee, who simultaneously keeps me thinking and laughing with his wit and wisdom, and Michael Williams whose institutional memory serves me well as chair of Comparative Religion, and whose sharp eye for detail has saved me more than once.

Finally, on the book itself, early readers of the manuscript were indispensable, including David Roozen, Lynne Baab, Jennifer McKinney, Matthew Keyes, Katie Corcoran, and finally and most importantly, Patricia Killen. Each offered important advice and edits along the way. In particular, Patricia read through the manuscript twice and commented on nearly every page. In light of these comments I rewrote the entire book. Thus, as always, I am responsible for the final product.

There were unexpected joys along the way. One was interviewing the leaders of these congregations. Many times, those outside churches fail to recognize the importance of pastoral leadership. Having been a pastor myself, few understand the enormous demands of this job that are mostly invisible and unseen, and thus unrecognized. But it is good work; the important work of caring for individuals, families, and those who have no one else to care. I admire these leaders and honor their service.

And finally, this book is dedicated to my two daughters. It is also a convention to thank one's family for sacrificing so that an author can finish a book. It implies a certain priority that I do not share. My family is my priority and no man or father could feel more blessed and privileged to have such lovely young Christian women as my daughters in his life—their stars inspire me daily. And I cannot finish without saying, that their mother, my partner, Annette, deserves most of the credit for helping them become who they are—no husband and father could feel more grateful.

Contents

12. The Spiritual Capital of Moral Worldviews, 271

    Notes, 285

    Bibliography, 291

    Index, 301

Prologue

Questions, Motivations, Purpose, and Plan

In March 2003, while visiting Venice, Florida, just after the U.S. invasion of Iraq, I walked past a Baptist church and witnessed a bold statement of evangelical support for the war. Along the sidewalk in front of the church, placards read "God Bless America," "Pray for Our Troops," and "Jesus, the Supreme Commander." This strong advocacy by evangelicals for state-sanctioned violence that confronts and deters what they perceive as "evil" was confirmed by a 2002 survey of 350 evangelical leaders by the Ethics and Public Policy Center, which found that 70 percent agreed that Islam "is a religion of violence," and 59 percent thought the United States should use military force against Iraq; 19 percent disagreed that force should be used.[1]

On October 31, 2004, two days before Election Day, George Regas, the Episcopal Rector Emeritus of All Saints Church in Pasadena, California—a liberal Protestant congregation—preached a sermon entitled "If Jesus Debated Senator Kerry and President Bush." On June 9, 2005, All Saints Church received a letter from the Internal Revenue Service questioning whether the church, because of the sermon, had violated its status as a nonprofit organization. Because of the nature of the sermon, the IRS said that the church had "implicitly opposed" one candidate (George W. Bush) and endorsed the other (John Kerry). The sermon eviscerated the Bush administration for its lack of concern for the poor and its warmongering—including Kerry in the critique and encouraging churchgoers to vote "their values."

This book comes from my attempt to wrestle with the internecine conflicts percolating in the American Protestant landscape. The dramatic rise of conservative Christians into the field of political power is a product not just of elites at the top, but of evangelicals at the grassroots level, advocating in their churches, and at times on their sidewalks, for the righteousness of their causes. While evangelicals have had some success, the voices of liberal Protestants have been, if not silenced, then at least muted in the public forum—and sometimes, as mentioned above, by organs of the government. It seems for many that the battle has been taken to a new level of intensity pitting liberal Protestants against evangelical Christians.

In this book I seek to get beneath the rhetoric and cut into the substance of these positions. I do an archaeological dig into the moral worldviews of evangelical and liberal Christians by asking these questions: What are the moral terrain and religious worldviews of American evangelicals and liberal Protestants? How are these worldviews created and sustained? How can one understand the putative "clash of cultures" between the two? This book makes clear that the clash of cultures is real between these groups, but not so simple. The moral worldviews of each of these movements share common structural features, though often reaching quite different conclusions. Moreover, in the process of analyzing the two moral worldviews I found myself seeing strengths and weaknesses in both and coming to a sometimes grudging respect for each of their perspectives. And, of course, I have my own perspective and motivations that I bring to this project.

In the late 1990s I proposed that my study of Fourth Presbyterian Church in Chicago, Illinois, was a counterexample of liberal Protestant decline. Fourth Presbyterian, when I finished the research in 1998, had nearly three thousand members; in 2006, it had more than five thousand members and it was continuing to grow. It was a liberal Protestant megachurch; a church with more than two thousand people attending worship on Sundays. I concluded that churches other than strict evangelical congregations could and would thrive in the American religious market. Fourth Presbyterian was fortunate to be in a dynamic and thriving metropolitan hub, not far from an impoverished African American community, whom they assisted through a tutoring program serving more than four hundred African American young people. The leadership of the church, clergy and lay, established a strong identity, an intellectually stimulating message of hope, and a challenging call of service to those left out and left behind. I argued in *The Gold Coast Church and the Ghetto* (Wellman 1999b) that the church neither advocated for systematic changes in the social inequality of Chicago's economic life nor in the system of American market capitalism, but in the midst of an aging and evolving Protestant establishment congregation, the congregation exercised the principle of noblese oblige. Class privilege in this sense was not dislodged; the ritual life of the congregation practiced an elite aesthetic format of music and the arts. The aesthetic tastes and preferences of upper-middle-class Anglo American culture were celebrated, embraced, and reproduced. Thus, I contended that the church duplicated the system of class culture, but mitigated the effects of this inequality by reaching out to those with less with programs and opportunities for young African Americans to advance themselves economically and socially.

When my family left Chicago and moved back to Seattle, it was a homecoming of sorts. My spouse and I had been raised in the area, and we both had been nurtured in a moderate form of American evangelicalism. We had been away for nearly sixteen years, leaving behind the Pacific Northwest (PNW)[2] and our young adult evangelical faith. My research and writing on Fourth Presbyterian was more than a professional affair; I served the congregation as a part-time minister and so it was a form of intense participant observation. In coming home to live in the PNW and to teach at the University of Washington, I immediately began to research vital liberal Protestant churches on the West Coast. My assumption was that the West Coast, generally known for its liberal or at least libertarian culture, would be a natural breeding ground for growing liberal Protestant congregations. I received grants to study twelve congregations up and down the West Coast. But to my surprise, I could find few liberal churches that were actually growing, financially or in membership. Eventually, twelve congregations emerged. None of these were megachurches like Fourth Presbyterian. Indeed, I limited my criteria of liberal vitality to churches that had maintained or at least come close to maintaining their membership and their financial levels over three years. I also sought out churches that had a sustained and distinct institutional identity led by a stable core of leaders, clergy and lay.

The twelve liberal Protestant churches I chose were dynamic and spiritually rich congregations. When I examined the spiritual practices of the leaders and laypeople, it underlined that this was a complex mélange of personal experience, creative interaction with the Christian tradition, and an innovative reformulation of what it meant to be a Christian in a modern and secular culture (Wellman 2002). Nonetheless, my difficulty in discovering vital liberal Protestant churches made me wonder why, in a region known for its progressive politics, there were so few thriving liberal Protestant churches? Moreover, in the process of my investigation, I stumbled across a veritable bouquet of thriving evangelical churches. This piqued my interest, both because of my own background, and also because it surprised me that in an "unchurched" region, known for its secularity, it was the Protestant evangelicals who were flourishing. This discovery was precisely the seed for the present book, comparing vital liberal and evangelical congregations in an open religious market, explaining and understanding their strengths and how they interact and compete with each other. This volume answers the question of how these two disparate types of Christianity and the moral worldviews they create and inhabit respond to the region, to each other, and to the wider American culture and politics.[3]

The plan of this book then is a comparative study of Pacific Northwest Christian subcultures. Readers who want to go right to the story and analysis of this study can skip the context, theory, and methodology elaborated in part I and read part II. In part I I explain the history and conditions of these American Protestant subcultures in the twentieth century. I argue that the traditional scholarly convention of a two-party system in American Protestantism tends to be overdetermined—correctly identifying that differences exist among Protestants but missing both the similarities in cultural processes and the diversity of opinion among American Protestantism. White evangelicals and liberal Protestants are two powerful American religious subcultures; they are among many that compete and battle for followers in American culture generally, and in the PNW specifically. Nonetheless, white evangelicals and liberal Protestants represent subcultures that affect American culture and politics, and so the manner in which they are formed and interact with each other is an important aspect of understanding the American cultural landscape and the PNW. I then offer my own definition and theory of religious moral worldviews that I use to describe, examine, and explain the religious moral worldviews of these two religious subcultures. I place these groups in the context of the PNW and begin to show how and why they grow or decline based in part on distinctive regional characteristics. The final section of part I gives the reader a sense of my method and the landscape of the data.

Part II invites the reader into the moral worldviews of these two subcultures. I put these two worlds into conversation and critique of each other on five separate dimensions of their religious moral worldviews: identity and moral logic; ideology and belief; ritual and organizational dynamics; outreach and mission, and, finally, religion and politics. Throughout this part of the analysis I examine how each creates and sustains its moral worldviews and how each sees the other—as each critiques and not uncommonly distorts the other's views—as well as, on rare occasions, finds common ground. The purpose of this analysis is to show the power of religious moral worldviews, and, in particular, how they work and function in a specific regional context. Most important, I put up a mirror to these two groups for their own examination as well as for outsiders who wish to understand the inner workings of these groups. My hope as a scholar is to expand mutual understanding, not simply to encourage a bland tolerance or create a false consensus, but to inspire respect for differing truth claims. In this sense, agreement is not necessary, but the understanding of difference and the recognition of strongly held moral convictions, I would argue, is important.

In part III I summarize how my theory of religious moral worldviews explains why these two groups grow or decline in the PNW, and what this analysis offers for an understanding of the PNW and of wider American religion. I end part III by describing how my mind has changed about these groups after spending a great deal of time with these data and the writing of the book. In this sense, scholarship is a moral enterprise—where one seeks to tell the truth about one's data, explain it as clearly as one can, listen to it and, on occasion, allow it to change one's mind. In this sense, I invite the reader into this same moral enterprise—to read carefully and listen to the moral worldviews of these two groups, and then make up her or his own mind.

PART I

Religion and Moral Worldviews in American Protestantism

I

The Shape of American Protestantism

The number of liberal Protestants has been in decline over the last
generation. Indeed, Protestant denominations in general, which include liberals and moderates, have lost anywhere from 30 to 40
percent of their membership (Roof and McKinney 1987; Hadaway
and Roozen 1995). What is less well known is that American Protestantism as a whole has lost its share of the American populace.
In 1993, the percentage of Protestants in the U.S. population was a
little more than 63 percent; in 2002 the percentage of Protestants was
approximately 56 percent. And depending on one's calculations, demographers have suggested that soon Protestants will no longer be
the majority religion in the United States (Smith and Kim 2004).
The reasons for this change are in part due to the fact that more and
more individuals are raised without a religion, increasing from 13 percent in 1973 to 29 percent in 1994 (Smith and Kim 2004, 8). Moreover, the number of Protestants who retain their faith has shrunk in
the 1990s from 90 percent (between 1973 and 1993) to 83 percent
in 2002. The decrease is particularly dramatic among young people
(Smith and Kim 2004, 9), and is occurring as well among evangelical
Protestants, though it is less pronounced (Smith and Denton 2005).
The general trends show some signs of leveling off. Nevertheless,
immigration accentuates the downward decline—while 10 percent of
the adult population is immigrant, only 24 percent of immigrant
adults come from a Protestant background. Thus, over the long term,
the trends show at least the potential for a continuing, slow decline.[1]

While the overall decline of mainline Protestantism is well documented, there are also increasingly diverse subcultures within the overall Protestant population. Robert Wuthnow's path-breaking work (1988) analyzed the "restructuring" of American Protestantism into categories of "liberal" and "conservative" over the second half of the twentieth century. The social and political issues of the 1960s and 1970s polarized Protestants. John Green (2004) has recently differentiated this polarization with empirical data, showing differences not only between mainline and evangelical Protestant groups but within them. He distinguishes mainline Protestants, evangelical Protestants, and Catholics by traditionalist, centrist, and modernist ideological categories, delineating political affiliations relative to them. Mainline Protestants, which compose 16 percent of the whole, are divided as traditionalists (4.3), centrists (7), and modernists (4.7). The political partisanship of these groups correlates to what I found in my study: modernist mainline Protestants (or "liberals" for this study) are affiliated with the Democratic Party by a margin of 2 to 1; and liberal Protestants share this same political affiliation with black Protestants, modernists Catholics, American Jews, atheists, and agnostics. This creates a politically like-minded group of approximately 23 percent of Americans. Green divides evangelical Protestants, who are 26.3 percent of the total American religious landscape, as traditionalists (12.6), centrists (10.8), and modernists (2.9). Evangelical traditionalists and centrists are affiliated with the Republican Party by similar proportions as liberal Protestants are to the Democratic Party. Evangelical traditionalists share the same partisan loyalties with the traditionalist Protestant mainline and traditionalist Catholics, creating a common political coalition of approximately 22 percent. The churches in my study can be situated along these same partisan lines; the evangelical churches are in the traditionalist and centrist evangelical tradition, mainly supporting the Republican Party, with the modernist or liberal Protestant churches showing a preference for the Democratic Party.

Labels are never perfect, but for convenience's sake, when I use the word *liberal* (liberal Christian or liberal religionist) from now on, I am referring to liberal Protestants, as I define them in the next paragraph (Wellman 2002). The meaning of this term for the most part is a theological perspective, but as will become clear, this group also tends to be loyal to the Democratic Party and to progressive politics generally. When I use the word *evangelical* (conservative Christian or conservative religionist), which I will define more thoroughly below, I mean evangelical Protestants. This is a theological identification but, again, it will become clear that this most often also refers to a political affiliation with the Republican Party. Further, the evangelicals in this study tend to be "entrepreneurial" evangelicals (Wellman 2004). Entrepreneurial evangelicals reflect the theological mentality of evangelicals generally but tend to be more aggressive in evangelism and church growth specifically. I am aware that there can be evangelicals in liberal congregations and liberals in evangelical churches, as well as both in Catholic parishes, but in this study I focus on Protestant congregations. Moreover, in my data, I found few if any evangelicals or liberals in churches that did not reflect their theological perspectives.

For this study, the liberal Protestant congregations are defined by a distinct set of ideological characteristics. They most often propose that Jesus is a model of radical inclusiveness—fashioning an ethic that emphasizes hospitality to those marginalized in society—justify themselves in their faith tradition as much by reason as by tradition or scripture, and leave decision making about faith or personal morality in the responsible hands of the individual. The moral worldview of these churches reflects a liberal theology that advocates for the concerns and rights of homosexuals; and supports justice causes such as peace, ending homelessness, and ecological stewardship. Even as the liberal moral worldview tends toward libertarianism in personal morality, it proffers stands on social justice and broader support for the "common good" (Wellman 1999a, 2002; Ammerman 1997, 2005).

Nonetheless, listing the characteristics of liberal Protestants tends to miss the complexity of this religious identity. My interviews with nearly 450 liberals and evangelicals from 34 vital churches in the PNW illustrate the complexity with which evangelicals and liberals negotiate their religious identities. In particular, remarks by liberal respondents disclose the nuance and personal struggle that often marked many of their comments. Liberal Protestant laypeople, even when they came from churches that were vital and that they loved, consistently struggled with how to define themselves, as an Oregon layperson shared while discussing his congregational church:

> I struggle sometimes with the noncreedal aspects of our church; I'm like a little bit of a box with loose edges on it, more than perhaps some of the people here. And I think that from this question, as well as some of the other ones, that one of the difficulties in not having that box is it does become very difficult to describe who we are. It makes it very difficult to take stands on things. Because I would think in some ways people might say "We'll take the more liberal, the more progressive stand," but I think we often avoid taking stands on things because we really have a "y'all come with all your opinions and bring it into the melting pot" [attitude]. But when I'm outside the church trying to describe who we are, or to defend who we are, depending on what that is, it becomes very difficult to articulate that.

I also think that not having a creed or a set of beliefs, that other
people are telling us, not that it has to be creedal, I think there are
ways that that can happen and it does happen at other churches that
many of us have left, is that if we say you can believe anything, we
also can say you can believe nothing and there's some danger in that.

Indeed, liberals are often known more for what they are not—*not* fundamentalists; *not* homophobic; *not* patriarchal—than for their positive characteristics. And, as the Congregationalist layperson explains, this liberal tendency
to accept difference, combined with the fear of creating an offense, undercuts
liberals' ability to take stands on some issues such as the Iraq War and on issues
of economic justice. Nonetheless, as I detail in this volume, each of the liberal
churches in this study has taken definitive stands as church organizations on
the support of gay and lesbian people. This relative diffidence is, in part, a
refusal to form a false consensus; liberals seek to avoid conformism and will
leave individuals with the task of making up their own minds. The unintended
consequence of this liberal reticence, as many lay liberals make clear, weakens
their ability to mobilize for principles close to their faith. Tellingly, the comments of the layperson above came from a church whose pastor I found to be
articulate on theological principles and on issues of social justice. Thus, the
ability of liberal churches to negotiate ambiguity and refuse simple answers is
institutionally both its strength and its ongoing weakness.

The natural question, in light of the decline of liberal Protestants and
mainline Protestants in general, is what about the growth of American evangelicalism? Many have suggested explanations, including moral and theological strictness (Iannaccone 1994), engagement with the larger culture (Smith
1998), superior forms of religious rewards, as well as the intense push for
evangelization and church development (Finke and Stark 1992). There is also,
however, striking quantitative data that invites further elaboration. Evangelical
families had higher rates of fertility than mainline denominational families
during the first half of the twentieth century, as well as higher retention rates of
their young people in their churches (Hoge et al. 1993, 1994). To some extent
this advantage leveled off with the baby boom generation of the midcentury,
but then continued after the peak of the baby boom. This evangelical boom in
fertility and in the retention of their children and youth in their churches has
created a formidable advantage for American evangelicals that continues into
the twenty-first century (Hout, Greeley, and Wilde 2001, 497; Greeley and
Hout 2006).

In fact, Hout, Greeley, and Wilde make the claim that ideology or engagement with culture has nothing to do with the growth of evangelicals in the

twentieth century. Evangelical advantage is purely "demographic." But as this volume shows, the growth of evangelical churches is at least due in part to the intense ideological focus on the family. Organizationally, evangelical ministries encourage fertility and lionize the nuclear family, and spend enormous resources on buildings and facilities for families. So, yes, demographics are an important factor. But is human reproduction unaffected by ideology? Forty-three percent of evangelical respondents in my study came from nonevangelical backgrounds, meaning they were invited or evangelized into these evangelical churches. Evangelicals in this study preach, practice, and promote the production of children and the reproduction of faith in children and youth. I found a high priority placed on children and family ministries in all twenty-four evangelical churches that I studied. In one urban Oregon church, the emphasis and focus on children for newly married women was a constant drumbeat. One new member described how she is asked at every church gathering of women whether she is planning on having children. For her, this was not an offense, but a sign that becoming a mother is a high priority:

> And also kind of the feeling of just maybe motherhood is this elevated calling—kind of like you're better because you're a mom, or what not. To me it's like a little bit of the church's reaction to our culture, which for the past thirty years or so has said that you're better if you work outside the home and to me it feels like our church's response to that is like a little bit to the other extreme and maybe a little more balance might...and I really appreciated when [our pastor] spoke about this topic. I think he was speaking about the roles of women and he said a lot of women come to him and say is it wrong for a woman to work outside the home and he said the question isn't Is it wrong for a woman to do that? the question is Why is she doing that? Is she doing that because the husband is lazy and won't provide, well then, yeah, it is wrong because he should be doing it. But if she's doing it because that's what fits for her family and she's able to and it's the best fit for them and what God wants them to do, then there's nothing wrong with that. And I think for me that was really freeing, especially I feel like I'm one of the few married-without-kids women at our church. So it was just really freeing to hear that from the pulpit, that now that I'm married my role isn't solely to have kids and be at home. I'm just not in a place where I'm ready for that.

In response to queries about children, this young woman sought out the pastor for guidance. But the response was just as interesting as the question.

The young pastor conditioned his response by first wondering why she would not have children—perhaps because her husband could not provide for the family adequately. Of course, if the woman felt it was her call to work outside the home, then that was okay. The implication is that it is better to have mothers stay at home and that this should be made possible by the earning power of the husband. The young woman celebrates this trend; the strong focus on family is a countercultural message that emphasizes the importance of motherhood in an urban setting, which ordinarily caters to young, single, professional men and women. Motherhood, in her mind, was something that was "elevated" in status by the church. Indeed, in another part of the interview of this urban, Oregon focus group, a young woman proudly asserted that church focus on bearing children bucks cultural stereotypes: "It's not the typical Gen X, wait until you're forty to have your first kid." So demographics make a difference, but an ideology of reproduction, whether in terms of evangelization or in bearing young children, also permeates evangelical culture.

Evangelicals have a symbolic and socialization reproduction advantage as well; studies examining the retention rates of evangelicals versus liberals make this clear (Hout, Greeley, and Wilde 2001; Hoge, Johnson, and Luidens 1994). Socialization is about ideology; it is a symbolic system (a worldview that I develop in this study) that is internalized and becomes the engine of repro- duction, facilitating fertility and nurturing specific cultural and moral values and actions. Thus, American evangelical Christians both produce more kids and maintain their children within their churches. Furthermore, ideologically, evangelicals no longer appeal primarily to the lower-middle class. In educa- tional and in socioeconomic terms, evangelicals have made recent gains in these areas and are nearly equal to the Protestant mainline and the Roman Catholic churches (Smith 2000; Greeley and Hout 2006). As I will show in this study, nearly a third of the fastest growing congregations in Washing- ton and Oregon are Pentecostal and charismatic churches—congregations that have traditionally attracted the American lower-middle class. However, I found that these congregations are now appealing to middle- and upper-middle-class individuals and families. Indeed, it is the Pentecostal churches in the study that stood most firmly in the "prosperity gospel" tradition.[2] As I have said, I use *evangelical* in this study as the overarching term for conservative Protestant church-goers, to include Pentecostal and charismatic Christians as well as Christians in the American fundamentalist tradition. I will explain shortly the history and relations of these various evangelical groups to one another.

The changes in the overall makeup of Protestantism have had significant effects on mainline Protestant churches. The rate of transfer from evangelical churches to mainline churches has dropped to its lowest level in the last decade, falling from 21 percent to only 9 percent, with no signs of any significant reversal. What makes this trend even more important is that demographers have found that "the trend toward staying in conservative denominations is strongest among the rising numbers of upwardly mobile conservatives" (Hout, Greeley, and Wilde 2001, 498). Thus, the stereotype of evangelicals being less educated or coming from the lower classes hits an inverse relation. In fact, evangelical churches are becoming attractive to those who affiliate with them precisely because of the churches' socioeconomic advantages, as my study reflects and as new research has shown; evangelicals have now entered the elite levels of American society in business, government, education, and even in Hollywood (Lindsay 2007). It is an ironic twist on H. Richard Niebuhr's early twentieth century complaint in his classic *The Social Sources of Denominationalism* (1975), which condemned mainline Protestants for catering to the wealthy. In the twenty-first century, as the mainline Protestant denominational churches have lost some of their class distinctions, evangelical churches are now becoming beacons of middle- and upper-middle-class status. Niebuhr's archcondemnation of class-structured denominationalism is striking:

> Denominationalism in the Christian Church is such an unacknowledged hypocrisy. . . . It represents the accommodation of Christianity to the caste-system of human society. It carries over into the organization of the Christian principle of brotherhood the prides and prejudices, the privilege and prestige, as well as the humiliations and abasements, the injustices and inequalities of that specious order of high and low wherein men find the satisfaction of the craving for vainglory. The division of the churches closely follows the division of men into the castes of national, racial, and economic groups. It draws the color line in the church of God; it fosters the misunderstandings, the self-exaltations, the hatreds of jingoistic nationalism by continuing in the body of Christ the spurious differences of provincial loyalties; it seats the rich and poor apart at the table of the Lord, where the fortunate may enjoy the bounty they have provided while the others feed upon the crusts their poverty affords. (6)

Niebuhr, along with many commentators at that time, assumed that American fundamentalism had lost the denominational battle. He grieved and denounced the fact that mainline Protestants simply catered to class interests. Indeed, scholarship has traditionally observed that fundamentalists appealed to the poor and uneducated. This was often a critique as much as an observation (Berger 1961; Winter 1961). It is ironic then, for multiple reasons, that the revenge of the evangelical success is its new class status. It is worth exploring, therefore, which I do at the end of this book, how American evangelicals, as a significant American subculture, are challenging mainline Protestantism as the center of the Protestant orb in American culture. To what degree are evangelical churches seeking to become what the Protestant mainline establishment church was in the 1950s? As this study makes clear, they have become a significant subculture with numbers, growth, and the desire to shape moral norms and to impact American political culture.

The decline of liberal Protestantism is real, demographic, and, I would argue, ideologically shaped. It is well known that American culture has moved in a conservative direction (at least ideologically) over the last decade (Lakoff 1996; Fogel 2000). Despite countervailing examples (Wellman 1999a; Ammerman 2005), liberal Protestantism is struggling to maintain and reproduce itself. Its message deemphasizes the supernatural aspects of religious experience and emphasizes inclusion and justice for sexual minorities and women. While it is responding to a niche in the American religious marketplace, its ability to reproduce itself appears limited biologically, organizationally, and symbolically. Whether this limitation is an intentional process or an unintended consequence of its theology and demographic realities is a part of the question of this study.

2

The Origins of the American Evangelical Subculture

Estimates of the numbers of evangelicals in America vary dramatically, from fifteen to twenty-five million adults by evangelical demographers and scholars, to 100 million by various contemporary commentators (Noll 2001; Baylor Religion Survey 2006).[1] Data that comes from the American Religious Identification Survey (ARIS) show that when adult Americans are asked to self-identify, 25 percent claim to be evangelical.[2] I follow ARIS estimates of evangelical self-identification in part because its figures are relatively conservative. Even so, the ARIS numbers translate into a substantial American evangelical subculture of approximately fifty million American adults.

When I use the term *evangelical* I am aware that evangelicals exist outside of Protestant churches and affiliate with diverse political parties. This is to say, evangelicals attend nondenominational churches, traditional evangelical denominations, Pentecostal and charismatic churches, and sometimes mainline Protestant and Catholic congregations. But again, for this study I focus on evangelical Protestants who present a relatively homogenous political orientation. In defining the term *evangelical* I follow Bebbington (1989) and Noll (2001) in using *evangelical* as the umbrella term for conservative Christians in American culture. Evangelicals are generally those who emphasize *conversion* (the need for a personal decision to follow Jesus Christ), *missionary activity* (the obligation to share with others this need for conversion), *biblicism* (seeing the Scriptures as the sole authority for belief and action), and *crucicentrism* (the belief in

Christ's sacrifice on the cross as atonement for human sin). As I explain further below, the river of this evangelical subculture has multiple tributaries: early twentieth-century American fundamentalism; the growth and development of Pentecostalism and the charismatic movement; and the rise of neo-evangelicalism at mid-century, and the subsequent growth of nondenominational churches and parachurch organizations. All of these contribute to the recent surge of the entrepreneurial evangelical congregations; churches that are much less sectarian than their predecessors and much more engaged in transforming American culture and influencing American political culture with a form of civil religion, which I define below as a "civic gospel." I outline the three main tributaries of present-day evangelicalism as fundamentalism, Pentecostalism, and neo-evangelicalism. I then define the civic gospel evangelicals tend to embody.

1. Fundamentalists

Under this broad category of evangelicalism, I place American fundamentalists. Fundamentalism is an early twentieth-century movement in American Christianity. From the position of American mainline Protestants, the fundamentalists "lost" the battle over the Bible with the Scopes Trial in 1926 (Marsden 1982). Fundamentalists separated from mainline American Protestantism and went "underground" to build their own social, educational, and religious infrastructure. As scholars have shown, from the 1920s to the 1950s fundamentalists were, in fact, far from defeated, but established their own growing subculture even as the mainline began its slow decline. Classically, fundamentalists have been labeled as "antimodernists" and even "belligerents" against modern life (Riesebrodt 1993; Lawrence 1995). Fundamentalists, partially in response to rejection by mainstream society, adopted a sectarian strategy creating their own plausibility structures and moral worldviews. However, Joel Carpenter, in *Revive Us Again: The Reawakening of American Fundamentalism* (1997) avoids the reification of American fundamentalist groups by showing their development and diversity within American Protestant subcultures. Fundamentalism has always been a dynamic and fragmented collection of groups with diverse responses to modernity. Thus, the lines of religion, culture, and modernity are much more porous and fluid than portrayed by scholars attempting to generalize about the field.

In this study, fundamentalists are represented by traditional evangelical denominations, and independent and nondenominational churches. None of the churches that I studied could be labeled as particularly belligerent or antimodernist. They do not reject modern culture per se; indeed, they criticize and condemn parts of the values of modern life, but they often use the fruits of modernism (technology and media, for example) to promote their messages. Indeed, they use modern technology with greater aplomb than their liberal Protestant cohorts. Moreover, if modernism is defined as the differentiation of social spheres, the rationalization of social processes and structures, and the development of market capitalism, so-called fundamentalists have accommodated to this movement quite effectively. They lionize a market mentality economically and religiously—seeking to expand their economic resources and at the same time taking advantage of open religious markets—particularly in the unchurched region of the PNW. Moreover, the fundamentalist concentration on personal agency as the vehicle of salvation accommodates the individualism and compartmentalization of the modern mentality. If anything, these churches show an affinity for the structures and processes of modernity.

Thus, the early sectarian nature of fundamentalism was more a necessary reaction to the rejection by mainline American culture. What is seen in the history of these churches is that they are quite willing to use the products of modernity to facilitate their movement. And with greater demographic success, they become less sectarian and much more willing to accommodate the wider culture and engage this culture with their message. In this sense, modernity is, in fact, not a barrier but indeed an instrument and facilitator of their development.

2. Pentecostals and Charismatics

The second grouping under the wider American evangelical movement are Pentecostal and charismatic churches. These churches have their origins in the early parts of the twentieth century, coming out of emotionally charged revivals such as the Azusa Street Revival in 1906, and spreading from California across the nation and the globe by entrepreneurial men and women preachers (Carpenter 1997; Wacker 2001; Jenkins 2003). These churches emphasized a democratization of the spirit, cooperating with nineteenth-century American populism and extending access to the "spirit" to include all ethnic groups, men and women, and every socioeconomic class (Hatch 1989). The movement showed that all could be called by the Spirit to exercise their gifts for ministry, healing, and evangelism. This early charismatic social movement took on denominational form relatively quickly. The Assemblies of God was formed in 1914; the predominantly white Pentecostal Church of God in 1919; and in the same period the Black Pentecostal denomination, the Church of God in Christ, was created. The racial integration of early Pentecostalism lasted into the early 1920s, but was largely undermined by the implementation of Jim Crow laws in the South. This "triumph of the spirit" embodied many of the same characteristics of early fundamentalist churches, emphasizing the Bible as the infallible word of God, the necessity of conversion to Christ, and the need for believers to evangelize, but adding to these factors the subjective and affective experiences of spiritual experience. The story is long and complex, but the "charisma of the spirit" did not end with Protestant Pentecostals but spread to the Roman Catholic churches in the 1960s and to the broader Protestant churches at the end of the century. In a recent Pew Forum Survey, 18 percent of all American Christians claim some form of "charismatic experience," many more than the 3 percent of Americans who affiliate with a Pentecostal denomination.[3] In this sense, labels come to be less meaningful in defining Christian experience at the end of the twentieth century.[4]

A third of the evangelical churches in my study came out of the broad charismatic movement. In these churches I saw both the greatest integration of ethnic groups and the clearest signs of rising class markers and an emphasis on the "prosperity" gospel. Ethnic integration *and* prosperity (spiritual and material) are taken as signs of God's blessing. The best illustration of this trend was the Pentecostal college group on my own university campus. It was one of the most ethnically diverse groups on campus, and had been intentional about being a multicultural leadership group. One lay leader said, "The faces of the leaders must represent the world." This young woman is African American; the six focus group members included one other African American, a young Hispanic man, and three Anglo Americans. It was by far the most ethnically diverse group among the twenty-four evangelical churches that I studied. The group was articulate and relatively progressive on issues of race and gender—speaking up for racial integration and women in ministerial leadership, supporting the Iraq War, and touting sexual Puritanism and other strong conservative Christian beliefs. These young people were ambitious about their faith and about their lives. One wanted to be a doctor so that she could take her skills into mission fieldwork, and several others wanted to go into public service. The pre-med student was a clear proponent of the "prosperity" gospel. For her, it was self-evident that "God, like any good father, would bless his children with material prosperity." For her there was no contradiction whatsoever between spiritual and material blessings—one led naturally to the other. Related to this was the fact that the respondents from the charismatic churches in my study expressed much less tension with the broader culture. The entrepreneurial nature of the PNW, a wide open market both economically and religiously, creates a natural affinity for these Christians with broad ambitions for evangelism and material wealth. Indeed, the charismatic churches appeal to northwesterners precisely because of the churches' emphasis on diversity, wealth creation, and individual initiative interwoven with a worship style that engages the body as well as the mind.

The University of Washington charismatic college group meets midweek, and the worship services include contemporary rock music that can similarly be heard in all the evangelical congregations in the study. But this group also includes the traditional Pentecostal practice of speaking in tongues, or glossolalia, whereby young men and women voice semantically random syllables that are believed to be God speaking to the church, and that traditionally call for interpretation by those with the gift of discernment. The group's services also call for spontaneous healing and expectations for miracles. In 2006 this fellowship of college-aged young people had nearly one thousand students in attendance. The young, charismatic preacher wore expensive casual shirts, he drove an expensive automobile, and flaunted his spouse (baby in tow), who was also young, attractive, and dressed in impressive but casual clothing. The Pentecostal preacher's message, recapitulating many of the themes among the clergy in my study, focused on the Scriptures, emphasized social conservativism (abstention from premarital sex; against homosexuality), celebrated a market mentality (emphasizing growth economically and evangelism for the church), and was laced by a strong support of the Iraq War (though, as he said, this was an "aside"). In fact, he mocked groups that he saw marching for peace. He said, "If we don't fight the terrorists over there, they will be coming to get us over here. And the first people they will shoot are those peace activists." This drew an approving shout from the crowd of young students.

The overall message of this Pentecostal college service in content and in style communicated that the good news of the gospel blessed one eternally, and also showered one with blessings in this life—sanctioning a conservative and politically powerful American state. This movement from fundamentalist, sectarian, and Pentecostal roots to a generic charismatic, entrepreneurial, evangelistic, and sometimes prosperity-based evangelicalism catches the broader dynamics of the entrepreneurial evangelical churches in my study. The evangelical churches in the PNW are enthused by an open religious market that coincides with a region that is entrepreneurial and unchurched. Nonetheless, many evangelical churches are in tension with the libertarian spirit of the region. The evangelical moral worldview grates against a region that authorizes the power of the individual to make up his or her own mind on moral values, actions, and projects. The moral message of personal purity chafes against what evangelicals interpret as a morally "permissive" spirit.[5]

3. Neo-Evangelicalism

The broader contemporary American evangelical culture of conservative Christianity has multiple sources in the American Protestant religious land- scape. This range includes the early fundamentalists and the Bible-based and nondenominational churches that flow from that stream; Pentecostal and charismatic variants that echo in the Calvary chapels and Vineyard "spirit"-led movements coming from California (Miller 1997); and less powerful though important sources that arise from the Holiness movements coming out of the Wesleyan stream of piety and sanctification. And finally, though less central to my study, this group includes the Christian Reformed movement, which is theologically and socially less conservative compared with the evangelical churches in my study. I intentionally left out the African American Christian movement. It is evangelical and conservative in theology but quite progressive on economic and some social issues. In particular, African American Chris- tians have come out overwhelmingly against the Iraq War (Baylor Study 2006), thus making them distinct from white evangelicals (on political issues) and liberal Protestants (for theological reasons) in this study (Greeley and Hout 2006).

The etiology of the contemporary white evangelical movement comes out of the 1950s in response to the sectarian and isolationist nature of early fun- damentalism and Pentecostalism. Moderate neo-evangelicals like Harold J. Ockenga, pastor of Park Street Church in Boston and first president of the National Association of Evangelicals (1942), sought not only to nurture deep evangelical piety but to evangelize American secular society and to go out in mission to the world. In this sense "engagement" became the linchpin that activated the movement to transform and evangelize "secular society" at mid- century (Carpenter 1997; Smith 1998; Hunter 1987). The most visible figure in the movement was Billy Graham. Graham was raised a fundamentalist. Early in his ministry he encountered conflict with fundamentalist leaders precisely because of his willingness to work with mainline Protestant congregations and to engage the wider American public. This broader neo-evangelical movement was symbolized and nurtured by such magazines as *Christianity Today* (1956) and schools such as Fuller Theological Seminary (1947). They each maintained a distinctive set of evangelical beliefs—the infallibility of scripture, the need for conversion, the blood atonement of Christ, and the call for world evangelism. However, they were intentionally *not* sectarian—seeking in the classical biblical framework to be "in the world but not of it." In part, this shift signaled a movement away from a premillennialist pessimism about the condition of the present world situation toward a renewal of the postmillennial hope for world evangelism. The quintessential example of this evangelical movement was the parachurch organizations, exemplified by Graham's leadership of Youth for Christ (1944), as well as other groups such as Young Life (1941) and World Vision (1950). These organizations concentrated on youth ministry, world missions, and service to those in need around the world. They embodied the willingness to move outside traditional denominational and institutional restraints, to use popular culture for the sake of "reaching" and serving a lost generation of young people. The disdain of, and perhaps more aptly, indifference to denominational structures percolates across the evangelical churches in my study. Most of these congregations are either unwilling or uninterested to name a denominational connection and are frequently loosely networked with broader evangelical movements. Contemporary exemplars of this movement include Rick Warren's Saddleback Church and his Purpose Driven Church Conferences, and Bill Hybels's Willow Creek Community Church and the Willow Creek Association that trains church leaders from across the globe (Sargeant 2000). In both cases, denominational affiliations are downplayed (Warren comes from a Southern Baptist background), and evangelical commonalities are emphasized.

4. Evangelicalism and the Civic Gospel

The political activism of the broader evangelical movement at the end of the twentieth century has been a surprise to many. The rise of American fundamentalism in the 1910s rejected the social reform movement of the social gospel as a liberal accommodation (Marsden 1982; Evans 2004). Fundamentalism built a strong grassroots network that was led initially by northerners, but blossomed in southern soil. The southernization of the national evangelical movement was accomplished by immigration. By 1970 more than 75 million southerners had gone north and west to establish evangelical enclaves outside the South (Dochuk 2005; Harvey 2005). Tellingly, the majority of the evangelical senior ministers from my PNW study trained at midwestern Bible colleges and seminaries, and many of these schools have southern roots (Carpenter 1997). In the aftermath of the civil rights movement, white southerners turned to the Republican Party, forming the grassroots of the Christian Right (Wilcox 2000). This movement sought not only salvation of souls but it also expanded its early moral conservatism and anticommunism to a broader social, economic, and political platform, aligning a conversionist impulse with a free enterprise culture to expand the domain of Christ and commerce

(Carpenter 1997; Marsden 1982). Finally, the prominence of southerners in the military knitted together evangelicalism with the American military, producing what we now note as the strong support of evangelicals for America's military goals and the vision of the United States as a "beacon" of democracy and freedom in foreign policy (Loveland 1996; Martin 1999; Marsden 2006; Wellman 2007).

In the 1970s, following the loss of Bible reading and prayer from schools in the 1960s, and with the passage of *Roe v. Wade* in 1973, the public muscle of the evangelical grassroots movement awakened. Its public power was exemplified in the presidential elections of 2000 and 2004 (Green 2004). Moreover, evangelicals have come to believe that engagement in public debate is part of what it means to be a faithful Christian. In surveys, American evangelicals believe their faith informs their politics by a nearly two to one margin relative to mainline Protestants, and they are by similar proportions more committed to "transforming" society than are mainline Protestants. Furthermore, more than 90 percent of evangelicals believe that religious people should "fight evil." The old notion of "separation from the world" has given way to intense engagement with the world. And self-identified fundamentalists and evangelicals are no longer sectarian; they believe that the world must be engaged, transformed, and converted (Green 2003, 15, 18; Smith 1998).

The most common critique of evangelicals in the 1960s from the liberal Protestant establishment was the failure of conservative Christians to make a pubic witness (Hadden 1969). While liberal Protestant denominational leaders joined the antiwar movement and marched for civil rights in the 1960s, conservative evangelicals were a part of Nixon's "silent majority," supporting the status quo and backing the Vietnam War. Today, with Republican George W. Bush in the White House, the strength, frequency, and volume of evangelicals in the public square has increased dramatically (Domke 2004; Domke and Coe 2007).

Consequently, evangelicals are no longer interested in silence or separation; they want to engage the wider culture. But what does this mean? What kind of civil religion are they advocating? Recent research has shown that there are sets of common evangelical cultural characteristics that have been called a "civic gospel." These characteristics include the belief that evangelical conversion will address and solve social problems; the government should protect America's religious heritage; the United States was founded as a Christian nation; it is hard to be a political liberal and a Christian; the promotion of democracy around the world should be encouraged; and evangelicals should advocate for economic, religious, and political liberty, and, by extension of these last two, support the war in Iraq (Kellstedt et al. 2003, 553; Wellman 2007). All of these characteristics are mirrored by the evangelical respondents I interviewed in the PNW. In 2007, mirroring the rest of the country, white evangelical support for George W. Bush and the Iraq War has declined; I will explore this more fully in the chapter 11 on Religion and Politics.

Thus, I argue that this civic gospel is part and parcel of the evangelical moral worldview that I address throughout this volume. But it also marks one of the ironies that this study reveals: the reversal of roles between evangelicals and liberal Protestants. The public voice of liberals is now relatively mute, less sure and focused than it was in the 1960s and 1970s; the evangelical voice is now what many take as the public voice of American Christianity (Domke and Coe 2007). This book opens a window on the complex changes and transitions in the moral worldviews of evangelical and liberal Christians, showing the conditions and consequences of these views on PNW culture in particular, and on the broader American culture more generally.

The evangelical community is no longer sectarian in the classic sense of isolating itself from the broader culture; it now seeks to engage culture, to change and transform it into its own image. And while liberal Protestants may no longer be one of the dominant voices in American public life, they remain an important voice in the American Protestant subculture. However, while the easy labeling of American Protestantism as a "two-party" system (evangelicals vs. liberals) is a popular model for some, I argue that it hides the complexity of the Protestant moral terrain. It is to this complexity I now turn (Williams 1997; Jacobsen and Trollinger 1998).

3

Complicating the Two-Party Protestant Explanation

1. The Problem with the Two-Party Model

The rhetoric of the clash of civilizations, or the simple two-party explanation of American Protestantism, stills resonates in wider popular publics, but in this study the story is more complicated. To begin, I am taking two subcultures, evangelical and liberal Protestant, and bracketing them out for comparison. This is *not* to argue that they are the *only* subcultures in American Protestantism. They are simply two distinct subcultures within the wider mosaic of American Protestantism. I argue that there are multiple subcultures that range across the ideological spectrum. A subculture, for my purposes, is considered to be a group with relatively homogenous social and symbolic boundaries; the communities within the subculture share that worldview that comprises a framework of moral values, actions, and projects. I am not arguing that there has to be perfect homogeneity; subtle differences exist within these communities. Nonetheless, I show that there is a coherent moral worldview developed by these subcultures. Moreover, the permeability of the boundaries within these subcultures varies according to context and history. As we have already seen, early American fundamentalists created hard boundaries, in part out of necessity because of their marginalization by mainline Protestant culture. Over time, with success and cultural accommodation, evangelical boundaries have grown more permeable—the sectarian nature of American evangelicalism has decreased and it is now more engaged in mainstream politics. In the 1960s and 1970s the moral worldview of liberal Protestants was clearer and liberals were more engaged politically. Today, liberals have become less publicly demonstrative and less engaged politically due in no small measure to their success in advocating for the rights of minorities, women, and gays. Thus, liberal Protestant withdrawal has been in part intentional; by definition the moral worldview of liberals tends to refuse exclusive or absolute moral boundaries even as they make their own set of truth claims about culture, politics, and God. Thus, I complicate the two-party dichotomy not because of political correctness, but because social reality demands greater subtlety than the generalizations often given to describe it.

The history of two-party dichotomies in the study of American religion shows how attractive it has been and its power to annunciate new factors in analyzing differences between the two groups. Table 3.1 shows the numerous variations on the theme.

Scholars over the last half-century have tried to explain, as Robert Wuthnow put it, the "restructuring" within American Protestantism (1988, 1989). As George Marsden has argued, in the nineteenth century American Protestantism reflected a relatively homogenous evangelical religious culture, which assumed that America was a Protestant Christian nation, or at least should be (Marsden 1982). Even in the midst of this Protestant hegemony, forms of

TABLE 3.1. Two-Party Dichotomies in American Culture and Religion

Theorist	Evangelical Protestant Religion	Liberal Protestant Religion
Wade Clark Roof	Locals	Cosmopolitans
Dean Hoge David Roozen	Traditionalists	Scientific humanists
Robert Wuthnow Joseph B. Tamney	Conservatives	Liberals
James Hunter Davison	Orthodox	Progressives
Robert Bellah	Utilitarian individualism	Civic Republicanism
Martin Marty	Private	Public
Richard Mouw	Evangelical	Ecumenical
Jeffrey Hadden	Conservative and Fundamentalist	Liberal and Neoorthodox
Harvey Cox	Metaphysical	Political
Christian Smith	Conservative Christians	Liberal Christians
Andrew Greeley Michael Hout	Conservative Christians	Protestant Mainline

Adapted and updated from Warner 1988, 52.

disestablishment rippled through American Christianity. It began with the early legal disestablishment—in 1833 the state of Massachusetts was the last state to cease state support of religion. In the early years of the twentieth century the cultural disestablishment of Protestantism was well on its way—reflecting a public fragmentation that has not been resolved (Wellman 1999b). More recently, a so-called third disestablishment, an organizational phenomenon, has been described as a movement from attachment to primary groups of family and church to secondary associations of friends and mutual interest organizations. This has also been interpreted as a transition from a group collective mentality to a more compartmentalized orientation, reflecting a preference for personal autonomy (Handy 1984; Hammond 1992). These waves of disestablishment facilitate and reflect the fragmentation of American Protestantism and the reality of diverse Protestant subcultures.

Larger social events and movements in American culture, such as the disagreements between the Northern and Southern Christians over slavery, the rise and influence of Darwinian theory, the immigration of Roman Catholics, the influence of the historical critical study of the Bible coming from German and European scholars, and the rising middle and upper middle classes in American society, undercut the Protestant homogeneity at the turn of the twentieth century. A powerful turning point for Protestant hegemony was the First World War. I have argued the trauma of the war challenged Protestant plausibility structures and brought to public consciousness theodicy questions of how to rationalize a good God in the midst of such horror. Protestant proponents of the war had a difficult time reconciling their rhetoric and the reality of modern war (Wellman 1999b). Moreover, during this period, disagreements over how to interpret scripture took center stage; the modernist-fundamentalist controversy of the 1920s undermined the Protestant cooperation, stimulating the Protestant tendency—a potential always present—for schism, conflict, and contestation. For evangelicals, to question the tradition of scriptural authority jarred their religious identity. Liberal Protestants sought to accommodate their faith to the modern world, to gain the acceptance of the elite classes, and to maintain their own standing at the center of American culture. I would argue that the most accurate description of the "battle" was that both sides suffered and had to accommodate dramatic cultural and social change. Liberal Protestantism began a slow decline; by mid-century the Protestant establishment begrudgingly accepted a Roman Catholic president. Protestant theologians such as Reinhold Niebuhr and Paul Tillich, who had political and cultural leadership in the 1950s, lost public prominence in the second half of the twentieth century. In the contemporary period, mainline Protestant public intellectuals are difficult to name.

In response to all of these dramatic social changes and in the aftermath of the modernist/fundamentalist conflict in 1920s, fundamentalists built their own culture, primarily in the Midwest and South. They concentrated on the construction of a family-centered culture, established a parallel educational system, and passionately pursued evangelism and mission in the United States and abroad. Conservative Protestants no longer looked to American mainline culture for legitimacy; they nurtured their own grassroots culture—creating plausibility structures independent of the mainline denominations and of secular American elites.

The fruits of this separate evangelical Christian culture can be best exemplified by the way evangelicals came to dominate the field of world missions. The world wars disrupted Western confidence that Christian civilization assured progress (Stanley 1990), while push back from indigenous peoples across the globe forced missionaries to rethink simple moral notions of good and evil. Mainline Protestants, in particular, "rethought" missionary impulses, responding to the critiques of colonialism with more inclusivist theologies (Carpenter and Shenk 1990). Finally, the women's missionary societies, always the backbone of mainline Protestant mission work, were displaced by mainline denominations for financial reasons (Roberts 2002).

In the process of this transition, the mainline Protestant contribution to mission declined dramatically from the 1950s forward. Indeed, there has been so much decline that over the last generation nearly 90 percent of missionaries came from American evangelical churches (Baptist, Pentecostal, and other traditional evangelical denominations, as well as nondenominational and independent churches). In the contemporary context, the number of long-term contemporary missionaries (those serving more than two years abroad) is approximately 120,000; a quarter of this number are sent to Africa, Latin America, and Europe, respectively (Wellman 2006; Wellman and Keyes 2007). Short-term missionaries, those serving anywhere from two weeks up to two years, are more difficult to count, but they are estimated at 350,000.[1] From the research in this study, the liberal churches supported less than a handful of missionaries; outreach for liberals is simply not about conversion so much as it is about social service (Wellman and Keyes 2007). On the other hand, every evangelical church that I studied supported multiple long-term missionaries who were sent to evangelize and serve the needs of people abroad.

The history of the twentieth century for American Protestantism will be written as a momentous period of change. The early twentieth century Protestant mainline hegemony was overturned; fundamentalists, Pentecostals, and numerous Protestant groups filled this vacuum and have established a new but quite fragile Protestant consensus. This delicate framework holds together

a diverse group of evangelical subcultures. They are a loosely networked association that creates a homogenous moral culture even as evangelicals lack
institutional accountability to one another. These evangelical subcultures resource one another and mobilize around moral causes, but are congregationally
independent. This American spirit of entrepreneurial and independent Protestantism has always nurtured individualistic and charismatic entrepreneurs.
Thus, organizationally, schism is the rule in American Christianity and not the
exception. This tendency toward division lies within the liberal and mainline
Protestants as well. Over the last twenty years, the Protestant mainline has
been in a constant state of internecine conflict over issues of gay ordination
and sexuality generally (Wellman 1999a). The United Methodist Church, the
Presbyterian Church (USA), and the Episcopal Church in America are all
threatened by schisms over these issues. Prodded by conservative interest
groups, liberals are now challenged by traditionalists in their denominations
from abroad (Jenkins 2003). It is in part out of this fragmentation that I have
come to a multidimensional sense of Protestantism within the wider field of
American religion.

2. A New Model of the American Religious Landscape

To describe and explain the multidimensional aspects of the field of American
Protestantism, I use Fred Kniss's work "Listening to the Disenfranchised: Toward a Multiparty Conception of American Religion" (Kniss 1997). His theory
of a "moral field" not only multiplies the dimensions of American religion but
also describes the interactions between marginalized groups and their effects
on the center of American culture and society. Kniss does this in large part to
explain the relationship of American religious minorities, in this case Mennonites, and their impact on the dominant culture. I would propose that applying Kniss's theory to Protestant subcultures, particularly those in the PNW,
gives us a greater purchase on understanding and explaining these subcultures
and their relation to the wider culture.

Subcultures, as I defined above, embody a distinctive moral worldview with
values, actions, and goals. Subcultures maintain symbolic and social boundaries that are relatively homogenous and predictable. Greater ideological consistency tends to rule in subcultures on the margins, whether religious or
secular. Nevertheless, history, context, and proximity to the centers of cultural
and political power affect moral boundary maintenance. As subcultures draw
closer to dominant political centers of power, their boundaries become more
porous; the farther away they get, the less permeable subculture identities

become. By definition, centers of political power develop as various coalitions gather around broad interests; each subculture gives up something for the sake of being a part of the governing party. Thus, as Kniss argues, cultural and political centers are "ambiguous middles" where political coalitions—through compromise and negotiation—are able to rule.

Kniss's map of the American moral fields uses crosscutting axes to construct a two-dimensional, ideological moral landscape. The east-west axis is the horizon of moral authority by which moral values are formed and deployed. These values, on the western axis, are embodied in groups, defined ideologically by modernism. On the eastern axis, values are sustained by collectivities, defined ideologically as traditionalism. Individuals and groups use values to construct goals and ends that shape core truth claims; they evaluate and judge what is ethically good and evil, and build what they interpret as aesthetically appropriate. I plot PNW evangelical and liberal Protestants on the wider moral map of American culture and religion, giving us a sense of how they relate to each other in terms of their moral values, and to the wider American religious and moral landscape.

If moral values shape the ends and goals of human moral behavior, the moral projects or actions are the means and endeavors produced by and for these moral values. Kniss develops a north-south axis for the moral project. The northern axis positions the individual as the object of the moral action, defined in ideological terms as libertarianism. The southern axis takes the collective as the object of moral action, ideologically labeled as communalism.

This moral field ends up with four ideal types that define the moral field of American culture and religious life. The southwest corner is typically the domain of the American left, defined by modernist and individualistic moral values with moral projects that focus on collectivities of the state; the northwest corner is the common province of therapeutic utopians, modernists who define their moral projects individualistically; the northeast corner is the traditional site of the American right, taking on traditional moral values that plot the individual as the moral project; and the southeast is the site of collectivist utopias, embodying traditional values with collective social projects, best exemplified in the American religious sphere by Mennonites and the Amish.

Kniss is quick to suggest these ideal types have some empirical application, but, in reality, the field is far less clear, because groups tend to embody multiple values and actions across these ideological spectrums. Kniss is not interested in closed categories, but in flexible and interactive cultural fields that overlap and borrow sources of authority and projects depending on interests and needs. For example, Jim Wallis, editor of *Sojourners Magazine*, uses the authority of moral traditionalists to construct a consistent pro-life ethic along with an emphasis on

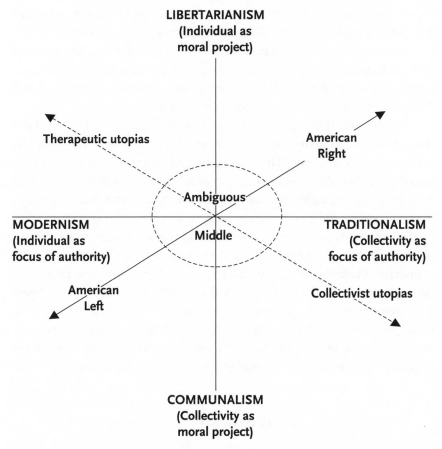

FIGURE 3.1. American Moral Landscape (Kniss 1997, 268)

communalism and the importance of governmental care for the poor. Liberals tend to pick up on Wallis's strong advocacy for the poor and his critique of the Bush administration's foreign policy, but they are far less sympathetic to Wallis's pro-life position on abortion or his ambivalence toward gay marriage. This variance reflects how liberals lean toward libertarian values of personal autonomy and freedom of personal moral choice (Wallis 2006).[2] Evangelicals may sympathize with Wallis's stance on abortion, but find his critique of militarism problematic and his suspicion of free market economics and the need for governmental intervention on behalf of the poor less attractive. This reflects evangelical tendencies toward traditionalism on collective and personal moral values, with a strong tendency toward libertarian and individualistic moral projects that, in part, produce their tendency to accept and sometimes endorse a laissez-faire economic philosophy. For evangelicals, however, on issues of national security a collectivist project is endorsed that advocates for a strong military interest in spreading political liberties to other nations. For their part, liberals may have interest in collectivist projects for the disadvantaged, but they are cautious about the military power of big government. However, on personal morality, liberals are starkly libertarian and individualistic. Thus, neither side perfectly embodies the ideal type of the left or the right.

This new moral map gives us the clarity of ideological ideal types, and also shows that groups can use crosscutting values that create moral actions that are sometimes difficult to plot. Thus, the dichotomized model of American Protestantism tends to distort more than it reveals. This is to say, there are multiple American religious subcultures in the American moral landscape negotiating the ambiguous middle of American political and cultural power. Depending on their proximity to this power center, the ideological stances of secular and religious subcultures reflect degrees of strength in their symbolic and social boundaries; the farther away from the middle, the harder their boundaries; the closer in, the softer and more permeable the boundaries become. I plot in figure 3.2 various American religious subcultures on this new map of American religious landscape to give a sense how each group relates to ideal types *and* to the dominant centers of American political power. A part of the problem, of course, is that each of these groups has changed across history and depending on cul-

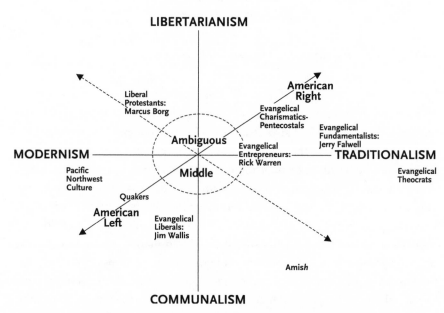

FIGURE 3.2. Mapping American Religious Subcultures (adapted from Kniss 1997, 266)

tural and political movements. This underlines the dynamic nature of subcultures to the broader dominant centers of power.

This experiment in plotting religious subcultures illustrates the complexity and dynamism of these groups. It also makes clear that each subculture must respond to a center of power, and that symbolic and social boundaries become more or less permeable the closer or the farther away the group is from the ambiguous middle of cultural power. The Amish and evangelical theocrats (in much different ways) are the most sectarian of subcultures and the farthest away from the center; and the entrepreneurial evangelicals and liberal Protestants are the least sectarian, the most accommodated (though in different ways), and the closest to the ambiguous middle of American power. But again, it would be a mistake to reify these placements; American religious subcultures remain in flux. In this way, as I argue in chapter 4 religious subcultures create moral worldviews that are relatively homogenous and predictable even as they express different levels of fluidity and permeability in how they manage their boundaries relative to dominate political centers.

4

Modernity, Religion, and Moral Worldviews

1. Modernity and Religion

In the 1960s scholars of religion argued that modernity had brought secularization, and institutional religion was in decline, receding into the private sphere of the human heart. Modernity as a process and ideology had overwhelmed, replaced, and displaced the need for religion. Modernity had rationalized systems and institutions, compartmentalized various social functions, and made society more efficient and effective in the delivery of goods and services. Ideologically, modernity affirmed the authority and autonomy of each person, making the individual the adjudicator of meaning and purpose for their lives, thus displacing religion as an authority for values and moral action. Modernity facilitated and even celebrated cultural diversity and religious pluralism that undercut the power and plausibility of religion in society (Luckman 1967; Berger 1969).

Peter Berger, who was at the forefront of theorizing secularization, has only recently changed his mind. The secularity of Europe, for Berger, is the exception in the world; in fact, for Berger, the "desecularization" of the globe is the strongest trend in global religious culture (Berger 1999). For Berger, what must be explained is not secularization but the failure of modernity to replace religion. Religion not only continues to flourish despite modernity, but in fact flourishes *because of* the pluralism in the contemporary cultural scene (Stark and Finke 2000). That is, in response to the fragmentation of modern life, humans want to believe in stable, moral worldviews supported by superempirical[1] claims that legitimate and justify these moral orders (Smith 2003). As Christian Smith has argued, evangelicals have developed "sacred umbrellas" to negotiate this lack of general societal norms, thus showing that religious subcultures have flourished despite the loss of a wider sacred canopy (Smith 1998).

These sacred umbrellas accommodate the personal autonomy of modernity and yet, as my study shows, evangelicals are nurtured within smaller religious enclaves.[2] The lived religion of evangelicalism has an intensely communal sensibility; the priority of small groups in the churches in the study was nearly as important as personal faith in Jesus Christ. In this way, even as evangelicals negotiate modern life by privatizing their religion, they are also networked and sustained by intense commitments to small groups within their religious communities. Subcultures nurture strong moral umbrellas that not only cover individuals, but sustain small networked groups. Thus, *sacred tents* is a more adequate and accurate metaphor to desribe how individuals in modern life are sustained by religious subcultures. Indeed, the tent metaphor underscores the causal nature of religious ideology as a process that originates in groups. Human beliefs and values in general are reproduced and nurtured by social networks, despite the fact that individuals frequently overestimate the power of their own personal agency in determining their values and beliefs.[3]

Liberal religionists in this study have also accommodated modernity, with its emphasis on personal autonomy and social differentiation. They are staunch supporters of the separation of church and state. And while liberals emphasize personal forms of spirituality, often using ancient religious traditions for their everyday religious practice, they nevertheless create their own sacred tents. Liberals consistently stress the importance of integrating their beliefs and actions; their faith may be a private matter and yet they consistently emphasize that it *must* infuse all aspects of their lives. For them, like the evangelicals in the study, religion creates a moral worldview, and while liberals are less apt to organize small groups, they do pursue more informal networks of interaction that sustain and reproduce moral worldviews within their own religious subculture.

2. A Definition of Religion and Moral Worldviews

Definitions by their nature are heuristic devices rather than settled proofs; they shape analysis rather than give the final word. At their best they prod thought and provide guidelines for investigation. I offer the definition to stipulate what

I mean when I analyze that which I call religion; to show that religion, conflict, and politics are related to one another in significant ways; and finally to connect religion to my theory of moral worldviews.

The working definition I have developed runs as follows: Religion is a system of symbols, composed of values and beliefs, embodied in ritual practices, developed in a communal setting, often institutionally legitimated that negotiates and interacts with a power or force that is experienced as within and beyond the self and group; this power or force is most often referred to as god/spirit or gods/spirits. The symbolic and social boundaries of religion mobilize individual and group identity by constructing moral worldviews that create conflict and, more rarely, violence within and between groups (Wellman and Tokono 2004; Wellman 2007).[4]

I begin with the discursive makeup of religion as a system of symbols that provides a narrative infrastructure whereby beliefs are constructed and values evolve. Humans form and are formed by systems of words that interpret their relation to others and to groups. God(s) and spirit(s) are one more aspect of that negotiation, constructed by and shaping humans in a reciprocal manner. This system of interpretation is never ending, reflected by the changing patterns of interaction with culture and politics that affect every religion and, in this case, Christianity in particular. Various leaders of the Christian religion have claimed that they represent the original view of the faith, but any cursory knowledge of the history of Christianity shows that St. Augustine is much different from Rick Warren; St. Benedict has little in common with Jerry Falwell; nevertheless, each of these Christian leaders would claim that their visions were and are the closest approximations of the faith. Words that describe the faith are shaped over time by the tradition, individual and group preferences, and the era's context, culture, and politics.

Words and actions function reciprocally; the two cannot be separated from each other. In other words, belief and ritual function in tandem related to and shaped by cultural context. The ritual life of the early church, though simple, was deeply influenced by Greco-Roman forms, just as the Ethiopian Orthodox Church reflects its own particular tradition through time and Brazilian Pentecostalism expresses in word and ritual a quite different variation of how one embodies the faith in action. The Calvinists of seventeenth-century New England would not recognize or approve of the contemporary evangelical megachurch skits. Thus, self-evidently, word and action are always shaped by context and the dynamism of historical moments. Moreover, the communal aspects of the development of religions underscores that language, by its nature, is a social act; individuals function, think, and innovate within networks of language, practice, and culture that cannot be disentangled.[5]

Institutionalization of religions is a matter of developing social complexity, including networks of elites. The differentiation of functions demands institutional rules and roles, proliferating with time and the growth of populations. We see this in the development of the early papal hierarchy, transitioning from a persecuted Jewish sect to a robust Roman institution, and finally to a political power player in the early medieval European world (Stark 1996). The Protestant establishment shaped American cultural and political life at the turn of the nineteenth century, extending its reach through much of the first half of the twentieth century (Baltzell 1964; Hutchison 1989; Wellman 1999b). The transition of the American evangelical church from a fundamentalist enclave of the 1920s to a political machine in the 1990s makes the same point. Religious elites, as they are able to succeed culturally and socially, will tend to expand their ambitions to wider cultural and political fields of power and, depending on context, opportunity, and leadership, will seek to become dominant cultural and political agents.

Every definition of religion is challenged for being too broad, and must be distinguished from broader cultural forces such as nationalism. But the fact that this is always a problem will be explained below. I argue that religion negotiates and interacts with a power or force that is experienced as within and beyond the self. I avoid saying a "supernatural" force because this word relates to and arises from the Christian tradition, and because many find this force or power within the natural world—or permeating multiple worlds—to include thinkers within the liberal Christian tradition (Borg 2003). I distinguish the power and force of religion farther from secular social life, by arguing it is most often referred to as god(s) or spirit(s). Of course, there is the problem of no god or spirit in some forms of Buddhism though it is also often said that within popular versions of Buddhism there are realms of deities. Moreover, the Buddhist experience of awakening is a force or power that overcomes or transcends the self and group; thus, even though Buddhism tends not to point to a spirit(s) or god(s) per se, it can be covered by my definition of religion (Wellman and Tokuno 2004).

A religion, by my definition, is a group process that creates symbolic and social boundaries that include and exclude.[6] These boundaries create tensions that differentiate the self from other, one group from another. In this sense religion shares much with other group-forming cultural mechanisms. Religion shares much with ethnic and political concerns that are well-known vehicles of identity formation. I would argue, however, that religion is an effective and persistent social boundary maker and marker. These boundaries can and do create conflicts and tension both internally (ascetic practices) and with others, whether with one's family, the tribe, the group, one's nation, or indeed other nations. Moreover, in all periods of history religions by definition must and do interact with political fields of power, and in the modern era with nation–states. Thus, the continual definitional issue mentioned earlier of how to distinguish religion from politics (Wellman 2007). And this is my point—the mixing of religion and culture is inevitable. As David Martin has explained, "[P]olitics and religion are isomorphic" (2005, 47). There is a necessary relationship between the two because one cannot be "in" a religion without being "in" a political culture, and of course modernity, by definition, puts one "in" a nation (Wellman 2007). Religions, by necessity, join or reject the actions of the political order and the power of the state. In order to survive, organizationally and as a system of meaning, religions must adapt to and address the powers that be. Of course, religious groups can distance themselves from centers of political power, as some sectarian groups do, but even here, being over against the other—as is the case of the Amish—remains a form of relationship that identifies the sect as a distinct communal organization separate from, as in the case of the Amish, a "secular" American culture. In this sense, religion is neither completely innocent of power nor can it be fully separated from the dynamics of political power centers.

Finally, my definition of religion affirms the power and durability of moral worldviews backed by and in interaction with a power or force that is experienced as within and beyond the self and group. By moral worldview I mean not only the ethical principles of what is right and wrong but also the symbolic boundaries by which values are shaped, behaviors are managed, and moral projects are constructed (Smith 2003). Analytically, I am not assuming that these moral orders are ontological givens; they have historical antecedents, are culturally created, and have a natural history. I use them as heuristic tools to describe and explain how evangelicals and liberals construct religio-moral orders.

This is not to say one needs a religion to have a moral worldview; my assumption is that everyone has a moral worldview, no matter how superficial or well thought out it might be. I am also aware that this is a debatable assumption; some would argue that humans are merely cost/benefit maximizers. In this framework humans employ values as ways to avoid costs and expand benefits; humans are purely instrumental in how they negotiate getting what they want. I am not persuaded by this perspective. I do not deny that cost/benefit analysis occurs. Humans have interests and make tradeoffs based on a long-standing and relatively stable set of preferences. However, my axiom is that human choices are always related to a moral worldview—a narrative system of symbols that guides and shapes action and produces truth claims—no matter how inefficient, fragmented, or banal that might be. Indeed, a moral worldview may be purely egocentric—though even here, the norm is the self and its fulfillment is taken as what is good, true, and beautiful (Frankena 1973, 17; Smith 2003). Again, a moral worldview does not necessitate a religious system, nor must all moral worldviews be legitimized by a felt sense of power or force that is beyond the self and group. Religion, however, does use this felt sense of power to construct, defend, and sustain a moral worldview.

My argument is that liberals and evangelicals in this study create and are shaped by religious moral worldviews, backed by a felt sense of a power or force that is beyond the self and group. These religious moral worldviews are quite durable (sustaining groups even as minority populations) and portable (particularly when I examine the way evangelical missionaries in this study are to carry their faith into foreign contexts and cultures) (Wellman and Keyes 2007). In this sense, religion, particularly in the modern period, is a kind of subculture that constructs social and symbolic boundaries over against and sometimes in tension with wider cultural norms. As other scholars have argued, tensions arising in a pluralistic context can and often do strengthen religious moral worldviews (Stark and Finke 2000). This does not mean people like to have their moral worldviews challenged. Religious subcultures seek homogeneity. Nevertheless, it is true that this homogeneity is sometimes enabled by conflict within groups and with outsiders (Coser 1956). In this sense, "engagement" with cultures, as Christian Smith has argued (1998), is a factor in evangelical vitality.

Religion, like nationalism or ethnicity, has the capacity to motivate and mobilize individuals and groups. In this sense religion is not unique relative to other cultural systems in creating group cohesion. But religion is a powerful force in human life. The affectivity and communal effervescence that arises from religious ritual creates an internal combustion engine that is the genesis of religion's power to motivate and mobilize individuals and groups (Wellman and Tokuno 2004). Thus, religion can empower even small groups to resist larger and more dominant social forces. Religious subcultures, as I will show in the study of liberal and evangelical Protestant Christians, give humans a moral worldview that persists and endures even against great odds.

Thus, I would argue in general, based on my data, that not only do individuals prefer a stable moral worldview and to associate in groups with homogenous values, they also desire that their entire society adopt their same values. This explains, as this study shows, the missionary zeal of evangelical Christianity; evangelism is a critical feature of what it means to be an evangelical in the churches in this study. Perhaps even more telling is the resentment that bubbles up to the surface of liberal culture (whether religious or not) against evangelical religious and moral advocacy. Liberal Protestants may trumpet tolerance and acceptance, but they do not want evangelicals trying to convert others. Liberals prefer everyone to be accepting as they are—that is to be liberal. Liberal Protestants tend to have an implicit larger agenda. This same liberal agenda is the cause of evangelical resentment against liberals; evangelicals accuse liberals of "intolerance" toward them, charging liberals with a form of hypocrisy in not allowing evangelicals to speak their mind in the public conversation. In either case, the decision to evangelize or to seek general civic tolerance is driven by moral conceptions and truth claims linked to worldviews that mirror those conceptions.

This theory has been constructed and developed in part to explain what I found in more than 443 interviews with evangelical and liberal Protestant Christians in the PNW. In an overwhelmingly unchurched region, evangelical religion has grown and creates relatively homogeneous moral worldviews that attract many to its tight moral communities. Similarly, though with less robust results at least numerically, liberal Christian groups attract individuals with distinctive moral worldviews that also seek homogeneity. The liberal Christians are less effective because their moral worldviews accept some internal ideological diversity and dissuade members from evangelizing liberal views in the name of liberal tolerance. However, liberal Christians are ambitious to have this moral worldview of tolerance and acceptance imposed on society. Thus, the importance of this study that investigates and explains the moral worldviews in the context of a unique region of the United States, the PNW, or what has come to be known as the "none" zone (Killen and Silk 2004).

5

Demographics, Culture, and Religion of the Pacific Northwest

The PNW is a unique part of the nation. The demographic story gives us a sense of continuity as well as discontinuity with other regions of the United States. Most northwesterners live in urban areas (80 percent; the United States, 79 percent), and there are similar age ranges and marriage rates to the nation as well. Caucasians are a larger share of the population (83 vs. 75 percent), with fewer African Americans (3 vs. 12 percent) and fewer Hispanics (7 vs. 13 percent) living in the region, although the PNW has slightly more Asian Americans, American Indians, and multiracials versus the national average. The PNW is also, on average, more educated; there are fewer individuals living there with less than a high school education (14 vs. 20 percent), and slightly more that have at least a bachelor's degree (27 vs. 24 percent). The region also has more professionals and slightly more farmers. The PNW annual median household income is higher than the national rate, and has a poverty rate slightly under the national average (Killen and Shibley 2004).

The demographic discontinuity, however, is striking and shapes the unique cultural and religious landscape of the region. The contrast in population density per square mile is dramatic (14 persons to 80 for the United States), thus, there is an objective correlate for the felt sense of wide-open spaces commonly mentioned by natives and newcomers alike. Indeed, there is a high influx of immigrants to the region. Washington ranks eighth and Oregon tenth in net domestic migration between 1990 and 1999 with nearly four hundred thousand

and three hundred thousand immigrants entering Washington and Oregon, respectively. Furthermore, Washington and Oregon rank forty-second and forty-third, respectively, in the percentage of those who are born in state, meaning that more than 50 percent of residents of the PNW were not born in the states within the PNW (Statistical Abstracts 2000). This discontinuity underlines the relative instability and mobility of the population, which creates a lack of traditional ties to the area, as well as fewer family networks and institutional attachments. It is no wonder that northwesterners often say they feel a simultaneous sense of isolation and exhilaration at the chance to start anew (Killen and Shibley 2004). This sense of isolation combines with a region that is well educated and suffused with entrepreneurial interests, organizations, and capital undergirded by a tradition of individualism and self-sufficiency. Merging with these characteristics is a regional commitment and access to outdoor recreation (Killen and Shibley 2004; Shibley 2004). By uniting these factors one can hypothesize that the region would tend to have a lower degree of interest in and commitment to institutions generally, and organized religion in particular.

Indeed, the differences between the PNW and the rest of the nation on church affiliation are remarkable. The regional differences with other parts of the United States portray a relatively unchurched population, with 63 percent of northwesterners religiously unaffiliated; this compares to percentages of the religiously unaffiliated in the Rocky Mountain West (48 percent), the Midwest (41 percent), the South (41 percent), New England (39 percent), and finally the Mid-Atlantic (34 percent), and Southern Crossroads[1] (33 percent). The latter two regions are mirror opposites of the PNW (Killen and Shibley 2004). Needless to say, the vast majority of the population of the PNW are unaffiliated; they have no official institutional membership in a religious body, or at least one that is acknowledged by an American religious denomination. Out of those 37 percent who are affiliated, 24 percent come from evangelical churches, as I have defined broadly. These evangelicals are, in turn, divided by traditional evangelical denominations. Baptists make up 7 percent, churches coming out of the Holiness/Pentecostal traditions (13 percent), and, finally, those from nondenominational and independent churches (11 percent). Roman Catholics make up 30 percent of the total affiliated with churches, and the Protestant mainline makes up 18 percent. Mormons compose 8 percent of total adherents (Killen and Shibley 2004).

While it appears that northwesterners are unique in their lack of interest in churched religion, the "none" label may be a misnomer. That is, even though 25 percent of northwesterners claim no religion (compared to 13 percent nationally), 67 percent of these so-called nones believe that God exists; 52 percent agree that God helps them; and 34 percent would say that they are "religious." Thus, even the "nones" in the PNW have a relatively deep sense of religiosity, and indeed belief in God and a God who is an active and interacting being. Mark Shibley has argued that "nature religion" is the dominant civil religion in the region. That is, a cultural ethos that takes its relationship to nature as its "ultimate value," creating a moral worldview that sacralizes nature as a way to orient as well as form the values that guide and shape lives (Shibley 2004, unpublished manuscript). I am less certain that we can generalize nature religion as *the* civil religion of the PNW. I have plotted it at some distance from the center of PNW power. But I would say that this is an important subculture of the region, which interacts with the region's dominant power centers, which I elaborate below.

This lack of religious affiliation in the PNW is part of a long-term pattern. Since 1970 the number of PNW adherents has only risen by 4 percent; the unchurched have decreased from 67 to 63 percent. The movements are slight, but what has changed is the rate of population increase from 1970 to 2000: for the nation, 32 percent; for the PNW, 70 percent. Considering these trends, people come to the PNW for a number of reasons. First, they are drawn by the lack of population density (even though most end up in urban areas), by economic opportunities marked by an entrepreneurial spirit and the promise of a flourishing network of knowledge workers and technology opportunities, by the natural environment that has long been an alluring aspect of Northwest culture, and finally by a desire to start afresh culturally, religiously, and even spiritually. Many newcomers come to the PNW and break with their cultural or family traditions. Often, once here, the bounty of the natural environment becomes more central to their lives. Again and again, among liberal and evangelical pastors in this study, the main competition for the loyalties of their flocks was the outdoors. The moderate climate in the PNW does not deter one from going out in either the winter or the summer. The sense that nature is elevated and in some sense sacralized runs hand-in-hand with what it means to be a northwesterner.

The challenge for churched-religion is how to draw and keep "believers" who seem to have little interest in "belonging." Or at least, as Shibley points out, people who see the beauty of the outdoors as their "sanctuary" and "chapel" (unpublished manuscript). As I go into at great depth in part II, liberals deal with the culture of the region by accommodating to the patterns of the PNW—shorter and earlier worship services, fewer demands on lay leaders, an emphasis on a rational basis for faith, an egalitarian and progressive focus theologically, and a consistent emphasis on social justice and gay rights in particular. Evangelicals deal with the uniqueness of the region by meeting the competition head-on; creating facilities that rival or substitute for public community meeting places; and developing their own family activities, sports groups, and all kinds of other groups. Indeed, evangelicals attempt to meet human needs at every level of human development and family makeup. Moreover, evangelicals in the study tend to rejoice in the fact that people in the Northwest have few church affiliations. For them, it is an opportunity to make new converts. For evangelicals, there is an intense ethic of voluntarism in nurturing individual choice in faith and in decisions about church. Voluntarism creates authentic commitments that are subjectively intense and organizationally and spiritually fruitful for church attendance and financial giving.

As I mentioned before, when I first arrived in Seattle from Chicago I was struck by the fact that in a region I had considered politically and culturally "liberal," churches in that ideological spectrum were difficult to find and had only marginal degrees of growth, both numerically and financially. The relatively robust nature of evangelical growth sparked my interests and made me curious about the "fit" between the PNW and American evangelicalism. In part, the answer to this question comes in the radical openness of the region, culturally and religiously. As Patricia Killen and Mark Shibley point out, no religious group "dominates" the PNW (Killen and Shibley 2004). Unlike most other areas of the nation, no religious group is putatively in charge. Numerous religious subcultures seek their part of the market. But to what center of cultural power must they relate? What is the ambiguous center of power in the PNW?

As William Lunch has outlined, politics in Washington and Oregon are shaped by three broad positions: "the new moralists, the old moralists, and libertarians." The old moralists represent a Republican party with a Christian base that is conservative economically and socially; they tend to be aligned with the older, natural resource-based economy (agriculture and lumber) that has traditionally dominated the region. The old moralists defend a traditional worldview, while new moralists (exemplifying the new knowledge economy of technology) advocate less social control while maintaining a moderately conservative economic approach to taxation and government. The libertarians represent the independent streak in PNW politics, with its generally liberal take on social control and advocacy to get government out of people's lives (Lunch 2003; Wellman 2004).

This mélange of cultural values is joined by a strong interest in preserving and sometimes even "worshiping" the natural beauty of the region. I argue that the region is best delineated by a pragmatic approach that generally distrusts government, lionizes the entrepreneur, nurtures a libertarian and individualistic set of values, and seeks the preservation of the region's resources and beauty. One notes the frequent difficulty in the PNW in funding large public projects (transportation and education). Thus, the region is not liberal in the sense of being communitarian or devoted to larger public projects for the common good. It is fundamentally entrepreneurial and libertarian; individual initiative is key and individuals are free to act as they may as long as they neither hurt anyone nor harm the environment. Tellingly, even the growing nonprofit, charitable service organizations and foundations in the region are organized by entrepreneurs with tight controls on efficiency and results—pragmatism trumps idealism and charity is managed for outcomes (Fleishman 2007).

This moving and sometimes ambiguous middle of PNW culture creates specific opportunities and challenges for the evangelical and liberal subcultures in this study. For evangelicals, the open environment creates opportunities to expand their mission; the individualism tracks with the evangelical focus on each person as the unit of salvation; the entrepreneurial spirit values the ambitious visions of evangelical pastors who tout results and value quantifiable outcomes; and the relative isolation and lack of traditional communal connections create the need for social connection. Evangelicals, as part II makes plain, create groups to meet these needs. Nonetheless, the libertarian nature of the PNW challenges evangelical moral traditionalism; evangelicals seek to defend and nurture traditional family structures—focusing on the development of children and youth ministries; encouraging young adults to marry, and advocating (sometimes politically) against gay marriage and for a culture of intact heterosexual families.

For liberal Protestants, the PNW culture creates a crisis of differentiation—how to make sure that they are *not* identified with the growing evangelical Christianity in the PNW and how to defend organized religion from the libertarian ethos of the culture that is individualistic and anti-institutional. The challenges are enormous; the central values of hospitality promoted by liberal Christianity (specifically for gay and lesbian rights) are already a part of the PNW culture. What do liberals add to the regional ethos? My conclusion is that in considering the culture of the region, liberal Christianity has had less success in taking advantage of the region's unique characteristics for several reasons: the complexity and bureaucracy of liberal polity eliminate entrepreneurial personalities; liberal theology mostly mirrors the egalitarian and inclusive nature of the regional moral landscape; and finally, the theological assumptions about God and grace as infinite resources dampen any liberal motivation to reproduce followers. I leave the in-depth analysis of the moral worldviews of these groups for part II; for now I describe my methods of collection and the data and demographics of the evangelicals and liberals in this study.

6

Method, Data, and Demographics

This study examines twenty-four of the fastest growing evangelical churches in western Washington and western Oregon that had shown substantial growth in numbers and finances between 2000 and 2005. These were compared with ten vital liberal Protestant churches in western Washington and western Oregon that had maintained stable congregational numbers, finances, and church identity during a similar time period. I chose the western parts of the two states, first, because they contain the largest population centers; second, because liberal Protestant churches are nurtured in urban centers (seven out of ten liberal churches were urban); and finally, because I found that growing evangelical congregations were strikingly evident in these same secular western parts of the states, particularly in suburban areas (twenty out of twenty-four evangelical churches were suburban). Once again highlighting the fact in a highly unchurched and purportedly "secular" region, evangelical religion is thriving. By vital and thriving I mean that over a three to five year span of time, churches have either sustained or grown their congregations (numerically and financially); moreover, the church leadership has been relatively stable and expressed a coherent identity and vision for their churches.

I am aware of the bias of sampling only churches that are vital or growing. The goal was to choose churches that exemplified liberal and evangelical Protestantism in the region. It was not to create a random sample of churches in the region, but to identify how these two forms of Protestant churches functioned in the midst of a unique region. How did each express the moral worldviews of these forms of Christianity? By not including declining or failing churches I am not able to establish a causal claim on the cultural factors that have led to the growth of evangelicalism. Nonetheless, my assumption is that vital and growing churches would express the core of these religious moral worldviews and would give me the best indicators of how religious organizations adapt and thrive in an unchurched region. Moreover, my experience has shown me that churches are constantly looking for models of success. The churches that I chose are the ones that other churches try to mirror; in the interviews with various clergy and lay leaders, they most consistently mentioned other "more successful" churches and church leaders in the region. Thus, I began to hear similar names mentioned, and larger churches identified as models. These churches then function as types that may not perfectly represent the region but are very much models of the hopes and dreams of Protestant religious life in the PNW.

For each church, my three graduate students and I observed church services, interviewed the senior pastor, and (in the case of the evangelical churches) an international missionary supported by the church. We conducted focus groups comprising churches' lay leaders and new members (those who had been members for less than two years). For the most part, the focus group members were suggested by the pastor; we asked for a representative group relative to age, ethnic background, and intensity of participation. We presented ourselves as interested and sympathetic investigators wanting to understand the Christian faith in an unchurched region. Why did liberal and evangelical Protestants churches thrive in an open religious market? What impact did these vital churches have on the region? How did these churches respond to the cultural and political issues of the day? The interviewees were asked questions regarding their faith, churches, politics, and views regarding the PNW region.

The liberal churches were identified by speaking to mainline Protestant executives who knew of liberal or progressive churches that were vital and even growing. We spoke with pastors and other laypeople who identified churches that met the criteria of having either grown or at least remained the same in numbers and finances over the previous three years. The set of ten churches included three Congregational and three Episcopal churches, and one each of the following: Presbyterian Church (USA), United Methodist Church, Lutheran Church (ELCA), and an American Baptist congregation. At the time when the churches were selected, each met the above-mentioned criteria. Toward the end of my study in 2006, only two churches had continued growth in numbers and finances; three had plateaued in numerical growth even as their budget increased slightly; and five had marginally declined in numbers but were holding their own financially. Three of the five declining churches had changed pastors and two of these were beginning to turn around their churches with slight increases in attendance. Nine out of the ten churches were averaging 280 congregants in attendance each Sunday; none of these churches had more than five hundred attendees on Sunday morning. One of the churches had nearly 1,400 attending five services spread out over Sunday morning and evening. This church had the largest annual budget: more than $2 million. However, in the last year of the study the church's pastor had to let go of two full-time ministers due to increased building costs and a stagnant congregational pledging level that had caused a budget deficit of $100,000. Five of the churches had budgets of under $500,000, and the other five had budgets of slightly more than $1 million. The annual giving for the liberal churches in mission was less than 10 percent of their total budgets. One of the liberal churches had a large endowment of nearly $20 million built up over the last generation and thus was able to give substantially more toward mission and social service. Nonetheless, this same church met its everyday expenses through annual congregational pledges of $1 million. Overall these liberal churches show some strength but also real vulnerability.

Institutionally, the liberal churches had a common characteristic that I did not seek out but discovered as I investigated the congregations. Seven of the ten congregations were officially designated "welcoming" to gays and lesbians. Depending on the denomination, the churches had gone through processes that stipulated that the congregation was "More Light," a "Welcoming Congregation," "Open and Affirming," or a "Reconciling Congregation." Four of the ten congregations reported that one-fifth to one-third of their congregational members were gay or lesbian. This became a marker of identity for these churches. Two of the ten senior pastors were female; one was a gay man who had made his sexual orientation clear at his hiring; and another church had suffered the loss of its pastor to AIDS. In each of these churches, leaders and laypeople, even those who were gay or lesbian, made it clear that this was not "the" marker of their church. In fact, as one gay lay leader said to me, "If this were known as a 'gay' church, I wouldn't stay."

The evangelical churches were identified from a dataset of more than 1,300 churches that supported the large Luis Palau evangelical festivals in Portland and Seattle (in 1999 and 2001, respectively) (Wellman 2004). Thirteen of the churches were in the western Washington area and eleven were in the western Oregon region. Eight megachurches were included in the sample; four from Washington and four from Oregon. Megachurches are defined as congregations with two thousand or more individuals who attend on a regular basis each Sunday (Thumma and Travis 2007; Ellingson 2007). The denominational affiliations of the Washington churches are one Presbyterian Church (USA), two Baptist, four Pentecostal (Foursquare and Assemblies of God), five non-denominational, and one Calvary Chapel. The denominational affiliations of the Oregon churches are one Presbyterian Church (USA), one Baptist, four nondenominational, two Pentecostal, two Church of the Nazarene, and one Christian Missionary Alliance Church. The distribution of denominational affiliations represents the PNW distributions that I detailed earlier, with a strong emphasis on nondenominational churches and a lower proportion of traditional evangelical denominational affiliations, particularly in the Baptist tradition. This underscores the independence of evangelical churches in the region and the relatively recent beginnings of these churches (nine out of the twenty-four churches were either started in the last ten years, or have seen the majority of their growth in those years). In interviews I saw little interest in denominational affiliations. Indeed, even when I investigated their Web sites, it was sometimes difficult to identify denominational connections. Need-less to say, laypeople downplayed these connections even more. This was not a negative identity either; when asked about denominational affiliations, lay leaders and new members simply showed little or no interest.

The vitality of the evangelical churches was clear from the numbers. The median growth rates of the twenty-four churches over five years were nearly 90 percent. None of these churches voiced any note of decline. Only one of the churches was losing its pastor; he was going to a larger church opportunity. It was too early to know whether this would affect that church's growth rate. The median budgets in these churches were $2 million per year; the median mis-sion budgets, including local and global mission, were more than $200,000 on an annual basis. All eight of the megachurches had budgets more than $3 million with mission budgets right at 13 percent of the overall budget, slightly more than the median for the total sample of evangelical churches.

The common organizational characteristic of the evangelical churches was the overwhelming focus on growth, outreach, and evangelism. In contrast to the liberal churches in the study that made only three missionaries available for interviews—all retired—every evangelical church supported multiple interna-tional missionaries, sometimes a handful, but most often thirty to forty, either part-time or full-time missionaries. We were able in the study to do interviews with twenty-seven full-time international missionaries who are affiliated with the twenty-four evangelical churches in the study (Wellman and Keyes 2007). I will discuss this group in the chapter on mission. The median length of stay abroad for this group was nearly six years in the field. There was also a greater number of part-time missionaries within the evangelical churches; groups and nuclear families would spend a week or two abroad in mission. One church encouraged nuclear families to alternate mission work with vacations—taking a vacation one year and doing mission work the next year. Mission was woven into the life of these congregations.

The missionary zeal was not simply going out to those abroad but also to the local community. Over and over again, ministers and laypeople voiced the ways in which the PNW was a mission field. As one Pentecostal minister said, "If you wanted to encapsulate what this church wants to be about, it's making God famous in the city of Seattle. People, when they come here, they sense that we're going someplace. It's not just about us, but about making Christ famous in the city of Seattle." In a word, these evangelical churches reverberated with ambition to "win" the PNW and the world for Christ. Thus, while liberal leaders might complain that the PNW had no tradition of church going and tended to discount organized religion per se, evangelical leaders would often comment with excitement about untapped opportunities in the region. The reality of the region's open religious market was not so much a problem but an opportunity for the evangelical churches. Thus, laypeople would say that they left another church (often a mainline Protestant or Roman Catholic church) because there was not enough focus on evangelical outreach. Underscoring this emphasis was the fact that according to interviews, 41 percent of all the evangelical informants' prioritized evangelism; in comparison, only one variable mattered more to evangelicals: small-group work (43 percent).

The only comparable point of emphasis for liberal church participants was a focus on outreach to gay people; 37 percent of our liberal informants mentioned this as a critical feature of what it meant to be a part of their church. It is a priority for the liberal churches in the study, but it is not the *only* feature of these churches. And indeed this liberal emphasis arises not out of a politically correct ethos, but a deeply felt, theologically sophisticated, moral worldview. As a liberal pastor explained:

> I think the question is a larger one than that and I think this con-
> gregation sees it as a larger one than that. I certainly do. I've angered
> some people who are gay and lesbian because I have not been out
> there crusading and preaching that from the pulpit as the issue.
> I don't believe that's the issue; I think it's one of many issues. This
> congregation was at the forefront of the movement around gender,
> in terms of ordaining women to the priesthood and allowing women
> to become bishops in this church. So the issue is theological. What
> does it mean as a church that practices infant baptism? When I
> baptize you as a child, do you become a full member of the body of
> Christ or not, or is that membership in the body of Christ conditional

upon something? Your race, your culture, your sexual orientation, your mental capacity, your intellectual capacity, your skill level? And I think the church as a whole is at a place, for the most part, of saying any person baptized into this church is a full member of the church, so that's the theological position out of which support of gender equality emerges. I think that the creation stories are another theological touchstone, if you will, that God has created each of us in the image of God, for starters, and the companion piece to that is that God has created us with the ability to make choices. So people here would say that free will is a God-given gift and the capacity to make choices is a God-given gift. I think it's a theological touchstone.

These reflections portray the deeply held theological worldviews out of which the moral values and projects of these two groups are constructed. As table 6.1[1] portrays, the demographics of these groups reflect the consequences of two distinct theological and moral worldviews.

The gender breakdown of the two groups is significant. Liberal churches reflect the more typical and expected gender proportions of most churches in which females outnumber males two to one. Forty-seven percent of my sample are male, with the higher percentage of males due in part to the sample including the clergy in the count—eight male to two female. Nonetheless, there is a sharp contrast with the evangelicals, where males are 60 percent of the total evangelical sample. The disproportion of males increases when evangelical clergy and lay leadership are separated; in this group males dominate by more than a two to one margin (102 to 48). In the evangelical clergy sample there was only one female pastor. The majority of evangelical churches either did not allow women to be ordained or were thinking about it but had not acted on the matter. The exceptions were most often the Pentecostal churches that were sometimes led by married couples, even though the husband performed most of the preaching. Nonetheless, reflecting their own heritage, the Pentecostal churches were by far more open to female leadership and were clear with their members that having females lead was a part of God's plan. As the one female evangelical pastor that I interviewed explained:

We do make it very clear at our membership seminars, you're going to be part of this local church, [female leadership] is a debatable issue in scripture, it is debatable and to some people it's not exactly mainstream. Our pastor has taken the position that it takes all people to win our city. We need men, we need women, we need young people, and so he doesn't put a limitation on anyone. We be-

TABLE 6.1. Descriptive Statistics, Percentages by Religious Group for
Socio-Demographic Variables

Variables	Liberals	Evangelicals	Difference
Gender			
Female	53.10	40.27	12.83*
Male	46.90	59.73	−12.83*
Total	100.00	100.00	0.00
Education			
Secular college	41.38	41.95	−0.57
Xtian college	6.90	11.74	−4.84
Secular grad.	40.69	9.40	31.29***
Xtian grad.	0.00	6.38	−6.38**
Total	88.97	69.47	19.50***
Location			
In-state	70.34	81.38	−11.04**
Out-state	29.66	18.62	11.04**
Total	100.00	100.00	0.00
State			
Oregon	51.72	48.66	3.06
Washington	48.28	51.34	−3.06
Total	100.00	100.00	0.00
Religious Upbringing			
Evangelical	13.10	34.90	−21.80***
M. Protestant	55.86	17.45	38.41***
Pentecostal	1.38	6.04	−4.66*
Rom. Catholic	9.66	13.09	−3.43
Unchurched	7.59	7.72	−0.13
Total	87.59	79.20	8.39*
Political Affiliation			
Democrat	7.59	2.01	5.58**
Republican	0.00	15.44	−15.44***
Total	7.59	17.45	−9.86**
N	145	298	

*p <= 0.05 ** p <= 0.01 *** p <= 0.001

Note: Variable definitions for choice variables: Secular college = percent of respondents who graduated from a secular college; Xtian college = percent of respondents who received a four-year degree from a Christian college; Secular grad. = percent of respondents who received a graduate degree from a secular college; Xtian grad. = percent of respondents who received a graduate degree from a religious college; In-state = percent of respondents who are natives to the state they currently live in; Out-state = percent of respondents who moved to the state they currently live in; M. Protestant = percent of respondents who grew up as Mainline Protestants; Rom. Catholic = percent of respondents who grew up as Roman Catholics.

lieve we are a model of a New Testament Church, and [our pastor] believes we should release women to function. So we probably are a little bit out there. But anybody that would come into the church, we ask them, do you have a problem with that? And if you do then maybe this isn't the church for you, because you will see women leading in their role. But our pastor says, "According to your gift." We're not releasing women to release women, but if you have that gifting, there's the calling, there's the talent, then we're not going to hide it just because you're a woman.

Other raw demographic data show striking results: 88 percent of the liberal respondents had completed some form of higher education (41 percent of this number included a graduate degree of some kind). For the evangelicals, 70 percent had participated in forms of higher education (16 percent of this number had some form of graduate education whether in secular or seminary settings). Both groups reflect a highly educated subset of PNW culture, with three-quarters of our total sample having participated in higher education, compared with approximately 25 percent of the wider Oregon and Washington population. But even when comparing these data, there was a higher propor-tion of liberal respondents who attained a graduate degree. As I will explore further, education has a higher priority for liberals compared with evangelicals. There is strong suspicion among evangelicals that education, and particularly public education, has a secularizing effect. This was a drumbeat among the evangelical respondents, that public education and public culture of the United States and the PNW in particular "scoffs at," "ignores," and generally "deni-grates" a "Christian" perspective on understanding the world in general, and science in particular. One evangelical respondent said:

One thing I find very interesting, one thing we have a very difficult time discussing in our society is the whole issue of evolution ver-sus creation. The idea is there has been this subtle belief that evolu-tion is built on scientific fact, and creation is built on nonsense. But the fact is, if there was a willingness even to consider, to look at it in a realistic manner, they would realize it is quite the reverse. There is no scientific foundation that disagrees with creation, but there is a fountain of information that disagrees with evolution. Evolution has no basis whatsoever in scientific fact. It is completely based on a spiritual belief system that says basically that there cannot and is not a creator, that all things happen by chance, even if that chance is not only improbable, it's impossible.

Many evangelicals in the study experienced tension over the perceived secularizing effect of public education in particular, and the culture in general. As I detail further in part II, evangelicals, in many cases, have constructed a parallel culture that includes education, entertainment, and worship. For evangelicals, this acts as a bulwark against the secularizing tendencies of the wider American culture. This does not mean that they do not want to impact and engage the wider culture, as my analysis in part II shows. For evangelicals, there may be tension with the wider "secular" culture, but this "world" is less a threat than an opportunity for evangelicals to expand their reach and to convert others to Christ. Evangelicals in this study have moved from a sectarian basis to entrepreneurial ethos, both reflecting the character of the region and capitalizing on the region's open religious market.

The PNW evangelical community is a religious subculture that, while not sectarian, does express distinctive social and symbolic boundaries and traditions. Many evangelicals come to these churches from an evangelical background (35 percent). Likewise, most liberals come from mainline Protestant backgrounds (55 percent). A higher percentage of mainline types have converted to evangelicalism (18 percent) than the percentage of evangelicals who have transferred to liberal congregations (13 percent). This is a reversal of the past trend of more evangelicals transferring into mainline denominations and it is congruent with the findings of Hout, Greeley, and Wilde (2001), who discovered that fewer evangelicals are transferring into mainline Protestant congregations than was the case in much of the twentieth century. Transfers of Roman Catholics to the liberal Protestant churches are similar (10 percent) to that of Roman Catholics to evangelical churches (13 percent). What is striking for evangelicals in this study is that when Roman Catholics make these transitions it was in every case self-described as a "conversion" to the Christian faith:

> I was raised Roman Catholic and became a Christian in college when
> I was eighteen at the Air Force Academy. I am eternally grateful
> to the air force. That was just one of those things. I was around some
> other guys that were believers and they invited me to go to a win-
> ter retreat. It was there the pastor from a little bitty town in my
> home state in Texas was the speaker and I just really related to him.
> That's where I heard really the first clear presentation of who
> Christ is and what Christ did for us and trusted him, and that's when
> I became a Christian.

A telling piece of the demographic data is that for liberals and evangelicals, only 8 percent of the respondents come from an "unchurched" background. It suggests that many of the newcomers to churches in the region tend to be immigrants (who are already religiously affiliated), looking to "connect" in a place that is relatively lacking in communal networks. This inability to attract the unchurched is predictable for the liberal churches, since they have no intention of evangelizing. But if we consider that evangelicals mention evangelizing as their top priority (by 42 percent of all evangelicals), the facts show that they simply do not attract or "convert" the unchurched at any greater rate than the liberals. This is not because of lack of effort. Pastors and lay leaders in particular mentioned attempts to attract "secular" types by creating buildings and programs that lack a "churchlike" feel. Indeed, as we witnessed, few of the evangelical buildings in this study reflect any conventional church architecture. They most often resemble schools or large public facilities. The interiors were equally neutral toward religious symbols and were quite often more like auditoriums or theaters. This is not to say that evangelicals accommodate when it comes to their message, but in terms of marketing their "brand," the religious message is muffled and recessed. Nevertheless, this strategy fails to attract the unaffiliated; instead evangelicals draw those from similar church backgrounds, newcomers who share the faith, or those from marginal religious backgrounds who seek a more intense form of faith.

My supposition is that liberal churches fail to attract the unchurched in part because they share so much in common. That is, as Mark Shibley's study has shown, the unaffiliated believe in God at similar rates to mainline Protestants; they pray as much, but they have no interest in religious institutions per se. They tend to be attracted to and involved in forms of "nature religion," and they hold relatively "liberal" social views on gay marriage, abortion, and other social issues of the day (Shibley 2004). Thus, even though there is a strong resemblance between the liberal Protestant churches in this study and the unchurched, the unchurched tend to see themselves as "spiritual but not religious." So, there is little reason to be attracted to the liberal churches because they already have what they might "get" from these churches.

Evangelical churches, on the other hand, do not fare much better with the unchurched. Evangelical churches sponsor attractive "family-oriented" programs, as well as groups that seek to appeal to people at every life stage. Nevertheless, the core theological and social messages of evangelicals are much more conservative than the beliefs and values of the unchurched in the region. Thus, what keeps evangelicals growing is the numbers of evangelical immigrants to the PNW, who, instead of defaulting into the unchurched ethos of the region, become active in these churches. Thus, evangelical churches work very hard to counteract the regional entropy toward disaffiliation, and, as part II makes clear, evangelicals do this by creating an institutional engine of biological, social, and theological reproduction. Evangelicals encourage and nurture larger families, and are more effective than liberals at keeping their children within the fold. Finally, evangelical leadership consistently emphasizes the need to reach out to newcomers and to evangelize both here and abroad.

Part II explores in depth the moral worldviews that these two communities create and how and why these two groups mobilize and motivate their members. In a series of five chapters, I investigate each group's religious identities, beliefs about God, rituals, and organizational practices, mission visions, and, finally, the consequences of each of their moral worldviews on the political position they espouse.

PART II

The Moral Worldviews of PNW Evangelicals and Liberals

7

Religion, Identity, and Moral Logics

1. The Organic Nature of Moral Worldviews

The metaphor that I use for the moral worldviews of evangelicals and liberals in the PNW is organic; they are more like onions than a toolbox. There is a tendency both for some analysts and for these groups to see the other's religious and moral worldviews as instrumental.[1] That is, moral values are acquired or discarded based on the benefits derived or how these values are adaptive to culture. However, the more I investigated these groups, the more stubborn and steadfast I found their moral worldviews. Each carries core convictions that are persistent and durable across time and against challenges (Wellman and Keyes 2007).[2] Moral worldviews begin with a core allegiance that forms the moral order of individuals and groups, giving them authority and shaping values and actions. Thus, my argument is that moral worldviews are layered organic structures centered on a moral core and in which certain values and opinions are given more weight than others. Individuals will give more weight to values and opinions they perceive as more directly connected to their moral core.

Each layer of the onion is perceived to be interconnected. Those who inhabit a moral worldview consider deeper layers more central, more important, and less negotiable than outer layers, where greater diversity is tolerated. This metaphor acknowledges that no two respondents' moral worldviews are exactly the same, particularly in the outer negotiable layers. Like onions in a field, the moral worldviews of the respondents are similar enough for me to categorize them all as a particular type of onion, but each individual specimen exhibits unique variations according to the soil it was planted in and ways in which it was nurtured. Moreover, unlike onions, preferences and tastes also account for differentiation. Nevertheless, I noticed again and again a relative homogeneity that underlined the historical and social construction of these moral worldviews from the two groups.

The organic metaphor illustrates, however, that these moral values, whether for evangelicals or for liberals, are deeply held and are not merely instrumentally rational. This is not to say that each group does not gain benefits from these moral worldviews, but that these positions are held at their core on a value rational basis. Individuals using this form of value rationality seek to verify truth claims based on their experience and maintain their moral worldviews despite the costs, socially, emotionally, or physically (Weber 1975). Nonetheless, each of these groups—evangelicals and liberals—uses the instrumental claim as a hammer to impugn the other. Evangelicals in this study, even as they assert the absolute nature of their truth claims, accuse liberals of being relativists. I found this not to be the case. Liberals, like evangelicals, hold a strong set of allegiances and values that they argue are relative to their time and tradition. This means they take their claims as "true," though not the "only" truth.

On the other hand, liberals often accuse evangelicals of using their "values" to win elections or manipulate larger groups. Now this may or may not be the case at the level of political elites, but my findings show that evangelicals hold their own values as central to their identity and are also aware of the way politicians manipulate them for their own ends. Evangelicals are loyal first to their values and only secondarily to their politicians.

I will first compare the moral worldviews of liberals and evangelicals by examining their core allegiance; second, I will explore the moral values that are derived from these core commitments; third, I will investigate the moral actions and projects that stem from these values; and finally, I will speak to the outer layer of the onion, the most negotiable part, the customs and aesthetics of this moral worldview, where adaptation and flexibility are at their height.

a. Core Allegiances

At the center of the evangelical moral worldviews is a personal relationship with Jesus Christ, based on an act of submission to the authority of their "Lord." This act of allegiance is intimate and intensely subjective. It is intimate in that this submission is not merely intellectual but also an emotional commitment that is cultivated endlessly through worship, prayer, ritual, and personal piety. It is subjective in that it centers on a personal decision by each individual that engages the core identity of the self. The intimacy and subjective nature of this core are not only continually nurtured but also normatively constructed. Leadership molds how these personal decisions should be made and how one should feel about them in the process. Indeed, the transformation of this personal core is the center of what many pastors and laypeople mentioned as an "authentic" faith. One lay leader tells the story of his conversion. He framed it with his own limitations and "sin" and ends with a personal submission to the "Lord," which was echoed in multiple stories told by evangelicals in the study:

> I'm an alcoholic and at age forty I felt like my life was really disintegrating. All the hopes that I had had were going down the tubes, and someone invited me to a home Bible study and I realized I needed to put my trust in the Lord and that he was worthy of my trust and would see me out of my alcoholism and see me through the problems I was having with my family. So at age forty I got serious. I did grow up in a very nominal church. We went to a church here for a while and there was a big problem in it, so we set out to find a church where we'd be happy and we ended up here. The reason that we love this church is because the word of God is faithfully preached. The people are very loving and supporting and it's a church of prayer and it's a church that reaches out into the community.

Context matters on how this core relationship is formed and cemented. It is within small groups and home churches where evangelical piety is nurtured, which I explore further below in chapter 9. A vocabulary is constructed in these groups that shapes and guides how one expresses the faith. A consistent theme molds the discourse of evangelical piety in these churches that faith is a "relationship and *not* a religion." The movement demands that an ascriptive and secondhand "religion" be replaced by a voluntary and firsthand relationship to Jesus Christ. The life of faith is made vivid and deeply experiential. The case of a new member exemplifies this transition. Despite the fact she had grown up in a devout Roman Catholic home, she explained how she had now converted to her newfound faith:

> I grew up in a very devout Catholic home. Very devout. We were in church whenever we were supposed to be and practiced the sacraments and religious holidays. It was my senior year in high school

that I was dating a boy that went to a Methodist church and went with him a couple times and began to realize that there was something different about other churches. I had never attended a different church other than the Catholic Church. And that began the practice of starting to question why I believe what I believe, why are we doing, say, the whole reconciliation confession? Why do we have to talk to a priest who is just a man? How can he forgive me of my sins? And just began questioning and asked my parents and my mom's answer was, well, this is how we've always done it. This is what we believe, this is our heritage, this is our tradition. And that wasn't an OK answer, because they taught me not to follow the crowd in the other decisions I made. Why should I do that with one of the most important things in my life? And through the guy I was dating, we had several conversations about religion and faith and he would direct me to the Bible, which I had actually never opened at that point. And his answers made sense and they were confirmed with what God's word was saying. And it was in December of '88, I was twenty years old, that I realized what the truth was and that I needed a relationship with Jesus Christ as opposed to pursuing a religion. And that was quite a big deal in my home. My parents felt like I was abandoning the family, the tradition, the heritage, and it's been thirteen, fourteen years now and they too realize that there is something different. Not all of them have realized that it's a personal relationship that they pursue, but they did see a difference. And they have come to accept it.

These dramatic stories of conversion to a "relationship" are common throughout the interviews. The personal and intentional act of submission is a critical element in guaranteeing that one is "saved" and that one has a vital faith. Of course, again, context matters; boyfriends, intimate others, as well as small groups help to guide these decisions. Nonetheless, personal and individual decisions mark evangelical piety.

This "relationship" with Jesus Christ is not only the necessary engine of personal transformation but of social change as well. This new self is thus the font of religious salvation, but also propels cultural and political change (Carpenter and Shenk 1990). Indeed, for evangelicals, social change that is not preceded by personal "repentance" is not only inauthentic but is even useless. This is the reason for evangelical ambivalence toward secular social programs and one of the sources of outrage among liberals who complain that evangelicals fail to support public services. For evangelicals, progress means submission to Christ; everything else follows from it. For evangelicals, liberal social action is superficial and destined to fail because it does not "touch the heart."

The moral core of liberals is less focused on a person, Jesus, then on the principles he embodied. The rhetoric of liberal inclusiveness sometimes hides its theological depth. For Christian liberals in this study, inclusiveness is at the heart of Jesus' message. Jesus embodies an "open commensality"; all are welcome at his table regardless of class, race, or gender (Crossan 1992, 262). Jesus preferred sinners and was sometimes labeled as such. Liberal churches move the idea of egalitarianism and open commensality to the very heart of their moral identity. One liberal pastor quoted Joel 2:13 as his core biblical rationale for his doctrine of God. He paralleled this to what he called Jesus' only "theological parable" of the Publican and the tax collector, where the Pharisee at synagogue thanks God that he is not like the tax collector. The tax collector prays and expresses his unworthiness and his repentance is his righteousness (Luke 18:9–14). The pastor argued: "God calls for repentance and brokenness and is merciful. God does not demand holiness first and then forgiveness." This framework is like a bell that echoes in almost every conversation with liberal laypeople and pastors alike—God is not the Holy One, filled with righteousness, but the loving One always already accepting and forgiving (Wellman 2002).

The consequences of this ideological differentiation go deeper than a negative identity construction. As another pastor put it: "Liberals demand inclusion and this means unity between the outside and the inside of the self." Nancy Ammerman (1997) has called this the "lived religion" of liberals or "Golden Rule Christians," but it goes to their moral core. Not only does behavior trump belief but, more important, the two must be integrated, so that the outer and the inner self are coordinated. Thus, one notes a high sensitivity to hypocrisy in liberal Christians, which so often bleeds into forms of cynicism and a backing away from organizational religion. Indeed, at one point I asked a group of laypeople why they would not use the Nicene Creed or any other traditional piece of liturgy in what they call their "celebration"—their church service. I received a ferocious rebuke for suggesting that they take on a tradition that is meaningless to them. This reluctance illustrates the powerful demand for consistency between a felt conviction and forms of tradition.

This ideological framework, moreover, affects the liberal Protestant theological perspective and how liberals interpret Jesus. When I asked how a group of liberals interpret their faith relative to other religious traditions, the univocal response was summed up best by the following remark by a liberal lay leader: "Jesus is a way that they follow but not THE way." Evangelicals might call this relativism or even heresy. But in conversations with the ministers and lay-people of these liberal congregations I was struck again and again at the depth of thought and struggle that had gone into their theological conclusions. Their beliefs center on the principle that Jesus presents God's way in the world. Another layperson said, "I believe in a little *c* Christianity. Jesus is the way but not the only way. Truth has come in other religious traditions." Yet another described her belief about Jesus this way: "Jesus came to reveal God and for 2,000 years we've got hung up on Jesus. He didn't ask us to worship him." Christ is not so much the Savior who died for the sins of humankind, but the one who challenges one to service, decenters the ego, and gives one power to imitate and follow a life of compassion (Wellman 2002).

Often in interviews with liberals they would describe their journey from a more conservative, evangelical faith in rather tortured terms. One told how he was raised Baptist, and "at age 14, I looked [at the church] and it was borderline psychotic." He left the faith for twenty years, only returning because he had children and his wife wanted him to go back.

> And so with great fear and trembling I entered the door. But the first sermon was on the love of God and I couldn't recall ever hearing that inside the church walls before and I was instantly hooked. I remember how a friend described how his neighbor, an evangelical missionary, went overseas and before he fixed the natives' teeth, would ask them to make a decision for Christ. For me [the liberal layperson], it's not so much about salvation. It's all about the way you live your life, the way you share with other people.

The liberal moral core demands the integration of belief and behavior. For liberals, salvation is the "wholeness" that this integration implies. Salvation meditates a life of integrity of word and action and thus is a thoroughly this-worldly message. Salvation is not about life after death but about the presence of God in this life. To be sure, not all are happy with the emphasis on a this-worldly salvation. Several liberal focus group members complained bitterly that a guest pastor at the church had come and debunked the notion of res-urrection after death. Even the most liberal of the focus members thought this was a mistake and simply "depressing." One of the pastors said that he had recently "come out of the closet" about his beliefs (at an Easter worship service) saying, "I actually believe in the actual resurrection of Jesus." Some congre-gational members were taken aback but many were relieved. What this means is not so much that Jesus had died for sin and saved the individual believer, but that Jesus "incarnates" the love and gracious presence of God on earth as well as beyond. Thus, even as liberals unanimously emphasize the integration of word and action in this world, some find great hope in the message of a world to come.

One of the liberal church's mission mottoes speaks to the focus on human experience as that which mediates the life of God: "Honest question, shared experience, and ancient traditions." Each of these churches emphasizes the complexity of human existence and the "sheer contingency" of human life. Over and over again liberals would share the labyrinthine reality of their "spiritual journeys," filled with issues and questions that have no easy answers. At least a quarter of the focus group members and four out of ten liberal ministers describe these journeys as moving away from evangelical or fundamentalist backgrounds. The reasons for rejecting this perspective are multiple but primarily center on how simple answers had failed them as they confronted contemporary situations. They consistently asserted that the resources of their conservative faith were no longer adequate.

Finally, throughout my conversations with liberals egalitarianism was a strong trend. For the women, it was in part a feminist critique of patriarchialism. Many women made the point that men had too often used religion to oppress women. Several women voiced that their having grown up in the 1960s made it quite difficult, if not impossible, to use or understand the word *Lord* used in relationship to Christ. It was simply a word that they found repugnant:

> The Lord and Savior brings out this kingly monarchical kind of image that I have difficulty with. That is, the monarch has all the answers and makes all the laws and everybody has to do that, but they are on such a pedestal, nobody could ever approach who they are and what they are doing. I've always liked the story of the Emperor's new clothes. The emperor is walking around handing out decrees but really doesn't have anything on. I guess I always see that as the other side of the Lord and Savior part.

Even so, five of the ten ministers were willing to embrace the language of Jesus as Lord and Savior. Nonetheless, for these pastors the Lordship of Jesus highlights the liberal egalitarian message of the Christian gospel. As one pastor related, her loyalty to Christ "relativizes all other values" and, in a sense, underscores the need for equality among all people. For another minister, this notion of Christ's supremacy (as Lord) creates powerful judgments against income inequality, inequality among nations, and the lack of opportunities for ethnic and minority groups. In each case the pastor calls for a radical turn to God and the recognition of God's "preference for the poor." The pastor's sermons were sprinkled with the demand that one must follow Christ and that to know God is to seek justice and equality for those left out of political and economic opportunity. This tough message of justice was not met with universal approbation by any means. Indeed, one focus group member in the church found this "dabbling in politics and economics, tiresome at best." In this sense, the complaint by evangelicals that liberals too often accommodate the message to contemporary culture and thereby lose the "offense of the gospel," is again a generalization that does not hold. Liberals were willing to offend and did risk offending their middle- and upper-middle-class congregations.

As we see, the core allegiances of these groups are neither instrumental nor superficial. In each case, they are based on theological convictions and truth claims, shaped by experience, which deeply inform their moral worldviews. At the same time, even as the groups arrive at their moral worldviews by a similar process, their content is quite different. For evangelicals, relationship trumps moral principles, and salvation by grace through Christ conditions and legitimizes moral action. For evangelicals, first and foremost, the sin of the self must be overcome. In light of a holy God, how does one come before God to find favor and grace? Evangelicals find that favor in Jesus Christ and his death on the cross. However, this is more than a simple transaction. It is, rather, a living relationship that restores joy to life, inspires one to share a message of hope, and creates stronger relationships with families, friends, and those in need. The evangelical approach is individualistic; at the same time, these discussions nearly always take place within a group context. The fellowship of believers shapes the discourse and nurtures the faith.

For liberals, on the other hand, there is less interest in the salvation of the individual and far less interest in small groups—liberals consistently accent the need for each person to interpret his or her own faith. The central question for the liberals is not so much about the sin of the self but how to motivate and integrate the self in such a way as to align it with the broader and more gracious ways of God. This God is all-loving and kind and, through Jesus, shows one how to live. To live is to treat others fairly and equitably, to love and forgive others as exemplified by Jesus, and to know the joy of God's presence as Jesus knew that presence. This is in line with the nineteenth-century liberal theological tradition of Friedrich Schleiermacher, who emphasized the importance of "God consciousness" over against individual salvation (Schleiermacher 1988). Liberals want to experience God, not so much as a savior but as an exemplar and presence that inspires one to full human integration and moral action. The evidence shows that both of these groups are struggling to embody a moral worldview that is demanding and sometimes daunting. We now move to the values that grow out of these core allegiances.

b. Moral Values

From this personal center arises a second layer of values respondents considered "moral." It is at this level, following Fred Kniss, that I investigate what the locus of moral authority is and what values arise from this perspective. Here one notes the greatest contrasts between evangelicals and liberals. Liberals embody forms of modernism and personal autonomy, while evangelicals advocate a stringent personal and scriptural traditionalism. Kniss captures this difference by distinguishing the individual as the locus of authority for liberals, and the collectivity as the seat of authority for evangelicals. I am less convinced by this distinction. Evangelicals are strongly individualistic when it comes to their core allegiances, even though they depend on groups for support. Liberals value personal autonomy but at the same time are convinced that public and communal social action makes the difference. Moreover, both groups spoke about their values in homogenous terms. Both groups came to their values shaped by a set of subculturally conditioned assumptions. Group consciousness was strong on both sides. Each group represents a moral worldview with core allegiances and with an authority that is socially and historically constructed. The values differ, though the construction of authority is similar.

For evangelicals, the second layer of the onion focuses on honesty, integrity, service, traditional sexual morality, devotion to family, and hard work. Respondents emphasized "relationships"—beginning with Jesus Christ, but including friends, family, and strangers as being pivotal for the formation of their morality. I do not claim that the values drawn by the evangelical community, or the liberal community for that matter, are inherent to Christianity or the teachings of the Bible; they are interpretive acts. For instance, contemporary, evangelical, American "family values" were not a part of the original Christian community or the medieval church, nor do they play the same role in contemporary liberal Protestant congregations (Browning 2000). One of the ironies, which liberals point out, is that Jesus was at best ambivalent about the family, even his own family. Thus, the focus of evangelicals on family as a central plank in their moral worldview is at least debatable.

Nevertheless, for evangelicals, this second moral layer calls for conservative and traditional values around heterosexual marriage over against what many evangelicals believe is the political imposition of gay marriage by elite liberal culture. Indeed, initiatives against gay marriage were being voted on in

Washington and Oregon at the time of the interviews; it was clearly a watershed moment for these churches:

> We have been facing, you know that in Washington and Oregon, we
> have been dealing now with same-sex marriage. We don't approach
> this as a political agenda. We approach this as a doctrinal issue that
> we feel strong about, about preserving the traditional view of marriage. So we had a little emphasis, we had a Sunday sermon, we did
> a petition signing. Not because we hate gays, because that is not
> the case. God loves them and he loves them as much as he loves us.

For evangelicals, homosexuality is a sin. But evangelicals believe that all people are sinners; they simply do not want what they call "sin" (gay marriage) codified in law. Of course, as was repeated again and again, it is not that they hate gay people; they love them and they want the "best" for them. That is, they want them to come into to what they call a "natural" (God ordained) heterosexual marriage and experience the joy that God has for them. Indeed, the issue is a difficult and painful topic for evangelicals. On several occasions, evangelicals expressed strong feelings of political and social oppression by the "liberal agenda," forcing them to accept the "gay" lifestyle, which they abhor. Moreover, some argued that there will come a time when Christianity, or at least their moral positions against homosexuality, will be outlawed and that they will be under legal persecution. One respondent said:

> But yeah, I mean, basically, what God's truth is the truth that I
> believe in, whether it's popular. I mean, if there comes a day, which
> I believe there will, that it's illegal to gather with other Christians
> or to believe in certain things, I don't care. I'll take a stand for God
> because eternity is waiting for me.

This was a common fear expressed by evangelicals that traditional marriage was under attack. This was in part the reason for the May Day for Marriage event held at Safeco Field in Seattle in 2004. Washington churches, led by many of the pastors and lay leaders in the churches that I studied, gathered together to hear speeches supporting traditional marriage. It was estimated that around twenty thousand attended the event. There was a special place in the bleachers for a small number of protestors, and many who supported gay marriage stood outside Safeco Field to protest what they called an act of "discrimination and prejudice." This protest was disturbing to many evangelicals in my study. They saw it as a form of secular and liberal hypocrisy: Seattlites, known for embracing a culture of tolerance and free speech, were intolerant of *their* free speech when it came to standing up for traditional marriage. For several evangelicals, it was the first time that they experienced "hate" speech against them.

> When you talk about a culture or a mindset in the Northwest, even in the paper yesterday, they had an article on Seattle as the number one most educated place in the country and we're the most un- churched in the country. So you put those up and go "For being so smart, why are we not grasping wisdom from the Lord?" And I think it's true, it's here in the head and hasn't made it to the heart. So we're kind of in a culture of knowing a lot and we can't make the distance from head to heart. And then this culture of tolerance, as long as I don't bother you, you don't bother me. And as long as we continue on that road everything is OK. And I see that in my workplace and even out in the grocery store. As long as we're just doing our own thing, everything is OK. The May Day for Marriage thing was the first time [for me] feeling hated. Walking into a place like, all of a sudden, I didn't have my so-called right to go in and express my beliefs and my faith because somebody was attacking me for that. And I've never experienced that before. Usually it's, you do your thing I'll do my thing. And this was flipped, like all of a sudden I didn't feel like it was OK for me to take my position.

Among the interviews, nearly 30 percent of evangelicals advocated against gay marriage, and another 22 percent spoke out against abortion. For evan- gelicals, these are not "political" issues but moral ones. Evangelicals consid- ered abortion a "tragedy," an "abomination," a "holocaust," and a "terrible act against the sanctity of life." These values were consistent across the interviews; even among some of the "liberal" evangelicals, gay marriage and abortion were rejected as moral options. Evangelicals considered their positions as "absolute" and felt them to be "unconditional." Finally, all of the evangelical respondents said that their moral values were based on biblical standards that they con- sidered "absolute" and "certain."[3]

The evangelical claim to "absolute" truth and "certainty" about these moral claims shields evangelicals against external criticisms and the values of cultural and religious others. This makes sense within the moral worldview theory. A worldview is a morally, psychologically, and intellectually ordering structure. Voices from outside the moral worldview are unpersuasive because within the bounds of that moral worldview they are illegitimate and incoherent. Thus, liberal moral worldviews and critiques make no more sense to evangelicals than evangelical critiques do to liberals. I do *not* assert that evangelical moral positions are immune to change, only that if change is to occur, voices of critique that might instigate that change must speak in an idiom that makes sense to evangelicals. During the interviews, the evangelical subculture was aggressive in fending off challenges to their moral positions, but again, liberals were equally demonstrative in attacking evangelical truth claims and defending their own. Thus, as noted above, not one of our evangelical respondents expressed an alternative perspective on either abortion or gay marriage. But neither did any of the liberal respondents come out against gay marriage. When evangelicals critique liberals as relativists, evangelicals are mistaken. Liberals hold their values every bit as absolute as evangelicals do. Of course, liberals do not say that they do this, but as one lesbian clergywoman said in responding to the evangelical position on the incompatibility of the Christian faith and homosexuality, "My spirituality is unassailable."

At this level of the moral onion, values are nonnegotiable, so it should not surprise us that we find perspectives that are held absolutely. When evangelicals seek to give moral authority to their values they always go back to the Scriptures. It is from the Bible that they gain their values, and in this sense they are expressed as sacrosanct and infallible. Liberals construct their moral authority from a combination of sources, including reason, personal experience, and their religious traditions. To think for oneself and to make up one's own mind is a "sacred" duty. It became something of a cliché in the interviews with liberals, but frequently liberals would say, "God gave us a mind to think for ourselves." The highest compliment a liberal can give to her church is "You don't have to leave your mind at the door." Liberals are children of the Enlightenment. For them, thinking for oneself is sacrosanct every bit as much as supporting traditional values is for evangelicals. The liberal perspective is held with a sense of pride, as is evident in one respondent's comments:

> I wanted to speak to something on a common thread. To me, it's more than just allowing each of us to explore our own theology, but it's actually requiring us, where there is this structure or box in more conservative churches, here, not only are the boundaries removed if we want to, they are removed whether we want to or not. There's a requirement and a demand on us to push ourselves outside our comfort zone and our box a little bit, where not everything this church does is going to make everyone happy. But what it does do is make you ask yourself questions; and most important, it's OK to ask questions, and that's why the person is back that next Sunday. It might not be what I want and I'm not comfortable with this, but I'm comfortable with the totality of what this church embraces, so therefore I will be back.

Again and again liberals spoke with a sense of near awe that their churches make them question. Evangelicals' churches give answers; liberals expect an intellectual challenge. Evangelicals want certitude; liberals know there is no final answer. Liberals will say that they take the tough road and evangelicals the easy one. Indeed, as one liberal lay leader said in speaking about theology, "We're in the majors; they're [referring to evangelicals] in the minors." Again, interestingly, evangelicals interpret liberal Christianity as an easy accommodation to contemporary culture. That is, liberals emasculate the faith and remove the "offense" of the gospel in order to appeal to modern people. Of course, both of these groups need to establish the legitimacy of their belief systems and rationalize their moral values over against the other. Liberals tended to comment more frequently about evangelicals than evangelicals about liberals. While evangelicals felt less challenged by liberal churches per se, evangelicals remained defensive against liberal culture in general. Liberal churches, on the other hand, felt directly tested by the numerical success of evangelical congregations, and frequently bemoaned this competition.

A second critical value for liberals is that of inclusiveness. For liberals, this principle comes not from "political correctness" but from the Scriptures, and most powerfully from the ministry of Jesus Christ. As was referred to earlier, the open commensality of Jesus and his willingness to speak and work with women and other ethnic groups in the Scriptures underlines the "radical openness" that liberals preach and try to practice. A pastor who retired during this study reflected with pride on what others had called him in his two churches in Oakland and in Seattle. He said, "In Oakland I was called a 'nigger-lover' and in Seattle a 'fag-lover.' But I stand and will continue to stand with those who are attacked and put down." This pastor had facilitated the racial integration of his church in Oakland, and in Seattle mainstreamed gay and lesbian people into the leadership at his church. He paid a price for these actions. In the last several years his denomination had voted twice to "disfellowship" his church for their support and ordination of practicing homosexuals. Both votes failed to get the two-thirds plurality, but it had been close, and the second vote was closer yet. For this pastor and for many of my liberal respondents, a part of their spiritual practice is to affirm and empower gay and lesbian people. This is a part of their advocacy for inclusion that they find voiced in the Gospels of Jesus Christ.

In direct response to conservatives who criticize liberal Protestants for their relativism and willingness to compromise, liberal pastors and laypeople say that they will not compromise on the gospel's demand to include all people, particularly those who are marginalized such as gays, women, and minorities. But even here liberals were quick to say that their churches were open to all, and that they did not want to be labeled as a church for gays and lesbians, but indeed a church that reaches out to many kinds of individuals who are marginalized in society. One person said:

> I don't think it's right to label this church as one that is just for gay
> and transgendered and all those other people. And I don't know if
> it's even fair to label the more mainline liberal churches as that.
> I think maybe we're considered liberal churches because we are open
> to all forms of people, ideas, discussions; open to all kinds of questions about faith, about Christianity. But I also think we're open to
> bringing in other faiths, like the Buddhists and the Hindus and
> whoever else might be of interest to us for various reasons; connected
> to politics, connected with the city and the homeless and the needy
> and at-risk youth and the mentally ill, all that kind of thing. So, I
> don't like the fact that you're trying to label us, or at least I get that
> feeling, that you're trying to label us as liberal only because we're
> open to gays and lesbians.

Once again for liberals the moral principle of inclusiveness goes to the heart of their convictions and to limit the breadth of this inclusion is to question their integrity and undercut their moral and religious values. In this same church, the assistant pastor, an openly gay man, was married to his partner in the sanctuary. It was televised on the local news during the time when Multnomah County, Oregon, was still giving out marriage licenses to gay couples. In response to this action, another layperson said:

> I was very proud when our minister married his partner in our
> sanctuary. That was a very thrilling day to me. And I was very proud
> of our church and how loving and accepting we were. But again, I
> don't think that is our whole identity. I just think that's like another
> day at our church. It was important because we love him so much
> and we were happy for him, but it wouldn't have mattered who he
> married, we would have been happy for him.

Consistent with the absolute nature of evangelical values, someone at a large evangelical church in the city commented on the marriage of the pastor to his partner: "This pastor is the most evil man in the city." It goes to show that on this issue of values the gap between evangelicals and liberals is wide and deep. On the issue of homosexuality there is a cultural clash that runs across these two groups. I saw no signs of possible reconciliation. Even when I interviewed evangelicals who were the most critical of U.S. foreign policy and the

Iraq War, when it came to abortion and specifically to homosexuality, there was no compromise from them on the issues.

Thus, at this level of the moral onion, moral worldviews can and do come into conflict. When the conflict is at the level of values—values that are nonnegotiable—it is a dangerous divide. Both sides feel the pain of this divide, and both sides stand firmly in their faith that what they are doing is right, true, and good. Of course, there are evangelical elites who are willing to compromise on the issue, but I found no evidence of any who did so in my study. I now investigate the moral actions and projects that flow out of these values.

c. Moral Projects

At this layer of the moral onion, there is much greater diversity. When moving from core allegiance to values, there was strong consistency in positions taken by evangelicals and liberals. Respondents argued with certitude on their positions. In the transition from moral actions to moral project, there is less assurance about how to translate core allegiances and values into actions. At this layer we begin to see the intersection of moral worldviews and politics. Positions are taken but with less certitude on either side. Positions are also conditioned by context, events, and local traditions. Thus, respondents are less willing to pronounce that their positions are right or wrong. What this also signals is that Christianity has never had a specific political agenda. It is difficult to construct a political philosophy from the New Testament (Hays 1996). Nonetheless, there are trends in each group that I will investigate. Specific political issues, such as war, I examine in greater depth in the chapter on religion and politics.

Economic and political positions that often stem from but do not completely coincide with moral positions are the third layer of the evangelical and liberal moral worldviews. Predictably, there is some diversity of opinion at this level among PNW evangelicals. Respondents supported both liberal and conservative views on political issues like welfare, taxation, and environmental conservation. While the "moral" positions mentioned in the previous section were sacrosanct among evangelicals, the American political conservative agenda is held less absolutely. Respondents proved able to criticize the conservative political worldview on issues including welfare, environmental policies, and even, though only rarely, the war in Iraq. Nevertheless, most evangelicals self-identified as conservative and Republican and argued for conservative political perspectives mentioned earlier: less government, stronger military, expanding economic markets, and advocacy for democracy. Socialism was rejected across the board. Support for forms of democracy and liberty was perennial and strongly stated. When it came to issues of war, evangelicals argued for the deterrence of evil, but even more often voiced the belief that the war was bringing "liberty" to Iraqis. Americans were "liberators" of an oppressed people, overcoming the "evil" of an authoritarian dictatorship, but just as importantly were opening up missions to the Muslim peoples of Iraq. The stated evangelical rationale for either support or dissent relative to the Iraq War was formulated directly from their morally orienting worldviews.

Following the trends in evangelical public engagement outlined in part I, evangelicals generally support greater political advocacy than liberals. Nearly 15 percent of evangelicals either practiced direct forms of political advocacy or supported the church doing so. Twelve percent of liberals supported forms of political advocacy, but in the interviews liberals tended to express greater caution about mixing church and state. Evangelicals, on the other hand, were less guarded but nonetheless wary of the results. Evangelicals believe that church and state should be kept separate but they increasingly voice the importance of engaging the public square with their views. One lay leader said:

> The church has to be careful about mixing church and politics because in this country we have a tradition of separation of church and state. And if we cross that line we'll be paying taxes on this property and everything else. And it's not just a financial thing, it's deeper than that. It's a national historical, it's one of the basis of our nation ... separation of church and state. I think the church should promote the idea of registering to vote and being a good citizen. The church better not cross the line and start supporting candidates or not, because that will be trouble, I think. That's my personal opinion ... that we'll cause trouble. But as far as us as individual Christians, whatever, talking about things in church or having a petition. It was done tastefully, there wasn't a problem, I don't believe, at least with that. That type of thing can't come from the pulpit. I just think that would be wrong and get us into trouble and we'd be headed down a slippery slope. Now I think it's great when the pastor says register to vote, do your citizenship duty and all of that. But if he starts to say "Hey, you need to go out and sign a petition because we need to get this elected official recalled" I'm saying time out, you've crossed the line. That to me would be wrong. We do need to be active politically. It would be great if more Christians ran for public office. I think that would be wonderful.

What this lay leader means by having a "Christian" running for office is someone who supports evangelical moral values. Thus, I heard no one advocating for a purely Christian theocratic state. In this sense the fears of liberal elites are overblown and exaggerated (Goldberg 2006; Hedges 2007). Evangelicals may believe at times that the United States is a Christian nation (or at least we used to be) but, at least in my sample, no one argued for a form of Christian nationalism.[4] At the same time, evangelicals sought to persuade others politically to their moral worldview and to provide a culture where their values would be protected and projected into the public square.

Indeed, if evangelicals feel oppressed and even persecuted (15 percent felt this way) then it is because of what they perceive is a "liberal culture," which for them is relativist and promotes immorality (pornography, gay marriage, infidelity, and the like). Of course, the irony is that liberals were equally concerned for their kids and about popular culture and how corrupting it is, which I will discuss below. Like evangelicals, liberals critiqued the consumerist nature of American culture. Nonetheless, evangelicals are at the same time aware that politics will neither end human social corruption nor be the solution to the problem of human sin. It is the human heart that must be changed. An evangelical said:

> We have a model that God is not political. We see this over and over again, that it is not an issue of politics. . . . We see that even when Jesus lived on this earth, there was a grand desire to pull him into the politics of that time that existed, but he refused to be pulled into that. He didn't speak against the Roman government, even though the Roman government was extremely cruel and he wasn't saying that what they were doing was right, but that the issues were not political. The issues were spiritual issues. It's challenging in that the danger is that when the church gets involved in politics, and I mean the organized church, not the spiritual church, but the church that is organized by people, that the danger is that they become simply another voice among several voices. There is a need to be involved in the process to vote for people, to pray for those people, to encourage them to make decisions that are principled, that hopefully are based on biblical principles, but the reality is that to not believe that you can somehow form or force a society into this form based on a political action.

While it is true that the moral project for evangelicals is not something that can be forced or even finally legislated, evangelicals are willing to push for and support legislation that aligns with their moral values. Thus, the liberal fear that evangelicals want to change public policies is not unfounded. At the same time, for evangelicals politics is always penultimate; the heart is the pivot point of moral transformation and without a "heart change," politics do not matter. For evangelicals, the moral project is persuasion to their moral values. These moral values, from their perspective, are best nurtured in open markets— economic, cultural, and political. That is, liberty is an important cornerstone of their political belief system. The connection and potential affinity between evangelicalism and American political conservatism will be discussed under the topic of religion and politics, but the overlap between the evangelicalism and political conservatism is real and potent. Evangelicals strongly support open markets where they can share what they believe. But political advocacy per se is not at their core; I found that only four out of twenty-four evangelical pastors were strongly supportive of specific political initiatives. And in each case it was about moral values. Moreover, evangelical pastors frequently felt used by politicians, who, after seeking them out in order to be elected, did little to forward conservative moral issues in office. One pastor in particular was discouraged that after thirty years of ministry and his strong backing of conservative social issues, no progress had been made. He invited a Republican candidate for the U.S. Senate to come and pray in his service. The pastor did not endorse him and he received some negative feedback by having the candidate participate in the service. But, as the pastor said, "If we're given a tax break by the government we're getting it for the wrong reason. Let's get this club off our necks. It's a muzzling kind of a deal." For him, the nonprofit status is a tax benefit, but the effects are to keep the church out of partisan politics and thus, for the pastor, out of electing people who can push Christian moral values. This pastor is simply saying, as I heard from many evangelicals, the moral battle for the sake of families and children is being lost. Thus, what mobilizes and motivates evangelicals is their allegiance to their moral values rationalized through selective use of scripture and inspired, as they say, by their relationship with Jesus Christ.

Again, consistent with my findings in part I, I found in my interviews with liberal Protestants a relative lack of interest in politics. In the 1960s and 1970s, the liberal Protestant church was on the forefront of civic engagement. They critiqued conservative Christians for their obsession with individual salvation and their tendency to stand back from the political public fray. Of course, much has changed in the evangelical circles since then. Today American evangelicals believe their faith informs their politics by nearly a two to one margin relative to liberal and mainline Protestants, and are, by similar proportions, more committed to "transforming" society than liberal and mainline Protestants. Furthermore, more than 90 percent of evangelicals believe that religious people should "fight evil." Self-identified fundamentalists and evangelicals no longer believe in "separation" from the world, but that the world must be engaged, transformed, and converted (Green 2003, 15, 18; Smith 1998; Lindsay 2007). Indeed, it is the liberals who tend toward privatization or at least compartmentalization of their faith. A part of this results from the fact that the civil rights movement has largely succeeded, women's rights have achieved general acceptance, abortion is generally safe and legal, and there has been some movement toward acceptance for the rights of gay couples, however uneven. American culture in general favors and overlaps with many of the "values" that liberals hold close.[5] In other words, liberals have won most of the public battles and there is thus less to fight over. Reasons to mobilize have decreased and in many cases disappeared.

But it is also true that liberals often cite the dangers of the mixing of church and state. Over and over again liberals expressed a general reluctance to take public stands. One urban congregation that had officially made a decision as a church to be open to ordaining gays and lesbians would not take a public position on the Oregon initiative defining marriage as being between a man and a woman. As the pastor explained, the church was quite cautious about creating divisions within its own walls:

> I think the church is effective when it's faithful and true to its spir-itual traditions and its understanding of its heritage. The issue of gay marriage is an interesting one in this congregation. I thought that this congregation would probably want to endorse gay marriage. We did not. We spoke against Measure 36, but we spoke against it say-ing that we believe that we have not yet discerned where God is calling us in this and that we should not be taking a stand on behalf of the entire congregation until we have more of a sense of common vision of where that should go. We've taken strong stands on is-sues that the community disagrees on and my associate and I and several of the rest of us infiltrated the James Dobson movement to prohibit gay marriages and we went there deliberately to sit in on the groups and not to disrupt them, but to say How do you get to the point of view you're at and why do you believe that? What's the evidence you have for that? And you know there are other people out there who have different points of view than you do. Just to make them a little uncomfortable with what they perceive to be the over-whelming dominance in the Christian faith of their point of view. There are very few issues that you deal with biblically and theologi-cally that are clear-cut.

This reluctance is reflected in the fact that only two of the ten liberal senior pastors could be called political advocates. One has since retired and the other is struggling with a church that is in slow decline. A part of this reluctance to be involved in politics stems from the fact that lay liberals simply do not want to hear about politics on Sunday morning. A liberal layperson who attended the church with the pastor who is most politically active complained to me: "I want to hear about God when I go to church. I don't want to hear about economics or social ministry or how I am not doing my part, when I feel like I'm dedicating my life to my kids and to cancer research. I feel like I'm hounded every time I come to church."

This emphasizes the idea that liberal laypeople are a less homogenous group than evangelicals are. The pastor of the fastest growing of the liberal churches mentioned that a small group of members was upset at the voiced opposition to the Iraq War coming from guest preachers over the summer in 2006 and sought to "hear less politics from the pulpit." The pastor obliged, based in part on his belief that politics do not belong in the pulpit whether from the left or the right. Liberal pastors frequently mentioned the political diversity of their congregations; evangelical pastors less so. Evangelicals are preaching to congregations in which they perceive greater moral consensus.

Moreover, ambivalence about political advocacy does not just come from laypeople in liberal churches. A liberal pastor expressed the struggle in his own denomination, which has a large percentage of African Americans. As a white male in the denomination he said he had to be sensitive to his African American colleagues who simply did not want to talk about homosexuality and generally have a "don't ask, don't tell," philosophy of ministry. Moreover, this same pastor spoke of his own frustration being a part of the liberal advocacy group in the PNW. He said there were nearly three hundred members, and fifteen of those members kept the organization going. He expressed what he felt was a lack of "urgency" in liberal ministers. For him, instead of working harder to counteract what he called "fundamentalism," liberals had "gone to sleep."

When liberals mention mission in their churches they mean social service and ministries of outreach, and tend to lionize these efforts. However, another striking finding was that there was slightly more voluntary service (separated out from evangelical mission work) coming from evangelical churches in the study (37 to 34 percent). It is simply no longer the case that liberal churches dominate service to the poor and the socially marginalized (Brooks 2006; Cnaan 2002; Hertkze 2004). Of course, there were examples of service in every interview that I did with liberals. In one case a church has led on a Seattle-wide mission to do away with homelessness. Another church has created a two-hundred-bed facility in downtown Seattle that assists homeless and mentally ill men, women, and their families in their transitions to independence. I saw ministries of all kinds working to relieve suffering and to care for those left out and left behind.

At this level of the moral onion, dilemmas abound. To what extent should the church interact, affect, and engage the state? What is the church's role in service to the poor and destitute? Should the church seek to convert individuals or simply serve them? Should the church seek to dominate politics and change the moral conditions through legislation? I investigate the institutional church dynamics of evangelicals and liberals in chapter 9. Nonetheless, some of the certainty and clarity of the core layers of the moral worldview are left behind when analyzing moral projects. In general, the core allegiances and principles of evangelicals and liberals are not negotiable, but the ways in which these values are implemented in their moral projects is much more complex than is acknowledged. Neither liberals nor evangelicals seek to dominate politics. Yet liberals take their cultural impact for granted. Evangelicals are clearer about the moral worldview they want to create, but how they get there is much less clear. Liberals tend toward inclusion and egalitarian principles, but how these values translate into culture and politics is less apparent than in the 1960s during the civil rights movement. For liberals, caution is the word since they both esteem diversity and inclusiveness even as they advocate for equal rights being unassailable. Some of liberals' strongest words are against evangelicals—again, a negative identity—in part because liberals find the moral values and projects of evangelicals intolerant and unjust and, in part, because liberals struggle with how to be tolerant and inclusive while advocating equality all at the same time. How does one support tolerance and take a strong moral stance? Evangelicals are less wary of offending those who disagree; they simply make their moral points. Each struggles with how to translate its core values into moral projects.

d. Aesthetics

The fourth layer of the onion is composed of culturally conditioned customs and aesthetics such as protocols of social interaction, practices of worship, tastes in music, the architectural style of churches, and what form worship takes (loud or soft music, dancing or no dancing, long or short services). At this level of the moral onion one would imagine that these nonmoral goods might allow for tremendous diversity and flexibility among evangelicals and liberals. That is, the farther one gets away from the morally orienting core of the onion, the more easily diversity is tolerated. And to some extent this is true. However, there is relative homogeneity within each group concerning religious customs and even personal and religious aesthetics.

On the evangelical side, buildings are important. In fact, a third of the evangelical churches were either building a new sanctuary or planning additions and remodels. Evangelicals pride themselves on building churches that look far more like warehouses, malls, or auditoriums than traditional American Protestant church architecture. The evangelical plan is to create a facility that reminds no one that this is a church. Of course, several of the congregations have inherited more traditional churches from their forbearers, but they tend to excise religious artifacts and symbols and turn their "sanctuaries" into theaters of worship, entertainment, and inspiration. One evangelical lay leader said:

> I think the building itself is certainly not a cathedral. It's pleasant to walk into, but it's not ornate, so trying to make the average person come in and feel comfortable, I think that's part of the design of the building. It's not high church, but it doesn't give the impression that we aren't very passionate about our faith. We have a very specific . . . I don't know if I want to say doctrine, but just scripture. We believe in the scripture. It's what rules our lives. So it's not that we're so open-minded that we let anything happen; that's not the case either. So we're very fundamental in our belief of what scripture means and that's one of our tenets, but yet we try to interpret that in a modern sense, but we don't compromise our faith to become more acceptable to the twenty-first-century person.

As this lay leader says, "make the average person come in and feel comfortable." The PNW evangelical style mimics the secular nature of Northwest architecture—its informal style; its multiuse functionality; its tendency toward impermanence; its openness to bring in the mundane into the sacred (coffee cups and muffins in worship services, and fast food malls outside the sanctuary space); and its focus on family, children, and facilities that meet the needs of families at every stage in life. Indeed, on several occasions, evangelism for these churches was achieved through the building itself, by tripling the size of the children's and youth facilities and then doubling the numbers of young people in the church. Many of the churches build a simulacrum of secular children's and youth activities, competing with, replacing, or complementing the secular community programs. As one lay leader commented:

> In some respects you could say a church is like business, too. I don't want to reduce my relationship to God as a business, but the church

corporate, the building, the finances, the church structure itself is run like a business. I've been on the board for ten years and we make a lot of decisions on church policy and direction of the church, direction of the services. We've made changes to the music program that have had both positive and negative results. You go to a younger type of music and we had a lot of growth in the youth area, younger adults, but we had a significant drop-off in the older families. And as you try to tone that down a little bit then you have more of the older people come back and then you start to lose out on some of the younger ones. So I think what we're doing now with adding our Saturday night service and saying, "OK, we're going to have a service that with no apologies is going to be targeted more toward that younger crowd and let the music be and let the type of service be exactly what this generation culturally needs to feel interested so that they too can express and learn more about their relationship with God." This is just as important as having a service that is geared more toward the older ones. So we've tried a lot. And only time will tell if this is successful. But, if church isn't in constant change trying to meet the needs of the congregation, it's going to die.

The usual critique of the evangelical churches by liberals is that they are too market conscious, adopting and adapting to the consumerist ethic of the culture. Seeking out and accommodating to contemporary styles to meet the needs of their "consumers." And, as the lay leaders above say, sometimes they fail; sometimes they succeed. At the very same time, evangelical lay leaders and pastors in the study were ferocious in defending themselves against these cultural critiques. For them, aesthetics and lifestyle customs of a community must be accommodated in order to attract families to the church. One megachurch pastor went so far to say that swearing in the worship service is an important way of being "relevant" in a coarse culture, enabling congregants to feel "comfortable." At the same time, the core of the gospel for evangelicals is the offense that one is a sinner who must repent. There are no exceptions. Of course, the ambience of these churches fully affirms and confirms many of the material desires and tastes of northwesterners. Thus, as we see later on there is no critique of "consumerism" in these churches. Sin is a matter of giving the "control" of one's self to God. But instead of creating persons willing to delay gratification, evangelical culture sees salvation as the door to gratification (within certain limits) in this world and the world to come. The offense then is the narrow and exclusivist door to salvation, by Christ alone. For evangelicals, the fact that liberals do not voice this exclusivist claim is the source of liberal decline and accommodation to secular culture. One evangelical pastor, a former U.S. marine, put it starkly:

> When people come, we teach it, we preach it, and we live it. And if they come to me with issues and bothers, I will help them work through their problem one time. But if they come back to me the second time and the third time, I finally tell them "You're not growing up. This is the same thing we were talking about a year ago. These are the same issues you had a year ago. If God is really helping you grow and you're really submitting yourself to the scripture, if I'm not further along today than I was last year, I'm not growing. If I'm stunted, there's a reason I'm stunted spiritually. It's because I'm not applying God's word." And so we just confront them with it and some people have left. But mostly, they'll say "You know, you are absolutely right" and there is a change in their behavior where they are growing. It doesn't mean that they get over it completely, but they are further along today then they were last year and you know, sometimes that's a hard line to live that if you don't live there, you constantly have babies in your church. And Paul talks about that. He said, "Man, you should have been further along now. You're still drinking milk and eating pabulum. You should be ready for steak and potatoes." And we teach that on Wednesday nights in our Bible studies, in the Sunday school classes. This is what we give to work with our teachers. Hey, we're talking spiritual growth here. We can't mollycoddle people. That's why the mainline church has been so weak for so long, because we've babied people.

There is an implicit iconoclasm in the evangelical style and aesthetic. There are typically no crosses in the front; no robes on the clergy; no apparent ritual (though I show a pattern of ritual action, however informal, in the chapter on ritual). Moreover, their rhetoric abjures complexity and disdains sophistication, focusing on the Bible and its application to everyday life—judging all things as they relate to the ministry and relationship with Jesus Christ. The lone icon then becomes the Bible. It is the Bible alone that deserves one's adoration and it is only through that Bible that the witness of Jesus Christ can be found, understood, and proclaimed. Not unlike their Reformed and Protestant forbearers, everything else beside the Bible is secondary. Though the Reformed tradition, particularly in the Confession of 1967, warns against biblical idolatry, the Bible points to the revelation of Christ; the literal Bible is not *the revelation* of God in itself.[6]

Furthermore, the evangelical aesthetic has all the markings of the American middle class—a simple, sober, clean atmosphere that does not draw attention to itself but gives space to promote a message of moral rectitude, personal transformation, family solidarity, and service to the cause of Christ. Organizationally, one might say, the brand is willing to change everything except for its central prop, the Bible, and its core message, salvation through Jesus Christ.

Liberal aesthetics are once again more complex and ambiguous than those on the evangelical side. If evangelicals support a strict doctrinal core and an informal aesthetic style, liberals support a relatively strict aesthetic format, but practice a more flexible ideological center. When I sent undergraduate students to analyze evangelical and liberal Protestant churches in the PNW region (churches in the study), they would inevitably come back saying, "The evangelical congregations were quite liberal; the mainline [liberal] churches were very conservative." What they meant, of course, was that the evangelical worship styles used music that they could recognize and the liberal churches most often used traditional Protestant hymnody, often coming from the nineteenth and early twentieth century. More to the point, one of the evangelical churches that they attended was theologically one of the most conservative within my sample—even though aesthetically it was judged as the most avant garde. This shows that in some sense evangelicals have achieved their goal in attracting northwesterners with an aesthetic look that appeals to their tastes, which keeps them coming, allowing the church to begin to socialize them into their exclusivist religious doctrines.

For the liberal churches in the study, the mix of a traditional worship style and a liberal ideological core occurred in nine out of ten liberal churches. The church services tended to be relatively formal, and liturgy was traditional and sometimes acutely so, particularly in the large Episcopal churches. To this point, three of the fastest growing and largest churches in the sample were Episcopalian. They sustained the mix of tradition and theological innovation in the most tactile form. Moreover, even when the Episcopal Church promotes a relatively liberal social agenda and a relatively liberal theological perspective (see Bishop Spong's [1992] views on scripture), it still puts the Eucharist at the heart of its worship service. As one Episcopal minister explained:

> The Eucharist is the center. That action, that sacramental action, is the center and not the scripture, for instance. But where do we first learn about that sacramental action from the story contained in scripture? So it's a very scriptural thing to do that and to do it as often as possible. We ourselves at this church have engaged in a lot of

innovation around the prayer book, but the Episcopal Church is pretty uptight about its liturgy at times. That's where the Episcopal Church goes from being nonliteral to literal. We change the language; we don't touch that prayer book. But we use its forms, because it's the forms of that eucharistic liturgy.... First of all it's ancient and they kind of have this hallowed ring to me for that reason. But also, if you step back and look at it as a rite; if you're a student of ritual you go "Yeah, it's got all the right component pieces." You know, the way you enter into it, the way you experience the Eucharist itself and then the way you exit from it is a good ritual form. Now the reason, for instance, that I like that kind of sacramental worship as opposed to what you might find in a liberal UCC church where maybe they celebrate the Lord's supper once a month, that kind of thing, it's primal, it's primitive, it's tasty, it's sensual. It has a kind of strange humbling effect. People have to hold out their hands and get fed like little birds. And it's embodiment. So, Episcopalians are often known for their kind of intellectualism, or at least their educational pedigrees, and yet here we are participating in this openly mysterious primitive thing. It's good for us, it's healthy. It's to say, look the ordinary things in the world: grain ground, leavened; you know, grapes, fermented, shared; and we don't even like to parcel it out on separate plates. The common cup thing that turns some people off. Everybody drinks from that same cup. Where else in this culture would bright, creative people do that. "Hey, you want some of this?" So it's good for us.

There is no doubt that this is a traditional vision of the Christian faith. Yet, at the very same time these churches perform covenant services between gay couples and allows for a traditional latitudinarian interpretation of the Christian tradition—the incarnation, the resurrection, and the nature of the trinity. Indeed, liberal laypeople in responding to questions of why they go to these churches said any number of times, "I can believe whatever I want in this church." Another said, "Today I don't believe in eternal life; all we have after we're dead is the memories of our lives. But I might feel differently next year." Sentiments like these were repeated a remarkable number of times with some pride: "I can make up my own mind when it comes to spiritual matters; what I love about our pastor is that she doesn't give answers, she asks questions."

Along with this celebration of personal exploration and theological innovation, there are great expectations for excellence in a balance of elements that were summed up well by a congregant at an American Baptist congregation. She had received her PhD in social work and was deeply committed to her church. At the very same time, she expected a great deal from it, and wanted it to be "intellectually challenging, deeply spiritual, socially engaged, and have beautiful music and liturgy." If nothing else, I saw from liberals a highly sophisticated form of consumption—a delicate balance of aesthetics, a libertarian sense of morality, a sophisticated taste in music and the arts, and a concern for egalitarian and distributive forms of social justice. In this way liberals make high demands on their churches and are clearly not patient with mediocrity and the lassitude of change and transitions that occur in most churches. In the liberal church in which its pastor retired, 150 members walked out with him. The congregants were unapologetically clear that they attended because of the pastor's sophisticated taste in liturgy, a flair for oratory, and a nature-based spirituality that appealed to the distinctive liberal and northwestern ethos that sacralizes the natural world.

The styles of worship in the liberal churches were relatively formal. Over half of the liberal congregations had organs and sophisticated musical programs with high-quality choral music. The middle- and upper-middle-class elegance was an important aspect of what attracted many to these churches. They wanted the liturgy to be "beautiful and elegant." As another said, "The liturgy is my spiritual life and religious obligation." There was extraordinary care given to liturgy, making sure it was true to tradition and well performed. This combination of social service, theological innovation, and high liturgy was critical to the lives of liberal churches. This is not to say that they were humorless or lacked spontaneity. As one who had grown used to the formality of churches in the East and Midwest, I was struck by the sudden informality in the midst of liberal worship services. During one service, the congregation began laughing in the middle of a reading of scripture, which recited a series of complicated biblical names. Afterward, the pastor said this reaction was "common in the community."

The liturgical traditionalism of liberal congregations was underlined by the fact that in every church the ministers wore robes, and in several of the churches the liturgy was intensely formal. Yet, at the same time, again when lay liberals were asked about their churches, the overwhelming answer to the question was how "inclusive" and "welcoming" the congregation was to everyone, and in particular to gays and lesbians. If evangelicals constantly seek and support new families, liberal churches tend to reach out most to gays and lesbians. Outreach to gay people was the third-highest noted characteristic of the liberal churches; 37 percent of the total liberal church sample mentioned this as a point of priority. But again, this was not their only emphasis.

The aesthetic ethos of liberal churches was also enhanced by a strong outreach to artists, both local and national. A number of churches spoke of the importance of "mainstreaming" artists within their community. Several of the churches, particularly those in downtown areas, sponsored weekly "jazz services" and traditional "choral music" including the Hallelujah Chorus, opening these events to the public and making the churches the center of community-wide activities. The point of reaching out publicly, however, was not to "evangelize" others so much as to "serve" the wider community.

The deeper moral values of evangelicals and liberals are once again reflected in their aesthetic and cultural customs. The liberal churches would often complain about the lack of children and youth programs (few had more than a handful of children and youth), yet they were unwilling to change their services to appeal to families, young children, or youth. Growth, for liberals, is not a primary goal; faithful service to an inclusive and loving God is their focus. In that sense, the aesthetics of these two groups come from contrasting core values that have consequences for their identities and their future numerical growth and general institutional health.

2. Conclusion

In this chapter on the moral worldviews of evangelicals and liberals I have shown the power and organic nature of each group's core layer of their moral onion. Neither of these groups holds its moral positions instrumentally; that is, the allegiances and principles that each group sustains have profound roots in moral worldviews out of which moral claims are made and moral projects are built. Moreover, neither evangelicals nor liberals are very accurate about the other. Evangelicals see liberals as relativists and heretics. Liberals think of evangelicals as being manipulative, narrow-minded theocrats. As I have shown, liberals hold their values with nearly as much certainty and conviction as evangelicals. Liberals have deeply felt principles that may not be as clearly articulated as evangelicals express them but are held with a deep sense of allegiance. Evangelicals pride themselves on the certitude of their faith and the absolute nature of their moral values. Evangelicals believe that moral values must arise from the conversion of the heart, and thus are generally suspicious of social change based on politics alone—though evangelicals are deeply committed to a political culture that supports their moral values. Liberals believe in an inclusive and loving faith, a moral worldview where individuals make responsible choices, and a public space that embodies an egalitarian ethos. Politically, liberals are reluctant to enter into political advocacy—in part for the historical reasons mentioned in part I—yet they strongly support gay rights, and push for political accommodations for homosexuals.

The aesthetics and customs of these two groups have produced religious communities that embody their values. Evangelicals use their entrepreneurial interests and focus on outreach to seek new converts and reproduce faithful members of their faith. The evangelistic focus produces numerical growth and fits with a PNW culture that thrives on change, innovation, and a market focus. Liberals have vital communities as well, though they are less willing to experiment with style, even as they innovate theologically, as I will show in the next chapter.

8

Religion, Ideology, and Belief

1. Ideology and Its Natural History

This chapter addresses the issue of ideological forms and beliefs of
evangelicals and liberals. Why not simply use theology? I will not
do so in part because religion is always tied in one sense or another to
social reality and thus political power. Every language system (and
thus religion) has a "natural history" (Davidson 1999; Geertz 1999). It
arises from group processes that involve scarce resources that must
be negotiated and distributed based on systems of power that are
controlled by elites. In more complex systems this involves laws and
systems of bureaucracy that control resources, distribute power, and
shape status in a group, state, or nation. Religion is no different.
Religion is isomorphic with politics and thus social systems tend to be
mirrored in beliefs and theologies (Martin 2005). This is not to say
that religions necessarily support the political status quo; they can
resist dominant ideologies as well as partner with them depending
on context and the varying beliefs, interests, and leadership of religions (Williams 1996). Thus, theologies are ideological as they shape,
control, and deliver religious rewards or what might be called "spiritual capital."[1] This kind of capital is a resource that empowers,
guides, and rewards human action; it is form of human capital developed communally, though its characteristics are subjective and
invisible, and thus difficult to quantify. Nonetheless, as I will argue in part III, spiritual capital has significant effects on human

communities. I will keep this in mind as I compare and contrast evangelicals and liberals on their beliefs about Jesus Christ, interpretations of the Bible, sin, and finally, the nature of their epistemological claims.

Evangelicals and liberals inhabit quite different theological worlds. Polemicists, and occasionally myself included, have thought that these are two different worlds—even two kinds of Christianities. In some sense they are. However, I prefer to call them subcultures or species of the genus Christian. Of course, it is disputed whether there is one genus known as Christian. Nonetheless, there are family resemblances between these two groups, disputes between them to be sure, but they are commensurate with each other; they live in a similar language world so that differences are clear. Yet even though they speak with the same vocabularies, there are misunderstandings. Each of these systems reflects fundamental interpretations of what is true and good—some with sophisticated self-reflexivity, others with a studied lack of self-awareness.

a. Jesus Christ

As we have seen before, relationships are at the core of the evangelical moral worldview. And the heart of that inner layer is a relationship to Jesus Christ. During the height of our interviewing evangelical churches, the movie *The Passion of the Christ* was playing in theaters. An evangelical student who had come to see me summed up my findings with evangelicals when she said, "The entire movie was like a prayer for me; I was in tears for much of it." The movie focused on Christ's shed blood. It was, in a tradition of the Roman Catholic Church, a meditation on Christ's crucifixion and his suffering. The evangelical Protestants in this study, who have traditionally been in tension with the Catholic tradition, found deep resonance with this meditation on Jesus' blood. For them, the blood was a sign of love; Christ's blood is the currency of their salvation, and it is symbolic of their intimate relationship to Christ. Indeed, evangelicals mentioned the importance of Jesus' blood nearly always in the context of their relationship to Jesus. Contrariwise, fewer than a handful of liberals mentioned a relationship to Jesus and fewer still brought up Christ's blood shed for sin.

For evangelicals, sin and redemption are the central theological drama. How one might overcome the corruption of sin and its consequences echoed throughout the interviews. Nearly a third of evangelical respondents shared stories of conversions; again, less than 5 percent of liberals spoke about a conversion. For liberals, faith is a spiritual journey that they often mentioned as a long, twisting path, but with no particular starting point necessarily. Evangelical stories often expressed the most dramatic moments when their lives changed, or times when having shared with a loved one, that person's life was transformed. One evangelical story typified the drama of conversion for evangelicals:

> I love this story because it happened. My mom and I had planned
> to go see that movie; my mom is in very bad health. I asked my
> mom, "Are you going heaven?" "Sure." But it didn't sound very
> convincing to me. And so I had planned to take her to go see *The
> Passion of the Christ*. Well, before we got the chance to do it, the night
> before we were going to go, she was in bad shape. They called
> from the hospital and said, "I don't think she's going to make it." She
> had pneumonia and she had like three organs that were going out
> and she was already on dialysis and her heart, it was just bad. So that
> was the night that the doctors thought she was going to die. So I
> drove to the hospital and on the way to the hospital I said, "Lord, I
> don't know if my mom is saved or not, only you do." I said, "If she's
> not, let me take her to see *The Passion of the Christ*. Let me just have
> this one chance to take her to go see that movie and then tell her
> about you." Well, she recovered and when she got out we did go see
> that movie. And after that movie was done, it was just her and I
> going, it was supposed to be a big family thing but it just ended up
> being her and I going. And I drove her home and I said, "Mom,"
> and I talked about Jesus on the way home, trying to explain the Bible
> to her a little bit. And I said, "Now Mom, last week you almost
> didn't survive and you are here today. Now let me ask you, if you died
> right now, would you go to heaven?" And she said no. I said,
> "Well, why not?" And she said, "Because I wouldn't." And right there
> in my car she accepted the Lord Jesus Christ as her personal sav-
> ior. And her face lit up and her eyes became alive.

In the evangelical interviews I frequently came across poignant stories about drug addicts who had been saved; dying children who accepted Christ; marriages that were saved because of conversion; young people who turned their lives around because of Christ. More often than not this was done in response to the love of God that evangelicals felt from and for Christ. Only occasionally it was also in response to the need to escape hell. Nearly 10 percent of evangelicals mentioned the reality of heaven and hell in the interviews. This threat of hell is in part what provides the urgency to "win" others to Christ. The vast majority of evangelicals would say if one does not make Jesus Christ one's

Lord and Savior, then one is bound for hell. Though evangelicals were also certain that love rather than fear motivates individuals to make decisions for Christ:

> The challenge is becoming Christlike, doing the things that Jesus did. How he helped other people. It's not about politics or anything; it's about helping people remember it's the soul that's in jeopardy here. Where are you going to spend your eternity? Are you going to spend it with Jesus and with God or are you going to spend it in hell? Hell wasn't made for us. It was placed there for the angels who rebelled against him [God]. Satan, I mean, imagine, one-third of the heavenly angels went and gathered with Satan. That tells you a lot. The fact that the social battle we're in here is about the soul, it's where we're going to go. I definitely don't want to see you go to hell. I don't. Really, that's our heart. Our heart is to reach other people, to let them see you've got to build a relationship with Jesus in order to get back that relationship with God and what he did.

Heaven is one's "natural home." "Hell wasn't made for us." From evangelicals I uncovered no Calvinist doctrine of double predestination. No one is "destined" for hell; one's true destination is heaven. In this sense the barriers to heaven seem less intimidating and more inviting, even more gracious, certainly, than their Puritan and Reformed Protestant forbearers. The question, "If you died today, where would you spend eternity?" was a common refrain for many evangelicals. But again, it was also frequently mentioned that conversion was not *because of fear of hell* but *because of the love of God in Christ*. It would be a misunderstanding of evangelicals to think that their faith is a morbid or even a sober affair. Indeed, my overall impression of evangelical services is one of intense celebration and joy. As one evangelical pastor said, "Mainline worship is like a funeral service. We don't do that." And this is true: evangelical calls for conversion are most often conditioned by the promises of a full life in Christ and, not uncommonly, promises of blessings, material and otherwise, on earth and, of course, in heaven to come.

The language of sin and redemption, which outsiders tend to take as a negative perspective, creates a powerful dynamic of "I was lost but now I'm saved." Evangelicals in the study percolated with stories of redemption. One evangelical leader related his own story of redemption from alcohol to President George W. Bush's story of his own deliverance from a destructive lifestyle. In particular, this evangelical respondent was inspired by George W. Bush's answer to the question of what philosopher influenced him most. Bush said, "Jesus Christ. Because he changed my life." The evangelical lay leader exclaimed:

> Well, in this specific case, as in the previous election, this comment is strictly personal, from me and means only what I believe, but when you have a candidate that when he's asked a question, Who is the most important person in his life? and he says, "Jesus Christ, because he saved me. I was a drunk." You hear that from someone and you know in your heart that he passionately believes in Christ and he's a Christian and in doing so, his direction comes from a higher authority than himself, it is impossible for me not to support that individual. Particularly when I see on the adverse side totally different values. In the case today, a man that's a Catholic but he supports abortion. These things make it such an obvious difference for me personally. Yes, I have to be on Bush's side. I absolutely have to be. I do not feel compelled to share that with everybody. I share it with some.

For evangelicals, the symbol of a relationship to Jesus Christ that has changed one's life is *the* central identity marker. Bush's quip was more than a signal to the white evangelical community; it communicated to them the central doctrine of the evangelical moral worldview: an intimate and heartfelt relationship with Jesus. As we saw above, this cemented, for many evangelicals, their loyalty to Bush. Later on, Bush explained the importance of his declaration of faith, "If you aren't one (Christian) than you just don't get it." And on this matter Bush was right. Absolute loyalty to Christ, to use a cliché, covers a lot of sin. It also helped Bush to receive the majority of white evangelical votes (Green 2004; Domke 2007).

This exemplifies the interplay of ideology, power, and religion. Evangelicals have used religious language and spiritual capital to persuade and sustain forms of cultural and political power. George W. Bush has mastered this dynamic in his interaction with white evangelicals that I will examine in chapter 11. On the other hand, liberals, who do not share this same Christocentric piety, tend *not* to understand the power of this religious piety. Some commentators believe this has led to the marginalization of liberals from political power (Domke 2004, 2007). And to some extent this is true; moral worldviews are more than words and can and do make political differences. The linkage between evangelicals, the American military, and politics has developed over time along multiple dimensions—it is neither natural nor quixotic, but historically constructed and deeply felt (Marsden 2006). But the relationship of religion and politics is also a fluid and changing enterprise. The fortunes of

Bush and the Republicans have risen as they have connected with white evangelicals, but this partnership is not a guarantee. Evangelicals may change their loyalties depending on their moral values. Moral values are sacrosanct for evangelicals; political parties and politicians are not.

The relationship of liberals to Jesus Christ is more complex. Liberals reject the evangelical take on Jesus, but do not want to give up on Jesus as a critical figure in constructing their moral worldview. Thus, there is cynicism toward the evangelical construction of Jesus, but also a longing to understand Jesus in a new way. As one liberal new member sarcastically described the evangelical idea of a personal relationship with Jesus, "I don't see Jesus as my imaginary friend." This same person went on to say somewhat wistfully, "This is something I have to do some spiritual work on." The term that many liberals use to label evangelicals is *fundamentalist*. It is a label that many evangelicals in the study have come to reject, interpreting it in the light of the American War on Terror (against Muslims) that is often couched in terms of "fighting fundamentalists." Nonetheless, I sensed that when liberals said demeaning things about evangelicals there was some longing in their voices, as in this case: "So anyway, the personal relationship thing sounds fundamentalist to me. One of the pastors was talking recently about his image of Jesus kind of on his shoulder and I had this little mischievous image of a parrot, with Jesus as the parrot. But the sense of Jesus always being there with him and . . . I don't have that in my life."

Thus, the series of cynical and at times snide remarks made by liberals against evangelical language about Jesus often ended in comments that exposed a certain yearning, revealing both a rejection of what are considered simplistic projections, but also a sense of interest and perhaps at times a point of envy. Liberals are suspicious that conversion to Christ is simply an excuse and a rationalization for inaction or a lack of social witness. As a liberal lay leader explained, "I think they [evangelicals] believe something like, 'I've accepted Jesus Christ, now I am saved.' Well, I call that cheap grace." She is referring to the German theologian Dietrich Bonhoeffer's distinction between cheap and costly grace. As Bonhoeffer said, "When Christ calls a man He bids him come and die" (Bonhoeffer 1949). Bonhoeffer suggested that grace without action is cheap; grace with action calls for sacrifice. For Bonhoeffer, who joined a secret plot to assassinate Hitler, this cost him his life. For liberals, faith in Jesus is *doing* God's work in the world. Belief, for many liberals, is cheap; the *real value* of faith comes in action:

> There's a second image that's almost as old and that is the image of Jesus as savior, but not necessarily personal savior. I came up and

came to personal awareness during the civil rights movement, in which the idea of Jesus as savior was not just simply, this was the guy that's going to get you to heaven, but this is the one that intervenes in whatever the heck is going on, who you can count on, look to, and follow. So the whole question of Jesus as savior also meant that he is intervening to aid, to rescue, to help. And it behooves us as a people of God to intervene. So that sort of served as part of the underpinning of my understanding of the civil rights movement and why religion was such an important part of us. If you have that sense of Jesus as one who intervenes with power. I want a God who's got some punch. So I say, gee, is there some other way that I can begin to have a place that we can talk about Jesus as the gentle teacher?

Jesus then is not an instrument of salvation for liberals, at least in terms of eternal life. Liberals tend to interpret the idea of eternal life for individual persons as a selfish act. As one liberal layperson said, "I think it's [speaking as an evangelical] 'I have to be saved,' as opposed to, 'Why don't we make the world a better place for all people?'" Jesus did not come to save souls but to be an example of one who seeks justice, who was willing to give his life for those left behind and left out. This perspective for liberals changes how they interpret not only Christ's death but how they envision what resurrection means in the tradition. Liberals express disdain and mainly reject the substitutionary model of Christian atonement. For liberals, the idea that Christ's blood is required as a sacrifice for humanity's disobedience and sin is a "repulsive" image of God. That is, the liberals in this study tended to believe that God's holiness necessitates no sacrifice for sin. God's character, by definition, accepts and loves unconditionally. Liberals also offered other reasons for Christ's death, which were more political than metaphysical. As one liberal lay leader explained:

> I have a lot of reasons Jesus died, as someone who was faithfully obedient and was killed by the very people and systems that he came to attempt to change. As the kind of overwhelming power of evil in this world that are subtle and not so subtle and the resurrection, which is what the early Christians focused mostly on, is about saying that God has the last word. That even these powers of evil, as powerful as they are, don't win in the long run. And that's very important. So resurrection is probably for me a source of hope more than anything else. Hope. Amazement.

For liberals then, the death and resurrection of Christ are not so much a transaction between God and humanity over sin, but an exemplification of the power of evil, which Christ confronted in his crucifixion and overcame in his resurrection. In the victory of resurrection comes the hope to transform evil. For liberals, the problem is not human sin and how to overcome it. The question for liberals is, How does one overcome the evil of injustice by following Jesus' way of justice and peace? Christ faced the "sin" of injustice and because of his righteousness was killed by those in power. Dominant political powers that injure and destroy the public good and the common people are the true enemies of Christ. Thus, Jesus' life and death are exemplary for liberals; he showed what it means to walk in peace and justice as opposed to seeking political power for one's own selfish purposes. Religious ideology, in the case of liberals, is used to resist forms of government that they deem oppressive or politically oppressive to minority rights—illustrating once again the inevitable intermingling of religion and politics.

As I have noted before, half the liberal ministers in the study had experiences of either conversion (often at evangelical venues) or what they described as "extraordinary" experiences of God's grace. In one case a liberal pastor experienced a healing in his teenage years at a charismatic service that he interpreted as a miracle from God. This, in part, motivated him to seek ordination as well as to take risks in ministry on behalf of justice issues. For this liberal clergyman, Jesus embodies a gracious, open, and affirming attitude toward life. Jesus is the embodiment of the ideal of inclusive love—gracious, impartial, and merciful toward all:

> My experience of God is one of incredible generosity and generosity expressed in embrace, in self-giving sacrificial love. I often think of Jesus as this incredibly joyful person who laughs a lot. We don't see him depicted that way in much of the artwork that is common. But I can't imagine that children would have wanted to be around somebody who was dour. I can't imagine that somebody who was not glad and joyful and filled with life would have gone to wedding banquets and invited people to feast in the way that seems to be so consistent. So I suppose from all that, the great sort of theological pillars for me is, What does it mean to follow Christ who is always inviting people in? Jesus is not about casting people out, but inviting people in. And he is surprising about it. He's always doing it with a sense of gladness and expecting that people will encounter God in one another. So that is central to how I understand the ministry I have been called to. Certainly part of the vision, and I think you would probably not be surprised to hear that from that some things flow out of it. I think the work of reconciliation is one of the major

works entrusted to the church and to Christian people. And I think
it's hard work. I think it's good work. I think it's glad work.

We see in this vision a living out of the message of Christian reconciliation. That is, in Christ all are already reconciled to God in Christ. Thus, to live
out the kingdom of God is to recognize and acknowledge this reality with gratitude and exemplify it in one's life. So, it is not merely to celebrate unconditional love but it is to usher in the "kingdom" with an inclusive and reconciling
lifestyle. Emerging out of this unconditional love was an initiative to end homelessness that came from several of the liberal pastors and rabbis in the city of
Seattle, including several Protestant senior ministers in this study. For these
ministers, the initiative puts into action the Christian work of reconciliation.
For liberals, the poor, in light of God's gracious love and profound hospitality,
must be welcomed into the common good, nurtured, and returned to health
and wholeness.

The separation from God because of sin that evangelicals often mention
simply is not recognized by liberals. Or rather, liberals argue the separation
may exist but it is a misperception about God that creates the separation. For
liberals God is always in communion with the world and so to follow Christ is
to recognize this reality and live it out fully in one's life and through one's
ministry and work of compassion and justice in the world. Sin, then, as one
pastor suggested, "is negligence or resistance to God's appeal." To become one
with God for liberals is to act in obedience to the gracious, loving hospitality
embodied in Christ. Or to use Bonhoeffer's terms, as one pastor did, "to become a person for others."

The differences between how liberals and evangelicals view Jesus Christ
expresses a fundamental divide between these two Christian groups. There are
core differences in how each group interprets Jesus Christ, the cross, and
resurrection. For evangelicals, Christ's work on the cross opens eternity for
them, overcomes their sin, and creates a "new spirit" within them of love and
forgiveness for all. This spirit sends evangelicals out to share this "good news"
in response to the "Great Commission" found in Matthew 28 of the New
Testament, where Jesus, in a postresurrection account, sends his followers out
"to make disciples of the whole world." Liberals do not quote this passage.
Indeed, when I asked one liberal pastor about evangelism, one who, in fact,
was quite open to the idea, he said that his church named this event "Outreach
Sunday." The concept of sharing one's faith is foreign to liberals. If it happens, liberals often reinterpret it as "meeting spiritual needs." However, when
asked about inviting others to church, liberals said they view this with some
moral suspicion. As one said, "It implies that the neighbor is doing something

wrong." A liberal pastor, who was new to the region, expressed his frustration with this liberal reluctance, which he interpreted as a "radical relativism, unique to the PNW." For him, the "postmodern situation allows everyone to speak their truth and let the chips fall where they may." Nevertheless, liberals emphasize the need to act out their faith but often feel morally constrained in sharing it precisely because they fear that it puts the other's truth claims in question.

Jesus Christ then is the one who brings evangelicals into a relationship that saves them, brings them joy, and sends them out to witness to him and serve others in his name. Most importantly, for evangelicals, how individuals respond to Christ makes all the difference for their eternal destiny; only those who name Christ as Lord are saved. For liberals, Jesus is the one whom they follow by including, serving, and loving others. Jesus confronts injustice and teaches liberals to overcome unjust systems. Jesus is the one who is for others, all others, no matter their sexual orientation, ethnicity, or gender. Most importantly, for liberals, this acceptance is unconditional no matter whether a person claims the name of Christ or not. If there is common ground between evangelicals and liberals, it is in the fact that these two groups point toward Jesus, even though what they see and respond to in Jesus is quite different. Moreover, each sees in their reading of the Bible the kind of Jesus that they seek to follow.

b. The Bible

If a relationship with Jesus is the core of the evangelical moral worldview, the witness to this relationship comes from the Bible. The Bible is the source of authority. The mediator of this authority is a pastor who preaches the Bible in a way that is perceived as convincing, powerful, and faithful to the scripture. Since there are few organizational structures to legitimize authority in evangelical churches—that is, bureaucratic associations or denominational structures—the personal quality of the pastor that enables him to preach from the scripture is the key element around which authority pivots. This biblically centered teaching and preaching is the most frequently cited reason that attracts evangelicals to their churches. In a sense the evangelical pastor has to be a virtuoso with scripture, quoting it, relying on it, and proclaiming it as *the source* of his ability to preach, and the prooftext for his points. I use the pronoun "he" because evangelicals rarely employ women as ministers, much less as preachers. I will explore gender issues further in chapter 9.

Scripture's importance is underlined by the fact that 38 percent of the evangelicals in my study mentioned, without prompting, that they believed in the "literal" interpretation of scripture. What *literal* means is somewhat of a moving target. It has been known for some time that when evangelicals speak of a "literal" interpretation of scripture it means that scripture is *their core* source of authority (Hunter 1987; Crapanzano 2000). Pastors and laypeople in the study were frequently aware that not every word of scripture was meant to be taken "literally," though the scripture is always the final authority.

One evangelical pastor, one of the most articulate of all the ministers, distinguished between "special" and "general" revelation of God. General revelation can come through our study and analysis of nature. Special revelation refers to scripture as the "final" authority. The Bible is God's inerrant word, written by men, but inspired by God. This means for evangelicals that the Bible is without error in matters of history, doctrine, salvation, and, a few said, in matters of science. However, the majority of evangelicals agreed that science "improves" our knowledge of the world. Indeed, an evangelical pastor was clear that the source of "general revelation" was God through God's creation. Thus, the general will of God is discovered by the scientific study of God's creation. However, the bottom line for evangelical pastors was that when special and general revelation conflict, scripture supersedes all other sources of authority. This is how an evangelical pastor explained these distinctions:

> The authority of scripture is our final authority for faith and belief, but not our only authority. That is really an important distinctive chararcteristic of evangelicalism, is that the scripture is our final authority for what we believe and how we live, but we also understand the importance of God's general revelation. His special revelation is in the scripture, but he's also creator and he has revealed something of himself in creation that is discovered through good scientific research. So we have a great deal of respect for the hard and soft sciences, because all truth is God's truth, so even though archaeology is based and grounded in the teaching of the scripture, archaeology is also informed and shaped by our understanding of the world as God made it. And so that's why our understanding of life is dynamic. I mean, there's things we are discovering through scientific investigation that helps inform our understanding of the scripture, but ultimately if what is purported to be true through scientific investigation is in direct contradiction with the word of God, then our final authority is the word of God and our understanding, our faith, at that point would instruct us that science is always growing and learning and discovering new things, and our faith at that point would say science has got some things to learn yet here. But

oftentimes the church has made the colossal error of very stupidly dismissing or not valuing science and general revelation. I think the church in medieval times is the ultimate example of that where Copernicus and Galileo were dismissed as heretics, when in fact their understanding of outer space and the nature of the universe was a whole lot more accurate than the Catholic Church. At that time I think the church lost the trust of the intellectual world at that point and it was really unfortunate. Oftentimes the liberal mainline, not always but often, plays down the authority of scripture. The fundamentalists play down the value of general revelation and research and so forth, and that's why fundamentalism is oftentimes branded as being a nonintellectual approach to theology because they say it's the Bible and is its only standard for faith and practice. Liberals would say, well, the Bible might be one of the books we look to, you know, the authority of scripture from the classic liberal standpoint is very weak. Evangelicalism, I think, has found its vitality and strength in that it has a high view of the authority of God's word, but it also has a high view of creation and what is discovered and known through science.

This pastor distinguishes evangelicalism from liberalism (which too often *relativises* biblical authority) and from fundamentalism (which makes scripture the *only* authority). Indeed, I found only one or two evangelical pastors in the research who held this fundamentalist viewpoint on scripture. Most, like the pastor I just quoted, interpret science as a legitimate form of knowledge. This underscores how evangelicals, and most of those in the study, did not want to be called fundamentalists or identified as such. In one case an evangelical pastor said, when I asked him if he identified himself as a fundamentalist became indigant—saying that he felt this was tantamount to being called a "nigger" (Wellman 2002). Quite striking language, but it also shows the length with which evangelicals have distanced themselves from the label—whether because of ignomiry that has come to be associated with the term through liberal discourse (proving one's ignorance) or through the associations of the word with religious extremists (proving that one is violent). In either direction, the interpretation of scripture has become a subtle problem for evangelicals. Most in the study continue to say that they take the Bible "literally," although they are quick to explain that scripture has various "genres" that have to be interpreted for their "authentic" meanings. One evangelical lay leader explained:

> One of the clarifications, we believe that the authors were inspired by God and they had a meaning for what they wrote at the time. We

know that there's poetry in the Bible, there's prophecy in the Bible, there's didactic teaching. All those things have to be taken in the context of which they were written. People talk about how you take the Bible literally, well, we take it literarily and how the author meant it to be. If it's poetry, it's symbolic. In Revelation there's a lot of symbolism; a lot of the prophets there's a lot of symbolism. It's obvious from the context that it is not a literal thing. It is a showing of things that we need to learn how to interpret what he's trying to tell us. So we try to get the meaning of what the person that wrote it meant, what God is trying to say, without just taking the words as they are written.

Throughout the study evangelical pastors and laypeople used a kind of generic common sense, or what some would call "the plain meaning of the text," to interpret scriptures that would otherwise be taken literally. In the same vein, most evangelicals searched for the "intent" of the scriptures, to discern their "true" meaning. One of the evangelical lay leaders tried to explain the apparent affirmation of the system of slavery in the New Testament. Paul's New Testament letter to Philemon, a letter written to the slave Onesimus, encourages Onesimus to remain a slave. For the evangelical lay leader, this is no way supports slavery or encourages it. Indeed, the letter's "true meaning is about welcoming back people into faith." As this lay leader says, "One must look at the inherent messages in scripture." Of course, the fact that evangelicals used biblical rationalizations on either side of the U.S. Civil War underscores the multivalent nature of scripture and the tendency of social context to shape interpretation (Noll 2006). Nonetheless, PNW evangelicals do not spend much time debating issues of scripture. Indeed, evangelicals asserted a consistent certainty in all issues of the Bible. And this is the point. One's moral and spiritual identity is confirmed and tested to the extent that one is able to accept and believe what scripture says. As one evangelical new member explained:

I think that's one of the problems that Christians have had ever since the beginning of time. Ever since Jesus was crucified and rose, Christians have argued about this point or that point and this has caused tremendous problems in the church. All churches, particularly the Catholic Church, have split several times over this. And Protestant churches have too. You can't believe in one section of the Bible and say "No, I don't believe this. It's impossible." You either believe what the Bible is telling you or you don't. And in a lot of the Bible is simply telling you what happened in that time; the Old

Testament leading up to the New Testament. And as I say, when Jesus was sent to earth, we must, if we're going to be Christians, we have to believe the New Testament. We have no reason not to believe it, and every reason to believe it. So these people who start nitpicking this or that, these are not true Christians, they're just not. They might say they are, but they are Christmastime Christians.

To question the authority of scripture for evangelicals is by definition to fall into error and, worse, to risk apostasy. Of course, not all evangelicals were quite so plain; most made this point implicitly. Others, including pastors, were crystal clear when it came to stating the authority of scripture. This clarity was one of the factors that made these churches and many of these pastors so attractive to members. In fact, one of the pastors who was most outspoken used bold and even vulgar language to make the point when asked about whether he believed in the inerrancy of Scripture:

Absolutely. Inerrancy, absolutely. There's one God. You cannot get to heaven without Jesus. Everybody is a sinful bastard. I'm old-school quasi-Calvinist. You're a piece of crap, Jesus is God, and you better tell him you're sorry or you're screwed. If you want the bottom line, I don't mean to be a dick about it, but that's where I'm at.

This kind of language does not show up in most of the interviews, but the tone of confrontation was not foreign to my conversations with evangelicals. This pastor's church was doubling in membership nearly every year, and, moreover, it was enormously attractive to young urbanites and particularly to young men in their twenties and thirties. There is at times within evangelicalism a flagrant disregard for cultural conventions and "politically correct" language of "liberalism." Politically correct language was often disdained as an "accommodation to liberal bias" and a "selling out" to liberal culture. God, for evangelicals, speaks directly and boldly from scripture and so pastors, by extension, quite often do the same, and certainly do so in ways that shock (outsiders) and attract and keep many (insiders) in these churches. And this use of nonconventional language has been a part of what it means to be "anointed" in the American evangelical tradition with its populist sensibility. Indeed, I heard countless times from evangelical laypeople that they felt relief that their pastors' stood for something; they know the "truth." Evangelicals feel that their leadership is willing to confront a culture of relativism.

For liberalism, as it is said, the Bible is "another story," almost literally. One of the consistent themes within liberal churches that I studied was their tendency to stand over against evangelical culture. This became most apparent when liberals spoke about scripture. Six percent (around nineteen liberals) came from evangelical backgrounds. Many of them spoke disparagingly about their upbringing, and particularly about the use of—or what they said was the "abuse" of—scripture. Several former evangelicals spoke about the "toxicity" of their evangelical upbringing that turned them into people who judged others and used the Bible to marginalize, shame, and injure others who happened not to believe in the "evangelical truth." In one case, a liberal lay leader said that he had gone to a Christian college, and had read the Bible intensively, but it simply brought him to a place of despair. He turned away from his past, and had only over the last several years begun going to a liberal church. He had not read the Bible for twenty-seven years and sounded as if he did not intend to do so again:

> Yeah, so, it wasn't long after I left [a Christian College] that I . . . and got out in the world that I just couldn't live with what I'd been brought up to practice. And I, you know, I had a really, you know, I would say deeply spiritual experience in my whole upbringing pretty much. But, it was the particular religious beliefs that didn't jibe with, you know, what I believed needed to happen. It was all the social impact things that my faith was constantly making me reject, or put people as wrong or whatever. So, finally when it was people that were so critical to me and I just couldn't really look at them and say, you know, you're going to hell and you're wrong and you can't get this divorce and one thing after another that I just really had to let go of that stuff. And when I let go of it, I mean I totally let go, baby with the bathwater; and went through a good twenty years of not going to church and I still haven't picked up the Bible yet. I mean, one of these days, you know, I probably will. But, so that's, that's been like twenty-seven years since I've been a Bible reader and I was, you know, I was a college student, at least an hour a day if not more up until that point in my life. Anyway, one of the things I think I discovered through that, and of letting go is that my spiritual life stayed, but my religious beliefs left. And I really feel that over that time that what I had that was real and genuine and religious beliefs that fit with my spirit, that those kind of crystallized. And I, you know, and finally came back to the point of saying, and even this can't fit with Christianity. And then to the point of saying, this is Christianity, that's what it's about.

This liberal layperson was deeply immersed in the evangelical culture. He knew scripture and understood the "demands" of evangelical culture. And in response to these demands—that he must call the ones "closest to him" to Christ or reject them—he was simply unable to follow through. I heard many evangelicals speak of their "duty" to call others to faith, but I never heard one speak of the necessity to turn away from those who had spurned the faith. In fact, I found the opposite. Many reached out to those who did not "believe in Jesus." Nonetheless, evangelical culture makes strong demands theologically and socially. Evangelicals are to "fellowship," that is, to be in community with, those who share and nurture them in their beliefs. Others, who are outside the fellowship, are not rejected, but they (even one's spouse) become objects of evangelization and of intense prayer. At one wedding I visited, the minister made a clear demarcation between the married couple, who had repented and given their lives to the Lord, and those outside this spiritual fellowship. After the wedding, the wedding party went into a separate room and began praying fervently for the couple and for the salvation of the unsaved among the "friends and family" at the wedding. The "spiritual" family divides, at least emotionally, believers from the "unsaved" in evangelical culture. The liberals that I interviewed detested these distinctions and the drawing of boundaries between the "saved" and "unsaved."

These distinctions that are rejected by liberals are a part of what liberals call the "misreading" of scripture. Here is the battle over biblical intent; evangelicals see one form of intent and liberals another. Liberals would often speak about the way the Bible is "used and abused" by "fundamentalists" to shame and push people away. For liberals, this form of literalism is intellectually insufficient and a form of misinterpretation. The Bible is not meant to be taken literally, and not meant to be used as a "baton" to hurt others. Moreover, the Bible must be put in its context. The historical and cultural methods of biblical interpretation are critical for liberals in order to place the Bible in a perspective that helps one interpret it appropriately. Again, liberals and evangelicals sound somewhat alike. That is, rightly interpreted, the Bible says what the group wants it to say. A liberal layperson defined who she was in relationship to the Bible based on her "right" to make up her own mind on scripture:

> I'm not a religious person; I'm more of a spiritual person. Although I was raised in the Presbyterian Church, one of the things that is important to me about this is it's not the strict dogma that appeals to me, and you don't find that here at our church. The basic Reformed tradition is that it is a relationship between you and God, which comes down to your own conscience. And that is what's important to me about this church. Regarding the Bible, I think it is an important

historical document. I think that the people who were writing it were struggling with their understanding of their relationship with God and what the things that were happening in their lives and in their cultures meant. But I think God speaks to us every day; it's just a matter of being able to hear. As I was coming here I was thinking about a singer/songwriter who was on a program one Sunday morning and he was talking about that God understands every language. And what he said was, the words really don't communicate what's going on, but luckily the bridge is being built from the other side, which means, God coming to us. In my life, I've felt much more tuned into that and the promptings of the spirit. I keep thinking of what that Bible scholar said, "The Bible really can be dangerous to your health." And I think it's a wonderful tool, but I think it can be a way of avoiding doing your own spiritual work.

Tellingly, in the last two quotes by liberals on scripture there is a critical distinction made: I am a "spiritual person" not a "religious person." When religious beliefs fade, what remains is spirit. One must do the "spiritual work" that sometimes "religion" causes one to avoid. Moreover, religious work is a function of adhering to doctrines and dogmas in scripture taught by "others," so that spiritual work is that which must be done on one's own. Similar distinctions are made by evangelicals, as we have seen; religion is ritual, while authentic faith is a relationship with Jesus. What this distinction means for liberals is that scripture is important, but one's own "personal spiritual work" can and *should* trump the Bible as an authority in one's life. In this sense the scriptures are valid and important as they teach about one's spiritual life and its development. Even in the churches that seemed to be "rediscovering" the traditions of scripture and the Bible, the language of liberal laypeople was put in the context of their own experience. Similarly, again, for evangelicals, one's "personal experience" with Jesus trumps all other sources of authority. Like evangelicals, liberals gain from scripture legitimation for their perspective. One lay liberal said in response to her pastor's biblically oriented sermons, "I understood Christianity and was able to find a place where there was a very inclusive message. A message that was quite countercultural. It helped me to discover a place where I was comfortable and where I felt very much at home." In other words, the scriptures become an authority for liberals as they confirm messages that liberals tend to believe in: inclusion, hospitality, justice, and social outreach. When the Bible is interpreted in such a way to express judgment, exclusion, or even violence, it becomes "dangerous," "shaming," and "unhealthy." It is exactly the "stronger" aspects of the Bible that evangelicals find most attractive about scripture. That is, it is precisely when the Bible "confronts" evangelicals in their sin that they "feel the truth." One evangelical commented that she "hated" it when liberal preachers tried to make her feel "satisfied" in her "sinful" condition.

Liberal pastors frequently spoke about the need to reclaim the scripture from "fundamentalism." As one pastor said, "The Fundies got the Bible; liberals got social justice." For him, "there must be a better sharing of the assets." As this pastor argues, the Bible is "uniquely regenerative" and thus liberals need this "story" to enable them to become "people of the story, redeemed by it to do the work of justice in the world." Another liberal pastor used quite traditional terms to narrate his use of the Bible's story:

> I see that the scripture is sacred text. It's not historic text. It's not scientific text. But it is sacred text. So it's Holy Scripture. I don't have any problem saying Holy Scripture. But it's holy metaphoric scripture. It's holy story scripture. The Bible says what it says. But when it says you are the salt of the earth it doesn't mean you're NaCl. The Bible right there is using metaphor. It's a form of spiritual text, but not sacred scripture. Part of what makes sacred scripture what it is, is that it is an identifier within the religious community, within a particular religious community. So I'm associated with the stories of the Hebrew and Christian text.

In this case there is within the liberal community much less interest in "proving" the Bible correct or accurate historically, scientifically, or even theologically. There is little talk about evolution and the need to establish Genesis as a true (even metaphorically so) account of human creation. Within evangelical circles there is a strong belief in creation by God, literally. Sometimes this literal belief is in what is called a "young earth" scenario—that God created the earth in the recent past. God's creative act is interpreted literally, but in symbolic terms. That is, God used the six days of creation (interpreting the days in thousands of years) as a way to create the earth and all that is in it. These discussions are moot for liberals. Science has the authority and cultural power to shape our beliefs about human evolution, the earth's development, and nature's workings. Frequently, liberals mentioned, "Why wouldn't God use evolution as a way to shape human history and the earth's movements?" Again, in itself it is not a topic that evokes strong opinions for liberals. It becomes intense for liberals only when they reject the literalism of evangelicals.

For liberal pastors in particular, the common comment is that "we take the Bible seriously but not literally." What this means in practice is that the "story" of scripture is the story of the church, God's people. Jesus is the "One for others." As a follower of Jesus the church is called to serve the outcasts of society and to include those who are marginalized. A common characteristic of liberal discourse is the need to expand boundaries, to move beyond us/them rhetoric. Moreover, liberals often spoke of the importance of using the hate against them to understand the ways they judge others. One pastor, who is gay and publicly known to be so by his congregation, was baffled by the vitriol of opposition to his ministry (he had received death threats), but he took it as an opportunity for spiritual and moral reflection on his own tendencies to judge others. He sees the obsession with sexuality as a rationale to avoid serving others:

> I find myself always asking the question, and I ask myself, it's part of my own spiritual discipline, when I find myself uncomfortable with somebody else, I ask why. If I'm in tune enough to be aware of the fact that I'm uncomfortable, Why? If I find that I have feelings of hatred or loathing, What on earth is going on here? What is it in myself that is perhaps being reflected from whoever or whatever group of people it is that's making me feel these reactions. That's a difficult process. I'm baffled by the way in which we seem to spend so much time on issues of human sexuality, when the scriptures barely mention it. The scriptures are filled with invitations to the table in the Gospels. Christ inviting people to banquets and to feasting and to fellowship. The scriptures, both Hebrew and Christian, are filled with admonitions about care for widows and orphans and the homeless and the hungry and poor; they are filled with cries for justice. The prophets talk about mercy and walking humbly with God. We sometimes find ourselves talking about money and we talk about money being evil, but the scriptures don't talk about that. The scriptures say that money becomes evil when the love of money is placed above all things. And I wonder when our obsession with money leads us to unhealth. I wonder if our obsession with sexuality, or any one thing, leads us to that place.

For liberals, the call from scripture is not only to do one's own spiritual work but to include those left out and to serve those left behind in society. In this way, evangelicals and liberals hear the same message from the Bible: the importance of service to others. Of course, this means quite different things for each group, which I explore more fully in chapter 10. Each group feels a strong desire to make "real" the call to provide hope to those who are hopeless, and indeed, they accomplish a great deal along these lines. At the same time, liberals and evangelicals differ dramatically on biblical authority. For evangelicals, the Bible is the inerrant word of God, perfect in every way. To question it is by definition to put oneself outside the evangelical community. For evangelicals, the scriptures are dangerous precisely because they confront sin and refuse rationalization of sin. For liberals, the Bible is potent and dangerous but in a different way. For liberals, the Bible must be rightly interpreted for how it calls them to ministries of justice and outreach; it is dangerous because it can be used to exclude and condemn the very people liberals include—gay people and others who are socially vulnerable. Liberals take the Bible seriously, but its authority is far from certain. In fact, to question the traditions and the Bible itself is a calling. Jesus did not "answer questions, but opened up new and deeper questions—the scripture makes that clear. He expanded the mystery; he did not diminish it." Moreover, liberals see scripture as a story that nurtures and shapes their spiritual lives. This spiritual work is "holy" work, and it challenges them to reflect on their own "inner lives" and how they can overcome prejudice and judgment against others.

In the end, however, the Bible demands interpretation. Evangelicals tend to hide this fact or even on occasion refuse to admit that they are doing it, since scripture lays out "its plain truth." Liberals, on the other hand, luxuriate in the art of interpretation. But both believe that they can come to the "true" intent of the Bible. They get there in different ways even as each wants to know what is "true" in the Scriptures. What this search for "truth" means is the subject of the next section on epistemology.

c. Epistemology and Truth

One of the fundamental aspects of religion is truth claims. In one form or another, religions make claims, whether implicitly or explicitly, about the ultimate nature of the universe and about human beings. In a sense, every one of us, as Christian Smith has argued, makes decisions based on our "moral worldviews" (2003). That is, all of us feel at least an inchoate sense that whatever one believes and does is what I should do (even if based strictly on one's own needs for pleasure). Thus, we make decisions on moral worldviews shaped by a combination of felt obligations, preferences and tastes, cultural contexts, and political circumstances. On occasion, people claim to be relativists (who make no truth claims) and they argue that all that they have is their perspective, which neither makes demands on others, nor puts moral obligations on themselves. Now some may truly be solipsists and therefore perfect relativists (knowing only their own perspective), but even here relativists make an implicit universal assertion. Moreover, scratch below the surface of an ardent relativist and one comes to core truth claims: no one should kill me or my family; I should eat; I should be able to make a living. All of these claims assume certain truths, no matter how limited.

When it comes to religion, truth claims expand and become global and even cosmic. In Christian terms the core story is filled with these claims: God is good and God made the world and pronounced it good. God created humans in God's image and gave them dominion over the earth. Humans were called to name the animals and were obligated and covenanted with God to worship God and love one another. There was one tree that humans were told not to touch and eat; humans did so, and as the book of Genesis says, they were excluded from God's direct presence. They were sent from the garden of paradise and were punished to work by the sweat of their brow and toil in childbearing. God continued to seek after humans to bring them into righteousness, but humans were stubborn and so God sent God's Son to redeem humanity, unveiling the kingdom of God and sacrificing himself on a cross to give new life to all who follow him. God's Holy Spirit, given by Christ, would dwell with God's people in a group called the church. The members of the church would prepare for the Second Coming of the Son by living lives of righteousness, and should spread the good news of Christ's message and live in love with all.

As with all religions, this summary of the Christian narrative contains any number of truth claims, obligating those who follow Christ to act on them and to live into them. And even my own synopsis has implicit constraints; I avoid using male pronouns for God, which assumes ultimately that God is neither male nor female—a truth claim. Religion in the classical sense "binds" individuals and groups to truth claims for which humans are rewarded and punished, treated with grace or with discipline, and based on their relationship to these claims and obligations, blessed or cursed. Truth claims are multitudinous in religions in particular and in the human population more generally.[2] Thus, this section brings to the surface various truth claims in the evangelical and liberal communities.

Claims about truth are critical to both liberals and evangelicals in the study. Indeed, truth claims were mentioned, in quite different ways, by 32 percent of evangelical respondents and 48 percent of liberals. What truth means to these groups is framed in distinct terms. For evangelicals, the claim that Christianity is absolute truth is an important religious identity marker. Evangelicals frequently argued that what made their churches attractive was that their leaders boldly stated the absolutes of their faith. Contrariwise, liberals were quick to reject this kind of framework by arguing that their faith is but one truth among many. Liberals rejected the exclusive nature of the evangelical claim. For liberals, this kind of intolerance goes against the true nature of the spirit of Jesus and is antithetical to their understanding of God. Hence, both groups make truth claims, but the basis of each creates distinct episte-mological trajectories.

The absolute nature of evangelical truth claims is a factor in attracting young people to the evangelical churches in the study. One of the unambiguous findings in my research was that evangelicals are rhetorically committed to recruiting, nurturing, and reproducing families, children, and young adults. They also show numerical success with families and young people. Indeed, more than half of the evangelical churches had large ministry programs (two hundred to four hundred participants) targeted at children, youth, and young adults. For the most part, liberal churches tended to have older adult member-ships, some families, and, more rarely, smaller though active youth programs (fifteen to forty participants). Only one liberal church in the study had programs for young adults in their twenties and thirties. The obvious question is, Why is it that evangelical churches often have such robust ministries to young people? The conventional wisdom for liberals is that young adults are too busy experi-menting with different lifestyles or simply not interested in church or God. Surveys show that this is not the case; studies of college students reflect strong interest in God, spirituality, and even religion.[3] To the extent that young adults respond to churches, however, evangelicals dominate this market. But the ques-tion is, Why would young people be attracted especially to churches that are more conservative morally and theologically? An evangelical young adult ex-plained why she thought her church was growing and it had to do with a specific set of truth claims (their absolute nature) and with how they are delivered:

I think so many people of my generation and my age, having been raised by a generation that sort of reveled in the denial of absolutes, or standards and morality, or basically a generation that ran from God, like all generations do. I think a lot of people are crying out or craving for someone to love and be a father figure and to disci-pline, because that discipline is a manifestation of love. I think that's a huge appeal of our church is that there's accountability, that it's not just another one of those superficially accepting, everything-is-subjective-type communities, which can't actually exist in reality. But the fact that our church does acknowledge that there are abso-lutes and that God is the absolute and that we have these systems of accountability and believe in truth, God's truth. That has a lot of appeal for people my age, I think.

I heard similar sentiments from other non-evangelical young adults. I sent out a group of 140 university students (most of whom were not churchgoing types, and who were either secularists or nominal members of their varied faith traditions) to compare a large, liberal, urban church with a large, evangelical, city congregation (both churches were in the study). The overwhelming majority came back "impressed" with the evangelical church, not just because of the livelier and more contemporary music but also with the fact that the pastor did not accommodate to what they perceived as "politically correct" moral norms. The pastor made demands and challenged them to rethink their truth claims. They did not say "truth claims" but clearly their implicit moral frameworks were being stimulated and they had to think anew about what they believed to be true.

Another young adult evangelical layperson explained that her attraction to her evangelical church was in part a reflection of having grown up with few explicit moral or theological "absolutes." She argued that young adults were attracted to the clarity and moral certainty of her urban evangelical church. She used the cliché "relativists" to label her parent's generation. Nonetheless, it was clear in my interview with evangelicals that certainty and the absolute nature of the moral and religious claims made upon them stimulated and challenged them. This may have resulted, in part, from the fact that young people viewed the confrontation with ultimates as new—a refreshing sense that choices had to be made and that these choices have consequences. These truth claims most often included calls to convert to Christ, to retain sexual purity (no premarital sex), or to share the faith with others. One of the ways that evangelicals tended to rationalize these truth claims was to say the minister or evangelical leader was speaking not to appease other humans but to please God alone. So evangelicals should also understand that causing "offense" to other humans was not his or her concern; he or she should only be concerned about offending God. An evangelical lay leader said:

> I think that we're more concerned about offending God and we're focused on just what the Bible says. I mean, listen to what [our pastor] says and what the elders stand on, it's very offensive to a lot of people for a lot of different reasons. If you come to our church for any length of time and go to a community group, you're going to hear things. People are very opinionated and passionate about their opinions, but at the same time, it's all about the gospel. We don't care about what people think, we care about what God thinks. But at the same time we want people to feel welcome. That's not the reason why we don't get involved, because we don't want to offend people. It's because we want to proclaim what we believe in and we don't want to stand for something other than Christ. Nothing else is more important than that.

The lay leader said this in part to defend herself and her church against charges made by other evangelical churches that wanted her church to take a stand on May Day for Marriage. Her church and its elders refused to participate, not because they did not support heterosexual marriage, which they do support overwhelmingly, but because for them it would distract from their concern to share the gospel. She felt that one should focus not on "issues" per se, but on leading others to Jesus Christ. The offense of the gospel should relate to God's truth alone and not peripheral "political" issues, which she felt were "distracting." The evangelical churches that actively supported May Day for Marriage were all suburban congregations. The urban evangelical churches—perhaps more sensitive to their own diverse urban surrounds that were antagonistic to the May Day for Marriage—tended to avoid needlessly alienating potential members. The urban evangelical churches at certain levels are unafraid of "offending" with the exclusive claims of Christ, but they are careful about which political issues they publicly advocate.

For evangelical churches in general, and particularly for suburban evangelical churches, their moral and theological truth claims forced them to negotiate liberal and secular publics. One evangelical pastor expressed his frustration that the evangelical community was getting pushed into a corner on the issue of gay marriage. For evangelicals, as I have noted earlier, gay marriage is anathema. In response, of course, they are accused of being "hateful" or "abusive," which came from some of the liberal respondents in this study. For this evangelical pastor, however, framing the issue was critical in establishing the truth of the matter and not being put in a losing situation in terms of public perceptions, particularly as he was one of the organizers for the May Day for Marriage event. As he recalled, the organizing pastors made sure there would be no "anti-gay" speech at the event from the speakers or the organizers, and yet, from his point of view, protestors against the rally were intensely hateful toward him and his followers:

> I think it's a battle or a war of words and the person who frames the issue has the upper hand. And they have learned that they can back people down, and Christians are about, you know, most Christians would say they're about love, so it's reprehensible to them to be pigeonholed or categorized with hatred, so it really intimidates Christians to be accused of hate. And they know that so it's a very successful ploy and they use it very successfully. Now is it true that there's probably some incidents, some legitimate incidents of hatred expressed by people who call themselves Christians toward homosexuals. I'm sure there is, because there's a wide, wide spectrum of

Christians and some of them are, I think, out of control. I certainly wouldn't condone what everybody who calls himself a Christian does or says. But on the other hand, in my experience in thirty-five years of pastoring, I have never seen or heard a single incident of hatred of homosexuals. But I have seen many incidents of hatred of Christians by homosexuals. So in my judgment, the reverse is true. But I am a bit biased and beauty is in the eye of the beholder.

For this pastor and the other evangelicals in the study, there are moral and theological absolutes that identify who "belongs" in their churches. However, when these truth claims are taken into the public light, opposition emerges. This tension, as other theorists have mentioned, reinforces the ideological perspective of evangelicals and solidifies their identity (Smith 1998). The tension confirms for evangelicals what Christ says in the New Testament: "You will be hated for my sake." But this does not mean it is easy for evangelicals, many of whom do not want to offend or hurt others. Indeed, evangelicals told me that they constantly remind themselves that they had nothing but love in their hearts for "sinners," which included gay and lesbian activists. And of course, this love is for the person but not the sinful actions—a distinction that liberals find unacceptable and hypocritical as I will explain further in chapter 11.

The "absolute truths" that evangelicals are so proud to proclaim also create a ready-made explanation for evangelical success in numbers; people want "absolutes." Evangelicals explain that liberal churches have emptied precisely because they have dropped the demands of the gospel and the offense it causes. In fact, one evangelical pastor suggested that evangelical churches have become refugee camps for discontented liberals, and this study shows that this is marginally true. Of the liberal churches in this study, 13 percent of their membership comes from evangelical backgrounds, and of the evangelical Protestant churches in this study, 17 percent of their membership comes from liberal Protestant church backgrounds. An evangelical pastor explained the numerical success of evangelical and liberal churches relative to how each negotiates Christian truth claims:

> I would say that the top three things that drive people out of churches, whether they are liberal or conservative, is number one, ideology. A radical change has occurred from a biblical-based authority to a culturally based authority where an authority outside of one's self gives way to relativism and the idea that the individual has the capability and the right to decide on their own truth. When that starts happening in a denomination, I think the people who believe there is absolute truth depart. The people who are attracted to relativism stay.

The whole idea of smorgasbord religion or Christianity where you come and take what you want, you decide for yourself, is very much part of the culture. It has been for several decades now and it's kind of a mix and match, designer Christianity. You make up your own mind. And the result is that no two people agree on anything. So there are refugees from that and some of those people show up here. I think there's a decay that takes place in the hierarchy of church organizations. Denominationalism has a history of imploding from the top. Like we say in Christian circles, the rot starts at the top. It starts in the schools, the seminaries, the denominational executives. And then it starts leaking down into the churches and so a lot of people have become very skeptical about what's going on at denominational headquarters or the denominational schools. Especially when they change their mind about things that the Bible seems to be very clear about. And then I think finally, egoism in the pulpit or in church government undercuts the Christian church. Sometimes it's the pastor who is a very controlling, authoritarian type of person and that drives people out, because he begins to act like a little king or pontiff and offends a lot of people. I think the attractive things about this church is that we're a very accepting group of people. We think of ourselves as a hospital. We expect that the people who are coming are going to be broken. Are going to have pain in their lives, are going to be the victims of their own choices. They've made big mistakes. Blown up big chunks of their lives, and they come here in deep need. And so we try to give them a safe place to heal, an accepting, healing community and to get healthy.

The pastor suggests that denominations, and here he means mainline Protestant denominations, have become less strict (moving from a biblically based authority system to one that is culturally based). Liberal churches practice a "designer Christianity" where individuals can choose what aspects of Christianity best accommodate their needs. And while it is true that this liberal accommodation to modernity (compartmentalization and individualization of interests) describes the liberal epistemological worldview, liberals in this study argue that the move toward individual choice and autonomous decision-making is morally more challenging and spiritually more elevated. That is, the individual must do the work on his or her own and not allow an external authority to make decisions for him or her. This type of authoritarian group think is precisely what liberals accuse evangelicals of doing; evangelicals follow their leaders instead of making up their own minds.

Evangelical pastors, on the other hand, react to these liberal accusations by arguing that in fact believing and following the "ultimate truths" of their faith is an overwhelming challenge. The evangelical faith contains moral and theological standards that no one is capable of fulfilling. And this is precisely what evangelicals leaders expect, the demands of the faith are absolute and all fail to meet the ultimate standard. The faith answers this dilemma with grace—undeserved favor from God—forgiveness that is effected by Christ's death on the cross. The church then becomes not a congregation of the perfect, but a "hospitable" for broken people. People who confess and repent the truth of their own limitations and in the process are made whole in Christ. Moral change is expected but perfection is not. The process and movement from confession to repentance, and then toward healing was a common theme in many of the evangelical churches. In fact, one evangelical lay leader said,

> At our church it's 100 percent truth and 100 percent grace; there is no trade-off or blending back and forth—and neither is it a compromise; within the limits of us as human that's how we can best do it, but that's hard. It's very hard.

This paradox of truth and grace is framed as a form of moral accountability, and church members are held to high standards. Leadership expects sinners but they must be willing to confess and change. This accountability was emphasized in every evangelical congregation that I studied, particularly on the issue of sexual morality. Failure is expected and accepted, and grace (by way of forgiveness) is given and is a part of the healing process. Indeed, evangelical laypeople were frequently amazed and impressed by the vulnerability of their leaders. In one case, an evangelical lay leader described how his own pastor was often vulnerable about his own sin in the pulpit:

> Oh, he's pretty real. He talks about his anger issues with his kids and his family. He talks about his own, I remember one time he was on his way to some vacation in a tropical place and he asked the congregation to pray for him for his purity of thought, because he was going to be around a bunch of women in bikinis. And he said, seriously, I would ask for you to pray for me. I remember this being years ago and thinking, that is so real, that he would just say that kind of stuff.

Personal vulnerability about weaknesses was common in the interviews with evangelicals. Truth for evangelicals means "transparency," in that one's sins are confessed and the need for repentance is expressed and forgiveness is given. On a regular basis, evangelical laypeople spoke endearingly about their pastors and how "real" they were with the congregation. The laypeople felt that they could "relate" to the struggles of the ministers. But relating did not mean to wallow in sin but was a way of saying, "Look at me, I am willing to be honest with my sin, and willing to confess, repent, and be healed." In several churches, worship services had the feel of an Alcoholics Anonymous meeting, where leaders and laypeople were quite open with their sin in public settings and sought healing in the community of faith. The mix of absolute standards (what evangelicals called the truth) and grace (unconditional acceptance based on confession and repentance) was quite real and tangible in these settings; evangelical congregants experienced and frequently expressed a deep sense of freedom and renewal.

To outsiders the evangelical rhetoric of absolute truth and high moral standards tends to obscure the therapeutic atmosphere of worship services and smaller group settings. Evangelicals hold together quite stringent standards of personal morality with modes of personal vulnerability that was many times surprising to us as researchers. Again, to those on the margins of these communities the two appear contradictory, but to insiders it is a powerful pattern of moral strictness, personal vulnerability, and unconditional forgiveness that many evangelicals said in the interviews was extraordinarily life-giving.

Indeed, a core critique of liberals by evangelicals is that liberals too often ignore sin and fail to confront it. Evangelicals are aware that liberals focus on the goodness of human nature. And it is true that liberals in this study frequently underscore the importance of discovering and recognizing the beauty and truth in human nature; they rarely emphasize or address human limitations or human failings. Thus, when it comes to sin (that is, behavior that is destructive or dysfuntional) evangelicals accuse liberals of denial and ignorance and, in this sense, evangelicals argue that liberals in fact "enable sin." An evangelical pastor described what he called "the liberal way," and he did it with some sensitivity, but he contrasted it in the end to the evangelical pattern of truth and grace and used the conversion of his sister from "a card-carrying feminist" to an evangelical to make his point:

> I think that one of the great strengths of the traditionally liberal
> mindset is inured in the compassion of Christ, the "give expecting
> nothing in return" model of Christ, and I think that it's hard to pop
> out liberal without getting into politics. But if we just take it as a
> general mindset, religious, political, whatever, I think the place that
> the liberal community misses is ignoring sin. Ignoring the ac-
> countability of individual humans for their actions. And I think it
> flows out into a lot of their solutions that end up enabling people.

I have drug users and alcoholics in my family. You have to love them, but not enable them. If you look at the mistakes that we're made with the Native Americans or Native Alaskans and then a correction of that mistake, OK, give them money. We're killing them. I don't like the fact that we killed them literally before, but what is done is done. And just like the dad who screwed up when he was a young dad and left his family and everything and then lets his drug-addicted twenty-six-year-old son live with him because he feels guilt about what he did in the past, you can't take away your own guilt. And I think some of the biggest mistakes I've made in life were trying to save people from pain that God wasn't trying to save them from. And I think that's what liberals do sometimes is they get confused that we can, well, a Utopian mindset, that we can make the earth a perfect place. It's never happened and I think evangelical Christians are this strange dichotomy of the greatest of pessimists and the greatest of optimists in the same. Whereas I think the thing that kills the liberals is that they tend to be optimists all the way to a place where they can't just look at what's not working and say, "You know, that's not working." And you know what, people do have accountability. And you know what, there's some people we actually can't help. But still, I think people live in this world, like my sister, she was full-on liberal, card-carrying member of the National Organization for Women, we lived in a relative amount of conflict for a while. Well at age thirty-six, she became an evangelical Christian. I was stunned. But as one who had worked and worked and worked for solutions and came up empty, empty, empty, the interesting thing was, she actually got involved in a business that had a bunch of Christians that said, "You are accountable for your life. You are responsible for where you are." And all of a sudden when she moved from victim mentality to responsible and account-able, there became a whole grid by which she could comprehend the idea of sin. So I think one of the problems with liberals is, I mean, it is wonderful to champion someone's cause who's a true victim. It makes me feel good. They like me. It's not as fun to tell somebody, well, the bottom line is you screwed up some things, just like I did, and you need to deal with them.

For this evangelical pastor, liberals function in society out of a state of guilt—guilt over past sins (whether toward the Native Peoples or toward African Americans). The evangelical pastor admits that as a culture we have sinned against these peoples, but where he differs with liberals is that handing over resources to these so-called "victims" has not helped but only enabled them in their destructive behavior. For evangelicals, confronting "sin" and dysfunctional behavior has to happen. It "may not be fun" but it is necessary if healing is going to occur. Moreover, not everyone will turn from their "sinful" ways, but confrontation with the behavior is necessary before help can truly be effective. In this sense, evangelicals like to say that they see both sides of human nature, how evil and "sinful" it is but also how confession, repentance, and forgiveness can bring a person to wholeness and health. Truth for evangelicals may strike outsiders as doctrinaire and rigid, but internally, the mechanism of truth and grace is rather dynamic and fluid. Salvation for evangelicals is not simply a function of conversion but a process over time.

One of the striking points of overlap between evangelicals and liberals is that for each the "truth" of their faith has nothing to do with religion per se. For evangelicals, the truth of Christianity is their relationship with Jesus that confronts sin, redeems it, and brings them salvation and blessings in this world and in the world to come. In a sermon by a liberal Episcopal priest, a similar claim is made about his faith: "As I like to say, Jesus came to do away with religion. Christianity is not a religion; it's a way of life." For this priest, religion is a way in which people mark themselves off as saved and safe, barricade themselves away from "dangerous others," and uses the language and acts of sacrifice "to keep God happy with us . . . not with *them*, but with *us* who keep the rules, who observe the regulations." This way of life, for this priest, means that "in Christ there is no more in and out." This distinction for liberals underlines the robust nature of Christian grace that includes all no matter what. It is a liberal theological truism often drawn in contradistinction with more "dogmatic" forms of faith (evangelicals) as in the case of this sermon. Indeed, liberals commented frequently on what they called "the fear-based theology of evangelicals." For liberals, making God's grace scarce is *not* what they are about; making God's grace abundant and for all is their modus operandi—the *veritas* of their faith.

The contrast that liberals draw with evangelicals comes out most pointedly in the liberal view of the self and sin. For liberals, evangelicals function out of a place of shame and guilt; guilt because evangelicals concentrate on naming and confronting sin, and shame because a Holy God cannot tolerate sinners in God's sight. For liberals, this creates a God who is "intolerant and abusive." And it demands from evangelicals a theology of payment for sin; Jesus' death on the cross substitutes for the death of the sinner. The proposition is flatly rejected in liberal circles. When I asked about the substitutionary model of the atonement, one liberal pastor explained:

I have trouble with that too. I feel like, I think Rita Nakashima Brock has said that a God that would do that is an abusive God. I don't use quite that language, but I feel that God is a loving God and does not need us to sacrifice his son in order to find reconciliation. We need to ask for forgiveness and we need to confess our sins and we need to change our ways when we're going in the wrong direction. But I don't want to stress that Jesus had to die for us. I think Jesus didn't have to die. I think Jesus died because we're sinful human beings and we often do the wrong thing to the good people who are trying to do what's right.

For most evangelicals, this statement alone puts liberals outside the ken of theological orthodoxy and outside the banner "Christian." For liberals, this is exactly the point: the relationship between God and humans is not adversarial, and it needs no mediator per se. The focus on shame and guilt only gets in the way of understanding the "mysterious and abundant love" of the divine. More to the point, the substitutionary theory of atonement not only paints a picture of God as an ogre, not able to forgive unless there is a blood sacrifice, it removes responsibility from humans for acting and doing what is right. Truth, for liberals, comes by way of individual exploration and decision. Humans not only have the capacity to do what is good, but they have the moral responsibility to act out with justice and compassion. Liberals are proud of the fact that instead of simple answers to questions of sin, liberals offer hope and belief in that humans can change and do what is right.

Mel Gibson's movie *The Passion of the Christ* is a kind of Rorschach test for differences between evangelicals and liberals. For evangelicals, the movie was emotionally moving, deeply pious, and showed God's compassion for humanity through the sacrifice of God's Son. For liberals, it was "primitive" in its sensationalism of Jesus' scourging; it falsely depicted the Romans as innocent and merciful while it made the Jews look rapacious and guilty; it did not capture the "message" of Jesus, but rather mired it in a sacrificial theology that is "superstitious and archaic." Needless to say, these are two different moral and theological worlds as one liberal layperson argued:

I think that the differences between us and evangelicals can kind of be summed up in Mel Gibson's movie. We are a community of hope and love and optimism. And the evangelicals seem driven by fear and guilt and anxiety that is so pervasive through the rest of society that it's a message that resonates easily with people. That if they comply with the rules then everything is taken care of and they don't really have to think about it. And we're all a community of people who really, deeply think about it and feel about it, have deep feelings about it, each and every single one of us and we allow those differences among us to be included and be perfectly accepted and fine. And there doesn't seem to be that in the evangelical community. I mean it's really fairly standard, and it's easy to market, it's easy to hype. There's an emotional message, a message of fear that resonates so easily with people and can be communicated easily. Ours is something more complex I think; it reflects deeper insights and requires more commitment on the part of the person to really think about it and know their feelings and share them and to be with other people who don't necessarily cookie-cutter stamp their beliefs and their theology.

A major critique of the evangelical community by liberals is that not only are the answers too simple but the messages (truth claims) are also created to be attractive and "appealing" to people. In others words, there is the belief that these messages are created to be easily digestible in order to manipulate the masses. This same critique, of course, is what evangelicals use against liberals; the latter accommodates their message to people by soothing their conscience with a "soft" gospel. Liberals respond that because evangelicals offer such simplicity they enfeeble those who consume these ideas; they give false security in a message that says that God will take care of you and the "Father" will give you everything you need. The infantilism of God in evangelical culture is rejected by liberals and is found to be intellectually and spiritually wanting.

This rupture is at the heart of the differences between evangelicals and liberals: What is the meaning of the cross? What is the core consequence of Jesus' life and death? For evangelicals, the truth of Christ is the recognition of sin, the need of repentance, and the hope of salvation through the cross. For liberals, the truth of Christ is his confrontation with evil (both personal and structural), and his death and resurrection are the victory over this evil, which both models how evil must be confronted and shows that in Christ grace is open to all. Jesus, in his life and death, excluded no one, and loved and forgave all. Both messages can come from scripture and from the Christian tradition. But each is a quite distinct truth claim with diverse consequences as we see throughout this book.

This distinction over these core truth claims creates divergent moral worldviews, and is claimed by evangelicals and liberals to be the path less taken. For evangelicals, the challenge of faith is the gospel's confrontation with individual sin and the need to submit to Christ. For liberals, the path of complexity and taking responsibility is not for everyone; in fact, because this way brings some discomfort it becomes a reason why many have a hard time coming back to liberal churches, as one liberal lay leader explains:

> I wanted to speak to something on a common thread. To me, it's more than just allowing each of us to explore our own theology, but it's actually requiring us, where there is this structure or box in more conservative churches, here, not only are the boundaries removed if we want to, they are removed whether we want to or not. There's a requirement and a demand on us to push ourselves outside our comfort zone and our box a little bit, where not everything this church does is going to make everyone happy. But what it does do is make you ask yourself questions and the question usually is, it's OK, and that's why the person is back that next Sunday. It might not be what I want and I'm not comfortable with this, but I'm comfortable with the totality of what this church embraces, so therefore I will be back.

For liberals, this "way of truth" is called "higher" and difficult, so that the challenge does not appeal to all and in a sense it cannot appeal to everyone. At the same time, I did come across several liberal laypeople who were quite aware of the evangelical critique of the liberal church. As one said, there is no "grit" to the liberal church's claims, so that few know "what we stand for." Indeed, more than a handful in these vital liberal churches did not know how to describe the church or the church's beliefs. On several occasions this was a problem, in part because the liberal laypeople "loved" their church but were quite aware that their church "was the best kept secret in town." In this sense, the inclusive, tolerant, and often libertarian nature of liberal churches tends to lessen the clarity with which liberal truth claims are reproduced, and mitigates the motivation to express and share these claims both internally and with outsiders. As I show in the chapters on organization and mission, liberals were hesitant at times to educate their own (children and youth) or share their truth claims with outsiders in any explicit way.

Nonetheless, theological truth is taken seriously by liberals. In research on West Coast liberal churches, I investigated at length the sophisticated spiritual practices and reflections of liberal laypeople and their ministers (Wellman 2002). Liberals care deeply about what they believe; they want something more than a rationalist understanding of the world. Liberals accept how the Enlightenment has come to explain the world, but they are also aware that modernity has its limits—there are areas of human consciousness that science cannot explain. Spiritual truths illumine these mysteries. It is precisely the multifaceted nature of liberal theology and its willingness to relate to modernity that are profoundly powerful for many, as one liberal lay leader described:

> I think that issue of complexity, to me speaks to why I am a member of this church and denomination. In terms of the term *liberal*, I mean, *liberal* isn't a bad word to me. In some ways I consider myself a liberal and in some ways I am much further to the left than that.
> I think a lot of people who belong to a church like this are people who believe that some kind of spiritual religious dimension exists and is important. They can't just take a purely rationalist view of existence. They know that they can't prove that there is a God. They are sometimes uncomfortable with God talk a little bit because they don't want to be viewed as just dogmatic types of people, but yet they also feel those who completely reject any kind of religious, spiritual understanding are being naive, kind of silly, presumptuous. There are a lot of people who struggle with living in a secular world, a rational world that think there is some kind of deity out there, and if we all talked about what we thought God was we might have some similarities and some differences. I think there are also a lot of people in this congregation and in more "liberal" congregations that believe that you have to live out your faith, you have to speak to those who are marginalized in some way. Like you were saying, the Bible is the kind of authoritative norm, that there is lots of room for interpretation, and there are other kinds of knowledge and learning and insight that are brought to it.

Liberals were quite often concerned that identifying as Christians made others think that they were "fundamentalists" and so they tended to avoid religious self-identification. But at the same time they are unwilling to give up their "spiritual journey" to secularists. Thus, there is a balancing act that goes on, which, as I have mentioned, at times makes liberals quite cautious in sharing their faith. Nonetheless, the theological distinctions that are made are based on much thought. There were a handful of lay liberal respondents who had PhDs in religious or theological studies. One argued that the Christian faith is the "fullest" embodiment of religious truth, but he was quick to affirm the contributions of other religions: "I tend to believe that Christianity is the fullest revelation of God. That doesn't mean from my perspective that I devalue other religions." I heard these careful distinctions often in liberal interviews, all in the spirit of ecumenism and, more important, as a part of a global liberal truth claim that argues that difference is acceptable and one can learn from those who are different from oneself. Or as one liberal lay leader said, "Difference does not equal disagreement."

The importance of dialogue and the "celebration" of the "other" is a part of liberal culture and this applies certainly to "other religions." Indeed, a common characteristic of new members in liberal churches, according to several liberal clergy, is the "fear" that new members have to "give up" their Buddhist beliefs and practices. It was not uncommon for liberals to say that they were "Buddhist Christians," or "Christian Buddhists," or "Budepiscopalians." And it was also widespread for liberal churches to have educational programs promoting understanding of other religions. One liberal pastor described this delicate ballet of laypeople identifying as Christians but also understanding the "good" in other religious traditions:

> Somebody said they noticed that for the current five- or six-week period we're in, we're hanging inside the nave, inside the main worship space of the cathedral, six banners from six major religious traditions, one of which is Christian. There's a Sikh, Buddhist, Jewish, Islamic, and Christian banner hanging in the cathedral, one for each of those traditions. And a person said in the newcomers class, "I love those banners, and I love what our church is about and I love seeing them there, but I've always understood Christianity to be exclusivist and those banners are inclusive. How do you reconcile that divide?" And of course we identified that "I am the way, the truth, and the life" is the main sort of text that has been used to promote that, but it's only one of many passages ascribed to Jesus from the Gospels. The other passages are much more embracing and welcoming of all people and so I think the question that we deal with all the time is, What does it mean to be in love with Jesus? What does it mean to say "yes, I'm a Christian," and yet to know that God is also at work in other religious traditions, and to be in a place where that doesn't make you feel insecure? And we're constantly grappling with that question. One of our Wednesday night classes right now is a four-week series on Islam 101, because people want to know more about Islam. Does it mean that people at our church want to convert and become Muslim? I don't think so. But it says that people want to know more. And they want to know where they encounter the divine in other traditions. At a newcomer's class about two years ago, there were thirty or forty people in the room one

Wednesday evening and I believe that every single person said they had experience in some other tradition, whether it was Buddhist, or Sikh, or Jewish, and the question was, Is it OK for me to bring what I've learned in those traditions to this place and to my encounter with Christianity? And some of them asked the companion question that I hear a lot, "I've been really bruised by the church in the past and I'm putting my feet back in the water in this place. Is it safe for me to be here and is it safe for me to bring my Buddhist meditative practice along with me?" And the answer is yes.

There were also voices among the liberal clergy that were less anxious to espouse this interreligious form of dialogue. As one put it, "People will say to me, 'I pick a little here and a little from there' and I say to them, 'You know, don't do that, that's disrespectful. Dive in deep here or dive in deep there.' I think the deeper you go into your own religious expression, the more affinity you have for other people who go deeply into their religious expression." This claim is that the more intense one is in the study of one's own religious tradition, the greater one is able to understand and relate to the religious expression of other traditions. For liberals, religious fundamentalists undercut this notion of a "deeper unity" between religions. This does not bother all liberals, but it certainly disturbs some, who rail against fundamentalists and how "they corrupt the true essence of the faith." Thus, liberals are not willing to give up their claims of a universal religious unity, even as they refuse to dogmatize about them.

This section has shown the intensity with which truth claims are made by both evangelicals and liberals. Each group argues for what is "true" about ultimate reality, the character of God, and the core of human nature. There is room to argue over who is more precise and articulate in their assertions, but there should be no debate that they both carry truth claims that guide their moral and ideological thinking. Each of these epistemological platforms has effects on their responses to wider publics and politics. For evangelicals, the strength and simplicity of their "truths" enable them to be quite clear about what they want and demand culturally and politically. In this sense liberals are correct about evangelicals; they are black and white in communicating their message to larger publics and are focused on reproducing these "truths" in their families and friends. Liberals, on the other hand, are also sure about their "truth claims" and seek to translate them into public policy, but, as becomes clear throughout this study, they are more cautious and reflective about these claims. This study shows that consensus on issues is not only more difficult for liberals but in a real sense not expected; each person should make up his or her own mind. The very nature of liberalism calls one to question "authority figures," and disrupts the capacity to mobilize politically or even to be motivated to reproduce one's ideals and ideologies. What effects this has on the ritual and organizational lives of these churches is the topic of my next chapter.

9

Religious Ritual and Organizational Dynamics

1. Defining Ritual

In many forms of Protestantism there is the tendency to deny that
Protestants "do" rituals. Of course, in the most narrow sense of the
term—dogmatic words and actions done by rote—this may be true.
However, using a broader sense of ritual we know that religions of
whatever type are full of ritual actions. Clifford Geertz's definition
facilitates this wider understanding of the term: "In ritual, the
world as lived and the world as imagined, fused under the agency of a
single set of symbolic forms, turn out to be the same world, producing thus that idiosyncratic transformation one's senses of reality"
(Geertz 1999, 201). Ritual in this sense is consecrated behaviors and
practices, legitimated by religious authorities, and traditions that
take "lived" forms and fuse them with imagined "worlds." The goal of
these practices then is to integrate everyday experience with worlds
that are above, beyond, and sometimes within this world in order to
transform everyday experience. It has been shown that Geertz's focus
on symbolic boundaries over social boundaries, and meaning over
power, misses the political consequences of ritual life (Asad 1993).
I have argued that rituals adapt to and shape social boundaries of
power and ideology as well as communicate meaning and purpose to
adherents, which confirms once again the intimate relationship between religion and politics. Nonetheless, in this chapter I emphasize

the symbolic over social boundaries, understanding the meanings of ritual action within these two communities of faith (Wellman 1999b).

For liberals and evangelicals, there are clear sets of behaviors and forms that are relatively homogenous in each community. Each group has developed ritual behaviors and practices over time that use religious traditions to imagine new worlds that are integrated into lived experience with varying degrees of success. I emphasize first in this chapter the symbolic forms of ritual life of these groups initially in worship, prayer, and finally on their Web sites. In the second section of this chapter I look at how liberals and evangelicals organize their groups relative to church fellowship, family and children, and issues of gender. In the final section of this chapter I examine institutional dynamics of clergy leadership.

a. Worship as Ritual

In liberal and evangelical congregations in this study, the ritual life of the community in worship was the focus of attention and energy. In both sets of churches the signs of their moral worldviews were often plain to see. The initial impressions of worship in liberal churches were that it was relatively formal and traditional according to each of the Protestant denominational traditions. Clergy were most often in formal robes of their tradition; traditional liturgies were followed, depending on the denomination; music was often traditional in the sense of coming from the high European culture of Bach and Mozart, and the nineteenth-century hymnody of the English and Americans. Finally, some of the musical liturgy came from more contemporary formal church music of the twentieth century; on rare occasions there was a mix of what is called "contemporary" American popular music. So on the surface, one sees, as many of my students have said, "these churches are very conservative and traditional." What they mean by this is that these churches have conserved the classic traditions of their denominations, the Reformed, Arminian, and Anglican in such ways that innovation in forms of liturgy and ritual are somewhat rare and when done, are quite subtle.

Nonetheless, the parts of liberal liturgies, when investigated at greater depth, reflect their ideological core and theological innovations. In almost every evangelical worship and Web site, one sees the importance of confession and repentance for sin. In only two of the ten liberal churches did I come across a prayer of confession and these were often prayers that addressed "fear" or "ignorance" or "reluctance" in living into one's "courage" or turning from what is "life giving" in one's being. Indeed, one opening liturgical prayer said, "Loving God, help us to believe that you accept us as we are, that we may accept ourselves. Teach us to affirm what is good in our lives and to grow toward what is worthy." The implication is that sin is not an ontological blot that needs the cover of Christ's blood, but a misalignment of the self that can be restored and renewed by a turning to that which is good, true, and beautiful. In liberal liturgy, the life of the self is good or at least is good in potential, and through education can be drawn out by the spirit and be united with the true self, the self made in the image of God.

Formal affirmations of faith were common as well in liberal liturgy. But these were also revealing of the liberal moral worldview and the kind of convictions and behaviors that they consecrate in their ritual lives. In one affirmation the traditional Trinitarian formula of Father, Son, and Holy Spirit was shifted to God, "the Creator Spirit"; Jesus Christ, "Spirit of God"; and finally, Holy Spirit as one who empowers "us to witness to God's love." Theologically, what is significant in this affirmation is that Jesus Christ may die on the cross, but his death is not redemptive of sin in the sense of a sacrifice or as a substitute. What killed Christ was the corrupt powers of the world, and in the process God's spirit is "poured out in fullness and in power/That the whole creation might be restored and unified." Christ is seen as a symbol of reunion of the entire creation rather than as the Savior of individuals. In the face of violence and exclusion, Christ offers reconciliation and inclusion. The conventional world of violence and revenge is turned on its head. In liberal congregations the metaphysical and ontological power of Christ is often expanded to include a "cosmic" dimension that is a source of unity that penetrates all of creation and, through this work, restores and brings hope for harmony and peace.

One of the most eloquent affirmations of faith is worth duplicating in full, in part because of its beauty and in part because it shows the trajectory of liberal liturgy and how the world is imagined in liberal churches:

> We believe in God above us,
> Maker and sustainer of all life,
> Of sun and moon,
> Of water and earth
> Of male and female.
> We believe in God beside us,
> Jesus Christ, the Word made flesh,
> Born of a woman's womb, servant of the poor.
> He was tortured and nailed to a tree.
> Knowing full passion and deep sorrow, he died forsaken.
> He descended into the earth to the place of death.
> On the third day he rose from the tomb.

He ascended into the heaven to be everywhere present.
And his kingdom will one day be known.
We believe in God within us,
The Holy Spirit of Pentecostal fire,
Life-Giving breath of the Church,
She is the Spirit of healing and forgiveness,
Source of resurrection and of life everlasting. Amen.

There are traditional aspects to this affirmation, but this is a congregation that refuses to use the Nicene Creed because it is too patriarchal and infused with the substitutionary atonement theory that they reject. Nonetheless, this affirmation of faith takes on some of the older aspects of the tradition, the Trinitarian movement, though named differently; Jesus is tortured on a tree, and in death Jesus comes to be present everywhere. The Holy Spirit is made female and becomes the "source of healing and forgiveness, source of resurrection and life everlasting." Using the feminine imagery is somewhat unusual, though not absent from the Christian tradition; forgiveness becomes a noun—an ontological power that absolves mistakes—and resurrection and life to come are named though interpreted symbolically. That is, eternal life becomes a state of being rather than a condition following death. In a focus group with liberal lay leaders following the worship where this formulation of faith was used, a gay man, whose "faith was salvaged because of this church," remarked on how powerful the use of a "feminine pronoun for God" was in his understanding of nature of God. For him, God is both male and female; God is the mystery that partakes of human complexity and its diversity. We see in this liberal conception of the Christian divinity a languaging of the Trinity not as "Father" or "Son" but a God who is mystery, though also shares in the full range of human differentiation. The liberal churches, in their liturgies, avoided literal anthropomorphisms for God, preferring abstractions and qualities rather than God as agent or person per se.

Notably, in two of our visits to liberal churches, the assistant ministers, both of whom were women, preached. Female leadership is not uncommon in these churches—the worship services expressed the core features of the liberal moral worldview. In one worship service, the outreach to homeless families was integrated into the worship liturgy. The congregation had a program that facilitated various families with children into transitional housing and invited these families to become a part of the church. The pastor introduced the families and afterward, in the middle of the service, asked for volunteers to complete the program, waiting until the sign-ups were complete. The sermon went on to emphasize the importance of Christ's outreach and focused on "inclusive hospitality" as the hallmark of Jesus' ministry. In another sermon, a genealogy of Jesus' birth was read from scripture. The pastor spent the sermon commenting on the women who are mentioned in the text, particularly Tamar and Rahab, both women of "disreputable reputations" yet a part of Jesus' lineage, once again showing the "radical inclusiveness" of Jesus' ministry and that "perfection" is not about "having one's plastic surgeon fix one's perceived physical imperfections" but about "accepting and celebrating the wonderfully messy" reality of the God-given nature of oneself and allowing God to empower oneself and follow the models of these "unusual" female biblical characters of righteousness.

In a sermon from a church that was the fastest growing of all the liberal congregations, the leadership intentionally made children, youth, and families one of the major focuses of the congregation. As the bulletin says, "Children are welcome and involved every Sunday morning, and services will often include special songs and stories for them. Children are not the church of the future; they are the church of the present." In the service I attended, the children's sermon was deftly mixed into the adult sermon, so the one flowed from the other, capturing the attention of children but also making adults realize the message was the same, only given at two different levels, but not in such a way to be in tension with the other. The sermon's question was taken from a Mary Oliver poem, "Spring," where she states, "There is only one question: how to love this world." Once again scripture was read and not ignored, but the "text" for the day became the poem rather than a biblical verse—sacred scripture is central in the congregation, but the "sacred story" dwells in other words as well, such as poems, stories, and words from other sources. The children's sermon ends with a "wondering question": "How do you love the world?" For the adults, it is the same question, the message in part being, "we care for each other by 'simply showing up' for one another." The pastor leaves the whole congregation with that question, saying, "Let it burn in your hearts," as the spirit burned in the hearts of the disciples at Pentecost.

Another liberal pastor made an arresting plea that liberals also want more than questions at times. Sometimes this pastor is quite direct. As she says, liberals sometimes want more than symbols. In an Easter sermon she used a contemporary image to describe and understand the resurrection, again relating a complex theological conundrum to adults and children so that both could understand, which would lead to a point that the pastor wanted to make—symbols point to and share in the reality of God's work in the world:

I used the example of [her son] when I talked about resurrection.
My son and I did this and this is sort of funny, when my son and

I, he's eight, we were talking about the resurrection and he says, "I'm Jesus, I've come back from the dead." And he starts kind of walking through the house like a zombie [from] *Night of the Living Dead.* So I said [in the church service], "Here's how my son views resurrection." I said, "That's not what we mean by resurrection, is it? With the flesh dripping off. So if it's not that, what is it?" On Easter I had John Updike's poem, "Seven Stanzas [at] Easter," which I've put in for years, where Updike is making this poetic plea that either we believe in the bodily resurrection or give the whole thing up. That it ain't no metaphor, Updike says. Sometimes I feel like I can provide answers in different ways. And the funny thing is that even thinking liberal people are looking for answers at times, but they don't want you to get there before they do. They're looking for a well-framed question first. And they're looking to know that you yourself are asking the question that they are asking. Otherwise they're not interested in your answers. I know, for instance, that we attract people who are interested in the questions first. Evangelicals grow more on the edge of people who are looking for answers first. And usually looking for answers to things that, and I don't mean this in a pejorative way, I think it's more descriptive than anything else, that they're afraid of something. One of the things we teach is that over and over again scripture says, "Don't be afraid, don't be afraid."

And even here, she differentiates the liberal perspective from the answers given in evangelical congregations—questions do not come from "fear" but from a source of curiosity, motivated by wanting to know and not by trepidation about a divine threat. But the sermon illustration along with the form of delivery gives a rare example among the liberal churches of a church that appealed to young people. I found that for the most part worship and ritual in liberal churches are focused on adults. With notable exceptions, there is a strong bias toward complex language and stories oriented as one lay liberal said, "toward a fifty-seven-year-old with a graduate degree." And indeed, demographically, this fits most of the laypeople among my liberal focus groups. The exceptions were one or two churches that made strong attempts at integrating rather complex messages to the level of children and youth. The ritual process of consecrating behavior and shaping mind and body to a theologically imagined world that appeals to adults *and* children is a subtle process; not all churches succeed in doing it.

Worship in evangelical services is ritually, in a literal sense, a different world. It is in part a product of the evangelical parachurch movement and independent evangelical churches of the 1960s and 1970s. These groups included

Young Life, Campus Crusade for Christ, and InterVarsity, as well as Calvary Chapel and Vineyard Church, coming out of California, that introduced an informal style of casual and contemporary worship. The parachurch movement jettisoned traditional church liturgy as rigid and "ritualisitic," and introduced contemporary musical instruments and relevant lyrics mixed with pop tunes that exploded in popularity in church services across the nation. The Christian music scene is now a strong niche in American music, competing with secular rock and roll for the hearts and minds of American teenagers and families (Wuthnow 2003). To varying degrees these forms of music and media have taken over evangelical worship. From independent ministry leadership organizations out of Willow Creek in Illinois and Rick Warren's Saddleback Church in California, churches have learned what appeals to middle-class Americans. And it is important to note, these are white, middle- and now upper-middle-class Americans. I found virtually no significant minority participation in most evangelical churches, with notable exceptions, mentioned earlier. A pastor in jeans or a Hawaiian shirt, with Bible in hand, preaching verse by verse, sometimes with an outlined sermon guide in the hands of congregants or sometimes with video clips in the background, is not only typical but expected in evangelical congregations.

In 2002, my family and I, while on vacation in a rural area of Washington, attended a Sunday evangelical church service where I expected mid-summer attendance to be low. The church was nearly packed, with more than three hundred people at the early service and even more expected at the second. Moreover, the crowd included large numbers of young families, including fathers, an anomaly in the liberal Protestant congregations in this study. The worship, largely a series of songs, was led by five female lay leaders at microphones. Lyrics were projected onto a screen. Featured songs were biblically based and intimate in their use of first-person pronouns. Women led the singing with some accompaniment by guitar, drums, and piano. There was no offering, although a missionary came forth to witness to his family's ministry to a tribe in Latin America. At his mission, he was translating the Christian Scriptures into the tribe's language and recruiting indigenous leaders in the area to lead a local congregation. In his presentation and body language he reflected a sense of joy and expectancy about what he was doing.

The pastor then gave the "teaching" part of a series on "lifestyle breakthroughs." The bulletin contained an outline of the talk with three points on how modern life is stressful and causes individuals to want what they do not need. The pastor gave secular and religious examples of individuals who had overcome these temptations and achieved a more "balanced" lifestyle that would be "pleasing to the Lord."

This was not expository preaching that took a book of the Bible and interpreted it verse by verse, but a topical teaching that used scriptures to make its point. The pastor was lively in his delivery. At one point, for every suggestion from the congregation of their own healthy lifestyle change, he threw out health food bars to them. He illustrated his points with personal examples of his own trials with stress. His preaching exemplified the evangelical preaching that I saw elsewhere, if not always biblically based than biblically defended, pointing to personal transformation (the salvation prayer for conversion was printed in the bulletin), and awareness of the need to address "the desires of the world" from which one must finally separate (Wellman 2004).

Of course, not every evangelical church mimicked this style or this tone. Nevertheless, as a research team, we found that nearly every evangelical church service mixed a celebratory style with a core doctrinal conservative Christian message that confronted sin in quite personal ways and at the same time offered ample opportunities for repentance and forgiveness. While the pastors could be combative, evangelical laypeople inevitably spoke about the "joy" and "energy" of evangelical services. The sense of expectation and gladness that I heard in worshipers' voices was palpable and seemed quite authentic. Evangelicals loved their churches and looked forward to going. As more than one minister and evangelical lay leaders said, "Northwesterners don't have to come to church; they want to come to church. I grew up in the South and believers here are more real than back home where everyone is expected to go to church." This theme of joy and authenticity laced many of the advertisements for evangelical churches. Ministers were described as "real" in the pulpit, which meant that they spoke from their experience and were full of "energy" and love for others. And the pastors I interviewed in the evangelical congregations—and they were all men who led the congregations—without exception were highly energized and passionate people about God, their church, and their future expectation of growth. Evangelicals were different from liberal pastors in that they expected and wanted growth in their churches. Most liberal pastors, on the other hand, were consistently anxious about "too much growth": in general, they said that they were not interested in having a larger congregation.

Moreover, evangelical pastors were quite concrete about appealing to young people. For them, liturgical forms, clothing, or any other impediment to attracting young people had to be abandoned. In one humorous but revealing tirade, an evangelical pastor told me why he did not wear a robe:

Yeah, because I believe, this is just my belief, that everybody wants some sort of rootedness, or historicity to their belief structure. And if they don't get it from their theology they have to get it from their expression. And I think that's what it is in the PNW. This region has the least churched cities in the country. It is definitely the least churched among young men. I think that's why young men don't give a shit about tradition; they don't give a shit about style or form. The only time they've ever seen a guy in a robe is when they got a DUI. So it doesn't conjure up warm images, sitting before a judge in some formal room where he's on a bench and you're sitting on a hard wooden pew and he gives you a fine for being drunk. That just doesn't conjure up anything real positive. So if you want young guys, the churches that go with the liberal message and the traditional form, they're not getting young people, they're not getting young men and they never will. They just can't. Because young people, they're about innovation and if you don't have innovation you're not going to get young people.

This evangelical pastor has been successful in attracting young men to his worship services, which are held in an old warehouse, now designed to be as dark as a nightclub, and equally powerful in generating Christian rock and roll. The sermons at this church were more expository but very topical nonetheless, in that verse-by-verse exposition occurred but contemporary topics were continually connected to the biblical stories. Indeed, the pastor was masterful in his sermons for his facility in moving from ancient Israel to the everyday secular life of twenty-five-year-olds living in a highly secularized urban setting.

Young people and families were attracted to this evangelical church and other similar churches in part because the arts and media are continually integrated in such a way that there is a relation between the aesthetics of contemporary American music and media and the life of the church. This is a core aspect of the ritual life of evangelical churches. The "imagined world" of evangelical piety is carried by contemporary musical and media forms into the "lived experience" of church participants. In a literal sense, in terms of time, evangelical services focused equally on music and media that were interspersed with prayer, and ended with a teaching or sermon. The arts used in worship, whether in visual or musical media, reflect a strong evangelical "mission" to integrate them into the church's piety and ritual life. As one evangelical lay leader described her ministry to artists in her city:

> The vision of the art ministry is that we would be connected to God's heart as artists, so God would inspire the artist who would edify the church in worship and teaching and support. Then the community would reach out to the greater community of our city creatively. So

part of our vision is to infuse creativity into all the different ministries, whether it be working with the children's ministry and working with kids being creative, or with the homeless ministry doing art
in the park and music and that kind of thing. Also the worship
ministry is huge, it's a big part of the arts including singers, song-
writers, writing worship music, and writers responding to their
faith in written ways. It's kind of a new concept to a lot of people
to connect art with their faith. So we try to do three shows a year: an
Easter show, a summer show, and then a Christmas show.

The use of the arts, music, and media are integral to evangelical worship
services. Another evangelical church had a thriving ministry to children and
youth, and had developed a college ministry that began five years ago with one
college student; it now has 300 students involved in five services on Sunday.
One of the worship services is channeled by video onto a wide screen in an adjacent room that has tables set up in a coffee lounge atmosphere so that young
families and young adults can drink coffee and interact with one another during the service, while young families take care of their toddlers and infants. On
numerous occasions the idea of coffee and worship were twinned as normal
and expected in evangelical churches. Coffee, as one evangelical put it, is the
"sacrament of the PNW, why not have it in the sanctuary?"

The evangelical congregation with the growing college ministry mentioned
it was in the process of raising nearly $6 million to remodel its sanctuary. At the
service to launch the campaign to raise funds for the remodel, the pastor used a
video in the service to make the pitch. It was spliced with contemporary
Christian music that was melodic and filled with sentiment about "our need to
worship God alone" and spliced with interviews with various people in the
congregation speaking poignantly about the impact of the church on their lives
and on their families. These interviews had various pictures of the future plan,
and the whole presentation was put together with sophistication and visual
power. As a result of the campaign, the church was able to raise in pledges $3.5
million in their initial campaign request from 349 families. The pastor was
thrilled and overwhelmed at the support for the new plan. One of the remarkable pieces of this campaign was the church's pledge to build a parking lot
that the adjacent public school could not afford. At first the public school and its
lawyers were hesitant over the deal, but soon the goodwill of the church won
them over and the school district agreed to it. I was told that the principal of the
school, who was not a member of the church, broke down in tears over the
generosity of the church. The church benefited from the plan because it could
also use the parking lot, even as it took on all the costs of the job.

Again, I was consistently struck by the joy and celebratory atmosphere of evangelical worship. This is all the more remarkable since a part of their message is a conservative and sometimes confrontational one, that humans are lost without God. Human disobedience is real and irrevocable without repenting and turning to Christ for salvation. The affirming messages of evangelicals are all conditioned on the fact that without Christ humans are doomed. Of course the evangelical jeremiad has a long history in American Protestant culture going back to the Puritans, reaching its peak with Jonathan Edwards in the eighteenth century. In the twentieth century the jeremiad echoes in the cries of moral degradation caused by abortion and gay marriage. In particular, in this study, evangelicals reject the "liberal talk" of the goodness of human nature as pointless and even foolish. An evangelical pastor in one of the most socially "progressive" evangelical churches that I came across gave a stern warning against liberal thought:

Robbie Zacharias [an evangelical theologian] said an open mind is like an open mouth, it's looking for something to bite down on, otherwise it's like the sewer, rejecting nothing. And as I look at our culture of open-mindedness, and as much as we want to uphold it as a value, I believe that biblically it says the heart that just keeps the open-minded pluralism is an empty vacuum and it's longing for something that's bigger than it. I'm not buying the whole Utopia of the American dream anymore. I'm going to become a nihilist, if anything, and say this is a joke, it's absurd. And the answer is that science has given us answers that modernity has given us about Utopia and technological and economic advancements and a place where we're all just these happy princes; it betrays the soul hunger in everybody. And as evangelicals who subscribe to more of an orthodox historical view of scripture, we say, "Jesus is truth. He's real, he came, he's present, and he calls you to live and to the way that you were made," then you begin to experience that life works and there are things like love and joy and hope in the midst of suffering and tragedy and the reality of this world and you're not just trying to one-up it through consumerism or whatever. So the mainlines gave away the Bible. Like they just said, "We're going to ordain homosexuals, or we're gonna undermine the truth of scripture." And to me it's like, I mean, when I became a believer, if there wasn't the God piece and the truth of his world to hold that thing together, I'm not getting up and going to church because I'm religious, or I like to sing hymns, I like to sit through boring sermons. There's just nothing in me that's going to join that club. But if it's true, then I'm stoked. I think what you have with the mainline is they said, "Well, it's not really true and it might not be true," and you got [Marcus] Borg and the historic Jesus Seminar stuff and all that. And so the church basically said that the foundation of this thing is suspect, the Bible and the reality of Christ and the whole Christology that has gone through the centuries. So of course the mainline is going to die, because religion sucks and the whole culture knows it.

For this evangelical pastor, who was the only evangelical who actually mentioned Marcus Borg, the fact that liberals question the Bible's authority upends the whole facade. It calls into question the "truth" upon which the church is built—without absolute biblical authority, going to church is absurd—precisely because the story behind it is not true. Evangelicals strongly argue that the core truth claims of what they believe are not a metaphor but are literally true; they know the "perfect truth." In this sense, the Scriptures witness to this perfection, though as I have mentioned before, this is not to say that some scriptures are interpreted symbolically. Though even here, the intent of these symbols is perfect as well. Again, by far the single most important reasons evangelicals were attracted to churches and attended worship was because the Bible was preached in its "perfection." Indeed, in several cases, evangelicals said their former church pastor was "charismatic" and an "entertaining speaker" who made "relevant points," but because he did not preach in a "biblical" way they searched for another church. Evangelicals demanded a biblically based preaching method. In this way, I found evangelical laypeople to be quite demanding of their pastors; if the pastor strayed from what was understood as a biblical principle, laypeople were quick to question him. My initial sense was that pastors in evangelical churches practiced "personality cults," but in listening to evangelical laypeople, a pastor's deviation from evangelical orthodoxy would mean either his transfer to another church or advocacy for pastoral change.

Evangelical worship though innovative in using modern media had its own kind of homogeneity. Contemporary Christian music once heard begins to sound quite similar. Moreover, the themes of God's love and redemption in Jesus Christ are repetitive and, at times, obsessive. At the same time the quality of the music has improved and has broken into wider markets and even onto secular radio stations. Nonetheless, the ritual strategies of evangelical Christian worship services reflected a patterned display. Contemporary music prepares the group for worship, followed by prayer, some scripture, and a "message." Occasionally a drama or testimony from missionaries is interspersed, but the sequencing is relatively similar even as it seemed "new" to outsiders.

Religious ritual is an imagined theological world embodied in consecrated action that seeks to infuse lived experience and thereby shape and guide human agency. This process of binding the imaginal and everyday world of congregants occurs in liberal and evangelical churches in different ways, but with similar ends. For liberals, the liturgical formulas of the tradition are largely retained, though innovation occurs theologically that reflects their ideological concerns. The integration of relatively formal ritual practices is mixed with "progressive" theological doctrines that emphasize the "human side" of Jesus' nature, his egalitarian ethical practices, and hospitality to the marginalized in society. Liberal liturgy remains more attuned to a literate culture, satisfied with read words in the context of a post- or late modern era infused with technologies that emphasize changing images and messages other than the spoken or read text.

Evangelicals, on the other hand, portray a ritual life with an antiritual rhetoric that heightens the "authenticity" of their liturgical practices. Nonetheless, their liturgies display homogenous forms that do ritual work by imagining a world that is intimately interwoven in lived experience. Evangelicals translate the theology of their evangelical traditions into the practices and aesthetics of contemporary Americans with sensitivity to the tastes and preferences found within popular culture. It is somewhat remarkable that the theological message of sin and redemption, which is certainly held with some suspicion and even offense in many quarters of modernity, is nonetheless well integrated with the forms and instruments of modern media such that any discord is downplayed. Prayer for each of these groups provides yet another ritual language to imagine these moral worlds and integrate them into the lives of congregants.

b. Ritual and Prayer

The life of prayer is an instrument by which one imagines the mysteries of one's religion and relates them to the exigencies of experience. How one interacts with and reacts to this "world" frames the moral worldview just as the moral worldview guides the interaction between what William James called the "more" of life and the lived experience of individuals and groups who develop languages that negotiate this relationship (James 1982). And not only do moral worldviews affect the life and language of prayer but also the larger physical and ecological environments. In both liberal and evangelical communities the ecology of the PNW was often mentioned as a source of inspiration and occasionally distraction in mediating the life of prayer in the lived experience of individuals and groups. For liberals, this was true in particular. Indeed, the word *prayer* itself was not frequently used in discussions by liberal clergy and liberal laypeople. As I investigated the transcriptions of interviews with liberals, the most frequent use of the word *prayer* was in relation to praying for participants and leaders in the Iraq War, often with the emphasis that the church was praying for the Iraqi people. But when it came to personal prayer, the comments were most frequently expressed in terms of spirituality, the "experience of God," or the "development" of the spiritual life. Of course, to be "spiritual but not religious" is hardly unique to the PNW, but it is more frequent in this region (Shibley 2004). As one liberal minister explained: "The thing that I hear most often is, 'I'm spiritual.' And 'spiritual' could mean anything. It's me with my shade-grown, fair-trade soy latte in the mountains rescuing salmon." He said this tongue in cheek but there is much resonance among liberal clergy to this comment. This same pastor went on to say as someone who was a relatively recent transplant to the region: "You can't live here and not have a sense that you're in the presence of something infinitely greater than anything we can imagine, whatever you choose to name that presence." And this was not just a description but a point of frustration with him and with many of the liberal clergy. Northwesterners are notoriously individualistic about their spirituality and, for many, spirituality comes in many ways and not only through their religious communities. Liberal clergy in the study often argued in one way or another, as one said, "You can't be a Christian in isolation." But this did not stop liberal laypeople from being just that.

When many liberal laypeople in the study spoke of "spiritual development" it was often in the context of spiritual retreats, frequently conducted in retreat centers from other religious traditions, including Zen Buddhist centers, sessions with Sufi masters, and sometimes with Christian contemplatives. There were several "spiritual development" centers directly attached to the liberal churches in this study. These centers brought in authors and activists from Christian traditions that included the Roman Catholic faith, but also Buddhist monks and practitioners out of the New Age movement. Many of these speakers had integrated what could be called "left" or liberal-leaning politics into their spirituality, so that this political aspect was often a facet of the discussion, either working on aspects of religious and spiritual nonviolence, or in support of women's rights across the world, or in validating gay and lesbian people.

But again I was struck by the caution among liberals to discuss how they related to God in personal terms. I do not think this was out of a need for privacy so much, since on many other matters, interviewees were quite vulnerable about themselves and their churches. For liberals, God is not approached in a familiar or casual way. One did not hear, as in conversations with evangelicals, about what the "Lord was doing in my life," or how "God had healed me," or what "God was teaching me." What became clear was that liberals did not ask God for this or that thing in particular; God is not expected to intervene in the details of one's life. As one lay liberal said, "I don't believe in the supernatural." Or as another put it, "How do we know whether or not there is an afterlife?" Or as another commented, "How can we know what God is like?" Now at the same time, the overwhelming comment about God from liberals was that God was loving, kind, and merciful. But did God do anything specific for them or for the world? For the most part my sense is that liberals did not expect or believe that God was in the business of "doing things in the world." If God did do something, it was to be present in the world. Indeed, one parent said, "It is not so much about me teaching my son to believe in God, but helping him to experience God's presence." Now this sense of "presence" is neither a superficial comment nor a throwaway line, but a powerful instrument of grace, love, and acceptance for liberals. For liberals, the world and all that is in it become "sacramental"—that is, the beauty, truth, and goodness of life point to a greater power that created it and sustains it. As one liberal pastor said, "I feel like I was born again many times in my youth—through charismatic experiences, by laying on of hands, through altar calls from Young Life leaders—but it was all of a piece, it was like life was infused with a sacred quality." So for liberals to compartmentalize the life of prayer, or to ask for specific things to happen for oneself or others, is in part too abstract or too instrumental. Life and spirit for liberals are of one piece and to separate out one's lived experience from God and one's requests from God's will is artificial or even manipulative.

For one liberal clergy, this seamless integration of prayer, God, and life comes out as part and parcel of her theology. Not all liberals would express it quite this eloquently or in such sophisticated theological terms, but it resonates with many comments that I heard:

> Where I am personally, I believe that Jesus Christ was more than just
> an exemplar. I believe that Jesus Christ is Jesus a person and
> Christ, in some way. Let me put it another way: the strong point of
> Christology for me is not the salvific stuff. It's incarnation. I'm a little
> more Eastern Orthodox in that way. So for me, the fact that Jesus
> was born is significant and the fact that Jesus died is significant,
> because those are two sure human experiences. The fact that I believe
> in some way that Jesus is God, and I do believe that, says that my

experiences as a human being of birth and life and death and all the stuff in between is that I worship a God that has been there and done that. But, sometime in the beginning part of the second century in Mass, some of the early church fathers said in one of the earliest articulated Christology in the Christian church, he became like us so we could become like him. And I just wish everybody would have shut up after that. Because the rest of the stuff, the virgin birth and the offering of the blood sacrifice and all that kind of stuff, as far as I'm concerned are metaphors from different communities of their attempt to try to explain it in their own time, which is what every Christian is faced with.

But for this liberal pastor, it is not that metaphors are somehow fictions, but they point toward a truth that cannot finally be fully captured, that is nonetheless quite real. This is the liberal critique of evangelical theology: evangelicals mistake metaphors for literal facts and thus make an idol out of what should be a sign. Of course, for evangelicals liberals do not have the courage of their convictions and claim "to follow metaphors" while evangelicals follow God. In any event, for liberals the metaphors are powerful reminders of the "truth" of God's presence in their lives that they refuse to manipulate or even label and only speak about with great caution and care.

I was curious how liberals would respond to evangelical God-talk categories; I asked several liberal focus groups and clergy about their "relationship" to God and whether or not, like evangelicals, they would make a "decision" to follow Christ or ask someone else to do so. The question was met more often than not with a blank stare. Although for one liberal minister, coming out of the Arminian tradition, the answer spoke to his tradition but also created a trajectory of ethical obligation at the same time: "Christianity by its very nature involves following the image of a Christ who was literally, as Bonhoeffer explains, the man for others." For liberals, the call of Christ is the call of service to others, so to believe is to act and there is little room between the two. In this sense, theology or prayer without action, to paraphrase the book of James in the New Testament, is fruitless. When I asked a similar question of another liberal minister who came out of the Anglican tradition, she framed her answer about a decision for Christ in light of the sacrament of Holy Communion. For her, to pray and to believe are to do ritual, to take the bread and wine, to participate in the ritual of the Eucharist: "We ask everybody to make a decision every Sunday. And we ask them to come forward to receive Christ every Sunday. And we also teach them that doubt is a necessary part of faith and that doubt is not the absence of faith. Questioning is a holy thing." So when in the presence of the Holy, the divine, and the mystery, liberals stand in the tension of their ideological tradition—faith is not so much an answer but a question; truth is near, though unverifiable and uncontrollable; the relation of lived experience to this "more" weaves together the majestic and the mundane, the sacred and the profane. The icons of faith, whether sacrament, Bible, or the everyday world, point to the divine mystery but cannot capture it, even as the mystery is as close as one's coffee or as beautiful as the mountain range in the distance.

Finally, prayer for liberals is private. At one point, a liberal lay leader said in reference to the spiritual and prayer lives of his fellow parishioners:

> But you often don't know what the person at the end of the pew
> believes. And it's none of your business; as one of our pastors says, it's
> none of your damn business. So we often don't know. Although
> there are a lot of people in this room I know quite well, I couldn't tell
> you anything about what they believe.

This was not said in anger so much as an explanation of the piety of this group. It is in part out of this piety that liberals express their moral worldview: "My life is my own and my relationship to God is a mystery." It is not the purpose of church to share one's most intimate thoughts about God or prayer. And a piece of this is that God is not there to be one's "doorman," to be at one's beck and call, but it is one's own responsibility to do what is right and to do good on behalf of the faith that one is given. It is a type of American individualism that is carried with pride and with a sense of righteousness in the liberal community. Moreover, it is in part the vestige of the Magisterial Reformation that touted God's sovereignty—one cannot manipulate God for one's own purposes, and more to the point, one should not do this. God must be approached with care, in the interior of one's heart—"Go and pray in your closet..." and not "in the streets." In the evangelical world of ritual and prayer, we see another story of faith, again, in contrast with liberals, reflecting a different moral worldview with its own sense of identity, ethical obligation, and relation to God.

The ideological world of the evangelical moral worldview prides itself in part on its clarity and certainty about what is true for God and humanity. Whereas for liberals doubt is a component of faith, for evangelicals it is more a problem and a sign of a lack of trust. Confidence, as Rodney Stark and Roger Finke argue, is always the major issue in religion (2000). How does one build a religious and moral worldview on something that cannot be empirically verified? For Stark and Finke, humans are willing to take risks and trust in an "invisible" force that they call God. This God is said to be both just and compassionate. In the Christian religion, this God is *the only God* and contains all that is good; God knows all, creates all, and loves all. For liberals, this God is more impersonal than personal, less interested in intervention, and more interested in the act of *being itself*. For evangelicals, on the other hand, this God is personal—the person of Jesus Christ; God is holy and just, so that sin is judged, but willing to intervene to redeem human sin. God offers his only Son who dies on a cross to ransom the human race. The rewards from God in the evangelical ideological worldview are far more explicit. For liberals, the presence of God in beauty and love is its own reward that is deeply meaningful, though a private and interior experience. For evangelicals, God is at work in their world, battling with diseases, guiding their lives in specific ways, fighting with Satan for the salvation of souls, and exercising control over human destiny.

This is not to say that evangelicals talked constantly about God in their interviews. They referenced God when it was appropriate to the question, and on occasion would proselytize me or other interviewers, often offering to pray for us. There was never talk about their faith being "private," as we saw with liberals, but they also did not gratuitously parade their piety. Nonetheless, when it was appropriate they were unafraid to mention what prayer meant to them. Most often it simply meant that they were praying for others, and this prayer most often came in the form of praying for healing, for safety, and frequently for the salvation of family members, friends, and others (including strangers, the world, and often Muslims). And this came up in simple circumstances. For instance, one evangelical lay leader prayed (silently) for her hairdresser during a two-year stretch every time she would go to visit her. The evangelical leaders said, "I never told her. And one day she said, 'I know you've been praying for me and I need to talk to you.' Great. She grew up in a cult. And she goes, 'You're not freaked out about what I'm telling you?' I go, 'Well, no.'" This evangelical leader went on to relate the story that she invited her hairdresser to church, and the leader was nervous because the hairdresser tended to dress "provocatively," and she did so, but the evangelical leader said, "My evangelical women friends welcomed her with open arms; they loved her into Christ." The hairdresser became an active member of the church. Numerous stories narrated these kinds of events, where strangers and friends were prayed for and eventually time and context created opportunities for evangelicals to invite them to church, and these newcomers were converted.

There is also awareness in the evangelical community that no matter how hard they pray, God does not always do what they want. This problem is rationalized as a matter of God's will and the need for obedience and submission to that will no matter what. Theologically, the task of faith and discipleship for evangelicals, as one evangelical pastor argued, was framed in terms of sin defined as "the misplaced self. It's the self out from under God. It's the child who says to his parents, 'I'd rather do it myself, don't tell me what to do. I'll make up my own mind.' It's the spirit of adolescence." For this pastor, this "sin" is often transferred into groups, churches, and even societies, which creates "anarchy and disorder." For him, this reality is amply illustrated in American culture, particularly in the breakdown of nuclear families, the advocacy for gay marriage, and the frequency of abortion. The evangelical moral worldview seeks a moral order that functions under a familial hierarchy of God the Father, who is in control; it is to this God that humans must submit. And it is only this submission that will assure a moral order and will lead to a thriving human community.

For evangelicals, there is real trepidation that they can do what is right without God. And this came out for one evangelical new member in relation to prophecy when several evangelicals were discussing how the Iraq War fulfilled prophecies from the book of Revelation. One evangelical said with some exasperation:

> And if Jesus said, "I don't even know the hour [when God comes
> to judge the world]," why are we pretending that we might be able to
> see into that? I think that's just dangerous territory to start draw-
> ing too big of conclusions other than, God's always in control. God
> can use any situation for good and then praying in that direction.

When evangelicals came up against a mystery or problem, the fallback position was always to say, "Well, I'll pray about it; God is in control." I never heard a liberal say, "God is in control." Indeed, even when it came to political issues close to the heart of every evangelical in this study, stopping gay marriage and abortion, one said, "Signing petitions won't move the hand of God; prayer is what moves the hand of God." Prayer is a leverage point for evangelicals, and if they do it enough, in the midst of other believers, evangelicals feel that they can change others, their churches, the country, and the world. But again, even if they are unable to get what they pray for, God's will is done.

The particularity of prayer requests came out most often relative to churches in the charismatic traditions, whether Pentecostal, Foursquare, or Assembly of God. On one Web site, the pastor, who had a form of leukemia, kept a daily update on his health asking for prayer that certain blood counts would decrease to certain levels. For these churches, God hears human prayers and wants followers to pray for everything in quite specific ways. Moreover, it is prayer with "purpose and power," believing that their churches can change the world: "Our church has a destiny; churches like people are created with a purpose, we're on a bus and there's a place we're supposed to go.... The destiny is to reach the world for Jesus." These churches, along with the other evangelical churches in the study, to one extent or another, were extraordinarily ambitious in their dreams for themselves, their churches, and the evangelization of the world. And this ambition also moved into less spiritual and more mundane areas of life. As one young college student leader in a Pentecostal church said:

> I think in our church we have a realistic idea of God and know
> that he's just like any other good father. I know my father loves to
> bless me. He loves to come over and help me fix stuff. He loves
> to pay for stuff and take me shopping. And why would my heavenly
> father want me to be poor and not get good things that are going
> to help me, or help me do things that I want to do, like setting up
> a skate park. And I think people have a false idea and a wrong idea of
> God. You look at men and women of the Bible like Abraham. Hello?
> He had cattle and sheep up the wazoo, and that's a sign of prosperity.
> And people suddenly think that when it comes to prosperity,
> that's not in the Bible. And it's like, have you read your Bible lately?

This explicit expression of the "prosperity gospel" was most common in the charismatic churches in the sample—in which blessings from God were asked for and expected. Some among the evangelical leaders in the study explicitly denied this kind of reciprocity, but the deeper logic of the quote resonates across the sample: God is *the* Father who wants his followers to make requests and will respond to these prayers. For evangelicals, prayer is efficacious. It is not simply a matter of putting oneself in the "presence of God" as in many liberal churches. For evangelicals, in scripture God calls people to "ask" for whatever they need and God presents himself as a "Father" who cares for his "children." This also fits into the broader ideological and moral worldview of evangelicals that one should "submit" to the "authority of the Father." Thus, the self (like a child) can ask for what he or she wants, but in the end, the Father decides and the Father is in control. Whatever happens then is the "Father's will" and, as one evangelical pastor said, "God is sovereign."

Finally, for evangelicals the spiritual life is not only about submission but also about conflict. Satan, which nearly 10 percent of the evangelicals mentioned in the study, is "real" and battling "believers" over the souls of individuals. Spiritual warfare is that simple: a struggle over the salvation of individuals. It is not so simple as to say, "Satan made me do it and I sinned," but for evangelicals, their theological worldview contains this notion of a competition over the souls of every person. This came out in particular on the issue of the Iraq War. Evangelicals were sensitive to the "liberal media" accusing them of "hating Muslims" and fomenting the conflict in the Middle East. Evangelicals in this study were adamant that "yes, there is a spiritual warfare going on in the Middle East over the souls of Muslims. But we are pro-Muslim. We want them to convert to Jesus Christ. The only answer to spiritual warfare is to pray." So Muslims are not thought of as evil, but simply misled by Satan; they need "rescue and not condemnation."

Prayer as a ritual process of integrating an imagined and lived world displays the substantial differences between liberal and evangelical Christians in this study. Prayer is an instrument of each of their ideological and moral worldviews, and by illustrating how each approaches prayer we understand how prayer expresses two quite distinct worldviews. If prayer is one of the most intimate acts of the religious life, in some ways the core of the ritual life, one can see why the clash between these two groups can become intense. At these fundamental levels the process and goals of prayer are distinctly different. For liberals, prayer is meditation on God's presence and the practice of moral principles that assure equality and openness toward all. For evangelicals, prayer is the vehicle for transforming themselves, each other, the nation, and the world; prayer can move God to transform the world. For evangelicals, in the end, prayer is submission to the Father who provides and takes care of them. For liberals, prayer empowers and enables them to make up their own minds and do works of righteousness for the sake of all.

c. Web as Ritual

A church's Web site is an electronic representation of how the church imagines itself and how it relates itself to the lived world of its members and potential visitors. Over the last ten years, Web sites have taken on a ritual-like activity, a repeated behavior that shapes and guides thoughts, feelings, and actions, while it mediates a vision and encourages the integration of these ideas into the lives of viewers. The Web in this sense goes beyond the description of reality to construct it, and directs what one sees and how it is seen. On liberal and evangelical sites there were degrees of interactivity and outreach to viewers who sought information, as well as what can be called forms of spiritual experience—prayer requests, visual art, and music. By interactivity I mean updates on information, texts and media that can be downloaded, as well as some reciprocal communication involving comments and queries directly on Web sites, whether in responses to a pastor's blog or calls for prayer. Thus, interactivity can be interpersonal but it most often is in relation to content (Bucy 2004; Sohn and Lee 2005; Stromer-Galley 2004; Stromer-Galley and

Foot 2002). The Web site has become a focus of communication for church organizations and integral to the way information is delivered. It is also a meeting point at which people interact, find meaning, and seek ongoing relationships. In all these ways, the Web site has a communal focus, an ideological interest, and has become an instrument of ritual life in religious communities and beyond.

In examining the Web sites of liberals and conservatives, I was most interested in the opening Web page of each of these sites. I discovered organizational priorities and gained a sense not only of what these groups were trying to communicate but also to whom they were trying to communicate. The liberal sites tend to be informational, emphasizing denominational identity, the mission of the church, and the importance of faith as a journey. Whereas almost every evangelical Web site had links for "newcomers," only one or two liberal sites addressed potential first-time viewers. Liberal sites were heavy on information links to various programs in the congregation, giving readers resources for events of the congregation and some content through sermon archives. On only one site was there a link to the sermon; one could download the message and read it or hear it online. Downloadable sermons and worship services were nearly universally located on evangelical Web sites. One obvious explanation for the simplicity of liberal Web sites is the church's smaller budgets relative to the evangelicals. And while this is self-evident when I compared the demographics and budgets of liberal and evangelical churches, it also reflects an ideological perspective. For liberals, outreach to new people or potential new members was not a priority—and Web sites reflected this disinterest. Liberal sites "welcome" those who come to their sites and they emphasize the "inclusive" nature of their church missions, but they do not encourage evangelism or exercise strategies of recruitment (Baab 2007).[1]

Evangelical Web sites nearly always bury denominational affiliations in out-of-the-way links. Liberal Web sites, on the other hand, either use denominational templates for their Web sites or offer links to their affiliations, whether with the Congregational, Lutheran, Episcopalian, or Methodist denominations. Evangelical Web sites emphasize the identity of the local church as a mission of Jesus Christ with few or no connections to other organizations. This is reflected in the links of each of the Web sites: for liberals, there are greater numbers of external links to wider national organizations; evangelicals tend to have more links but they are overwhelmingly focused internally on their own organization. Liberal churches are bold in their claim to be connected to the broader Protestant mainline church; the several congregational churches in the study used the United Church of Christ theme of "God is still speaking..." to lead off their Web sites and to emphasize that God is present to God's people who are called to serve, worship, and educate. The use of denominational affiliations tends to give liberal Web sites, at least in my eyes, a "generic feel." For liberals, this direct connection to the wider denomination underlines a web of connectionalism and accountability that is a traditional part of most mainline Protestant denominations. Evangelical Web sites, on the other hand, emphasize a local quality that takes advantage of Web designers within local congregations, reflecting again a greater budgetary priority, as well as messaging that a church, as one site said, "always has an eye on potential new members." In many of the larger evangelical congregations, Web site managers were on-site and updated the Web sites on a weekly and sometimes daily basis.

On the Web site of the fastest-growing liberal congregation there was a greater degree of interactivity—at least in terms of content—that used local talent within the congregation to keep parents and friends informed daily about a youth trip into the mountains of western Washington. The Web site showed a daily diary of the trip with pictures of the young people and their leaders that enabled viewers to get daily updates on their youth. The intense nature of interactivity, both in terms of the Web site and in other modes of communication, correlated with church vitality and growth in both evangelical and liberal congregations. The written communications of this same liberal congregation were also highly sophisticated and engaging to the eye and reflected a "local design" that did not use denominational templates. Thus, whether in liberal or in evangelical congregations, I found that local rather than generic media design correlated with greater congregational vitality.

Ideologically, the liberal Web sites were consistent with what we have seen before: a strong attachment to inclusion, the expression of religious belief as obligation to help the needy, and the reinforcement of religion as a spiritual journey. The themes of liberal Web sites almost unanimously communicated a welcome to all, arguing that their churches had "no circles of exclusion"; one church used Matthew 25:40 to exemplify its ministry, quoting Jesus, "As you did it to the least of these you did it to me." Again this same pattern is reflected in a national study of evangelical and liberal Protestant Web sites (Baab 2007) that showed that all liberal Web sites mentioned "justice" as a critical factor in church identity; no evangelical Web sites mentioned justice. At the same time, evangelical links to service opportunities outnumbered liberal service links. This pattern of a liberal rhetoric of justice with limited service opportunities is the same pattern I discovered in my research on outreach in chapter 4 (Brooks 2006).

Most liberal churches proclaimed their status as "open and affirming" to gays and lesbians, but they also asserted that "God's welcome transcends all human distinctions" whether based on class, race, or sexual orientation. This welcome was followed by invitations that each of these churches is a "community of faith that explores what it means to follow Jesus Christ." Another said in its mission statement that "Jesus Christ represents the clearest form of God in our experience." Thus, Jesus Christ was central to the "experience" of faith as a sign of God's presence, and this "sign" must be "explored." Christ is central not so much as the answer to a question, but as a mystery to be explored and a life to be lived—again, the integration of faith and life is at the core of the liberal message.

What liberal Web sites emphasized was that moral actions must follow from being identified as a follower of Jesus Christ. In one case, a peace rally was being sponsored by a liberal church to protest the goal of a "military victory in Iraq," and arguing for a "peaceful resolution to the civil war in Iraq." On another liberal Web site, a link to the children's vacation church school was next to the link for participation in the "gay pride parade" in the city, which was happening simultaneously with the children's program. A congregational Web site posted an adult education opportunity on the "cost and joy of Christian discipleship," reflecting again the emphasis on "action" as an integral aspect of Christian discipleship found in the thinking of Dietrich Bonhoeffer. In only two cases did a liberal Web site reach out to the wider city context—in one case extending a "citywide" service of mourning for an attack on a Jewish charity. Liberal congregations in this study are no longer the "public voices" of their communities, even as several remain "one" public voice among many in their communities. This is not to say that evangelical churches have taken over this role. None of the evangelical churches in the study attempted "to speak" to or for the city. These churches remain subcultures in the PNW. They know they do not speak "for" the culture but only occasionally to it. For instance, in several interviews with evangelical pastors, they spoke about their relationships to "city managers" and the way in which "God had called them to have a regional footprint." This meant not so much manipulating the local government but being a gathering place for the larger evangelical community for the sake of service and outreach.

Finally, for liberals the Christian faith is a "journey." This came out in an adult education series on "faith journeys," advertised on several Web sites, illustrating through the lives of people how the faith became "real" in everyday life. Several churches advertised how they "seek alternate ways to know God." This statement was in part a response to "fundamentalist" ways of knowing God, but also speaking to communities that related more to "spirituality" than to "religious dogma or doctrine." One church expressed its mission as being "companions on the spiritual journey." A part of what this meant was for the church to sponsor annual public "celebrations of creativity" for local artists, not necessarily related to the church or to Christianity, but to the "spiritual creativity in us all."

The tenor and trajectory of evangelical Web sites was remarkably different than the liberal Web sites. While the liberal Web sites tended to be defensive in expressing what their churches "weren't," and where they had come from (denominationally and historically), evangelical Web sites were fully committed to what their churches are and what they intend to be in the future. That is, the evangelical Web sites advertise a vision and imagine themselves as growing, expanding, and reproducing networks of "believers." The enthusiasm of the evangelical Web sites can be detected in their relative sophistication and quality versus that of liberal Web sites. Evangelical Web sites frequently feature photo slideshows, short music videos of baptismal events that just occurred, messages of the most recent services ready to download, and podcasts and broadcasts of ongoing events ready to be viewed and shared. Again, larger evangelical budgets count here, but so does their motivation to mobilize and attract newcomers to the church.

In terms of audience, evangelical Web sites expected visitors and thus were constantly changing and adapting their sites on a weekly and sometimes daily basis so that viewers had a reason to return over and over again. On liberal Web sites that I visited, only one church changed its Web site during the monthlong period between my first and second visits. Evangelicals reflected in their Web sites a vision of interactivity; in more than half the sites one could either join a conversation, sign up for the church blog, or view the minister's blog. Church building projects were updated and prayer requests were clarified by many of the churches, often on a daily basis. The communal and interactive nature of the evangelical Web sites integrated users or at least gave the opportunity for viewers of the Web site to participate in and join the imagined vision of the church in their own experience, facilitating connection and creating a ritual experience that is one of the ways many Americans "do" their religious lives.

Indeed, evangelical Web sites were quite sensitive to individual contexts. For churches in smaller towns, the emphasis on family, youth, and children was illustrated by photos that showed young families enjoying worship, and participating in camps, Bible studies, and baptisms. On most Web sites families were pictured prominently, often intergenerationally, and not infrequently showing ethnic diversity. This diversity was also seen on liberal Web sites, though the liberal Web sites were visually more generic and static. I observed the liberal Web sites for more than a year; only one of the sites changed the images that it used over that period.

The ideological makeup exemplified on the evangelical Web sites was consistent with what we have seen before. The sites emphasized the centrality of the Bible as the "sole" source of authority, the "inerrant Word of God," and the "inspired" witness to Jesus Christ. This theme was followed closely by the importance of confession and repentance. The opportunity to confess and repent was always a part of the pastors' messages, and it was also frequently followed by notes of encouragement, surrounded by terms of "empowerment," "joy," "celebration," and "renewal," expressing to believers the opportunity of a "second chance." The most striking note of these Web sites was the invitation to "worship" God, which was always filled with supportive comments and affirmation that worship was "meant to build up and equip believers to do the will of God." As one blog participant said, "I loved the opportunity to worship at your church and to show my love to God to let God love on me." This vocabulary of "love on me" was frequent in describing worship and the personal intimacy that evangelical liturgies nurtured. "True" worship of God was associated with a "real and authentic" experience of God's presence. This was illustrated at times through stories of healing, and particularly in the charismatic congregations, where there were explanations about the experience of "speaking in tongues," and how "this can happen for you." At times the language and expressions in the blogs were personal and vulnerable, expressing dramatic personal and family needs; the evangelical Web sites were places where individuals sought to fulfill their spiritual and emotional desires. The Web sites were for many a communal place of support and ritual activity of confession, repentance, and renewal. Personal and intimate talk was nearly absent in most of the liberal Web sites, where concern for privacy seemed to be paramount and, indeed, achieved.

The trajectory of the evangelical Web sites was also dramatically future oriented. By "future oriented," I mean their message was presented not just in terms of salvation, promising that God can save those who repent, and offering eternal salvation, but on a more mundane and practical basis these churches were ambitious to expand and grow. Most of the congregations strongly encouraged missionary activity, whether short- or long-term, and frequently mentioned or advertised teams going to Senegal, Guatemala, China, or other places. This aimed to encourage the youth and families of the congregations to "do" mission not only abroad but locally, whether in urban renewal movements, outreach through sports to the local communities of children and youth, or as local charity organizations, Habitat for Humanity, or homeless shelters and groups that feed the hungry in their cities. These mission trajectories were illustrated in quite dramatic terms in several churches (four out of twenty-four churches) that sought to be a church with a regional imprint.

That is, these churches sought—at least in their advertising—to be *the* church in their cities, by buying buildings in several locations, and using large screens to communicate the "message" of the pastor in multiple locations. In several of the churches, the branding of these multiple sites was done through a specific type of aesthetic that in the urban contexts had a postmodern ethos to it, and the Web sites tended to be designed with minimalistic features, muted colors and texts, and sophisticated Web designs intended to appeal to a younger audience. Nonetheless, even in the midst of the aesthetic minimalism, the vision and ambition of these congregations was, in the cliché terms of the nineteenth-century evangelical generation, to "win" their cities for Christ. Contemporary forms and media were adapted to the tastes and preferences of a "young, hip, digitally sophisticated" twenty- to thirty-year-old, but with a theologically conservative framework. In two churches, a "Calvinistic" theology was proclaimed as the way "to engage" the secular and unchurched region of the PNW, even though it was mixed with an Arminian message about personal decisions for Christ.

The ambitious dreams of these evangelical churches with multiple sites have attracted resources and entrepreneurs with financial capital, many giving large sums to see the vision happen. In one case, it was said that the total real estate holdings of the church were "21 million [dollars], with a debt of only 10.5 million [dollars]." This was followed by a strong campaign to pay down the debt and the request that if "every family gave $300 more each, the debt could be retired." But this retirement was not intended to stop building new churches, but to build more. This same church communicated in its literature that it had already "started more than 100 churches in the United States and many more overseas." Only one of the liberal churches in this study had sponsored a new church.

In analyzing these Web sites I have argued that they deliver information, but also become a medium of communal networks, ideological guidance, and ritual activity. The interactivity of evangelical Web sites is positioned for feedback and conversation among members as well as for opening avenues of communication to newcomers. The evangelization of the world is integrated into the lived experience of evangelicals by Web sites that advertise opportunities for mission, provide space to share stories of successful evangelization, and offer resources for organizations that have this goal of evangelizing the world. Repeated viewings of these sites reinforce this vision and make this imagined world real, habituating viewers to these dreams. The ideological vision of liberals is more about faith as a journey of inward development as well as a means of providing resources to help others in need. The vision of an inclusive world that is hospitable to the "least" and to the "last" in society is communicated through images of diverse groups connecting, stories of social outreach, as well as opportunities for liberals to serve the powerless. The bridge between the imagined world of inclusion and the lived experience of liberals has fewer mediating links, figuratively and literally. For liberals, outreach is filtered through a theology that is centripetal rather than centrifugal; liberals nurture circles of inwardness all the while reaching out to those on the margins even though, as Stephen Warner has noted, liberals do not bring outsiders in (1988). While liberals create organizations that at times work against numerical growth, evangelicals, on the other hand, express ambitions to grow not only on their Web sites but also through organizational dynamics that invite others in.

2. Organizational Dynamics

Groups' organizational dynamics tell us about how moral worldviews shape social structures and how group systems mold moral worldviews relative to context. Most important, organizational dynamics show how groups are mobilized by these moral structures. Sociology in its essence is the study of group construction and destruction and what processes facilitate one or the other. In this section I compare liberals and evangelicals on how they organize themselves as groups. I examine how each facilitates children and youth activities, and how these groups relate to their ministries to families. I examine gender dynamics within these groups, and what happens to gender in-group settings. Finally, I address pastoral leadership, what models of leadership they employ, and what processes and goals leaders use to pursue their goals.

a. Group Dynamics

In interviews with clergy and laypeople in the liberal and evangelical churches, I asked what attracted them to their churches and what kept them involved. The answers were diverse, and many centered on preaching and music. But in this section I focus on how liberals and evangelicals organize in groups, whether informally or formally. I coded responses on groups under the category of the "church is family-like." A sense of community was important to both groups; 32 percent of liberals mentioned the importance of community and 30 percent of evangelicals referenced community as a priority. For liberals, community means a felt sense of the group as a whole. For evangelicals, perhaps in part due to the larger nature of their churches, the sense of community centered on a small group. Forty-three percent of evangelicals talked about participation in a small group whereas less than one percent of liberals were active in a small group. The small group movement is nothing new to American culture; it is widely noted as being a central part of American group life, with nearly 50 percent of Americans in one form of small group or another, whether religious or secular (Wuthnow 1996). Even as liberals made no explicit mention of small group activity, they did express the importance of connection with the "church." Group action and a family-like ethos are important parts of the liberal congregations in this study.

A sense of inclusion is a critical term in the self-definition of a liberal church. Because it is used so often, it can become abstract and even cliché, but it is quite real for liberals. One new member wanted to make it clear that the inclusive nature of his church was not superficial but deeply felt and powerful for him and others:

> I think some common themes I hear a lot are words like openness, inviting, welcoming. For me, it's much more visceral here than in other churches. Terms you won't hear, which I think are quite surprising, you don't hear terms like tolerance and acceptance. I say that in a positive way. Terms like tolerance and acceptance make it sound like there's something wrong and you have to tolerate or accept it. I don't feel there's any sense of that here. The openness is embracing, it's gracious. It's not an acceptance of people or lifestyles or values that you don't like. It's an encompassing of all different viewpoints and you're always hearing people from all sorts of different backgrounds and viewpoints. They are being listened to, paid attention to, heard, invited, and encouraged. I feel the environment here is encouraging, not accepting or tolerating. It nurtures, it draws those different viewpoints out, and turns that into its strength, as is manifested in the programs, the preaching, and the way people interact.

Liberal churches seek to rise above a mere bland acceptance of difference to argue for a "celebration" of difference and the importance of learning from the "other." Not all spoke in such eloquent terms as this liberal layperson, but one could sense in these congregations that individuals felt "safe" as one said, and that there was a feeling of "devotion" in educational groups that was not about piety but about nurturing others in a "responsible and ethical lifestyle." At one point, I said to a lay liberal couple in one of my final interviews, "Evangelicals with their certainty and doctrinal clarity are able to mobilize their people more efficiently than liberal churches." The liberal laywoman without a pause said to me: "I think we lack efficiency by choice." She argued that the product of the liberal church is not a "saved individual, . . . It is a thinking, critical, responsible human being. Well, how do you create that in a Sunday? Well, you don't. I'm a liberal Protestant so I can say it's a tough road."

This embracing of difference and celebration of critical questions and reflection for liberals is not formulated in small groups so much as in informal occasions—adult education courses, coffee hour conversations, and informal meetings as friends over dinner. And for many liberals, the action of worshiping together and "doing" ritual together was a powerful "spiritual experience" that was done in the setting of the community. But even with those most committed and most intentional about their participation in the liberal liturgical life, comments such as the following spoke to the tentative nature of affiliation: "I felt like I can be here and I can leave here and I can come back here and there's going to be no question about where I've been and why did I leave and why did I come back." This liberal leader said this as high praise of her church, speaking to the sense of freedom she felt that the church community embraced, not expecting her to have to "explain" herself or justify her decisions to be a part of the community or not.

The inclusive nature of liberal community life was also critical for gays and lesbians in these congregations. It was always important for them to voice the idea that "this isn't a gay church; it is a church for all people, no matter their background." Nonetheless, the attraction of many liberal churches was precisely their "open and affirming" stance toward gay and lesbian people. In one case a church put out a pink ribbon on its church sign. But in most cases word of mouth led gay and lesbian people to these congregations. Indeed, in another case a liberal lay leader spoke about her "acceptance" in the church community and her relative distance from the gay community. She made it clear by her actions that the church community was more important and indeed vital to her and her partner:

> I'm here on Sundays, I'm here every Tuesday for the church board or church board planning meeting, as a leader, and every Wednesday night I teach a Companions in Christ group. My partner is also very involved so we spend a lot of time here. Our friends are starting to see us as Bible thumpers, because they ask us to dinner [and] we tell them we can't, we have to go to church. But definitely, this church is a big part of who we are and why we're here. We had a choice to leave the city about a year and a half ago and the church was actually a central reason we chose not to leave. I'm an out lesbian and this place, being in a friendly church, has been important to me. I'm an oddity in my community for being a Christian, much more so

than for being a lesbian in this community. I'm very well accepted
here and not very well accepted in my community being a Christian.

The fact that she and her partner felt "at odds" in the gay community was
not a frequent comment among gay laypeople, but the complexity of multiple
affiliations was apparent in other situations. In another church, a transgendered individual who had been ordained in a more conservative Protestant
denomination and had been defrocked for her new female identity told the
story of how she struggled to know how to fit in theologically to her new liberal
church. She was in fact "uncomfortable" with one of the clergy on the staff who
was openly gay. In time she came to accept him through a series of long
conversations they had together, which convinced her that he and the church
were sincere and were not "dumping" the liturgical and theological traditions
of the church. In time, this transgendered woman became a key member of the
confirmation process for adult education in the church and became, as she
said, "a den mother for new Christian initiates." The complexity of this story is
not uncommon in liberal churches and it underscores the difficult negotiations
of identity, theology, and group dynamics that occur in these churches. For
liberal churches, the assimilation of people of "minority status" is a critical
action of hospitality and community that embodies their ideological perspective and fulfills the demands of their moral worldview.

Of course, liberal group dynamics are not without their tensions and limitations. In several cases, liberal churches were chosen by members not because
the churches function so well but because the liberal churches are the person's
"last chance." Thirteen percent of liberal church members I interviewed came
from evangelical backgrounds. Many of these liberals spoke of their past in
dark terms. The said their former churches were "psychotic," "dysfunctional,"
"shaming," and generally unhealthy. Thus, as one said, for her, the liberal
church is "the church of the last resort." Some make the choice for liberal churches in spite of the fact that these individuals are deeply suspicious of
churches in general. Another new member reported that she had to stick with
Christianity because that is what she grew up with and thus must find what is
good in it and discard the rest:

> I feel like Rosemary Radford Ruether [a Catholic feminist theologian]
> has said, that because I was bred in this tradition, I need to work
> within that tradition to help rescue what is gold in it and save it from
> all the misunderstandings and the misleading and the militarism,
> the support for patriarchy, the wrong attitudes towards the earth and
> our relationship to nature. And I think as a psychologist I'm pretty

well equipped to help with that kind of struggle. So I stay in
this denomination, but I do my social action work with Unitarians.

Again the tentative nature of membership for liberals creates a relatively
ambivalent affiliation. That is, out of the broken parts of the Christian tradition, a few pieces can be spared. Churches are important to the degree that they
take "social action"; programs of social justice become a litmus test for valid
Christian belief. Belief itself matters less than how the church advocates for
those on the margins of society. In this way membership for some in liberal
churches is a fragile bond. As many of the liberal clergy complained, most
liberal laypeople have many commitments, the "church being one of those."
This contrasts with the evangelical congregations that I studied that tended to
demand (at least of those who had gone through the membership processes) a
more intense form of loyalty.

The marginality of membership is not always by choice. There were very
few young adults in the 148 liberal respondents—fewer than five. One of the
young adults was a young woman from a local liberal arts college who chose
the liberal church because of its theological complexity and nuance and also
because of its social action. She studied the classic Protestant theologians of the
last two centuries and was articulate about her belief in Protestant liberalism.
She spoke of her invitations to friends to join her at her liberal church, but no
one returned with her. She was frustrated by the lack of young adults in the
congregation, and also was discouraged by the lack of a "liberal" community of
Christians on her college campus (a secular liberal arts college):

I'm involved in the Christian student group on campus and it definitely is more of an evangelical group, but because that is the only
Christian student group, if I want to interact with other people
my age, I'm forced to look to the more conservative side of things if
I want to have that sort of community. And it would be nice to
have that fellowship with people from my own tradition, but it's just
not there.

If this young woman could have been involved in a liberal Christian group
with young people her age, she would have done so, but there were no opportunities at her liberal church or on her secular college campus. And so her
choice to continue to be involved in her church underscores the seriousness
with which she took her commitment to the congregation but also underlines
the limited opportunities for "liberal-leaning" young Christians to find Christian associations in their age group. In all the work I have done in Washington
and Oregon I have come upon no active liberal Christian college communities

with more than ten members. The most active college groups on my own campus are the Pentecostal fellowship group I mentioned earlier and a moderate evangelical church with a large Christian student fellowship, each having between eight hundred and one thousand young adult members.

In part because of the liberal moral worldview and the way it shapes Christian associations, liberal churches are relatively limited in their mobilization of groups in general, and groups of young people in particular. Only two of the churches in my study of liberal congregations had active youth programs, usually with ten to forty youth involved. It is an anomaly for liberal churches to have strong youth or young adult programs; it is not impossible but rare. This becomes clear in contrast to the evangelical congregations.

The conventional perception of evangelical churches is that they are doctrinal, rigid, legalistic, and judgmental. At least this was the assumption of many liberals in the study when making comments about evangelical congregations. In fact in self-reports it was common for evangelicals to say that they felt no sense of judgment in their churches. Indeed, in interviews with evangelicals, when asked what attracted them to the church, many commented on the "relational," "dynamic," and "graceful" aspects of their congregations. Relationships, as we have seen, are a key theologically and ideologically. That is, one's "relationship to Jesus Christ" is what saves, redeems, and empowers one to live, love, and transform one's community. The moral worldviews of evangelicals pivot on this relationship, and this "power of relationship" is transferred into congregational life through church fellowship and small-group activities. A key aspect of successful small-group work is trust—a nonjudgmental ethos of acceptance, encouragement, and care. *The Purpose Driven Life* (2002) by Rick Warren, an author most frequently mentioned by evangelicals in the study, lays out a sophisticated and in-depth process for developing small groups within Christian congregations—premised on a nonjudgmental though morally accountable process of trust and nurture. The leader (or facilitator) is far from a dictator indoctrinating the Bible into his followers; what he or she does is facilitate honest sharing of one's intimate life experience in a group setting that is "confidential" but open, morally accountable but "merciful," accepting but ethically "encouraging," fully aware of "human frailty" but expecting the "best" from one another (Warren 2002). One is struck by the power of these groups and the "ethos" that they engender in evangelical communities, as one evangelical lay leader argued:

> It's very much a turnoff for us to be involved with a legalistic kind of
> an approach to Christianity, the dos and the don'ts. This is a very
> grace-oriented congregation without the watering down of church.

Stick to good, solid, biblical foundational truths, but yet allow for sin, we're all going to commit, we're all sinners, we're recovering sinners. And we accept that. We have good solid standards, but we recognize we're all in the same boat together. We just come around people, working with them through the struggles we all have and small-group orientation to get relationships with other people. It's a big church and you get dropped through the cracks and having intimacy in relationships allows you then to practice grace and be a part of people's lives.

These comments resonate within many evangelical interviews, stressing the importance of truth and the confrontation with sin, but more important, that all are a part of the reality of sin and that all are in the process of healing through the redemption of Jesus Christ. Pastors and lay evangelical leaders constantly mentioned their own vulnerability, perhaps aware of what outsiders might think of them, but determined to make the point that their communities were neither legalistic nor rigid. This process of being "convicted" in one's sin was common in every group—men, women, and young people—that I spoke with. Men, in particular, mentioned the "power" of meetings where they could confess their sin:

At men's retreats people are open to confess areas where they have been struggling in sin and there's a freedom to seek forgiveness. Personally, I have been able to go to our pastor, even as an overseer, and tell him areas where I have struggled in sin and the response has not been, "Get out of here, you're a sinner," it's been, how are we going to work to get this straightened out. And that's been very freeing.

And this sharing of sin was neither superficial nor easy. Again and again evangelical members mentioned the importance of their churches in overcoming every form of addiction, drugs, alcohol, and emotional obsessions. Comments about the fact that "our church seeks to meet every need," were common across the interviews. Again, in comparison with liberal church communities where I did not hear or note this kind of intimate sharing, evangelical groups at times and in many of the churches encouraged individuals to repent, ask for forgiveness, and receive this in the midst of a confidential and caring small group. The group ethos of evangelical congregations supported the identification of sin, and its confession and forgiveness, as well as encouragement to rise above their struggles.

Of course, liberal church members would condemn evangelicals for their insistence that homosexuality is a sin; evangelical churches, in response, would not flinch from what they see as a biblically based standard: humans are meant to be in faithful heterosexual marriages and the expression of sexuality is meant for these covenanted relationships. Evangelicals, however, were also quick to say that for them, everyone is a sinner, so that they are no different than homosexuals—evangelicals would simply offer that they are "repentant sinners." Evangelicals further argue that they "love the sinner and hate the sin." Liberals found this distinction hypocritical and even hateful, but it is a central quality to the moral ethos within the evangelical community. Needless to say, no homosexuals confessed in evangelical circles that I heard about. Nonetheless, the vulnerability of evangelicals is a distinct and powerful convention for evangelical pastors and laypeople in this study. Indeed, in one case, following the revelations of the extramarital homosexual relations of the Reverend Ted Haggard (the Colorado megachurch minister and former president of the National Association of Evangelicals), a pastor in a megachurch in the PNW preached on the issue. He mentioned his own experience of sexual abuse (that was apparently already known by most parishioners) and outlined that equally powerful issues were likely going on within his own congregation:

> Every one of us, at some point in our life will need the healing hand of God. Whether it is divorce, rejection, having abortions, abandonment, drugs, pornography (studies show that half the men in this congregation are addicted to it), and any kind of brokenness.... The revelations of Ted Haggard were not shocking to me; Satan will often target those with the most power. What shocked me was hearing Ted Haggard say that he had been dealing with it his whole adult life.

That is, pastoral vulnerability is an important attribute of successful ministries in this study—but confession of sin has its limits—it would be difficult to imagine an evangelical community forgiving an extramarital homosexual relation in their pastor. Moreover, as the pastor said above, it was most shocking to him that Haggard had been dealing with this his whole life. It seems to imply that homosexuality is not a condition of one's being but more an occasional and momentary temptation. As I explore more thoroughly later, homosexuality as a sexual orientation is not "normal" for evangelicals, but is considered an attack by Satan and is a sin that can be overcome. That Haggard had not overcome it was a sign of his weakness and a problem that was not addressed in evangelical circles. Nonetheless, this sense of vulnerability and honesty in evangelical circles, however expressed in conventional terms, was a critical element that attracted evangelicals to their churches, as one evangelical lay leader explained:

There's also an enormous amount of honesty. Almost everyone who has talked about it has touched upon there's no taboos at the church. There's no one thing you don't talk about. It's an open dialogue constantly. It's a constant, we want to share what's real in our life and we want you to share with us what's real in your life, regardless of whether or not it's pretty, regardless of whether or not you put perfume on your problems before you come in. It's a constant open dialogue that allows you to feel comfortable. It allows you to see the reality of what Christianity is and what's real for the pastor, is the change that's happened, in his life and in the lives of other people that you meet.

Taking evangelical self-expression at face value is in part the task of this study; to give evangelicals a chance to "voice" their perspective and to reveal their moral worldview. But when this evangelical says there are no "taboos" in the evangelical community, one has to wonder. As I just discussed, homosexuality as an orientation cannot be confessed in part because it is thought not to exist. This is clearly a form of denial—a social taboo. Moreover, why did we as researchers never hear about challenges to economic justice? Why no call within evangelical churches to confront social and economic inequality? It seemed to us as researchers that this was another taboo within the evangelical community. One does not trifle in matters of free market capitalism. Although I will address this issue further in the chapter on mission and outreach, for now it is true to say that evangelicals worried most about "personal sin" and overcoming personal temptations. That is, the evangelicals decision to avoid social and structural inequalities was intentional; for them to talk about social structures is to avoid the issue of personal sin; to avoid the issue of personal sin is to flounder and fall into "self-deception," the deception that somehow by changing the "outside" one can change the "inside." This American theme of personal improvement and curing the "self" is a central code in evangelical circles. In a sense liberals also participated in this same code by privatizing their inner lives for the most part. Liberals did not speak out on public issues as I had anticipated in my initial approach to these congregations. While both evangelicals and liberals tended to privatize their ideological rhetoric, as I will show in the chapters on outreach and politics, evangelicals entered public debate in a more robust way than liberals, not so much as prophets fighting structural sin (economic exploitation or political oppression) but most definitely as moral advocates against what they see as the moral corruption of the culture. Indeed, my findings reveal that evangelicals are more engaged in the public square than liberals, whether locally, nationally, and most certainly, internationally. In this sense the relation of liberals and evangelicals to public life has reversed over the last fifty years.

Nevertheless, the organizational life of the evangelical community communicates an emotional ethos that is a "warm and welcoming" environment. Any number of evangelicals mentioned how their churches facilitated places to share and talk—one mentioned the "bistro" downstairs that invited groups to meet together, while others talked about the "coffee shops" that were frequently in the lobbies of evangelical churches, including one church with a Starbucks outlet. Another evangelical said, "This is what this church is good at—making connections." This, of course, hearkens back to Max Weber's reflections on his early twentieth-century visit to the United States, when he commented that in order to be a part of the business of America, one should make the church one's first stop "to make connections" (1946). And to some extent this is true, although I did not seek out to find how individuals used their churches to make business connections, it is certainly an aspect of the evangelical organizational lifestyle. Rick Warren's book *The Purpose Driven Life* lauds the evangelical entrepreneurial business-types as "wealth-builders" for the kingdom of God. As Warren says, some individuals have the "talent to make money" that can be used to spread the gospel (2002). Again, as we saw above, Warren never warns again economic inequality, but indeed assumes it as something God can use to further the church's evangelical mission.

At the same time, on several occasions, evangelicals in the study mentioned how their participation in these churches had transformed their priorities. For one, "making money" was no longer *the* priority but one among many, which was now subsumed under the worship and love of God. Indeed, several men spoke about the transformation of their lives based on their participation in evangelical groups, how they've created new priorities in their personal and professional lives, as well as how they've discovered new ways of treating others, especially their spouses and children:

> I have become a more compassionate, caring person. I can see
> somebody on the street that is in need and feel compassion for
> that person. Another thing that is difficult for any of us is when
> somebody does something against us that maybe hurts us, not nec-
> essarily physically, but emotionally and mentally, how we deal with
> that. I think this is something that in the process of my spiritual
> growth has impacted me greatly, that I can be more forgiving and
> caring for that person. If I'm wrong, then I deal with that in another

way too. But I think that's where the important thing in my life has been is my transformation with other people, and with my wife. I think when any of us get married, you think when you first get married everything is going to be perfect and everything is going to be calm and so you learn through that process. But there is a relationship there that can develop if you look at the biblical principle; the biblical pattern for a husband and wife. There can be a tremendous change in the relationship there, because we honor and respect one another and it works.

The group life of evangelicals eloquently expresses the moral worldview of evangelicals that focuses on relationships, the acknowledgment of sin, the need for repentance, and the hope of healing and reconciliation. This moral worldview and organizational ethos mobilizes evangelical church growth. A consistent theme, which I cover more thoroughly under the section on leadership, is the "empowerment" and "equipping" of members for ministry. It was mentioned on a frequent basis that the skills of evangelical members are nurtured for ministry. Ideas that come from parishioners are encouraged in evangelical churches and leaders affirm these new initiatives. Rick Warren's program of the Purpose Driven Life was mentioned by nearly one-quarter of evangelical respondents. Most evangelical leaders used parts of the program, taking "what works" and accommodating it to their needs. This program is about discipleship, equipping members for ministry, and creating small groups for "Christian accountability." One of the results of this program in one evangelical church was the dramatic increase in volunteers for the church. One lay evangelical leader said, "This church probably has a higher percentage of volunteers, I would say, two times of what the average church has—maybe 40 percent of members volunteer compared to 20 percent in most churches." These, of course, are round figures and probably exaggerate the numbers, but it was mentioned frequently among evangelical churches that members were encouraged to "use" their gifts and that leaders "did not get in the way." New members in particular were attracted to these evangelical churches because they were "dynamic and fun, full of energy." One sensed this vitality in the focus groups. The French sociologist Emile Durkheim spoke about a social "effervescence" that is the glue that mobilizes groups—it creates a momentum of its own, catching people up in its wake. We often felt this vitality within evangelical focus groups, less so in the liberal focus groups in the study. In the liberals focus groups, the stress was almost always on the struggles to gain enough volunteers, and the fact that liberal leaders were often "burned out" by being in charge of too many things.

Groups are created and are destroyed in part by the energy within them. This energy is created and shaped by the moral worldviews that they embody and envision. Liberal group structure is far more informal than evangelicals.' If community occurs for liberals, it often results from as an unintended consequence of church activities, rituals, and meetings. For liberals, privacy factors and an ideology of individualism lessen the need for this kind of group life per se. Liberals, however, find great strength in informal meetings, whether at coffee hour, adult education, or in one another's homes. The inclusion of people that have traditionally been excluded, particularly those who are gay and lesbian, creates a feeling of "safety and inclusion" for many.

In gross numbers, evangelicals in the PNW are growing, and liberals (churched liberals, that is) are in decline. Evangelicals have an ideology that is centered on growth, and is in relationship to the self, to God, to the family, the church, and the mission of the religion. Evangelicals have accommodated styles of group work that appeal to northwesterners because they activate a sense of belonging and moral accountability. The personal vulnerability of evangelical group dynamics is nested within a sophisticated system of group organization. Evangelical ideology of growth within a group setting motivates them to invite their families and friends to church, and to serve others in the community in entrepreneurial and enthusiastic ways as will be shown in chapter 10. In a region that is not only unchurched but relatively "ungrouped," evangelicals respond in ways that many find satisfying, energizing, and morally hopeful. How these moral worldviews function in families and around gender issues opens one more lens on the complex function of how moral worldviews work within these two distinct forms of Christian religion.

2. Family, Children, and Gender

One of the telling experiences I witnessed on a liberal church family retreat was a woman talking about how she felt that it was not her "place" to "force" her teenager to be confirmed since she wanted her son "to make up his own mind." Ten minutes later, she said she had decided to send him to a Missouri Synod Lutheran confirmation class at a church down the street from hers, because her son felt more comfortable with the kids at that church. This kind of ambivalence was not unusual in liberal churches that I studied. On the one hand, there is a principled resistance to "forcing" religion on anyone—even one's children—but on the other hand, there is an awareness that their children and youth are exposed to quite diverse and at times destructive media outlets and so there is a desire to "expose" them to a religious and perhaps, more importantly, a "moral" framework whereby they can make good decisions.

Nevertheless, the moral training of liberal youth seems haphazard and ad hoc. Other comments from liberal parents confirmed this; many said that since their teenagers did not enjoy church they simply left the teens at home; the youthful "unhappiness" ruined the parent's experience. Indeed, one of the significant findings of my interviews with liberals is that concern for outreach to gay and lesbian people outweighed how they prioritized outreach to children and youth, by a margin of 37 to 10 percent. For evangelicals, if children and youth are not enjoying church, it is the church's fault and evangelical parents either find a new church or try to improve their youth ministry. For liberals, the tendency is the reverse; if youth do not find church interesting, it is the youths' problem. Our findings showed that evangelicals are far more interested and invested in reproducing the faith in their children and youth and their churches reflect this priority.

In reading through the interviews of liberals, I was struck by another finding: there was a near complete absence of references to spouses or heterosexual marriage. Indeed, for this section, I wanted to mention how liberals would address heterosexual marriage and I could find no data to make a particular case on the matter. This confirms what Don Browning found in his extensive studies of religion and family: liberal and mainline Protestant denominations, over the last generation, have stopped addressing heterosexual family issues in a direct way (Browning 2000), either because of a lack of interest or because it is not politically correct. Most commonly, the conversations with liberals about marriage were in reference to political arguments over governmental definitions of marriage in the gay marriage debate—arguing that homosexuals should have the same rights to marriage as heterosexuals.

This relative lack of attention to family and children among liberals translated into church programs for children and youth that had good intentions but in general had little impact. For the three to four liberal churches in the study that did have active children's and youth programs, and in two cases a relatively dynamic program, this lack of attention paid to youth often made for an uphill battle for those in charge. As one liberal leader of a large children's ministry program said, "The (denominational head) really resisted the hiring of a youth leader. He would say to me, any kid who sticks with the church in their teenage years is a nerd," implying, of course, that youth did not belong in the church in the teenage years because they needed "to grow up." This dramatic statement did not stop that church from hiring a youth leader, or keep the church from developing a robust youth program with nearly forty teenagers. Nonetheless, this kind of attitude percolated throughout many of the interviews—never expressed in quite such explicit terms, but through a type of benign neglect toward children and youth.

Liberal clergy were quite aware of their inability to attract young people and thus young families. As one said, "I don't think we're always good at presenting a good story in a compelling way as far as children and young people are concerned." Another liberal clergy, who had led the marketing and media unit for a large mainline Protestant denomination, commented that his favorite reading was from Marcus Borg, but he knew from his work in marketing that Borg and the Jesus Seminar authors (another popular group for liberal churches) "appeal to post-50 men." Of course, this is a relatively select demographic group comprising white men who are highly educated and have the economic capital and thus time to do this study. In this sense it should be no surprise that Borg's *The Heart of Christianity* (2003) makes no references to families, children, or youth. Nonetheless, liberal clergy know quite well that they must address children and youth and their families, and in the churches with late baby boomer and older Gen-X clergy this was happening. Indeed, in the liberal churches in which I saw the strongest growth, the focus had become young people—though not to the exclusion of older adults. In fact, the fastest-growing liberal congregation was ministering to both. As the minister said, "Our largest growth area is empty nesters or near empty nesters; they come here for community." And he was clear on what attracted these adults:

> But I still think that, I feel this more and more, in a Western culture, especially in an upper- and middle-class culture in America where we seem to be hell-bent on fragmentation. You know, we're waving our hand over here on this street corner saying, "You know, tired of fragmentation, feeling a little alienated?" Every Sunday morning you can find a group of people who are doing whatever they can to satisfy their need to be in community. So I would never say we're in the business of saving souls. We do save lives.

And for this liberal clergy, welcoming children into the liturgical life of the community was crucial. Any number of his congregants mentioned how he made young people feel welcome. When I visited the church, the children's sermon was a short story that the children could relate to. It was told with the pastor sitting with the children in the middle of the sanctuary, which had moveable chairs placed in a circle, surrounding the clergy and the children. The minister deftly ended the children's message and then immediately addressed the adults, but the transition was smooth and subtle so that the children's and adults' sermons blended together. The pastor's laypeople all commented on how "delicious" this experience was for them and for their children. When I told this liberal minister the story of the liberal parent who did not want to "force" her child into confirmation, he argued:

Well, I'll say, you bias your kids in everything else, you don't allow them to make their own choices about whether or not to go
to school, or whether or not to go to this school or that school. That's
silly. I try to be nice about it but as I have less and less time in a
day I'm less and less nice about it. That's a silly argument and
the studies show that it opens kids up to, well, let's put it this way, on
a positive light, the studies show that a part of what kids need is
asset development. Being a part of a religious community is almost
always asset building in the life of the kid.

Like this liberal clergy, a Gen-X liberal pastor argued similarly that in a
"postmodern culture, there are no given cultural systems of epistemology,
therefore we need to present our religious perspective as persuasively as possible and let the chips fall where they may." In other words, for these younger
liberal clergy, there is a recognition that American young people are faced with
a plethora of ideological systems, most of them secular, and that if they are left
on their own, they will choose a secular epistemology, one that tends to be
oriented toward a consumerist and hedonistic moral worldview. A religious
perspective, and a liberal Christian point of view, must be taught since it
certainly is not a "given" in the culture. The task then of the liberal church is to
socialize young people into this ideological perspective that emphasizes justice, compassion, inclusion, and outreach to those who are marginalized.

The liberal churches in this study are caught between times. On the one
hand, the mainline Protestant church with its moderate liberalism, in which
many grew up, was once the putative reigning ideology in American culture.
This was a "vital center" that once supported civil rights for minorities—
including blacks, women, and, though with less strength, homosexuals. This
vision, however, has become diluted and has declined as *the* center of American culture. The new American culture, as the liberal clergy alluded to above,
is fragmented and eclectic, particularly in the PNW, where it is difficult to
know what values sustain, reign over, and guide culture. In the main, the PNW
is a libertarian mix of cultures that lionizes an entrepreneurial spirit, tends to
dismiss local government, leans to the left on social issues, and is relatively
conservative on government spending. Its popular culture is a hodgepodge of
boutique interest groups that range from environmentalists to anarchists; and
from social conservatives to the right-wing survivalists. In this sense, as was
mentioned above, it is an open religious market and to a large extent an open
cultural market.

When we move to gender, we see that on the liberal side, the churches in
the study seemed on the face of it almost "genderless." That is, feminism that

was a concern of the 1960s and 1970s has dissipated not in that is has disappeared as an issue, but that it has been integrated into the culture and its concerns normalized. This shows up in the interviews in many ways. Two of the ten senior ministers were female and in neither case was the choice controversial for the churches. Indeed, as one lay liberal leader said commenting on the diversity of his church's staff, "We have three women and one man. Two white women, one white man, and one black woman; and a gay man. But they weren't chosen because of this, they were chosen because of their qualities and I really like that." This resonated across the liberal interviews, with lay liberals assuming diversity not because of some explicit criteria but because it was how things worked out in the process of bringing in the most "appropriate people." Thus, there was little expressed concern about gender in general. It was taken for granted that clergy spouses or partners may or may not be involved in the churches. Clergy occasionally mentioned this when they said their spouses felt "no pressure" to be involved in their churches. In fact, in two churches, spouses attended other churches. Lay leaders did not mention the spouses or partners of their clergy whatsoever. This was assumed to be a private matter very much in line with the liberal moral worldview of autonomy.

Relative to language and gender theologically and liturgically, the most frequent comments came from self-identified "older feminists," one of whom had this to say:

> One of the things that has changed over the last thirty years politically and culturally is that words like *Lord* and *Savior* have a very different meaning to people of the generation forty and under than they do to the generation of forty and over. It's just hard, I am going to speak for my generation, it is very hard for us, particularly women, to hear *Lord* with all its intended meanings.

Another lay liberal leader spoke about the "problem of the monarchial language and how oppressive it feels to some of us." And clergy, particularly those over fifty, seemed quite sensitive to this issue, not using *Lord* in their prayers or in their sermons. Another woman spoke of her own journey out of the Roman Catholic Church, after having been a nun for twenty-five years and a major superior to five hundred women:

> There are many things that came together in my decision to leave. One of the primary reasons why I am no longer a Catholic has to do with the reasons why you [another focus group member] are no longer in your former denomination. That the patriarchy and the sexism [are] so thick you can cut it with a knife. Even in the best

of circumstances, and I certainly was exposed to the best of circumstances, Roman Catholic women are disenfranchised in their church. For me, that was a personally painful thing and driving me crazy.

Ten percent of liberals came from Roman Catholic backgrounds and several mentioned the "abuses" and "corruptions" within the Catholic Church. Gender was mentioned as an issue of concern though it seemed to be taken for granted that the Roman Catholics were wrong on gender equality and that any thinking person would know that equality was natural and normal. For clergy and liberal lay leaders, liturgy should of course try to reflect gender-neutral pronouns and prayers should do the same. Names for God should be female and male, which was appreciated by lay liberals, particularly by gay members, who commented on the frequent use of feminine images for God. In the younger liberal clergy there was talk about reintroducing "traditional language" and using more "traditional hymns" in worship. It was not so much to reintroduce a sense of patriarchy, although one might argue this, but that the battle over gender equality had been won—thus, let's recover the full language of the tradition. Of course, not all lay liberals were going along with these movements, so the future remains to be seen.

In contrast to liberal church interviews, the emphasis among evangelicals in the study on family was overwhelming. More often than not when evangelicals were asked why they were attracted to their churches, it was because of its focus on the many "young families," "the excellent youth program," the many programs for the needs of families in general. And, as liberals sometimes suspected and as outsiders might surmise, the picture of the evangelical family was a traditional nuclear arrangement, generally with the father as the sole breadwinner and the mother frequently homeschooling their children. This was an ideal for evangelicals, but the reality, as evangelicals were the first to acknowledge, was fragmentation and, as they often said, "brokenness." Indeed, one of the core emphases among the evangelical respondents was the sense of "vulnerability," "openness," and "honesty" that impressed them about their churches. There was one story after another of single mothers, divorced fathers, and every type of "sinner" accepted and "embraced" by these evangelical churches. In one case a father talked in detail in an evangelical focus group about his addiction to pornography and explained how, through his conversion and the fellowship of the church, he had overcome this sin. The evangelicals in the focus groups consistently mentioned the importance of their families to their faith and the transformation that occurred because they married faithful Christians, as one lay leader explained:

I grew up completely unchurched. In fact, my mother was very involved in the occult and so when I was sixteen and got saved things
got very exciting. I had a horrible life until I met my husband
that I've been married to for nine years. He grew up a Christian.
He's like a fifth-generation born-again Christian, so when I met his
family I was like, "So did you fly these people up from California?
Are they actors? Do these people all really like each other and look
this good?" And I just didn't buy it; I just thought this was crazy.
And they kind of took me under their wing and we went to their
church for a while. And I realized it was for real.

From my own perspective as a researcher I shared a similar feeling at
times that the evangelical community was too good to be true. The claims to
authenticity, vulnerability, acceptance, and love—all of this seemed to be expressions of "trying too hard to impress the outsider." And this impression was
confirmed in part by my interview with a college professor at a PNW Christian
college commenting on her students, many of whom come from evangelical
churches in the region:

Anecdotally, all of us in the subculture can tell you stories of the
number of our students who get abortions (with their parents' support) because the informal norms and stigmas are so strong against
having had sex before marriage, that all agree in the end that it's
better for no one to know about your sin and get the abortion (keeping up appearances) than to deviate from the norm—even when it
goes against the moral choice evangelicals believe above all others.
We often joke, sadly, that it really is about image and the image can
be very bankrupt (not always, but it's what we see again and again).

Nonetheless, similar stories of expressions of brokenness and acceptance
just kept coming up in the interviews. It can be argued that this was also
because I had chosen vital and growing evangelical churches, or that this discourse is a convention of these communities. And all of this is true—not all
evangelical churches are this way—yet, in this sample of twenty-four churches
the data reflected an unending series of stories of community life that nurtured
strong, functional family life.

What is the ideological core of this family model? One of the evangelical
senior pastors argued that the church's task is to speak out against oppression.
He listed a number of categories that the church was called to confront, including the oppression of children, the environment, racial minorities, the
"victims of abortion," and, in particular women. In the churches in the study,

the valuation and empowerment of women was an important aspect of the rhetoric of pastors. One evangelical pastor explained the role of women in his church and the role of men in relation to women and the family:

> But in terms of ministry and leadership in the church, we believe that, outside the office of elders, that is determined by God's gifting. Women preach in this church, women lead, they teach, they council. Ministerially, they function in any capacity that a man does. But, I'm standing in the New Testament at this point, and I say at this point, because we're willing to grow and learn here, is that the office of elder was designed by God and men are designed by God to lead in giving that oversight and that protection to the church. In the new world, in the new creation, there will be no distinction between male and female. Paul makes that very, very clear. I mean, here is an apostle that says, on the one hand, there is no male or female in Christ, and on the other hand, in his instruction to the local church, he's pretty clear that godly male leadership is what God desires for the office of elders. Hence, within the home, a godly husband is to be the leader in the home. Now that doesn't mean he's the boss, that doesn't mean he's the final authority, that doesn't mean he makes all the final decisions, that means that there's a responsibility of leadership there that really is a submissive role of serving his wife and children with his life.

This is not to overstate the role of women in leadership in these churches. Again, there was only one woman who shared a senior pastor's position among the twenty-four churches in the study. Males dominated the pulpits in evangelical churches, and most of the preaching, even in the church that had a shared ministry, was done by the males. Nonetheless, female leadership, particularly among women and with youth and children, was prized and understood as an aspect of "God's plan." Ministry is ideally dictated by the "gifts" God gives and not by gender. As the evangelical pastor said above, in the "new creation" there is neither female nor male, thus in the redeemed world without sin, gender hierarchy is overcome. But in the world of sin, the Scriptures have made it clear that the position of "elder" is set aside for males. Not every church in the study affirmed this point; the charismatic congregations seemed more open to ordaining women precisely because of their tradition of doing so, but only one of the charismatic churches in the study had gone ahead and ordained a woman. One sensed that evangelical women themselves were on both sides of the issue of female leadership. In one new members' class we attended, in response to a question about women elders, the pastor said, "We do not believe

that this is biblical." Before he could even finish his answer, a female participant in the class exclaimed her relief that "the church takes this biblical stand."
Nonetheless, in interviews with lay evangelicals, women in particular were
sensitive to how women were treated in the congregation. One said, "Women
are valued here; this is not true in all evangelical churches." Another said,
"I joined this church because a woman started it." She was referring to her
Foursquare congregation (led now by a male pastor), but the denomination
was begun by Aimee Semple McPherson in the 1920s. When this evangelical
layperson was asked how women were treated in her church, she said, "We are
asked our opinion and listened to; all you have to do is be in our service this
morning and see how our pastor treated his wife with such respect." The
modeling of spousal relationship between pastor and wife was noted by evangelicals in the study, in stark contrast to liberal congregations where talk about
spouses in general and clergy spouses in particular simply did not occur.

Families, youth, and children matter in these evangelical congregations.
Nearly 10 percent of evangelicals mentioned homeschooling their children.
Mothers who did this work felt it to be a great privilege, a way to protect their
children from a "corrupt" culture, and a countercultural action since it meant
less income for the families, as one evangelical lay woman explained:

> It's a challenge deciding, because not only is it an overwhelming job,
> but you have to kind of buck society and say, "You know what, we're
> gonna be a one-income family." So that makes some pretty signifi-
> cant changes socially, let alone economically. But I think it's a neat
> trend because I mean in this room, it's pretty obvious, but it's oc-
> curring more and more where people are wanting to take responsi-
> bility for their families and for their growth and I think that's perhaps
> part of the reason we're even here, because we're seeing that start-
> ing to happen in churches too. Yes, and chasing the golden ring
> is not what it's about. And so being willing to maybe not try and one-
> up our neighbors with getting the next boat or the next motorcycle
> of whatever, but actually to spend more time with the family.

In contrast again to the liberals in this study, evangelicals were strongly
committed to children's and youth ministries. Frequently evangelical laypeople would mention the importance of parachurch organizations—Young Life,
Youth for Christ—in their own lives. Twenty-six percent of evangelicals made
mention of personal conversions to their faith; these were more often than not
in their teenage years. Only a handful of liberals mentioned a conversion experience. Evangelicals are aware that many conversions happen in the younger
years, and so they focus their ministerial resources on this age. As one pastor

said, "We choose our most talented people to lead our young people." I did not interview a youth pastor in the evangelical churches, but it was clear from the numbers of children and youth involved in the ministries that their leadership was attracting many young people. This focus and energy to reach out to youth also showed up in the young people who were in the focus groups who spoke about how much they "loved" their groups and how committed they were to them. Adults hearing how much their children loved their churches was often a reason that adults had started attending these churches in the first place; when their teenagers were already involved, the parent(s) would come to find out what was going on. In interviews it was frequently mentioned that youth had preceded the adults (their parents) into church membership. It worked the other way around as well. One single mother explained the consequences of her conversion to the Christian faith on her children: "You'd be surprised how they pick up on it. My daughter became a Christian by watching me and wondering why I was so happy [when] I had nothing to be happy about. So both my daughters are now Christians. It moves mountains. I never thought that would change anybody, but since I changed they're changing." There is no hesitation on the part of evangelical adults to share their faith with their children. Indeed, one might say the purpose of evangelical parents is to do one thing: raise one's son and daughter in the faith. Moreover, the purpose of evangelical churches is to reproduce the faith in young people. As one minister explained:

> Our senior pastor has from the very beginning recognized that
> there's a generational pipeline; it's always our job as a pastor to look
> at the whole pipeline. How are we doing? From the input in the
> nursery, is that first-class? Is there a spirit of excellence there? And
> that's a requirement at our church that everything is done with ex-
> cellence, whether it's printing a mailer or something like that, the
> graphics, everything is done with excellence. So in the children's
> nursery, is it clean, neat, is it sharp graphics, the whole thing, all the
> way up to, we're really going after our fifth and sixth graders. We're
> really going after that age, because that's where kids get their faith.
> That's where our son got his faith, in fifth and sixth grade. He's
> riding on the faith of his mom and dad, but in fifth and sixth grade he
> took ownership of his faith. Then taking him onto that next seg-
> ment of life, seventh and eighth grade, junior high, that's a squirrelly
> age; we've got a great youth pastor, role models, men and women
> around those kids.

I will show in the section on leadership that evangelicals consider "excellence" in ministry an essential aspect for selecting pastors. It is often described in terms of doing the best they can to "witness" to the gospel of Jesus Christ. For evangelicals, the message can be distorted by a "poor medium," and so with children and youth, the form is critical in communicating and passing on the faith. And in this way class aesthetics come into play. At one evangelical church, one of my graduate students, who is knowledgeable of media, observed that the audiovisual equipment for the congregation was all state of the art; the "outboard A/V equipment alone was [worth] $100,000." There was an eighty-person choir, and two separate bands with sophisticated media equipment, appealing to the tastes and preferences of both adults and youth. As the pastor exclaimed in worship, "Do we have the best tech gurus around here or what!" He later added that with the new upgrades, "This church is *the* place to be on Sunday." The whole sense is that the church and its message are not only relevant to the culture (the PNW is a center of the new knowledge culture) but take the features of modern consumerism to the next level, so that one's preferences for these goods are affirmed, confirmed, and celebrated. One is encouraged to get these things, enjoy these things, or believe that one has the potential to do so all in the name of God.

In this way the "form" of worship must be "fun" and "relevant," and use the popular culture to communicate the "unchanging message of Jesus Christ." These "methods" not only confirm the tastes of adults, but at times submerge children and youth into aspects of consumerist lifestyle that evangelicals at least say they want to avoid. In one case, a church had created a booth in which young people would enter if they had memorized a significant number of Bible verses. Once inside, dollar bills would be blown into the booth and children and youth could grab as many as they could. In other ways, youth camps sometimes took on the flair, flow, and flamboyance of "Club Med" resorts with every imaginable sporting gear and luxury comfort all in the midst of an evangelical "spirit." Children and youth were socialized into an upper-middle-class lifestyle. In the chapter on missions, we find that international missionaries from these churches were quite aware of this tendency in their stateside churches. The tensions of accommodating to popular culture are a critical issue for evangelicals, which some have responded to but others have ignored.

Gender for evangelicals, as in liberal churches, is downplayed in comparison to the importance of family, children, and youth. This is not to say that gender roles are not clear, but in a sense the argument over gender was not *the* burning issue. But what was emphasized was the evangelical stance against gay marriage and against what evangelicals perceived was the "normalization" of homosexuality in civil society. For them, this was a critical issue because in their minds it undermines their values, the teachings of scripture as they interpret them, and the strength of the family. The arguments that evangelicals make against gay marriage are hardly unique and seem to come from other national evangelical associations such as Focus on the Family. For one minister, if the definition of marriage were to be changed, then the marriage between a man and woman "loses its sense of sacredness or being special. And I think I want to preserve that. We think that a marriage is a healthy place to raise a family, between a husband and a wife that are committed to one another in a covenantal relationship." This was a frequent argument along with the point heard commonly among national evangelicals: "Homosexuality is a distortion of the ideal of creation. God made us male and female. We were created to embrace the 'other' not the 'same.'" In response to liberals who claim that moral values and laws must evolve, evangelicals assert, "Time has nothing to do with morality. Either there is a Creator and therefore an ultimate point of reference or there is no creator and no ultimate point of reference." This either/or thinking on establishing values was a common epistemological argument in the evangelical churches; the creator cannot will two things at once. Divine law is set in scripture, which is inerrant and infallible. Of course, for liberals, as I have detailed before, this argument is petty at best and inhumane at worst. For liberals, God is dynamic and living and therefore God's judgments are made in relation to the lived experience of God's creatures; God's views must change by definition with time and context. For liberals, this dynamic and situational logic does not contradict ultimate truth but *is* ultimate truth. "Ultimate" cannot be limited to one thought, one idea, one dogma, or one doctrine.

This clash of moral worldviews on family, children, youth, and gender is profound. Each of these groups follows the logic of their ideological cores into embodied experience, connecting to the most intimate aspects of human life, sexuality, reproduction, gender, class, intimacy, and relationships. Each envisions quite distinct forms of what these mean for persons, groups, and churches. Each expresses moral worldviews in distinct ways with intended and unintended consequences on their churches. Evangelicals do all they can to reinforce and stabilize a certain type of family structure, desiring to reproduce this structure across time and generations. The evangelical vision is a middle- and upper-middle-class utopia, marked by moral discipline, economic success, and a heterosexual nuclear family. Growth and reproduction of faith and people are keys and one is not surprised that in an entrepreneurially oriented PNW culture, evangelicals have found a niche that they have exploited. Their growth in numbers is real; their tendency to recapitulate capitalist and consumerist values is an acknowledged problem, which, rather than confront they exploit. Liberals also understand their cultural niche: championing the rights of minorities, and empowering sexual minorities as legitimate and beloved members of their communities. Gays and lesbians feel at home in these churches. They thrive, take on leadership roles, and "witness" to the compassion and justice of a faith that they believe at its heart is about hospitality, equality, and freedom. In ways that are largely unintended, liberals are ambivalent about certain aspects of family, children, and youth. The consequences are less growth among young families and fewer young people participating in their churches. For each of these groups, their moral worldviews are sacrosanct, powerful, and divinely inspired. How leadership creates this vision and sustains these moral worldviews is the subject of the final section on organizational dynamics.

3. Leadership

Leadership counts. For many reasons, sociologists want to downplay the power of leadership to mobilize and shape groups. For instance, in sociology personal agency as a causal unit is questioned; systems and structures, and material and symbolic forms guide and determine culture. And while I find this argument persuasive at times, in my research on religious organizations, over and over again, leadership matters, whether lay or clergy. The key question is How does the leader embody the moral worldview of his or her followers? Does the leader inspire "followership"? Does the leader have the interest, passion, and empathy that followers want from a leader? Does the leader have the requisite talent to creatively organize a vision and facilitate or "equip" other leaders? Without strong, competent leaders, organizations, such as churches, begin to decline. I argue that the more competent, creative, and energetic the leader, the greater the chance for the group's mobilization and growth. What I am not saying is that good leaders do it all. By definition, effective leaders embody and have internalized the culture they lead; they have intuitively recognized and stated clearly the goals for the group. They are able to do this because of their native talents to set out a vision of the future that anticipates the needs, desires, and preferences of the group. Thus, systems and structures matter, but the mobilization of systems and structures depends on competent leadership; the one cannot be done without the other. Thus, both good leadership and cultural and social systems work in tandem by necessity (Reiff 2007).

In this section I focus on clergy leadership. Lay leaders are critical for the success of these churches, but for the reasons mentioned above, clergy count. Liberal clergy in the vital churches I studied are a relatively energetic and creative group. But in part because they have all come through their denominational "systems," one notes the constraints they bear and put on themselves.

Interestingly, while they each wanted to create vital and dynamic churches, they each put limits on numerical growth. Most either voiced reluctance about the church growth in their congregations or said that they did not want their churches to grow. In one case, a minister said, "If we grew much more, we would have to start another service and we would lose the community and intergenerational feel of the present service." Another simply said, "I would never want to be a megachurch; I would like to grow another 100 members [from around 200] but that's it. Enough to meet our budget needs." The pastor at the fastest-growing church said, "Every church has a size, every pastor has a size. You know, we're bigger than I want to be, but I'm not against getting bigger." The liberal minister with the largest church had the most entrepreneurial spirit. In the interview he ruminated on how to move from five to six services and how the new service might meet the needs of a new group. Another pastor who had just come to his congregation had a goal of "growing the congregation by 25 percent over five years."

Liberal leadership even among those with the most entrepreneurial energy tended to reflect a more bureaucratic organizational model: cautious, playing by the rules, and limiting the goals of the organization. This leadership style reflects the training of mainline Protestant seminaries and the rule-following nature of those who move through the nearly labyrinthine gate keeping of Protestant denominations. In a sense, as one layperson said to me, "If you had one ounce of entrepreneurial spirit you could not put up with the ordination process in mainline denominations." It is not as if all evangelical clergy were entrepreneurial by nature, but the culture of evangelicalism tends to demand growth—thus, one must grow a church if one is to gain status. This kind of growth is not necessary in liberal congregations, and in fact, the pastor with the fastest growing church spoke about his denomination's "disinterest" in growth. Thus, systems again shape and count in how leadership functions and what goals they embody and achieve.

There was also a particular strength and ideological core in liberal clergy that was expressed in the interviews. One of the woman clergy, early in her career, had to deal with sexual harassment as an assistant, and was faced with the decision to report her senior pastor and endanger her career, or keep quiet and "ignore her conscience." She did the former and this strength enabled her to lead her congregation in supporting gay and lesbian people in her denomination—a denomination that is at best ambivalent toward gays and at worst has ruled organizationally against the ordination of "practicing gays and lesbians." As she reported, a young woman from a conservative church in her denomination had come to one of her church's adult education sessions on sexuality. The young woman had been warned by her conservative church that this "liberal" church was "evil." This liberal clergywoman lives under the "threat" of being put up on charges of ordaining gays to her boards and/or the "blessing" of Holy Unions of gay and lesbian couples. In other words, liberal clergy were doing acts consistent with their moral worldview that put themselves and occasionally their churches at risk. This can be categorized as a form of moral courage.

Another liberal pastor who came to his present church as an "openly" gay man had to deal with many threats—even death threats because of his sexuality. He shows courage in facing down these threats, as well as bucking complaints in his own church. Homosexuals within his own congregation at times were upset with him because he did not advocate enough for gays and lesbians. But for this liberal clergy there is a deeper ideological and theological reason that he argued guides his thinking on the "radical nature of inclusion within his church":

> I've angered some people who are gay and lesbian because I have not been out there crusading and preaching that from the pulpit as the issue. I don't believe that's the issue; I think it's one of many issues. This congregation was at the forefront of the movement around gender, in terms of ordaining women to the priesthood and allowing women to become bishops in this church. So the issue is theological. What does it mean as a church that practices infant baptism? When I baptize you as a child, do you become a full member of the body of Christ or not, or is that membership in the body of Christ conditional upon something? Your race, your culture, your sexual orientation, your mental capacity, your intellectual capacity, your skill level? And I think our denomination as a whole is at a place, for the most part, of saying any person baptized into this church is a full member of the church, so that's the theological position out of which support of gender equality emerges.

As this liberal pastor suggests, the liberal moral worldview frames the issue of inclusion in a sacramental system that asserts that in God all are created equal. Moreover, in the practice of infant baptism there is no discrimination for God's grace from the beginning, so why start at any stage? Inclusion is the essence of grace that favors all unconditionally. In this sense, for liberal clergy, forgiveness is always already given, so the human decision to "follow" or "accept Jesus Christ as one's Lord and Savior" merely affirms what is already a "metaphysical reality" that "in Christ," which by definition all are, all are by definition in grace and thus "saved," which for liberals means all are empowered to be what God made them to be. For liberals, this means in the case of gay and lesbian people to practice this sexual orientation as a "gift from God," and to be faithful to it. And this is no different than someone born with a heterosexual preference; grace is with them to become who they were created to be.

Thus again, the moral worldview of radical inclusion and hospitality in liberal churches is not a superficial and "politically correct" slogan, but for liberal clergy in particular a powerful and "ultimate" point of truth that guides their thinking and leadership and pushes them to "equip" their congregations to be places that are open to all, regardless of class, race, sexual orientation, or human capacity. This moral worldview creates moments of exquisite courage, beauty, and truth in liberal churches, which are present, as we will see, in evangelical congregations as well.

But there is another, less obvious, aspect of liberal leadership that intentionally inhibits or limits the "ambitions" of liberal clergy. There has been a reckoning of sorts within the liberal Protestant tradition, which is in part a confrontation with the spirit of the postcolonial critique of Western dominance. It is a dominance that many liberals identify with the Protestant establishment in the mid-twentieth century and on a larger scale with the tendency of the United States and Christians in general to "lord it over others." I pushed one liberal clergy on the issue of why he did not seek to return to the days when his church did speak for his community, and his answer was theologically grounded in the idea that the goal of the Christian is not social and political dominance but humble service to those in need, which in part meant relating to and empathizing with those who are the "least, lost, and last."

> I'm not saying, "Don't be involved in social reform," but I don't think you're involved in social reform because you want to get power; I think you're involved in social reform because you want to change conditions that are treating people in a way that's less than God would have them treated. Every time the church has dominated a culture, go back to Galileo and how the church repressed thinking. Every time the church has gained social and political power, it has become what Walter Wink would say is the domination society. I think the ideal church is one that is spiritually open to where the spirit is calling in that particular age, and then responds as faithfully and as clearly and as definitely as possible. Martin Luther King Jr. is an example of that. He became powerful in the effect that he had, but his methods were not the methods of power that society would have. He organized people, but he also would not accept

violence as a means of doing things. There was friction and conflict within the black movement about his methods and styles, but
what King said was, "It's more important for me to be faithful
than it is to get power the way you're talking about it. I'm not part of
the black power movement," he says, "I'm part of the movement
of love." Or, it's an Abraham Lincoln saying "The Union can win the
war, but lose the nation." And power allows you to win certain battles, but it's more important to have the nation, in Lincoln's case,
or in our case, it's more important to be faithful to what we perceive God is calling us to be. The missionary movements of the
nineteenth and early twentieth centuries, they got a great deal of
political power because the capitalists saw that as a way of extending
economic interests into Third-World countries and underdeveloped
countries, but you start looking back at some of the things some
of the missionaries did and it was devastating. The church was not
being the church in some of those cases. Go to Kauai and find
out about the missionary family that dominated Kauai for many years
and still does to a large degree. I'm embarrassed to have the name
"Christian" with them, even though it would be far more important
for me to be faithful than to be wealthy.

Some would call this a "liberal guilt trip" but for liberals it is in part the
learning from the development of liberal theology in the second half of the
twentieth century that emphasized a Marxist critique of Western dominance in
general and capitalism in particular. This paralleled the development of liberation theology in Latin America and in many parts of the world that grew
apace the American civil rights movement. The latter sought not only to bring
political freedom to minorities but also to free them spiritually so that in their
rise they would not simply recapitulate the role of former capitalist oppressors.
This critique of Western culture and Christianity in particular affected and
continues to affect the liberal church in the United States. It mitigates an easy
relationship with the entrepreneurial spirit of the PNW and forces liberals to
think twice when creating ambitious plans, making them question whether
they are simply falling into the model of Western capitalism and other models
of cultural and religious dominance. To some extent, the decentered reality of
the Protestant mainline makes this temptation beside the point, but one hears
the echoes of these concerns in the liberal clergy of this study.

While mainline Protestants have felt—at least in the near past—a cus-
todial role for American culture, evangelicals for most of the twentieth century have been fighting an uphill battle against what PNW leaders take as the

"liberal secular elite" and a liberal Protestant culture that has "sold out" to this liberal elite. In other words, one hears from evangelicals the ethos of an "underdog" status and a ferocious ambition to "engage" and "transform" the culture. Evangelical leaders present themselves as "transparent," "entrepreneurial," and "humble" ministers of the gospel, seeking to evangelize the unchurched of the PNW. Nonetheless, for evangelical leaders, their time to lead is now and they have no hesitation in making the most of their opportunities.

The differences between liberal and evangelical leaders are distinguished by their self-presentation, motivations for ministry, visions and goals, and the strategies that each uses. Whereas liberals expressed how they took on the "role" of minister and moved through the professionalized processes of denominational bureaucracies, evangelical leaders more often than not, "felt a call to ministry." In this way, one is reminded of Weber's classic distinction between bureaucratic and charismatic leadership (Reiff 2007). For liberals, denominational rule following ensures organizational success; whether this translates into congregational growth is often unimportant. For evangelicals, by definition if there is no "call," the ministry becomes "moribund." In one case, an evangelical minister left a highly successful commercial real estate position to start a church because he felt "God's call on his life." Success in terms of growth legitimates the charisma of the leader; without it the "call" becomes suspect. One evangelical explained that he was in a horrific traffic accident as a result of drinking alcohol, and in what he thought were his last moments, he made a promise to God and went from life in a bar to life in the church:

> And so we went off this cliff, or this sand dune, this embankment
> and flipped the truck in midair and we were trapped, sandwiched in
> there. And in midair I pulled my head lower than the dash. So we
> were trapped in there and panicky and I prayed and I said, "God, if
> you get me out of this, I'll give you my life. You can do whatever
> you want with me." We were upside down and I finally crawled out of
> the side window. The rest of them got out and I walked up on a
> sand dune, looked up into the stars and said, "That's it, God. I'm
> done. Take my life, whatever you want to do right now." So that's my
> conversion right there, you know? But still having some of the
> same desires to drink and party and not knowing, I didn't know any
> Christians. So I was trying to figure this thing out myself and,
> long story short, I got on the side of my bed and just started praying
> every night and bought a Bible and started reading it. So I needed
> help with the alcohol side. So I prayed and asked God to take it
> away. Well, two weeks after that I stopped and never had a desire,

never had a temptation to do that again and one of the last times
I was at a bar, and I had just started going to a church and they
had this ministry training center, so I literally got out of the bar on
Saturday night, was at this church on Sunday, signed up for this
training center, and was in Bible school on Monday morning.

This same evangelical minister started a Foursquare Church and in less
than five years grew his church from 200 to 1,300 members and in the process had "planted five churches," including one on Harvard University's
campus, that ministered to students in the college. But *his* mission, as he stated
it, was "to really messed up people; so we have a mix of really messed up types,
professionals and young people." Another evangelical minister spoke about his
church's ministry to "gnarly people." On one occasion reported by an evangelical lay leader, a woman stood up in the middle of the service and "gave him
the middle finger, and he loved it! He approached her afterward and they had a
long conversation; she now comes to the church."

I found this same particular mix of "honesty," "transparency," and "authenticity" to be an engine that motivated many evangelical clergy. This mix
was of course wedded to a passionate "mission" to "witness" to faith—attached
as well to a strong leadership philosophy that "empowers" other lay leaders and
calls forth potential ministers within their congregations. Again, all characteristic themes are found in the ideal type of a charismatic leader. But of
course, personal charisma means little if the leader has no followers. Empowering a followership legitimates and constructs charisma. Another evangelical pastor changed his bylaws and created a small board to oversee the
church's lay leadership so that they and he could make decisions more "quickly
and effectively to meet the needs of the growing church." The evangelical
minister was proud of the fact that many of the programs in his church were
started by laypeople who simply "wanted to express their gifts in ministry; I
love the idea of unleashing people to express their unique gifts for others." This
form of facilitating lay ministry was a hallmark of the evangelical churches in
the study; they grew in large part because laypeople were invited and challenged to serve as "they were led by the Spirit of God."

This entrepreneurial spirit became a drumbeat in the interviews with
evangelical leaders. Entrepreneurs "don't wait, they act," and "their path may
go kind of left, right, left, right, but always forward." Evangelical clergy were
quite often quick to admit failure; one said that he was a poor leader, preacher,
and teacher; his gift was that he had "a small ego." He only preached 75 percent
of the time, so others had the chance to "exercise their gifts." His strength was
that he had "a thick skin," could make decisions quickly, and was able to put up

with criticism and move on. Liberals tended to assume that evangelical chur-ches were "personality cults," and as I said above, leadership counts, but evangelical lay leaders demanded a great deal from their clergy and oversaw their ministries as partnerships. Thus, one had the sense that evangelical leaders were on a "short leash"; deviation from a biblically based and socially conservative theological and ideological perspective would not be tolerated.

This sense of nurturing lay leaders by clergy was a consistent theme in interviews with evangelical senior pastors. In one situation, an evangelical pastor had "twenty-five to thirty-five potential leaders who feel that they might be called to full-time service and our goal is to always have twenty-five to fifty leaders ready to plant churches or be sent out into the mission field." In contrast to liberal churches, where at best there was a handful of students preparing for the ministry in the ten churches combined, the disparity could not be more telling. In at least a quarter of the evangelical churches there were extensive church-planting efforts taking place, with five, ten, and sometime more than fifty churches that had either been planted or were in the planning stages. One church was using resources from the Harvard Business School to test individuals for their entrepreneurial capacities, and training the church staff in skills of entrepreneurial management. Although liberals might chal-lenge this sense of using "corporate management models" as a part of a "co-lonialist enterprise," evangelicals were not unaware of the postcolonial critique of missions—making it clear that creating indigenous leaders in foreign countries was integral to the mission of the church, though this concern did not mitigate their evangelistic motivations, as one evangelical pastor explained:

> We don't like the idea of sending an American overseas for an in-definite period of time, partially because they never really accli-mate to the local culture. Their diet, their doctor, their education, they tend to set up a compound. Additionally, I feel like it's kind of co-lonial and patronizing. And part of it is as well, we like to invest the money and then get the money back. So we make a two- to three-year investment and then that church needs to be self-supporting. So the only time we'd send an American would be to a place that does not yet have a church. Send them in for the purpose of begin-ning a church and [get] out.

For evangelical clergy, the problem with evangelism was not that it had been tried and failed, but that it too often had planted a church but had not indigenized leadership. Missions, for evangelicals in this study, must become "self-sustaining" quite quickly. Unlike liberal churches that tend to try and preserve ministries and ministers, evangelicals have no hesitation in letting churches die and ministers fail. This kind of "corporate attitude" that seeks "results" and the "strategies" that will help achieve their "goals" is a part of evangelical culture. This extends to the fact that evangelical clergy resist "babying their flock" or their fellow colleagues. The churches that do not produce fruit should fail; clergy who are mediocre should not lead congregations. Evangelical leaders do not apologize for what they see as demanding or even "ruthless" expectations. For them, Jesus made demands on his disciples and there were consequences for "sin." Moreover, for evangelical clergy, the great mistake of liberal ministers is that their people are "coddled in their sin; it's not healthy." An evangelical minister explained that if people come into the church with their sin and it is not confronted, confessed, and redeemed, it destroys them:

> I've got a sexual hang-up, or something, pornography or immorality, or whatever it is. And it's tearing my soul apart. I don't care if the whole culture says live with your girlfriend, my soul is telling me, "Sure there's the physical thrills," but my soul is telling me, "I've got a conflict." Well everybody else is going, "Hey, I've got this great new girlfriend and we're moving in together" and sure it's exciting for a while. The Bible talks about the pleasures of sin for a season, but eventually, we are not designed to live without moral guidance. We are not designed to live contrary to God's laws. So we have this conflict. We try to be authentic and deal with that reality. It needs to be done kindly. We don't say, "You rotten sinner, you're going to burn in hell." It's "Look, there's an answer to your problem." I can't force it on you, but I have an answer and it's right here in God's word. If you're willing to listen and you're willing to let God work in your life, you can not only be delivered from that sin that's tearing you apart, but God will give you a purpose in life.

What one finds in the evangelical ministers in this study is passionate dedication to the core of their moral worldview—to confront sin, to make others aware that "we are a damn mess," and to share with them the "good news" that in Christ one is "made whole for this world and saved for the next." As one evangelical pastor explained, "This is a mission that I am willing to die for. I am not just trying to get people to be nice, but to reach them for Christ." This kind of clarity and perseverance were a part of every interview. And some were quite aware that the "hard boundaries" of their belief systems were exactly what they "needed," as one evangelical clergy revealed: "I need boundaries. So I live on that and I know in my own personal life, my discipline, it comes from what I learned in the Marine Corps." Only 7 percent of the evangelical respondents were involved in the military either as soldiers themselves or with a family member. I expected to find a much higher percentage. On the other hand, liberal respondents had less than 1 percent involved with the military. Nonetheless, the command and control ethos of military life was an important aspect of evangelical life, particularly in the sense of felt obligation, discipline, and hard work. Any number of clergy said that they took "no days off," and only stopped working to be with their families. For them, the ministry was not a "profession" but a "calling" and they spoke about it as a privilege. Liberal clergy voiced similar feelings of awe for their career choice, but they were more attuned to its bureaucratic and professional ethos. And indeed, one liberal clergy complained quite heartily about the "lack of urgency" among his colleagues, decrying their lack of passion "for justice," and the sense of "selfishness." I noted a therapeutic vocabulary that was a consistent theme among liberal clergy: If "I don't take of myself, how can I care for others?" The liberal clergy in my sample were enormously dedicated to their "positions," but that is the point; they were in positions. The majority of evangelical clergy had either created their churches, or had so distanced themselves from their denominations that they spoke as if they no longer were related to these larger bodies. The latter act was intentional at times in part because evangelical clergy knew that their laypeople were largely indifferent to denominational affiliations or relatively negative toward them. I found in liberal laypeople less indifference toward denominational bodies and even some positive feelings for them. For liberal laypeople, it made sense that their clergy saw themselves as professionals. In liberal culture there is a greater sense of compartmentalization of the private and public, thus one's beliefs are private, one's role as a professional is public, and the two do not necessarily coincide. For evangelical clergy, this compartmentalization is anathema. There is within evangelical clergy a strong sense that to believe in Jesus Christ as Lord demands a "total commitment," and if one is not willing to do this, as one evangelical clergy said, "What's the point?"

The evangelical commitment to their calling leads evangelical clergy not only to give their time and energy but their creative minds to "reaching people where they are." In this sense, evangelical leadership used every form of communication and media to make their point. As one pastor said, there needs to be a "What the hell factor?" in every one of his services:

> We place a huge value on creativity here. We talk about the "What the hell?" factor on a Sunday morning. And by that we mean we want every Sunday [for there] to be at least some moment in the service that catches people [by] enough surprise to say, "What the hell

was that?" And not out loud, hopefully. So as an example, I have
set a mole trap on stage. I have had piles of dirt behind me which I
hid to demonstrate the difference between mole hills and mountains.
I've started up a chain saw when I was preaching on [how] the ax
is laid at the root of the tree. I said, "Listen, that was 2,000 years
ago, we're in the PNW. This is the home of the loggers." I mean, we
don't have axes, we have this. And I pulled this up and I'm in my
robe and start this chain saw, *vroom, vroom, vroom.* We often are
thinking, What are the takeaways as you leave worship? So we give
people a rubber band to snap to remind them about the people
that they hate and that God loves. I have a video team, in fact our
whole worship creation is a very collaborative effort. And so every
Sunday morning I've got ten people out there saying, "That was my
idea," or "I had a part to do in that." But the heartbeat of it is you are
putting a vision before people that, first of all, Christ makes a difference in your life and Christ makes a difference in the culture. He
wants to change the world and he wants us to be an agent for that.
I remember my first meeting with my elders when I came here
back when we had 185 in worship. I said, "Just imagine if God could
have his way with us in five years, what would that look like?" So
we began to dream. And there in 1987 we set a goal of 2,000 by 2000
in worship. And we didn't quite make that, but we almost made it.
It's a shame to present that in a way that doesn't captivate people's
hearts and imaginations.

I consistently found in evangelical leadership a willingness to take risks, to
use as the quote above says, "audacious" means to communicate a message.
And again, every form of media was tried in order to reach the goal of communicating the "good news" of Jesus Christ and to "engage" and "transform"
the culture. Evangelical leaders also recognized the power of setting a vision and
ambitious goals to mobilize their people, and to a great extent evangelicals
achieved results when we note the average rate of growth among the twenty-four
evangelical churches at nearly 200 percent over a period of more than five years.

The logical question with any social movement is that after the initial
stages of "effervescence" fade, what happens when the early "charismatic" leadership grows older, relocates, or retires? Do forms of "domestication" and
"bureaucratization" naturally follow? And is it a logical question and one worth
pursuing? At the same time, this is not a longitudinal study, though of course,
its sets down a layer of data on the nature of evangelical culture in the PNW
from 2001 to 2006. From here, other scholars can sift through the records of

these churches in ten or twenty years to note what has occurred. My sense as a student of American church history is that the ebb and flow of American Christianity is to be expected. Some churches rise and others fall for many reasons that I have already outlined. Liberal leadership, particularly among the younger generation, seems to understand what it takes to communicate their message to younger adults, children, and youth. But as I have shown, the overwhelming effort and robust nature of evangelical networks that evangelical clergy have created is impressive. Their hard work, vision, and perseverance against difficult odds paid off, particularly in the context of a secular and un-churched region. Nonetheless, the 2010 U.S. census will tell how much progress they have actually made in expanding their market share of churched individuals in the PNW. I now turn to comparing the outreach and mission of liberals and evangelicals, and the particular nature of each of their relations to culture and what missions, local and global, flow from each of their moral worldviews.

10

Religion, Outreach, and Mission

1. Religion and Culture

To investigate the relation between religion and culture, I first compare how liberals and evangelicals fit within the wider history of the association between Protestantism and American culture; I then examine how each of these groups approaches the PNW culture in outreach and recruitment. What methods do they employ in these forms of "evangelization"? Finally, I analyze the meaning and strategies for mission, locally, in terms of service to their communities, and then globally, investigating the methods of proselytization of those abroad and service to those in need. Once again the distinctive moral worldviews of each of these groups form the symbolic boundaries of their ideology, and shapes and guides how they relate to the wider symbolic and social boundaries of the PNW culture. Religions, by their nature, are always moving within cultures and they identify themselves in this relation; in this sense religions are always mirroring, resisting, and accommodating to a wider culture, some with a degree of reflexivity but most unconsciously. Religions, as I have argued before, are therefore subcultural systems, by definition, in the modern era.

In H. Richard Niebuhr's classic study *Christ and Culture* (1951) he outlined five types or models of the relationship between religion and culture:

1. Christ against culture, a sect that stands against a dominant parent culture, the best example of which was the early church;

2. Christ of culture, the Protestant liberalism of nineteenth- and twentieth-century elite Christian religion, which made Christ the implicit goal of culture;

3. Christ and culture, recalling the Catholic synthesis whereby religion and reason would complement and complete each other;

4. Christ and culture in paradox, emphasizing the fallen nature of humanity and the grace of God in Christ that redeemed individuals and held out hope for the created order in the light of the Second Coming of Christ; and

5. Christ the transformer of culture—Niebuhr's preferred model— whereby nature and culture are marred by sin but redeemable and reformable by Christian men and women willing to do the work of reconciliation in the world (39–44).

Niebuhr, of course, was a master modeler of lived Christian religion. But I am less taken by his work than when I used his theological language to organize the patterns of twentieth-century American Protestant church history in my book on Fourth Presbyterian Church (Wellman 1999b). His categorization of Christ is too abstract; the word *Christ* itself is culturally constructed, so that I do not posit an independent Christ—hovering above culture, inspiriting the Christian church, and working in relation to "secular cultures" formatted in various models. I would argue that the field of religion and culture is more complex; lived religion always disrupts theory, whether theological or sociological. And the relation of church and culture, and religion and society changes rapidly and continually over time. Nonetheless, my task is to give some sense of this relation in the liberal and evangelical churches in this study.

The relation of liberal churches to the PNW culture is unlike any of Niebuhr's models. Perhaps this is in part because the PNW was relatively unlike any of the social contexts that Niebuhr had analyzed. The level of interest in spirituality in the PNW is high; spiritual but nonreligious people are, in fact, not that different in their beliefs from church-affiliated northwesterners, as we have seen. Historically and culturally, throughout its history, when people have come to the PNW they most often left behind their church affiliations— whether because they always wanted to or because they felt no reason to recreate them, or the religious institutions did not exist in the region. No doubt it is a combination of these factors, but the difference between the rest of the country and the PNW in terms of church affiliation is obvious not only statistically but also subjectively for those who come to the region, as one lay liberal newcomer said: "When I left Utah I was actually relieved not to have one of the first questions people asked me [be] what my religion was. And I was actually relieved. And then when I started looking around for a church and was thinking about bringing the children it almost got to be a little bit of a question about whether it was discouraged." That is, the PNW culture is not only a de facto secular (but spiritual) culture, but there are aspects that militate against church affiliation. There is nothing in the culture that creates a "sacred space" for the church or that gives it unique status. In speaking with any number of liberal or evangelical clergy, a consistent refrain of those who had come from other parts of the country was that there were no "perks" from communities for clergy in the region—no automatic memberships in athletic, golf, or entertainment clubs; no deference given or paid to clergy per se. It was not so much a negative attitude toward clergy but an indifference to them.

For liberal clergy and lay leaders, this indifference has meant several things. One is that since membership in churches is not taken for granted or expected, the usual "rites of passage" that would draw families to the church—baptism, confirmation, and even marriage—do not exist. People simply find other leaders, civil or New Age, to do "spiritual" ceremonies, including blessing children, houses, and marriages. As one liberal clergywoman lamented:

> There's a really strong unchurched ethos. You see it if you try to do anything in colleges or sports, Sunday is just another day of the week. There's no sense that maybe we should do it Sunday afternoon so people can go to church. Maybe that's all over, but I feel it's more around here. At the same time, people flock to hear authors and theologians and spiritual gurus of every kind. There's kind of a hunger for something. But my sense is a lot of people feed that hunger by going to a lecture and not building it into their lives in a permanent way. And that's probably judgmental, but that's what it feels like.

This means that when someone joins a church it is a choice on his or her part, relatively uncoerced and intentional. Thus, as one liberal clergy said, "So when somebody here says, 'I'm a member,' they really mean they're a member." This liberal clergyman took this as a boon to his church and the community. But not all liberal clergy and lay leaders find this helpful. Since liberals do not evangelize, as I show below, new members are difficult to come by. Indeed, one liberal newcomer to her church struggled over whether or not to "baptize my children; I don't want them to be coerced. I want them to be comfortable." I sensed in liberals, as I have mentioned before, an aversion to coercing their children and a kind of fear that they could somehow "offend" their children's sensibilities.

The PNW is daunting to understand for outsiders and even for those, like myself, who were born in the region. Typically, most assume the "liberal" nature of the culture, and this is true in part, but one liberal clergyperson pinpointed factors in the culture that changed her mind about it and her way of approaching the culture generally. She grew up in the Midwest in a family of deeply committed Marxists who organized unions and as she said, "radicalized them," leading to a series of arrests and a quite unstable early family life. In the summer she was sent to "socialist camps, sponsored by Eugene Debs." Her dad talked continually about the "new world order," calling Catholic priests "bloodsuckers," who baptized the capitalist status quo. At one point in her teenage years, she said to her father, "Well dad, I don't think the new world order is going to happen. I watched my dad's whole world drop away." In other words, she knew radical politics from the inside out; she also saw their abject failure. Her conversion to the liberal Protestant tradition came at the behest of an African American ordained Protestant minister who challenged her with the idea that Christianity combined a compassionate and prophetic tradition that not only led to political liberation but spiritual freedom. She ended up being ordained. So when she came to the PNW she expected a liberal politic and what she said she found was an intense "libertarianism." For her, the bottle law was an example; one had to recycle bottles in her state, but as she said, "Well, of course the bottle law only really worked when they attached money to it, so one could benefit from it." That is, for libertarianism to work it had to be combined with a utilitarian ethos. For her, this meant that there was much less of a communal ethic in the PNW than in Minnesota. In the PNW, for her, the differences are pronounced: "There's much more the sense that you don't give the poor a handout, you give them a hand up; and if they're not going to respond to it, the hell with them. Whereas in Minnesota, maybe because of its Scandinavian connections, you worry your head over all these poor people who choose not to respond. And here, they don't give another thought." As a liberal clergywoman, her sense was that one of the strong attractions of the evangelical church was precisely this appeal to individual salvation—a kind of libertarian and utilitarian spirituality; the sense that one must take care of oneself—that is one's own salvation. My own take is that liberals overstate individualism within evangelical communities; I found that within evangelicalism there was an appeal to the individual and his or her salvation, but it was deeply interlaced with a communal obligation and a pattern of small groups that created intense social networks. And indeed, one of the strong appeals of evangelicalism was these networks and communities that embraced families, children, and youth, compensating for the individualism and felt cultural fragmentation of the PNW.

In any event, liberal churches, in part because of their moral worldview, face dilemmas in responding to the culture of the Northwest region. The moral worldview of these churches tends to tilt toward a libertarian perspective—that is, as we have seen, a privatistic ethos around personal beliefs and behaviors, particularly sexual orientations. There is, as I show, a strong ethic of social action among liberals and an ethos of "making the world a better place," and in some churches, a push toward the importance of communal worship as a "key component" of one's spiritual life. But to a large extent liberal churches mimic or mirror many of the elite liberal cultural attributes of the PNW culture, such as the belief in the power of the individual to take care of oneself and to make the world a better place; a strong sense of egalitarianism and fairness for all; the belief that each person should think for himself or herself and become critical and self-reflective; the belief that life is a spiritual journey that involves a connection "to something bigger than oneself"; the sense that one cannot know or be certain of how to define this "spirit," thus creating ambivalence and great caution about naming it. All of this adds up to a liberal religious community that resembles the wider "spiritual but not religious" culture. Naturally then, how does one make one's religious community distinct from and attractive to this wider culture?

The reality in liberal religious communities is that the liberal moral worldview by its nature undercuts the assertion of explicit theological truth claims that would distinguish liberal churches from the wider "secular but spiritual" culture. In liberal churches one can endorse one's faith as one among many ways to approach the divine mystery, but to lift it up as the most plausible or persuasive approach is not acceptable. Toleration and the celebration of difference are applauded much more highly than an explicit affirmation of the uniqueness of one's faith. Thus, there is little or no tension with the wider PNW culture by design. In fact, there were in the study a handful of liberal leaders who responded to questions about the decline of the "liberal church" that perhaps this was for the "best." This was rare but arresting and, in part, it came from the liberal moral worldview that contemplated the history of Christianity and its many abuses of "minorities" and wondered, as in this case, out loud that perhaps the church must die for what it has done. In part, this response came from liberals who were particularly offended with the evangelical support for President Bush and the Iraq War, which I examine in the chapter on politics. But it was clear to me that liberals were struggling with how to be a "Christian" without being identified with parts of the church that they rejected. In fact it was a common complaint among liberal laypeople that when others found out they attended church, it was assumed that they were "fundamentalists." More than a few liberals simply kept their affiliations to themselves, compounding the problem of declining membership. Needless to say, the moral worldview and the relationship of evangelicals to the culture of the PNW were dramatically different.

A critical finding of this study is that among the twenty-four evangelical churches, I found nearly no one who was classically sectarian in that they sought to "shun" or "reject" the secular culture of the PNW. Frequently, secular liberals would ask if I was studying "fundamentalist" churches in the region. I rejected this label for several reasons: first, evangelicals themselves refused this label as a way to describe themselves; second, historically, fundamentalists have sought to distance themselves from the broader culture and evangelicals in this study sought to engaged the culture; and finally, as an analytic category I find the term itself overdetermined, that is implying a total explanation that in many cases hides reality rather than illuminates it. The evangelical churches in this study were nearly the opposite of sectarian—they were aware of the fallen nature of humanity, but this seemed to mobilize them even more to transform it, though always with the notion that "God is in control." Most of these churches in their central belief statements are "premillennialists," believing that Christ's Second Coming will precede Christ's thousand-year reign on earth. Typically, premillennialists are less interested in transforming the world, and yet the evangelicals in this study maintained a strong passion for civic engagement and deep interest in the common good. Moreover, the evangelicals in this study evinced an "entrepreneurial spirit" that expressed a "world-conquering" sensibility rather than a "world-weary" one. Heaven may be their home, but the earth and the culture of the PNW inspired them and mobilized their passions to evangelize and "save" it.

This is not to say that there isn't tension in the relationship of evangelicals to the PNW; but the tension is because of engagement rather then tension because of rejection. Christian Smith has argued that tension and evangelical engagement with culture are causal elements in evangelical vitality (1998). And indeed, I found the more I studied these churches what made them dynamic was not so much their "negative identities" but their positive moral worldview. So in analyzing their relationship to the wider culture, evangelicals often talked about the positive aspects of the secular and unchurched realities of the region. In fact, on several occasions, evangelical lay leaders who had come from the South and other parts of the nation that are more traditionally "churched" spoke in glowing terms about Christians in the region; one evangelical lay leader argued in response to a comment about the lack of dedication in church membership: "I am diametrically opposed to that comment, because of the strength and the depth of the churches, and not just ours, the lifestyle of those people is much stronger, in my opinion, than many places that I've seen in the South and other parts of the country." Other lay evangelical leaders rejoiced in the fact that secular people in the region were quite demonstrative about their feelings toward religion, and Christianity in particular. For one evangelical, this was a "blessing" since they did not reflect a "lukewarm" spirit and were clear about their decisions: "I pray for that to continue. For people to either be passionate about God, or let it go until they can receive his love and acceptance." Evangelicals argued that northwesterners chose member-ship not out of obligation or a family tradition but from a deep sense of "conviction."

There was also recognition that the PNW was not a "joining culture," and this formed two different but related responses from evangelicals. Evangelical leaders, knowing that it was a radically open religious market with few "props" to buoy the interest or need to join a church, sought to attract new people by a deep engagement with the culture:

> We engage the culture of today and we contextualize the gospel to today's culture, which means everything from dress to music to is-sues and style. We don't take an against-the-culture approach and we don't take a for-the-culture approach. We take a real people before a real God, and people who live in this world and the difficulties with finances and economics and relationships.

Thus, I found no evangelical churches in an "attack" mode on the culture per se. Indeed, many said that they felt "no tension" at all with the secular PNW culture and readily said they "never experience persecution or bias against them." That is, in a libertarian culture of "live and let live" evangelicals took advantage of this freedom to engage the culture. Indeed, many evangel-icals felt at home in the culture—relating to the libertarian social and economic spirit of the PNW. Many evangelicals combined the fiscal conservatism of libertarianism with the social conservatism of their moral worldview, creating a powerful moral cocktail—as one evangelical lay person said, "I believe in re-sponsibility and that means that each individual can take responsibility for their own actions, for my family, and my church." Or as another evangelical new member argued: "If you don't work, you don't eat today. That's what the Bible says. And you don't take care of the sluggard who doesn't want to work. You don't feed him. People are buying into this philosophy that somebody who has wealth owes you something. We are to go to work everyday, we're to do it in joy, everything for the Lord and not expect a free ride."

Not all evangelicals would have said this, but at the same time it resonated with the entrepreneurial nature of their churches, the focus on individual responsibility for life and faith, and the importance of the church providing community and services to those in need—even as they attached strings of responsibility to their charity.

Evangelicals in the study often celebrated the freedoms found in the American Constitution: the freedom of speech, the freedom of religion, and the freedom of association. In many ways this backbone of freedom resonates with the northwestern spirit of "making it on our own," and "every man for himself." It was precisely in places where evangelicals felt that their "freedoms" were being limited that tension with the wider culture arose. Because of their stand against gay marriage, a handful of evangelicals argued that in the not too distant future Christianity would be "outlawed" in American culture. Some evangelicals argued that there was a "liberal bias" against them so that their "opinions" were being censured. As one said, "I think the Democratic Party, the ACLU, the more liberal side tends to, it feels like, tries to hush and silence people whose views are premised on biblical perspectives." And of course, evangelicals argued that their positions were "based on absolute truths" that were a part of "God's order," so abortion and gay marriage are "unnatural" and "disordered" forms of morality, that "violate God's freedom." Thus, many evangelicals felt a strong desire to engage the public square over these issues, and yet at the same time this desire was mitigated by the belief that "God ordains the civil order." Hence, evangelicals have an ambivalent relationship to the secular civic order that makes them feel called to transform it, but at the same time believe that God is in "control of history" obligating evangelicals to obey the social order. This is in part what makes rulings such as *Roe v. Wade* so difficult to accept for evangelicals—because they feel both the moral need to change it while at the same time the religious obligation to accept civil decisions. This ambivalence also tends to undercut most forms of extreme political action—making most evangelicals rather benign political players—in part because they believe in the end that God's way will prevail whether in this world or the world to come.

The relation between religion and culture for each of these groups is complex and not easily captured by Niebuhr's models of Christ and culture. For liberals, the relationship is relatively sanguine. To a great extent the civil rights movements of the 1960s and 1970s made legal the movements for justice that liberal Christians hold dear—rights for ethnic minorities, women, and homosexuals. The latter remains a group that liberals argue continue to be stigmatized and thus worthy of advocacy and support. But to a great degree, tensions between liberal churches and a secular but spiritual region remain rather low. Ironically, if there are tensions, it is with "fundamentalist" Christians that liberals disdain, in part because of evangelical "dogmatism" but also because of their conservative social policy. Evangelicals, on the other hand, tend to feel "sorry" for the liberal Protestant mainline, counting them as "misguided" and even "heretical" though relatively harmless and in decline. For evangelicals, the goal, as always, is growth and engagement with the culture to convert and transform it. This entrepreneurial spirit fits with the PNW though the social and moral conservatism of the evangelical moral worldview create tensions, particularly on public issues such as abortion and gay marriage. But evangelicals do not carry over the strong "sectarianism" of their American fundamentalist forbearers. Evangelical churches, in fact, share much with the libertarian and entrepreneurial spirit of the region—causing them to focus on growth and a positive vision that is family-focused and morally traditional. It is to the methods of how liberals and evangelicals grow in this region that I now turn.

2. Recruitment and Outreach

Recruiting new members, known as evangelism in the language of the Christian religion, is for liberals complex, subtle, and very much entwined in their moral worldview. In a sense, as one liberal clergy put it, most new liberal Christians are "recovering." That is, in the instance of one downtown church, out of forty-seven people, a third were former Catholics, another third were former "fundamentalists," another handful were gays and lesbians, and another "six who grew up totally secular." This is relatively representative of the group that liberal churches attract, but the question for this section is How do they come to these churches and why?

To begin, liberals condemn outright evangelism that accosts individuals about the eternal state of their souls. Liberals do not try to "save souls," which one lay liberal found "self deceiving and selfish," that is, a form of religion that "promises a fantasy to come," and merely looks out for the interests of the individual to get what's good for him or her. The libertarian streak in liberals in the study was deep. "I guess the way that I think about it is that all paths lead to the same place and it isn't my job to go out and try to make someone else think a different way, nor is it somebody else's job to convert me in that way." The moral worldview of liberals demands that one make up one's own mind. Moreover, there is great resistance to "campaigns" for new members in part because of the market overtones. As one liberal clergy said, "It's a turnoff because it's corporate America, we're going to lose our soul to corporate America and we are the countercultural voice of religion now and are we going to lose that?" There is great concern among liberal laypeople and liberal leadership that the liberal church must grow, and yet there was a refusal to focus solely on families and the "narrow, parochial concerns of conservative family values; if that's the price you have to pay to grow, I don't want to grow." I heard these lines particularly from the first-generation baby boom pastors, resisting what they felt was a "sellout" to church growth specialists and a compromise of the "countercultural values of the gospel." Several lay liberal leaders argued, "If we have to expand our parking lot, then I think we simply say we won't grow." In a sense there is some pride among liberals that they do not grow because they have remained loyal to their core moral worldviews. And this may be true.

And yet, there were other voices among the liberal churches in the study, percolating up from younger clergy and lay leaders, realizing that times have changed and that methods must as well. However, the changes were subtle and complex. Liberals must argue for a reason that people should come to their churches. Their core theological truth claim that asserts the "truth" of God's essence and yet does not prioritize one religious tradition over another is both difficult to advertise and tends to echo the "spiritual but not religious" ethos of the PNW region. Thus, the question Why come to church? For liberals, there is no simple answer. For one liberal clergy, it is that there are a "variety" of religious and nonreligious traditions to draw on, and "I have chosen one: Christianity. I do think that human beings, myself first and foremost, are programmed to be religious. It's hardwired into us." When I asked him what being religious means, he said, it is "a form of communal spirituality." That is, for him, while being aware of the spiritual but not religious cultural ethos, "spiritual practices" done in community enable one to enjoy the "numinous that pervades everyday life." The mission motto of his church comes from this experience of "profound" mystery in four words: "Inclusion, service, discovery, and gratitude." But these relatively abstract terms cannot be fully experienced in isolation, so this clergyman argues that there is a need to practice them together, in service to one another and to the community. Or as another lay liberal leader asserted, "For us to invite someone into communion is to welcome someone into the kingdom of God thing, there's a little piece of it here, Why don't you come and taste and see?" This is both an invitation to the Eucharist and the "taste" of a spiritual community, set apart to practice "inclusion, service, discovery, and gratitude."

Again, this is a subtle invitation by liberal church leaders and most often only those who are already familiar with the tradition would find it appealing. Statistically, liberal churches draw no more "unchurched" types than evangelicals do. Liberals tend to draw "recovering" Catholics and evangelicals who have quit or rejected their tradition and want something religious that participates in the tradition without the "dogmatism" and "literalism" of Catholicism or conservative forms of Christianity. The most theologically positive and expansive call I found from liberal church leaders was from a clergyman whose church had the largest Sunday attendance. He argued that the core challenge is to define a theological reality that has profound effects of both transforming the participants as well as motivating them to serve those in need:

> I think it's good work, I think it's glad work. But I think the core of it
> is, What does it mean to us to acknowledge that we've been made
> in the image of God and that God yearns for both mercy and justice
> for all people and that Jesus invites us to be transformed, not to
> simply be placated? So while it's important that we feed the hungry,
> What does it mean for us to say we're going to feed the hungry
> and then ask why people are hungry? And how are we part of ush-
> ering in the kingdom of God in this world? How is the kingdom
> breaking in through what we as Christians do in our daily life? So I
> suppose one of the great themes for me is we are each invited to be
> bearers of Christ in the world, no matter where we are; as school
> teachers, fire fighters, software writers, whatever it is that we do.

On several occasions liberal leaders argued that Christ is not so much the focus of worship but the one who "bears the kingdom" and so obligates his follower to do the same. This means in the liberal moral worldview to live lives of compassion and justice. This means in part for liberal churches the inclusion of gay and lesbian people. One liberal lay leader defined the liberal church in just these terms: "Specifically, it means that anyone is welcome in this church, and very specifically that sexual orientation is not a reason for exclusion." In many of these churches sexual orientation was *the* reason for inclusion, making real what it means to follow in Christ's footsteps: "I come to this church because I'm in a same-sex relationship and it is a really comfortable place for the two of us to worship." A frequent side comment from liberal clergy was their significant ministry of officiating at gay "Holy Unions" enabling homosexual couples to make their relationships "sacramental." Of course, none of these gay couples remained legally married in Oregon after the Oregon Supreme Court nullified marriages in Multnomah County in 2004. However, this outreach to homosexuals is a powerful source of recruitment and ministry for these liberal churches, and yet it remains a source of some tension.

In one case an assistant minister to children and youth was called as an ordained pastor by a downtown church. He was clear about his gay identity and the church was clear and public about his sexual orientation as well. The senior pastor related that this move "caused some families to leave the church, though it attracted others." A liberal lay leader expressed the fact that she was sometimes concerned that the church's emphasis on gay rights "kept some people away.... We can be a church for anyone, not just gays and lesbians; and it's a little scary to me that we might be excluding people unintentionally." She did not want to reject homosexuals but she was worried about how the church might continue to attract heterosexual people and families. One clergyman in the American Baptist denomination expressed concern about the issue, explaining, "More than half the denomination is African American, most of whom don't want to deal with the issue of homosexuality; there is a don't ask, don't tell policy, even though many of our black leaders are quite progressive on most of the social issues." Thus, for this clergyman, his strong support of ordaining homosexuals was controversial not only for conservative white evangelicals in his denomination but also for African Americans with a long tradition of discomfort over the gay and lesbian issue.

A younger liberal clergyman, while remaining a strong advocate for gay inclusion, suggested to his leadership that they recruit those whom he defined as "spiritually purposeless." What this means for liberals is recognizing the importance of integrating individuals into a communal spiritual practice and a community of faith that is challenged to serve each other and to serve others. But it remains to be seen how liberals expand their recruitment rationale and the results from these initiatives. When I asked liberals about the word *evangelism*, it was rejected out of hand. For evangelicals, needless to say, evangelism was their raison d'être. Gaining new recruits validates their ministries. One might say without growth evangelicals lose their identity.

In coding priorities, evangelical outreach was by far the most important characteristic of the evangelical churches in the study. Forty-one percent of respondents mentioned the value of sharing the gospel. Indeed, the concentration on growth and "sharing" the gospel was a virtual drumbeat in the evangelical interviews. The evangelical moral worldview obligates those who believe in this core relationship to Jesus Christ to share this news with others— because it is *the truth* and it is the *only truth* that will save one's soul. For the most part, evangelicals tended to emphasize this "good news" of salvation; only 8 percent of evangelicals mentioned the threat of hell. Nonetheless, hell's reality and finality of death lurk in the shadows of evangelical motivations to share their "saving truth" with others. One evangelical pastor explained the difference between A-level doctrines (which are indisputable) and B-level doctrines (which are negotiable): "The fact that hell is final, I think that's A-level. What hell is exactly is secondary. But the fact that a holy God will judge sin one day and those without Christ face hell, now that is A-level. It is also A-level that Christ paid the price full for that sin and offers his righteousness as a gift to undeserving sinners who put their trust in him." It was not unusual for an evangelical pastor or layperson to mention that his or her life was changed by someone asking, "If you had two or three hours left in your life, do you know the destiny of your soul?" This prodded and pushed more than one minister into the ministry and preceded the conversion of more than a handful of evangelical laypeople.

Of course the threat of hell was constantly overshadowed in the interviews by the hope of heaven and the joy of Christian fellowship. In these vital and growing evangelical churches, I witnessed no fire-and-brimstone sermons, no modern-day version of Jonathan Edwards' "Sinners in the Hands of an Angry God." Evangelicals overwhelmingly expressed the power of uplift from the gospel and the fellowship they experienced and wanted to share. One of the misconceptions of liberals is that evangelicals spend their days "button-holing" people to coerce them into Christ. I found only one example of this behavior. In one evangelical focus group, one of the member's ministries was to walk around as a "human billboard," particularly at public events of groups he judged as "sinful," such as gay marriage rallies or pro-choice marches. The sign (which he wore to the interview) on his backside read "Jesus Saves" and the front read "Attention, Jesus Mighty God, Everlasting Father, Prince of Peace, Isaiah 9.6." For this man, the message of the gospel is an offense and, as he says, "The Bible says the gospel is offensive to those who are perishing and quite often they're offended because they don't want to turn from their sin and receive the forgiveness that Christ gives us for our sins." The man went on to speak about his public confrontations, particularly with politicians, one of whom was Jim McDermott, a self-described liberal Democrat U.S. representative from Seattle. The evangelical sign-carrier told how he would "admonish" McDermott every year for walking in the gay pride parade, knowing that McDermott's father was an evangelical preacher. The man would berate McDermott: "Shame on you for being up here and encouraging these people in their sinful behavior. What would your father think? He was on fire for Jesus Christ!" And then later on this evangelical related how the "Lord had put it on his heart" to go up to McDermott and "just love him," confessing to McDermott, "I've been real hard on you over the last few years and I want to apologize. I've blasted you and I really loved your father, he was a great man. And Jim McDermott was lis-tening, focused in on what I was saying." The man then immediately invited McDermott to a screening of *The Passion of the Christ*. For most liberals, of course, this whole interaction would be repulsive and ugly. And to a degree, even this evangelical man had realized he had stepped over the line, and he apologized to McDermott, although this had not stopped him from continuing his "ministry" as a "sign-bearer" for Christ. Moreover, even as he realized he was too hard on McDermott, he made one last pitch to have McDermott attend the Mel Gibson movie and to consider proclaiming faith in Jesus Christ. Of course, it never occurred to this evangelical that McDermott may have been showing support for gays and lesbians because he was "following Christ." Although I do not know McDermott's religious persuasions, liberals in the study would recognize McDermott's advocacy for the rights of sexual minorities and his stance against the Iraq War as being in line with how they view the mission of Christ.

I give the example of this "human billboard" to underscore how one evangelical can come to stand for "all" evangelicals in the minds of liberals. But in this study of evangelicals this was the rare case. Evangelicals tended to be deeply enmeshed in their churches, groups, and family activities. Indeed, many evangelicals would have balked at the activity of this billboard carrier and would argue that "coming alongside," "being a friend," and taking time "to listen" to others was the best form of evangelism. And there were countless examples of this "friendship evangelism" in the study. One church surveyed its visitors on Easter morning and tracked how many returned. They boasted at their "rate of return" and counted their success on the fact that most visitors had been "personally invited." One evangelical who had been in heavy metal bands and then become a Christian and joined the band at church. He invited his old friends to church, saying to them:

> "Hey, do you want to come watch me jam this weekend?" And they
> say "sure." "Well it's in a church, but you've got to come." And
> they would. Well, we have such a church that is so easy to walk into
> that's a really big thing. I think some people want to go to church, but
> they're scared. Are they gonna make me stand up, are they gonna
> make me put a hat on? What's gonna happen to me when I walk in
> there? And our church is so loving, it's open, the messages are so
> practical and so applicable to life. Like bringing my dad, he's never
> been into a church and every time he comes, he's, like, that was
> fantastic. You really enjoy it, you really talk to people.

One of the keys to evangelical success was that they thought from the point of view of someone who had either never attended a church or had had a bad experience with one. Evangelicals tended to know their market and asked how they could not only get people in the doors but how they could make them feel at home when they came. Their buildings were open, warm, conducive to people talking with one another, and their services were, as one evangelical leader

said, about "worship evangelism," which tried to make "real" one's "relationship" to God, so that it was fun, meaningful, and powerful. And this evangelical outreach and ethos were working for the churches in this study. Two of
the evangelical churches in the study came from the Presbyterian Church
(USA). This is a mainline Protestant denomination, though at the same time
deeply divided over social issues and in tension over theological ones as well.
These Presbyterian pastors spoke as evangelicals, over against the liberal lean-
ings of their denomination; one was in the process of considering his church's
"separation" from the wider denomination. One of the pastors commented on
the "evangelical wing" of his denomination and how well it was doing:
"There's only fifty churches in the country that have over 1,000 or more in
worship in our denomination on a Sunday morning. With the exception of four
or five, all the rest are evangelical. So these evangelical pastors and I meet
together on an annual basis to support each other, compare notes, brainstorm
and so forth." This Presbyterian pastor defined *evangelical* as "orthodox theology" that counts Christ as the only way to heaven—a belief he attached to his
firm stance on the "infallibility of the Bible." Like the other evangelical churches in this study, these Presbyterian churches were entrepreneurial and devoted to evangelism and their growth—numerically and financially—reflected
by their success.

The evangelical spirit of sharing the gospel was evident not only by the
churches in the study but also in how individual evangelicals approached their
jobs and their lives in general. As one evangelical lay leader outlined, his task—
along with that of his spouse—was to be a minister in every aspect of his life,
and his words reflected the words and action of many in the study:

> I feel strongly that Christ has called us as ministers; we're all min-
> isters and we . . . there is no secular or spiritual separation necessarily.
> I mean, we all live in the world and whatever we're doing there's
> a spiritual side of that. I work for the government and in the past,
> working for the government [meant] you couldn't have any display on
> your desk or any of that, that showed a religious background or a
> preference and that's changed now. It's different now than it was ten
> years ago. I approach work not as a platform to beat somebody about
> the head and shoulders with what I believe, but to be available to
> people to help them go to the next step that they want to go to. People
> are hurting, we go through hurtful times, everybody does, and to
> be there and just a simple, "I'm praying for you," and then they'll
> open up and you talk some more and see what needs they have
> and you try to meet those needs. So I think when you're real and

people see that, it opens up tremendous opportunities to take them to
the great healer, Christ. And we do that in our neighborhood, we
try to go to neighborhood get-togethers and people bring drinks and
they party. But we go, and we spend time with our neighbors and
it's been a great opportunity to build friendships and just let them
know that we're there when they need us. It's ingrained so we don't
separate the secular and spiritual that much.

This was a common refrain among many lay evangelicals, telling about
their experiences in their everyday worlds. They sought in their lives to reach
out to people wherever they found themselves; one spoke about praying when
she was at Home Depot. She asked God to show her how to witness to her faith
even as she was buying products for her church—expressing the numerous
times she ended up inviting fellow shoppers to her church. Another mentioned how his coaching his children presented him many opportunities to
invite families to his church. Another expressed the power of his ministry at
a prison; his church had come up with ways to integrate families of prison-
ers into their church. Another evangelical mentioned how she evangelized at
her job:

> I've saved, I can't tell you how many young women. Two years ago
> my boss came to me and [said], "We can't afford to pay for janitorial
> service anymore, we're gonna use trustees from the jail. Are you
> comfortable with that." "Yes, I am." If my boss asks me to do that
> I will find a way and we'll work around it. So I had my Bible in my
> office and the first girl, I didn't talk too much about religion to her.
> We were trying to learn this whole thing, how I wanted to clean up
> cleaning service. But the second girl I thought, "I need to get away
> from all this bad language" and I just told them, "I am a Christian."
> "Oh, you are?" And the first thing they want to do is hug you and they
> want to know about God. Here's my Bible. And most of them
> have Bible classes in jail. I've had them take my Bible and go in their
> little laundry room and turn the light on, and it's noisy with that
> fan going, and they work their little Bible study. It's such a wonderful
> feeling to do that and to talk to them about God. You know, you're
> sittin' in jail, you know about jail, it's terrible. And when they can
> get out and reach out and talk to somebody, oh man, they blossom.

While liberals talked about membership in terms of being a "recovering
Christian"—whether from a bad experience in more conservative churches—
evangelicals spoke about how they were "recovering sinners." Evangelicals

sought to live "within" the Christian worldview, interpreting their entire lives by virtue of their biblical meaning and theological significance. The Christian faith seemed to penetrate evangelicals at a very deep level; one even spoke of how her church was "like an epidemic," from which she always gains something "wonderful." "There's something here I'm like, wow. So if somebody would have told me a couple years ago that I'd be doing this, I would have said, there's no way."

I mentioned earlier the "effervescent" nature of evangelical groups, I heard and saw again this same "power" of group worship and action in evangelism. This came out explicitly in charismatic congregations where members spoke of the "gift of tongues" as a process of "falling in love" in praise with God. Like all the evangelical churches, God was "made real" in this process and through it one was "fully converted" to Christ. It is not difficult as an outsider to see why evangelical churches are growing; they want to. They know what methods work, their message is clear and to the point, and it has a reward attached—fellowship with other believers and eternity with God. Liberal churches, for the most part, struggle with recruitment in part because they are not always sure that they want to grow, their message is more complex and not easily distilled in a yes or no package, and the rewards in their communities of faith are also less clear. Nonetheless, they do offer a fellowship of faith and social action on behalf of others, and they are most clear about their love and inclusion of sexual minorities. In general, however, the liberal faith is a difficult one to reproduce; it is intellectually demanding as well as morally altruistic, and offers no clear eschatological or metaphysical rewards. I now turn to how these two groups work on their missions locally and globally.

3. Mission and Social Service

The moral worldviews of liberal and evangelical churches in the PNW are reflected in how they understand their mission on behalf of others, locally and globally, in service, social action, and outreach. For this study, social action means public policy advocacy; social service identifies actions taken on behalf of those with fewer economic or social resources; and outreach most often refers to evangelism—sharing one's belief system with another. How each group conceives its mission is just as important as what it does. I cover each in this section. To begin, despite the fact that liberals tend to talk a great deal about social service programs and accuse "fundamentalist" churches of being "internally focused," the data tell a different story. In coding church priorities, 37 percent of evangelicals mentioned the importance of social service on behalf of the poor in some form or another; for liberals, it was prioritized in 34 percent of the interviews. Now these are relatively close, but I expected liberals to emphasize social service more emphatically. Moreover, this is just one part of the overall evangelical mission, since for them "evangelism and missionary work" are even more critical; that is, 41 percent of evangelicals mention the importance of evangelical outreach compared with liberals who discount these forms of ministry. Nonetheless, the raw data show that both groups are categorical in the importance of caring for others, locally and globally, even as they approach this goal differently.[1]

a. Local Mission

Liberals are deeply ambivalent about mission as a form of religious outreach. One liberal layperson asked, "Should we share our faith and does this assume that there is a lack in [the] other person's perspective?" Another liberal in the focus group, speaking generally for all the liberals in this study, replied, "Faith is a private matter; we must be respectful of others and so we should not share our faith." Liberals spoke glowingly about the opportunity to care for others— but not, as we have seen, to bring them into their churches. If liberals think about the reproduction of faith, they would realize this only happens through actions rather than words, as one said, "To transmit the faith by living it." I did not hear of one case where a liberal had evangelized another person into faith by word of mouth. Moreover, in sifting through all the ministries of the liberal churches, particularly in the local mission area, I came across only one ministry that had the goal of transmitting the faith symbolically. This was the one new church plant in the ten liberal churches in the study. It was a small congregation, funding a single female pastor of Asian American ethnicity, with the motto "Multiracial, Multicultural, and Intergenerational Church." From what I heard, the church was struggling and small, but embodying the terms of its mission in its first five years. But in no other cases could I detect a local liberal ministry interested in recruiting new members from those they served.

Liberal churches in their local ministries are quite similar to nonprofit, secular, social service programs. They function very much in a secular mode of operation though there is at the same time a spiritual intent, though this is rarely made explicit. Liberal clergy in the study strongly supported this volunteer social service in their laypeople: "They're in Habitat for Humanity; they're on school boards, so that's good. I want people to be out there in the community doing things. They are in homeless shelters. So given the choice, I wouldn't want them to be on a committee at the church if they could be out doing other things."

In this sense the action of social service and political advocacy is more important than service to the religious organization per se; the religious mission of churches is deprioritized and social engagement with the needs of the community is made the central mission of the church. Liberals do not "force or coerce" their faith on anyone, but give without expectation of conversion. In this sense they are consistent with their moral worldview and it's imperative to do one's duty regardless of outcome. This begs the question of how liberals identify themselves as religious institutions. Mission in liberal churches is shadowed by the question Why should anyone do social service from the church when other local agencies already have similar volunteer operations that are ongoing? The more I explored what liberal churches actually do in social service, the more I found a great overlap between their activities and local social service agencies—and again, this was the point, there is no difference and, for liberals, there should be no difference. Liberals do not share their faith; they do works of compassion and justice because it is right and good—and because it is an expression of their faith. Indeed, the penetration of the local, grassroots nonprofit organizations by church members was a source of enormous pride for liberal churches:

> Politics though is really a very grassroots thing for a lot of us. We know from the organizational structure of the church that we're tied into the very earliest form of grassroots democracy in the country. This is how our church was modeled on the early colonial method of doing things. Consequently, we tend to have a church here where these people are probably on other planning commissions in the city. They are probably on boards of people who make decisions at the grassroots level. They've been educators. The tie-in to having an effect on society is pretty widespread, and that goes to some of what you said with our pastor being on board after board. Not just a member in good standing, but a legendary member of these nonprofits for various reasons. You should dig into those stories. So from the really grass-roots level through all of the issues, we're involved. We won't tout a candidate from the pulpit, and I'm surprised to see that happen on the other side.

Liberal churches in the study were deeply involved in local social service agencies, sometimes funding them and sometimes acting as recruiters of volunteers for these programs. The various programs included local food banks, food pantries at the churches, holiday meals served by congregants, family shelters (at one church), a mental-health chaplaincy that served the special needs of homeless mental-health clients, small (eight to twenty bed) transitional housing units for homeless women along with transitional counseling for jobs and childcare, teen feed programs, and nightly meals served from a downtown urban church. And this is but a representation of the many programs these churches created. As one lay liberal leader said about her church's shelter, "I think my biggest challenge so far in this parish is meeting hungry people who come to the door. We have a pantry two hours every day and give them food and looking them in the eye and offering food and conversation and welcome and some sense that they belong in our parish, even though they may not come to services, we're happy to have them here." It is a "humble" approach to ministry to the poor in the sense that liberals tended never to assume that they were "better than," or "knew more than," or were "more righteous than" those they served. Liberals practiced a sense of presence with others that was "inclusive and compassionate." Just as God is present for liberals, so they are to those who have nothing; it is a simple but profound witness. One liberal laywoman spoke with great eloquence about her ministry in hospice, where again her actions were one of presence rather than any explicit offerings of prayer. She felt a deep sense that she should sit with the dying: "If there is somebody dying, so they don't have to die alone, I can sit with them." This was a form of "spiritual practice" for liberals, embodying the "numinous" in moments when people were in greatest need. At the same time, the larger liberal churches in the study took on wider and sometimes quite ambitious local advocacy campaigns. As one liberal clergy outlined:

> We were at the forefront of the living wage movement. We certainly
> have been involved in issues in Central America over many years,
> have been engaged in questions around Palestine and Israel, and of
> course around issues of homelessness. The church has over the
> last several years convened the committee, or gave birth to a process
> that allowed the committee to end homelessness in the county to
> come into being and that just a few months ago released a really bold
> ten-year visionary plan to end homelessness as we know it in this
> county. So the church has always played that role and I think many
> people belong to this place because they want to be part of a religious
> institution where faith and the issues of the world interconnect.

Homelessness was a powerful motivator for liberal churches, particularly those in the large urban centers of the PNW. These larger more ambitious plans of eradicating homelessness were done in collaboration with other religious bodies, the cities, and with secular social service agencies. The ecumenical ethos of liberal churches was always a piece of their local outreach. This is both a part of the liberal philosophy of working with others to take on larger projects, and also a necessity since these liberal churches cannot act on their own. Thus, most of the churches in the study commented that they no longer "spoke for the city and community" on social service, cultural, or political issues. In fact, at times, focus group members would caution that liberals could occasionally "exaggerate their power."

More often than not, I found liberals "doing" social action in response to more conservative movements, whether religious or political. At times, the two were combined. For example, in the case when several lay liberal leaders from one urban church picketed a large evangelical congregation that was one of the sponsoring churches for the nationwide Justice Sunday program in which Senator Bill Frist made a speech from a conservative church defending the "conservative moral values of Christian people." In this way liberals were very much up against larger cultural trends over which they felt they had little or no effect.

Even as liberals ministered to those on the "fringe" of society, and protested conservative religious and social trends, they were proud that their social action was often controversial, whether ordaining homosexuals or blessing gay Holy Unions, or in another case defending a local mosque from what a liberal clergy thought was "harassment from the federal government." Following 9/11, a liberal clergywoman had developed a close relationship with a local mosque, and the two congregations had come to share some activities together. As the clergywoman said, "I am more comfortable talking with the imam from our local mosque than I am talking with conservative Christians." The church and mosque had started a mutual service project and in the process members had come to know one another. One liberal new member was attracted to the church because of this relationship with the mosque: "I thought there's no better way to learn about each other in a nonconfrontational way; to work on something that your values both feel is a worthwhile thing." This sense of mutuality in mission was a constant theme in interviews, whether ecumenically with other religious bodies or with other social service agencies working in tandem to struggle with wider issues, whether they are homelessness, hunger, environmental stewardship, shelter, employment, a living wage, or health care.

In another case that was "unpopular" in the wider community, a liberal church had come to the aid of a policeman who had had "sexual relationships" with two women while on patrol. The policeman and his family had become involved in the church and so the liberal church had come to know and care for him, his wife, and children. The clergy and lay leadership had come to the policeman's aid, defending him in the press, and negotiating with the courts on "an alternative sentencing process." The church had argued that the sexual relations were not "coerced" but "mutual and consenting" and that the women came from "shadowy" backgrounds involving pornography and the like. Of course, to the courts this did not matter. The church presented to the court an intensive probational process whereby they would take over the "rehabilitation" of the policeman, which would mean he would be discharged from his position, but would be able to work and take care of his family—as opposed to going to jail for six years and leaving his family destitute. The court disagreed with the church and scolded the liberal clergy and the church publicly in court for its "naïveté." Not all members of the congregation agreed with what their pastor had done, but the majority of the focus group at the church admired the pastor's courage and tenacity—in large part because it was not the "popular" thing to defend the policeman, but it was the "right" thing to do. The church was committed to caring for the wife and children during the policeman's imprisonment.

All of the liberal clergy in the study were left-leaning in their politics and three or four had come from relatively radical political backgrounds. Even so, most of the liberal clergy voiced sympathies with such politics. One clergy had lived in communal social action ministry; another had been a labor organizer; another was a part of a national political protest movement; another voiced sympathy with Latin American liberation theology and the benefits of early Christian communism; and several supported church exchanges with Cuban Protestant churches, speaking about the benefits of Cuban society on the lives of the poor. What struck me was that these concerns were only occasionally reflected in liberal laypeople. Generally, the liberal laypeople were left-leaning, but most were moderate Democrats. Additionally, there was a fair share of "quiet" Republicans who either kept "silent" when issues like these came up, or "libertarians" who took the philosophy of "live and let live" to heart. But in terms of local mission, liberal clergy tended to be "out in front" on more radical ideas of social transformation, and if these ideas came into the pulpits they were not always welcome by laypeople. At the same time, I noticed the newer liberal clergy seemed less wedded to "liberal" ideas and more open to traditional social, liturgical, and political forms. Indeed, one of the new "liberal clergy" was seen as more conservative than his left-leaning congregation. In general, the distance between liberal clergy and their congregants was greater than what I saw between evangelical clergy and their laypeople, and this came out on issues of mission and social action. If anything this caused liberal clergy to pull back from their own deepest convictions at times, whereas I saw none of this same self-censorship in evangelical clergy. A part of the reason for this was that most evangelical clergy had either come from the community that they served or had been trained at Bible colleges and started their own churches. If they had graduate education, it was most often from a conservative seminary and received while they were in ministry. Educationally, then, most evangelical leadership had not received a "dose" of Enlightenment training in a secular college or seminary. For them, the plain language of scripture was "perfect" and applying it to everyday life to grow disciples in Christ was the point of ministry. And it was no surprise that this is exactly what evangelical laypeople wanted: a biblically based sermon, applicable to their lives, that would preach good news, provide hope, and challenge them to grow. The mimetic relationship between evangelical clergy and laypeople was summed up by one evangelical layperson: "When I'm listening to my pastor's sermon I feel like he has been reading my mail." Indeed the moral worldviews of evangelical clergy and their laypeople felt very much in sync, particularly when it came to local and global missions.

The more I investigated the mission and ministries of the evangelical churches in this study, the more I realized that they have created a kind of "shadow" culture in the PNW. By this I do not mean a sectarian culture—that is, one that was utterly separate from or in confrontation with the wider culture—but a parallel culture formed to engage, transform, and convert the PNW. Unlike the liberal churches in this study who tended to "join" with secular social service agencies, evangelicals tended to create their own ministries that were not utterly unlike the secular social services groups—they performed similar functions, but evangelicals did all their work in the name of Jesus Christ.

To begin, it was rare to find in the twenty-four evangelical churches in the study a partnership with a nonreligious, nonprofit social service group. I found that on several occasions evangelical churches celebrated partnerships with Habitat for Humanity—an organization that has nurtured a relationship with secular communities as well as churches. Habitat is a Christian nonprofit that works nationally and globally to partner with families to build new homes. But more often than not evangelical churches had created their own groups to serve the poor, feed families, and help them transition into stable situations. Moreover, I found that these kinds of services of feeding the poor and sheltering the homeless were always tertiary ministries within evangelical churches; they were but one aspect of their overall mission and not *the* mission enterprise as they often seemed to be in the liberal churches in the study.

Indeed, local mission in the evangelical churches in this study tended to be nested in ministries to groups, evangelism to neighbors, and spontaneous acts of generosity and kindness to strangers. For evangelical churches, local outreach is a matter of creating groups that meet the needs of individuals at every stage of the lifecycle. That is, in every church in this study, there were groups for children, youth, men, women, married couples, divorced and separated people, singles, older adults, and people in recovery. In a sense these evangelical churches saw their churches as missions, as centers of care, conversion, and transformation. As one evangelical lay leader said, "Well, this place for a lot of people—and it was for us too when we first came—it's kind of like a hospital." The theme of recovery is a leitmotif among evangelicals and it means recovery from sin of course, but it also means recovery from every kind of mishap. In several churches, the Saddleback Church "Celebrate Recovery" program was used, based on Matthew 5:3–12. It has eight stages:

1. Recognize one is not God;
2. To believe in God's existence;
3. Consciously commit one's life to Christ;
4. Confess one's faults;
5. Submit to the changes God ordains;
6. Evaluate one's relationships;
7. Spend daily time with God; and
8. Yield to God in every way.

It is a Christian version of the Alcoholics Anonymous twelve-step program, though it is Christocentric unlike AA. Celebrate Recovery emphasizes reconciliation with Christ, repentance, and submitting to God's will. I saw these themes across the small group culture of evangelical churches, who used this method to treat addiction, divorce, and every kind of malady. One cannot help being impressed by the multiple layers and outlets of care and concern in these churches. They seek to meet every human need and relate that need to what they call the "good news of Jesus Christ." Indeed, to underline the multiple public outlets of these evangelical churches, one evangelical church estimated that there were more than "120 meetings at his church" each week. My guess from examining the church's Web site was that he was exaggerating, but even if he were half right, which seemed to be closer to the case, an enormous amount of human care was occurring in these churches.

This Christian therapeutic culture is a potent formula for many in this study. I could repeat any number of testimonials about the healing power of these groups, whether helping individuals to overcome addiction to drugs, alcohol, or pornography; helping them to work through the loneliness and devastation of divorce; "saving them" from homelessness or hunger; or bringing them into a "new family." But all of these programs of care serve a larger purpose for evangelicals: Unlike liberals who consciously refrain from verbally sharing their faith, evangelicals seek out ways to talk about the "good news" at every opportunity. One lay evangelical spoke about her small group and how it led to charity and her thoughts on opportunities for her to witness:

You live out your faith and for me, being involved in a smaller group really allows me as well as the group as a whole to express our faith in the way that we reach out, support, and help each other. One of our small group members, her husband died and we were able to rally around her and pray with her and support her. When we had the big ice storm just a few weeks ago, she has a huge—and she's in her seventies—has this huge cedar tree and a portion of it broke out and two of the gentlemen rushed over with their chain saws and cut out the dead branches that had broken. So, it's just wonderful to have an opportunity to live out your faith in helping one another, whether it's a fellow believer or even a nonbeliever, where you can in a situation that they may be going through, asking if it would be OK for you to pray for them. Sometimes it opens up doors to share your faith with others.

In any number of cases, evangelical laypeople had created opportunities to serve others. One group had spontaneously started painting houses for those who could not do it themselves, and served individuals who were not members of the church. Another group had started building houses locally with all-volunteer labor and selling the houses at a modest profit, using the money for missions, locally and abroad. Another evangelical had started the "parking lot ministry group" helping the disabled to make it to the church from their cars. Or in more individualized circumstances, evangelicals explained how their "life in Christ had softened their hearts" and allowed them to "smile in grocery stores," sometimes getting into conversations and "sharing their witness in the cereal aisle." In another case, evangelical lay leaders spoke movingly about how their teenage daughter had been empowered "by their pastor" to become "an interpreter" for her deaf friend and her family. The pastor noticed it and had begun to advertise it to the larger community and the church had gained more than seven families with deaf members. A similar process had occurred in the church when a layperson had offered to do Spanish interpretation of the worship service; it immediately began to attract Spanish-speaking families to the congregation. This process of discerning member's gifts and using them for "evangelism" was a critical aspect in these evangelical churches, which had the purpose of stimulating leadership, recruiting new members, and expanding the diversity of the membership. Nevertheless, evangelicals were consistent in admitting the fact that their congregations tended to be ethnically homogenous, not dissimilar to the liberal churches in the study. In each case, evangelicals and liberals wanted to diversify but both sets of churches had limited success in doing so.

Again, everyday life for evangelicals became a context for ministry and evangelism and often in quiet, unassuming ways. One evangelical lay leader spoke about how he was learning to witness and minister to the lesbian couple next door and how his "kids would go back and forth between their houses." In the latter case the evangelical lay leader never made it clear that this meant that they sought to change the lesbian couple, but I believe that was implied. Nonetheless, separation from the secular world, or the "sinful world," was never a part of the evangelical rhetoric in this study. It was quite the opposite; evangelicals were fully engaged at every level but on their terms. That is, instead of partnering, as the liberals did with community organizations, the evangelicals simply created their own organizations. The exception for evangelicals was that when they partnered with outside organizations, such as Christian ministries to prisons, youth outreach ministries to young people on the streets, Christian clothing closets, or Christian weight accountability programs—whether locally or internationally—they did so with only evangelical Christian groups.

Nonetheless, I think it is important to underline the fact that the liberal critique of evangelicals as being internally focused is partially correct. Evangelicals in this study always began with the premise that individuals needed conversion (an internal process) before they could go out and serve. Thus, at every level of the life stage evangelicals began with "spiritual growth" groups that had as the goal to "convert" and grow an individual in the "love of God." Now, once this process was under way, evangelical churches' ministries moved to the next level: to "present every member as fully mature in Christ" and "to equip each member for ministry." In the fall of 2006, a number of the evangelical churches in the study began with large "equipping" meetings to "kick off" the year. One of the themes for this kind of event was "go big for God." This kick off was led by a popular and successful Christian athletic coach to "empower" volunteers and to help them "find their gifts" and "learn to use them for Christ." Conversion, of course, was the theme that was virtually universal across evangelical churches, but the consequence of conversion must be action in evangelism, service, and loving others "into Christ." I was struck again, when I checked all the church Web sites at the end of August 2006, that every evangelical Web site had geared up for fall with splashy visuals and appealing images of "returning to church," while not one of the liberal churches in the study had done the same on their Web sites.

The local urban evangelical churches in the study generally followed the patterns of the other evangelical churches, but I noticed certain accommodations that they made to their specific context. They carried with them the same moral worldview with its core theological message, but always with a slightly more sophisticated appearance and postmodern motif. That is, in one case an urban congregation had developed an elaborate outreach program in the arts. On the one hand, it reflected a quite sophisticated sensibility, using modern themes, but always in light of an epistemology that celebrated the "source" of human creativity as coming from "God in Christ," and so even here an evangelistic theme was muted but still expressed. Another urban church had this same aesthetic sophistication but was less artful in its theological communication. The church focused its ministry and mission on young urban men and doing "preventive maintenance" (keeping them out of trouble with the law or with "sexual immorality") so these young men would come "to know Christ" even as they maintained their urban roots and creative and somewhat "raw" aesthetic. Indeed, this urban pastor, who used language that many students who attended his church found appealing and "relevant," counseled young people: "Get married, have sex all the time, love your spouse, and have some kids. Totally. Absolutely. We're all about that. In the city, teach your kids how to play guitar and grow up to be good tattoo artists and love Jesus. So that's where our cultural liberal comes in." In other words, one's heart must be "for Jesus," but one's aesthetic can be a "punk, tattoo artist, jamming for Jesus." When I responded that it sounded like he was trying to create "suburban-like" Christians in an urban setting, he was again quite forthright and consistent with the evangelical moral worldview in that his goal was having people come "to know Jesus" and everything else should go by the wayside, although he said it with greater bite:

> I love Jesus and I want people to love Jesus, I really don't give a crap about anything else. Christianity has gone to bed with Western society and they give birth to civil religion, which is to me just an ugly bastard child; so everybody is sitting around saying, "How do we preserve the bastard child?" Well, I don't know if we should have had that kid in the first place. I don't know if civil religion is, I don't have verses for it, it's not in my Bible. Heaven is my home, not America. I don't believe all the founding fathers were Christians, a lot of them were Deists. If they were Christians it's been 200 years and it's far in the rearview mirror. I really don't care about preserving the Western democracy, I don't care about traditional values, I don't care about upholding capitalistic principles. I don't really give a crap. I have one goal. I want people to meet Jesus.

He wittily avoided my question but made the larger point: he was not wedded to the usual cultural and political platforms with which outsiders accuse evangelicals; his goal was to create "relationship" with Jesus Christ.

After the interview, he went on to make the larger point that by creating a marriage culture and encouraging young evangelical men and women to have children that evangelicals would simply "out-reproduce" liberals in the long run and "take over the city because liberals don't have children." As we have seen demographically, there is some truth to what he is saying. It gets to the larger point of mission; one can do mission through the reproduction of family, that is, producing more children who will begin to dominate the culture demographically. This pastor's strategy was not vocalized explicitly in other evangelical churches, but it fits with the larger evangelical moral worldview of growth and expansion. And it is not that this pastor wants his young parishioners to simply "know Jesus," he wants them to engage, change, and transform the wider culture. This is an implicit aspect of his mission. So this urban pastor's style and rhetoric would not work in the suburban evangelical churches in the study, but that in part makes the point about evangelicals—context and local culture always matter and one must accommodate to these cultures to make an impact, to transform the culture, and to make it over "for Christ."

In the case of liberal and evangelical churches, the local mission of these churches was consistent with their moral worldviews. Mission for liberals meant caring for the marginalized in humble forms of service that met the needs of the hungry, the homeless, and those in life crises. In order for liberals to respect other's perspectives, one refrained from sharing one's faith with another; each person must be understood and accepted as he or she is. Of course, the consequence of liberals' refraining from evangelizing those they help is that even as liberals served others, they did not bring those in need into their churches. Liberals also worked with secular social service agencies, partnering with their local communities to serve those with less. Liberal church outreach mirrored secular social service in these communities. This was not a problem for liberals; in fact, it was a mark of their moral virtue. They served without expecting to change others' religions or expecting anything from the other, and maintained their sense of moral duty and altruism by forgoing their interests in either the reproduction of their faith or their institution.

Evangelicals, on the other hand, were consistent with their moral worldview, serving those with little in their communities by feeding the hungry and clothing those without, but their core ministries were about meeting the needs of their own. That is, these churches become hospitals for every human need, from preschoolers to older adults, from the separated and the lonely to those who are addicted and in bankruptcy. If you are broken in any way you come to these churches for healing and they try to meet your needs and in the process share the "good news of Jesus Christ." There is no doubt that evangelicals do what they do because their interest is in evangelizing the "unsaved" and churching the "unchurched." One church in the study was about to "possess the land"—build a new building—in the fall of 2006, referring to God's promise to Abraham of the "promised land." Their budget for the new building was $8 million, and they were on their way to meeting that number. But the goal for the expansion was to reach out to the "60,000 unchurched in the 30-minute radius of their church." Their motto was "Connect All to Christ." Local mission to these evangelical churches is the ambitious vision of Christianizing the PNW. They do not use that early twentieth-century term *Christianizing*, but the rhetoric and strategy of these churches is about that goal. In this sense there is a consistency between their goals and their global outreach; anyone who is not in Christ is and should become a target of evangelism. This comes out most potently in their international evangelical ministries.

2. Global Missions

The analysis of global missions presents a dilemma for the broader comparative analysis of the liberal and evangelical churches in this study. In each of the thirty-four churches in the study I attempted to gain access to interviews with international missionaries. I was successful in nineteen out of the twenty-four evangelical congregations and in two of the ten liberal churches. The simple fact was that the liberal churches either only supported a denominational missionary program in tangential ways—that is, without any real connection—or they did not sponsor missionaries from their churches. In the two liberal churches, all three missionaries were retired: one had been an active short-term missionary during her working life (making multiple month-long visits abroad), while the other two were a couple who had done long-term missionary work in Bolivia, lasting more than four years. Thus, I begin my analysis with the findings from the limited liberal data, and then focus on the results from the interviews with evangelical international missionaries. The disproportionate number of evangelical missionaries is predictable in part because the moral worldview of liberals is cautious about sharing its symbolic system with others. The task of mission for liberals is not to pass on the faith, but to work for justice and peace, supporting the rights of others to do and *believe what they want*. The evangelical missionaries in this study do not deny the importance of peace and justice and the support of human rights but they have no doubt that passing on their belief is their chief motivation and the core warrant for their existence as missionaries.

The dominance of evangelicals in global missions and the decline of liberal and mainline Protestant missionary presence are a reflection of the twentieth century. In the early twentieth century most American Protestant mainline denominations had thriving global mission programs. My earlier study on a large liberal Protestant congregation in Chicago, Fourth Presbyterian Church, showed a puissant global evangelical outreach program in the 1910s supported by congregational annual giving of more than a half million dollars directly for world evangelism. By the 1960s and 1970s, Fourth Presbyterian Church no longer sponsored any international missionaries, except through their general giving to the wider denomination (Wellman 1999b). This precipitous decline in resources and energy toward global evangelical outreach commenced following the First World War. In the 1920s, moderate to liberal mainline Protestant churches began to move away from global evangelical outreach. The reasons for this are multiple and complex,[2] but by the mid-twentieth century, Protestant denominations had substantially cut back their missionary programs. Evangelical denominations and nondenominational organizations and churches now dominate the field. Over the last generation, approximately 90 percent of missionaries came from American evangelical churches (Baptist and other traditional evangelical denominations, as well as nondenominational and independent churches). Today, long-term American missionaries (those serving more than two years abroad) number around 120,000; a quarter of this number is sent to Africa, Latin America, and Europe, respectively. Short-term missionaries, those serving anywhere from two weeks up to two years, are more difficult to count, but they are estimated at 350,000.[3] This same evangelical dominance is reflected in this study. The average number of long-term missionaries supported by the evangelical churches in the study was twelve; these churches supported fifty-eight short-term missionaries each year as well. The latter group included youth groups and short-term adult missionaries who went on one- to three-week trips both in the states (such as Mississippi and other troubled spots hard hit by natural disasters) and abroad to Latin America, Africa, Asia, and Europe.

The liberal churches in the study supported short-term work trips to the Gulf Coast to rebuild following the Katrina disaster; one church actively supported its denominational missionaries who were working on issues of "justice and peace" in the Middle East; and another church was significantly involved in the Heifer Project (supplying people abroad with animals for reproduction and food). Liberal churches were also involved in microlending activities to support Latin American farmers hit by bankruptcy due to transnational corporations as well as sponsoring rallies for human rights in Darfur. Again, the liberal moral worldview was mirrored in their international concerns: a stress on human rights; the relief of immediate hunger, health, and environmental dangers; the responsibility to preserve a healthy global ecology; the concern for

indigenous small businesses that were threatened by multinational corporations; and finally the strong support of education, for women in particular,
including family planning and learning new skills. Indeed, the number one
concern of the liberal missionary couple was to educate the Bolivian Indians to
whom they were assigned. This was no doubt difficult and important work in
part because the Bolivian government, before 1952, did not allow indigenous
peoples to be educated. For these missionaries, it was about empowering the
Indians with education, something that these liberal missionaries did with great
passion. But even in this case, as they said, once the Indians were educated,
"we helped them to take over and now there's not many missionaries left
anymore, which is good." For these missionaries, the passing on of the Christian symbolic system was not the point. They continue:

> We attended the local church there. My husband was a Sunday school
> teacher and so forth, but I think evangelical Christians would say
> we were not really missionaries because we were not saving souls for
> Christ. But at the same time we thought we were improving the
> people's lives. We were doing it for the church. We knew that we
> would have gotten far better income in the States. But even here at
> our shelter, we do not say to the people "You have to come to wor-
> ship service. We'll only feed you if you come first to this worship
> service." I'm opposed to that. I would like to give, I would like to see
> them giving and thinking, maybe this is what they would want to
> do. And many have joined the church.

This missionary couple took great care to carve out an identity separate
from evangelical Christians. They were passionate that they were not "fundamentalists," and that they did not serve the "Indian peoples to save their
souls." Nevertheless, they were also very clear about what they believed theologically and what they thought this meant in the world: "I think Jesus is the
only way, really. But when I say the only way, I don't mean you're damned if
you're another faith. It's just that his way makes a lot of sense." For this couple,
the nature of Jesus' way in the world was a passionate commitment to the poor
and the marginalized, but, different from other liberals in the study, this conviction was based almost entirely on their reading of scripture and what Jesus
would have expected:

> Protecting your neighbors, protecting the earth, loving your neigh-
> bor, feeding the poor, taking care of the widow and the orphan,
> visiting in prison—that's something we haven't done, visit in prison,
> we've never been a part of a prison visitation program. Jesus made

it very obvious, and I think he also made it obvious that we need
to rebel, we need to speak up and rebel when we see it going wrong.
In this country if you rebel, your closest friends and my brother
might say, you're nonpatriotic, you don't love your country.

Among the liberal interviewees this couple was the most distraught about
the Bush administration, haranguing the administration in the interview, arguing that its record of caring for the poor and making war could not be farther
from the "way of Jesus." For them, "conservative Christianity is stealing the
faith" supporting big business, going to war, "torturing innocent people."
The liberal missionary couple in particular was adamant in their disdain for
the Bush administration and "conservative Christians" who supported the administration. They were deeply involved in political protest. The husband had
gone to protest the School of the Americas in Georgia (renamed in 2001, the
Western Hemisphere Institute for Security Cooperation); this military base
trains Latin American army officers. He told about how he had been arrested in
one of his trips to the camp and that he was told that if he ever came back
again, "I would be put in jail. I hold the bail order at home as a souvenir." They
reported how they had seen the "dictators" in Latin America up close and the
"terror" that they had caused to the indigenous peoples and how the United
States had supported this oppression. The husband had also been involved in
labor organizing and he lamented the "decline of the labor union movement in
America." All of these activities were for them a response to their faith in Jesus
Christ that called them to educate indigenous peoples, to support human
rights, to protest against what they felt was an "unjust" government, and to
speak against a "corrupt" president. These former lay liberal missionaries were
some of the most theologically articulate liberals in the study and some of the
most politically radical as well. Many of their conclusions would have been
supported by other liberals, but few of the other liberal respondents would have
said that "Jesus is the only way," and fewer still would have been as arch in
their critique of the U.S. government.

    In arresting ways this liberal missionary couple was similar to evangelical
missionaries. That is, their level of belief and commitment to their faith was
intense and high; their willingness to take action because of their faith was also
clear and unwavering; they tended to be more aware of the global issues than
other laypeople in the study; they were willing to critique governments (their
own in this case) that did not live up to the standards of the Gospel; and they
had opinions about politics that were informed and precise. This same combination of characteristics can be seen in the evangelical international missionaries in the study: intensity about faith; a willingness to take actions that

were risky; and a critical eye for political bodies and sometimes others in the faith. The conclusions that evangelical missionaries came to were quite different, but the passions were high as well. Liberal and evangelical missionaries embody the most intense notions of each of the liberal and evangelical moral worldviews.

Another retired liberal short-term missionary was quite passionate on a number of issues as well. She was a critical leader in the move to establish her church as a "More Light" congregation, encouraging the ordination of homosexuals and supporting the blessing of Holy Unions. She was committed to the Jesus Seminar and had "read Marcus Borg." Her theology reflected the complexity and ambiguity of the liberal worldview, but also a radical commitment to compassion and justice in the world. She read and listened to Jim Wallis, the editor of *Sojourners Magazine,* an evangelical author and speaker for social action. I found only two people among the evangelical respondents who mentioned Jim Wallis in the study; a dozen or so liberal laypeople mentioned Wallis, and nearly half of liberal clergy had read him; and two liberal churches in the study had had Wallis come speak at their churches. Wallis's relatively conservative theology did not appeal to liberals, but liberals resonated with his antiwar and antipoverty campaigns. This liberal short-term missionary also was deeply committed to socially responsible investing. She had read David Korten's *When Corporations Rule the World* (1995), which documented the exploitation of the poor by multinational firms. Nonetheless, she found few within her own local church willing to take action on this issue. Finally, she had developed an annual program of exchange with her denominational church in Cuba. For her, this was an eye-opening experience:

The hospitality wherever we went was the very best that they could provide. The spirit in those people was what affected us the most. They have so much joy, singing, dancing, and music making and you just wonder "Where does this come from?" Their poverty is different than poverty in the rest of the world. They're all poor, but they all eat and they all have shelter and medical treatment. So there's a difference. What we learned, or what I learned anyway, was that this joy that they're able to express through their creativity has to do with relationships. They care for one another. They don't have that value of independence in our country that causes us to become so estranged from one another. So that's about it. They have needs and we have tried to help them. We met the people and became so bonded to them that the same group of people with one or two new people went again the next year. And it was just like going home and visiting our nearest and dearest relatives. It was wonderful. The second year we visited a church that we were considering to be sisters in partnership with. We had a wonderful time visiting them and getting acquainted with them. But they have limited communications. They don't have any computers; they don't have any way to communicate with us. So we hadn't heard from them, but we did hear that their pastor had a brain tumor and is apparently close to death now. So that's very sad. So we weren't able to go this year because we didn't have a license and next year we expect to be able to go again. And I may not be going.

For this liberal short-term missionary, the Cuba trip was a moment not to evangelize but to learn from her fellow Christians and to be in fellowship with them. At the same time, in that same church, no other liberal laypeople mentioned the program or seemed interested in it. It was not a critical element for the church or for the senior pastor. Nonetheless, the mission activity fit with the liberal moral worldview because it was not about sharing the faith, but about being a "presence" with others on the margins; learning from them and being in service to them. However, even as I heard profound stories of service in global mission from liberals, there was only a handful who shared this passion in these churches.

The data for the evangelical missionaries came from twenty-seven missionaries (including seven husband and wife teams) representing a total of twenty interviews. The twenty-seven missionaries represent nineteen of the twenty-four evangelical churches in the study. Most of the interviews were face to face, six were conducted by phone, and two were accomplished solely over e-mail. The missionaries who participated only by e-mail responded to a general questionnaire followed by further clarifying questions. They were asked about their professional and religious background; their reasons for missionary activity; a summary of their missionary experiences; their perspectives on American evangelicalism; their views on American politics and the war in Iraq; and their thoughts on the interaction of church, American culture, and politics.

I originally assumed that the initial effect of being abroad for evangelical missionaries would be a critique of American foreign policy, influenced by alternative perspectives they encountered overseas among other international missionaries and in response to the native populations in the nations they encountered.[4] What I found was quite the opposite. The missionaries in the study, with few exceptions, found their conservative cultural and political moral worldviews reinforced. Nonetheless, international missionaries were distinct from the stateside evangelicals in their potent critique of American popular culture and its impact on evangelical churches in the PNW. Even here, however, their critique centered on Christian character as opposed to political systems; once again, a perspective that is consistent with the evangelical moral worldview. I was struck in the research on international evangelical missionaries by both the portable nature of the evangelical worldview and its durability no matter the context (Wellman and Keyes 2007).

In order to identify and separate out the evangelical moral worldview as *the* reason for evangelical perspective, I analyzed each missionary's background carefully for his or her demographic origin, social class, denominational affiliations, education, length of stay internationally, contact with saved or unsaved peoples, as well as contact with missionaries abroad. Descriptive statistics for the missionaries are found in table 10.1 below.

All of the evangelical missionaries in the study, except for one, were supported by organizations, denominations, and churches related to and affiliated with the evangelical churches in the study. Five of the missionaries were sponsored by one denomination (5/27). Many were involved in interdenominational organizations (10/27), such as Food for the Hungry International or the Wycliffe Bible Translators. Many operated independently of any organization whatsoever (12/27). All of the missionaries except one were American citizens who had served or are currently serving abroad. The other missionary was born in Africa, spent most of his life in the United States, and now leads mission and humanitarian teams to Africa. The missionaries served multiple functions abroad, including church planting, humanitarian aid, and other auxiliary roles within the missionary community (e.g., these included teachers at schools for missionaries' children, and an engineer who spent his life building facilities for missionaries, including landing strips, power plants, hospitals, schools, etc.). Two of the missionaries had participated only in short-term missions (less than a year). The rest served long-term missions to various destinations around the globe. The median time spent abroad by the sample was six years. Five participants had served for twenty or more years. Of those who served long-term missions, six had served in Europe, eight in Africa, three in Asia, seven in South America, five in the Pacific Islands, and two in Jamaica. Most of these missionaries had served long-term missions in multiple locations and sometimes on multiple continents.

The missionaries were relatively well educated, reflecting the PNW in general. More than half of the respondents had a BA degree or higher, with six holding an advanced degree (MA/PhD). Seven had less than a BA, though all of them had at least attended some college or Bible training certificate program. Missionaries were classified by class affiliation according to their current or

TABLE 10.1. Descriptive Statistics for Missionaries

	%	(n)		%	(n)
Sex			*State*		
Male	51.90	(14)	OR	40.70	(11)
Female	48.10	(13)	WA	59.30	(16)
Class			*Contact with International Missionaries*		
Working	14.80	(4)	No/little	36.00	(9)
Pastoral Only	25.90	(7)	Yes	64.00	(16)
Professional	59.30	(16)			
Sociopolitical Views			*Primary Contact with Locals*		
Unchallenged	7.40	(2)	Nonbelievers	16.70	(4)
Changed	18.50	(5)	Believers	45.80	(11)
Strengthened	74.10	(20)	Both	37.50	(9)
Education			*Region of Origin*		
Below BA	28.00	(7)	Urban	44.00	(11)
Seminary Degree	20.00	(5)	Suburban	36.00	(9)
Secular BA/BS	28.00	(7)	Rural	20.00	(5)
Advanced	24.00	(6)			
Years Abroad					
0–4	40.70	(11)			
5–10	29.60	(8)			
11–19	11.10	(3)			
20+	18.50	(5)			

N = 27

Note: Percentages under or over 100% are due to rounding errors. Ns that do not total 27 are due to missing cases. Variable definitions for choice variables: Region of origin = region where IMs' home church was located; Contact with IMs = whether IMs had contact with other IMs during their missions; Primary Contact with Locals = whether IMs had contact primarily with nonbelievers, believers, or both.

recent occupations. All of the missionaries had worked or were working in a pastoral capacity as missionaries. The majority of the missionaries (16/27) also had professional backgrounds as teachers, engineers, corporate consultants, or social workers. Only four of the twenty-seven missionaries came from working-class backgrounds in construction or the military.

There was a time when conservative Christianity was popularly identified with working-class affiliations and lower levels of education. This is perhaps a product of the early fundamentalist retreat from the world. However, the evangelical missionaries in this study underscore the fact that evangelical identities are no longer incompatible with higher socioeconomic norms, habits, and education. In other words, evangelical churches embody many of the same markers of middle- and upper-middle-class identity that evangelicals might have sought in mainline Protestant congregations in the past. Moreover, this underscores the fact these missionaries had choices in their professional lives; to be a missionary was a matter of choice not necessity. These were people who could have done other things, made more money, and accumulated greater prestige, certainly in the eyes of the secular and libertarian PNW.

I divided the missionaries into three groups according to how their experiences abroad affected their sociopolitical views. The first group included five missionaries who changed their sociopolitical views in response to their experiences abroad. These were the exceptions among missionaries; they were by far the most critical of American foreign policy—unusual relative to the other missionaries in the study as well as in comparison with stateside evangelicals in the study. The second group included twenty missionaries whose beliefs were strengthened or reinforced in response to the challenge of being abroad, and in many ways reflected the views of the stateside evangelicals in the PNW. The remaining two respondents served only short-term missions and their views were both unchallenged and unaffected.

The first group consisted of five missionaries who went abroad and relativized their cultural assumptions in response to a different host culture. One example was a missionary couple who served in South America. Both mentioned coming from conservative political backgrounds, and both attended the Moody Bible Institute—a mainstay of the early northern fundamentalist movement (Carpenter 1997). Yet both reported a striking change in their values. The husband characterized his experience in this way:

> Anybody [in South America] from the president on down to the trash collectors, they have an opinion about everything and they want to be heard. And it's reality. Everything they have to say is valid. So I guess, coming to the point of how am I changed, is that I've learned to respect other opinions and I've learned to expect other points of view. Because I grew up very black and white and I grew up very dogmatic and judgmental . . . I need to calm down and make my gray area a little bigger, where I can respect more people.

This missionary's experience abroad not only changed his political persuasions but even called into question the moral black and white binaries that often characterize the evangelical moral worldview that I have covered in this study. Of all the missionaries, he was the most critical of American foreign policy:

It seems so depressing that the United States gets involved in other countries for our own good. It's not for democracy. For instance, with Iraq, it's not for democracy. It's for oil. There've been other dictators that we never messed with, we never touched. And why is that? Because they weren't a threat to the United States and we could always get what we wanted from them. . . . I think we exploit and it's just too easy to do. We exploit for our own good.

This missionary was again unusual not only for the missionaries in this study but compared to stateside evangelicals in the PNW. As I show in the chapter on politics, few stateside evangelicals made this critique. Another missionary who worked with Muslims in East Asia recounted a similar experience of being challenged and changing his opinions:

There were people from Europe that were believers doing mission work, people from Scandinavia, from Germany, from England, Australia, so all over the place. So one thing that I did do is I started saying, "Wow, people come to the Bible from their own political view, from things that are getting fed from their culture." So that really caused me to say, "What cultural baggage do I take in when I interpret the scripture, when I look at the Bible?" And I saw a number of things.

This missionary began to recognize that while the Scriptures are still inerrant, his interpretation of them was distorted by "cultural baggage" that needed reappraisal. As he was confronted by international Christians with different perspectives, he reevaluated his views on the death penalty, spanking children, and the war in Iraq. Although he did not make explicit declarations about any of these issues, he expressed much more ambivalence than was characteristic of the stateside evangelicals and particularly other members of his home church. This same missionary also expressed discomfort listening to conservative talk radio and even some of the sermons at his sponsoring church that were quite conservative culturally and politically. Nonetheless, even in instances such as this where contact with diverse perspectives changed the missionaries' views, it never changed their core theological or moral worldviews. Rather, it honed or deepened them toward what they felt was the "true" meaning of the faith.

Another evangelical missionary representative of this group served in Jamaica, the United Kingdom, and Africa. In response to this service he too showed the beginnings of critical thought about the cultural and political consequences of what it meant for him to be an evangelical:

Because we're evangelical Christians we're kind of expected to be Republicans and to just say whatever the Republican agenda is, that's the Christian agenda. But because we lived in Jamaica when it was coming out of a strong Socialist, it's still Socialist, but in the 70s had a very strong Communist influence, and because we've lived in the UK, which is a strongly socially oriented economy and government, I guess I'm just not as Republican as I ought to be. I tend to see both sides of it.

This missionary was skeptical of the conservative agenda in the United States, but on the other hand, he said that seeing "a very high percentage of third-generation welfare-dependents" in the United Kingdom did not enamor him with liberal fiscal positions either. He expressed some ambivalence about the war in Iraq, but did not criticize or oppose it. Although some of these missionaries were critical of the Bush administration, *none* went so far as to oppose it. None mentioned voting against Bush or made political defections to the Democratic Party. The few missionaries who did come out against the war in Iraq did *not* waver on their core moral worldview or the values identified with it such as opposition to abortion and gay marriage. Again, the core allegiance to Jesus Christ, the inerrancy of the Bible, and the moral values of the tradition were nonnegotiable. Political issues were somewhat more negotiable, but most often reflected the elective affinity between conservative Christianity and conservative Republicanism.

The second group, which was by far the largest, said that their experiences abroad strengthened their political persuasions. This happened in one of two ways: They saw things that confirmed their political views, or, in response to alternative political positions, they strengthened and defended their own. One missionary, when asked whether his political views had been changed by his experience abroad said that, "my political views have been hardened to the point where I'm probably a more conservative individual than I would have been, although I was pretty conservative before that." He said that this change was because he had seen the problems of Communism firsthand in Nicaragua, Socialism in Scotland, and corruption in Africa:

When you go to a place like Nicaragua where the Communists
had been in place for ten years and you see a whole nation demor-
alized by the effects of Communism, you realize what that system
does to people. . . . My time that I've spent in Scotland hardened
once again my view of not allowing Socialism to creep into our
governmental system because I've seen what it does over there.

It's pathetic. Everybody's on the dole, so to speak. Getting rid of that is even more important to me now than it was before.

This was a common reaction among the five missionaries who served in former Communist countries. Their beliefs in the American ideals of democracy, liberty, and free markets were strengthened by what they perceived to be the deleterious effects of Communist regimes. In these cases the experience of another culture confirmed rather than weakened their political biases.

The one missionary who identified herself as both a liberal and a Democrat found her experiences made her "more of a Democrat." Even with her political affiliation she strongly opposed abortion and was passionately against gay marriage. Nonetheless, she criticized President Bush for alienating other countries, for being stubborn, and for his environmental policies. Like her conservative counterparts above, she noticed things abroad that only confirmed her opinions. In her case, it persuaded her to a more liberal form of state economic policy. She said, "I was not a big fan of welfare in the States because it got abused," but that she would prefer to see a welfare system abused than to see children "dig through a dump to try to find something to eat. . . . I think going back I'll be more a supporter of government help-type programs such as welfare and things like that."

The cultural and political biases of some missionaries were confirmed *in response* to external criticism. A missionary to South America said that locals had challenged her support of the war in Iraq but that after rethinking her support she concluded that she was right after all.

Their viewpoints of war were different from ours. And most of them really condemned Bush for the war in Iraq. . . . It actually made me more belligerent, more on Bush's side because I felt like so many of my Peruvian friends and acquaintances were bringing me that and talking about how wrong they thought it was. Yet the more I talked with them the more I realized that what they were saying was not founded on the Truth, not even the truth about what actually was going on, so yeah, it changed me to stand farther away on the spectrum from them.

This missionary went on to say, "Mostly they didn't understand the concept of war and when war is just. So I think if they had a more, well, in my opinion, if they had a more biblical understanding of war then they would have maybe developed a different opinion." I noted again that most often when evangelical missionaries were challenged about their theological and ideological perspectives, the opposition, short of producing an actual conversion of that moral worldview, strengthened their moral worldviews, causing them to re-articulate their views more persuasively and coherently in response to the challenge. This is reflected in the standard comments from missionaries that their perspectives were biblical and thus absolute, such as in the above question.

The views in opposition to the war in Iraq mentioned above caused another evangelical missionary to reexamine his views and further strengthen his original moral worldview. He justified the war using two moral arguments: "When stronger parties (Saddam Hussein) encroach on weaker parties (the Iraqi people) it is our ethical responsibility to intervene and protect the weak." He also said his pro-life position against abortion—which he judged as biblical, moral, and absolute—motivated him to support the war because of all the lives that were being lost under Saddam's regime. Thus, in response to challenges he integrated what was originally a political belief with his core values and made it a "moral/biblical" issue.

None of the evangelical missionaries in the study changed their opinions on issues they felt were moral, biblical, and thus absolute. A minority of missionaries became critical of their political biases but *not* to the point that they would actually oppose the Bush administration or its conservative political agenda. The largest group found their political opinions confirmed for various reasons. In light of these findings, the durability and portability of the missionaries' moral worldviews is consistent and confirmed by the analysis. This moral core, echoing Brian Stanley's observations (1990, 173), is perceived as absolute and above culture. The values are held with absolute certainty, often confirmed by and in reaction to opposition.

Indeed, I found that the missionaries who had experienced greater cultural and religious diversity (and thus opposition) at home were more resistant to change in their encounters abroad than those who came from more homogenous backgrounds. The consistent variable that distinguished those missionaries who changed their views while abroad from those who reinforced them was their exposure to diversity and challenge at home. Those who experienced more diversity in America while at work, at school, or in their community showed more resilience while abroad. Table 10.2 shows how these two groups compare relative to their region of origin, class affiliation, and educational background.

Participants who changed their views were drawn exclusively from suburban and rural areas, whereas almost all participants from urban areas found their views strengthened by their experiences abroad. Smith (1998) and Rodney Stark (2000) suggest a connection between the location of participants' home churches and the strength of their commitments to their moral worldviews. The plurality inherent in any metropolitan environment creates tension

TABLE 10.2. International Missionaries: Region, Class, and Education

	%	(n)		%	(n)
Strengthened (N = 20)			*Changed (N = 5)*		
Region of Origin					
Urban	55.60	(10)	Urban	0.00	(0)
Suburban	22.20	(4)	Suburban	80.00	(4)
Rural	22.20	(4)	Rural	20.00	(1)
Class					
Working	20.00	(4)	Working	0.00	(0)
Pastoral Only	20.00	(4)	Pastoral Only	60.00	(3)
Professional	60.00	(12)	Professional	40.00	(2)
Education					
Below BA	33.30	(6)	Below BA	20.00	(1)
Seminary	16.70	(3)	Seminary	20.00	(1)
Secular BA/BS	33.30	(6)	Secular BA/BS	0.00	(0)
Advanced	16.70	(3)	Advanced	60.00	(3)

Note: Percentages under or over 100% and Ns that do not total 20 are due to missing cases. Variable definitions for choice variables: Region of origin = region where IMs' home church was located; Pastoral Only = IMs who had held only pastoral occupations; all other IMs are classified by recent or current secular occupations.

with evangelical worldviews. This was exacerbated by the tension between supporters of gay rights and conservative Christians in both Seattle and Portland. It follows that missionaries from urban areas who experienced more tension and challenges to their values when home were more likely to solidify and strengthen these values, thus making them more impervious to change abroad.

A seeming discrepancy in the general trend could be drawn from the fact that four respondents who affiliated with the working class found their views strengthened. As working-class affiliation and conservative sociopolitical views are associated (Gans 1988; Lipset 1960; Warren 1976; Zuckerman 2005), one would expect these subjects to be more susceptible to change as they likely encountered little tension in the workplace. However, all four of these missionaries came from urban home churches that had directly participated in the evangelical movement against gay marriage by sponsoring the "May Day for Marriage" rally at Safeco Field in Seattle on May 1, 2004. Thus, all had encountered significant conflict and diversity in the context of their urban home churches.

Finally, this same counterintuitive trend is displayed in the educational backgrounds of the missionaries. Advanced degrees were disproportionately

represented among those who changed their views. This may seem to contradict the larger trend that would have predicted that those who exposed themselves to more diversity through advanced education would, like those who
experienced more diversity in the workplace, display more resilience in their
moral worldviews. In the case of college degrees this is precisely the case: All of
those participants who graduated from a secular university found their views
strengthened. However, on a closer look, this is also true of those with advanced degrees. Without exception those who reinforced their views attended
secular schools (University of Texas, Texas A & M University, and Bentley
College). Similarly, *all* of those with advanced degrees who changed their views
attended Christian schools (George Fox University, Biola University, and
Wheaton College Graduate School). Thus, exposure to diversity solidified the
sociopolitical views of missionaries rather than weakened them. Thus, coun-
terintuitively, the moral worldviews of those who stay within the conservative
Christian tradition either in their schooling or in their workplace are more
susceptible to change when confronted by diversity abroad.

Finally, the primary critique that evangelical missionaries make of the
United States is a cultural and spiritual critique of consumerism. The evangelical critique is subjective and personal rather than social and systemic. The
form of critique was consistent with what I found in stateside evangelicals—
the tendency to criticize character traits rather than systems. However, missionaries, while they were critical of the "lifestyle" and "morality" of popular
American culture, took their critique one step further and questioned the
impact of American culture on PNW evangelical churches. Missionaries in the
study focused their concern on the deleterious spiritual effects that consumerist culture had on American evangelical Christians. Indeed, nearly half of
the missionaries brought this up without being prompted and discussed
it at length. One of the missionaries to South America said that although he
enjoyed the United States, its consumerism brought spiritual emptiness:

> It also feels like too much. I mean, you've heard it, too many options,
> too many choices, too many malls, all of those things. And then
> something else that has crossed my mind . . . people have so much
> that it feels like they think that they . . . have everything . . . but at the
> same time they can be terribly spiritually empty and maybe be much
> less aware of it than people in other countries.

This missionary worried that the *material* fullness of American life numbs
Americans to their *spiritual* emptiness. Another missionary who had served in
South America and Africa expressed a similar concern: "We don't have to trust
[God] as much here in America. . . . We are so affluent for the most part with

money.... [But overseas] they learn to trust the Lord to get them through those things and times and families. And we don't pray like they do, we don't trust like they do. *We're so far behind them in spiritual development* (emphasis mine)."

Both these missionaries expressed concern that the affluence and excess of American culture were stunting its spiritual growth. A missionary to South America and Africa expressed the concern that this aspect of American culture threatened families: "It's not that we're antifamily here, but our job situation takes us to Chicago or San Diego, we move around so much, the affluence, the automobile, private homes, pushes everybody away."

Another area of concern was the acquisitiveness of Americans. Almost all the missionaries reported being surprised by how "happy" less affluent people seemed abroad.[5] Many missionaries found not only that they could survive with less than they thought, but that they enjoyed life more that way. One of the missionaries to South America reported: "It's amazing what I can live without and how much happier I am. There's less stuff in my mind—we're less busy in our minds."

Yet another common critique was of how "busy" Americans were. Missionaries explained that Americans were so engaged in work, tasks, and errands that they had no time for things like building relationships with friends, enjoying the weather, entertaining guests, or reading. Two missionaries talked about the importance of learning to "sit around and drink matte"—a drink shared communally in South America. By this they meant that one should take the time to enjoy one's company whereas "sometimes as North Americans we just want to go in and get it done and go on out." They critiqued this "busy" task-oriented aspect of American culture primarily because it detracts from relationships: "Planning everything out and having everything really set is really an error. Because that puts time and schedule and program above people... relationships should be our primary concern, and the intensity of getting the material done is really erroneous." Relationships, as noted earlier, play a central role in evangelical moral worldviews and this is an instance where an evangelical missionary found an alternative value to be more coherent with his moral core and thus adopted it.

Missionaries picked up similar themes in their critiques of American evangelical churches. Many criticized American evangelicals' preoccupation with "superficial" things like programs, facilities, and the "production" of worship services. Almost all of the missionaries said that the things American Christians could learn from international Christians were "simplicity" and the power that suffering and going without had in their lives. One missionary to Fiji said that he was discouraged by the practice of putting rooms with video games, pool tables, and pinball machines for youth in American churches.

"How does that challenge the youth to be heroic?" he asked. As one missionary to Africa admonished, American evangelicals need to find "joy in the midst of suffering, in the midst of poverty." In all these cases they highlighted values that run directly against the culture of American consumerism.

The missionaries' critique of American capitalism was not a structural one. None were concerned with the systematic disadvantages capitalism posed to the poor—differentiating them from the American Protestant social gospel tradition (Evans 2004; Hughes 2003). Rather, it was a critique of the cultural and spiritual side of capitalism: The negative effects capitalism had on the consumer by forcing them to pursue a narrow set of unfulfilling objectives and stunting individual relationships with God. In this way their critique of consumerism was not all that different from what I found in liberal churches. Many liberals in the study "abhorred" popular culture, which they thought too often encouraged materialism and selfishness. Nonetheless, like the evangelicals, few liberals questioned the economic system as such.

The missionary critique of the excess and affluence of American culture is not unique to missionaries. However, the reason that missionaries gravitated to this critique *is* based on their particular moral worldview. I argue in the next chapter that the moral structure through which they understand the world shares an elective affinity with conservative political systems that presuppose that capitalism, democracy, and a limited but militarily strong government are structural "blessings" and "benefits" to society. Thus, evangelicals seek to redeem the American economic, social, and political system by restraining its excesses (materialism, moral relativism, and the welfare system) while supporting its core values of freedom, self-determination, self-discipline, and the defense of economic, political, and religious open markets.

The theology and moral worldview of the missionaries make it unlikely and even unnatural to make structural or institutional critiques of capitalism, democracy, or of a strong military that can deter evil (Wellman 2007; Marsden 2006). On the other hand, the evangelical moral worldview does give evangelicals a vocabulary in which to launch a moral critique of the cultural excesses of consumerism, the moral relativism of popular culture, and what they call the "socialist" tendencies of political liberals. The evangelical development of moral and ethical character within the family and church system can not only act as a prophylactic against the excesses within the larger cultural and economic systems but can redeem these systems. Thus again, moral and spiritual rectitude can restore systems as opposed to systems undermining moral character.[6]

For liberals, the very core of their ideological caution undercuts and even paralyzes their willingness to move out into global mission. Nonetheless, liberals take their stand on the importance of human rights, particularly for women; the alleviation of human need with social service; the support and willingness to learn from others, whether an alternative religion, cultural system or political ideology; and the responsibility for ecological, social, and economic stewardship in the United States and abroad. Evangelicals, on the other hand, support a global mission that, while aware of the tragic consequences of colonization in early mission work, is enormously ambitious in its goal to evangelize the globe. Today's evangelicals seek both to evangelize the world and in process plant churches and pass on the reins of leadership to indigenous Christian leaders. Evangelical missionaries are also deeply concerned with social needs abroad; even as evangelicals witness to their faith many work to assuage suffering. Indeed, there is a powerful and growing partnership of service and evangelism in the many Christian NGOs that now lead the world in taking care of human need (Hertzky 2004).

At the core of the evangelical moral worldview is the relationship to Jesus Christ, repentance for sin, and new life in Christ. Above and beyond all else evangelicals seek to spread this seed and reproduce their evangelical faith—this missionary drive has not only achieved results in the PNW but has made impressive progress particularly in the southern hemisphere. In the twenty-first century the heart of Christianity may soon no longer be centered in Europe and America but in the Pentecostal and charismatic churches of Asia, Latin America, and Africa (Jenkins 2003).[7] This transformation has its roots in America and historically in Europe, but its consequences on culture and politics in particular are hard to predict. I now turn to the chapter on religion and politics—twin sons of the same mother—mimicking, fighting, and partnering with each other in the evangelical and liberal churches of the PNW.

II

Religion and Politics

In this chapter I build on David Martin's argument that "religion and politics are isomorphic" (2005, 47). Just as politics binds the body politic by a combination of consent and coercion, legitimated by law in the modern world, religion binds groups by persuasion, though not uncommonly by force, legitimated by tradition—that is, law, ritual, and belief. The two (religion and politics) are by nature entangled in each other, which means they, by necessity, mirror and react to the other. Thus, my argument for this study is that religion as a subculture develops its own center of power and functions as an identity-forming mechanism, constructing moral worldviews that mobilize individuals and groups with the potential for conflict and peace in relationship to other centers of power. Religion, like politics, shapes group identities and thus the two cannot help moving in relation to each other, sometimes antagonistically and sometimes in tandem. Politics, power, coercion, and religion may be strange bedfellows, but they are structurally linked. The challenge of this chapter is to make lucid the complex interactions between religion and politics between liberals and evangelicals. I begin with a short review of twentieth-century Protestant mainline and evangelical history, showing the changing relationship of religion and politics. I then move to a discussion on how liberals and evangelicals in this study view the issues of abortion, the environment, gay marriage, and the Iraq War. I end with a section on how each group creates, responds, and engages their enemies.

1. A Short Modern History of State and Religion

In my work on Fourth Presbyterian Church in Chicago, I situated that church in the context of the Protestant establishment in the twentieth century. I gave a short history of the decline and the displacement of the Protestant establishment. This establishment reached its apex in the 1920s, but just as it did so it plunged into a series of damaging internal conflicts beginning with the modernist-fundamentalist controversy of the mid-1920s and continuing in the rest of the century with fights over theological orthodoxy (the nature of Jesus Christ and the various models of the atonement), tensions over women's ordination, conflicts over the civil rights movement, and, more recently, debates over the ordination of homosexuals and battles over gay marriage (Wellman 1999a). The remarkable fact is that in the 1910s the Protestant mainline was more or less unified theologically, morally, and socially. In the 1990s it was anything but; the twentieth century saw the fragmentation of the mainline into multiple groups, competing and conflicting with one another.

However, it must be said that Protestant "establishment" was always something of a fiction—that is, a Protestant elite that ruled the church. The American religious culture from at least the nineteenth century became robust precisely through competition and an open market that in intended and unintended ways allowed for multiple groups to compete in the market of religion (Finke and Stark 1992). With Roman Catholic immigration, minority Christian sects, and, at the turn of the nineteenth century, various figures representing the world religions, the Protestant establishment tried to maintain its hegemony theologically, socially, and politically. This was best symbolized in the mid-twentieth century with theopolitical leaders such as Reinhold Niebuhr, Dean Acheson, and John Foster Dulles—early architects of the cold war. They carried their Protestant vision into government and represented what Arthur Schlesinger called the "vital center" of American culture and politics (Schlesinger 1949; Hutchinson 1989). But this Protestant dominance cooled, particularly with the election of the first Roman Catholic president in the 1960s and with the removal of Bible reading and prayer in the public schools in the same period. All the while, shadowing the Protestant establishment were the fundamentalists, who, while defeated in the modernist-fundamentalist debates in the 1920s, did not quit. They created their own religious culture that blossomed and in time partnered with other mid-century evangelicals. These various evangelical tributaries eventually were joined in the 1980s by Pentecostals and other independent and nondenominational churches to create the large conservative Christian culture that I have put under the umbrella of evangelicalism.

The once "defeated" evangelical culture now carries a specific set of cultural traits that is becoming the "voice" of Protestantism in America. This rise of the evangelical subculture is one of the most important *cultural stories* of the twentieth century and confirms how religions as subcultures create their identity in relationship to political centers of power. The case of American evangelicals is illustrative: First, they resisted religious and political powers and more recently they informed and even shaped the American political center. This set of common evangelical cultural characteristics, outlined earlier, is called a "civic gospel" that includes the priority of evangelical conversion as the mechanism of solving social problems; the assertion of the United States as a Christian nation; the irreconcilability of political liberalism and Christianity; the promotion of and advocacy for economic, religious, and political liberty around the world; and the support for the Iraq War that I examine in depth shortly (Kellstedt and Green 2003, 553).

Nonetheless, as I have said before political interests (candidates and political parties) are *not* the primary area of concern for evangelicals or, for that matter, for liberals. Indeed, each group argues at the level of values (rather than policy) when addressing politics; the interest in political advocacy is frequently a secondary concern. And these values represent the moral worldviews that I have examined throughout this study. Liberals seek an administration that is compassionate toward homosexuals, women, and minorities. They ask, "Is the administration evenhanded in tax policies and generous in its social programs? Is the government fair in its foreign policy, considering the interests of Americans as well as other nations?" But again, liberals show enormous caution in trying to implement religious policies into political discourse and polity. Indeed, liberals are *more tentative* and reticent than evangelicals in this regard. This reserve reveals the fundamental political heterogeneity in most liberal congregations. Liberal leaders, whether clergy or laypeople, cannot assume a common political agenda in their congregations, particularly around hot-button issues. Moreover, liberals in the pews are less interested in political issues than evangelical laypeople.

Evangelicals, on the other hand, are not as hesitant about influencing politics, particularly when it comes to what they consider "moral" issues of abortion and gay marriage. In general, the ethos of government should uphold the civic gospel—underlining and illustrating the power of the elective affinity between the evangelical and conservative American political moral worldviews. In other words, what I found in the study was that evangelicals take for granted a specific cultural and political system that they judge, whether consciously or not, to be natural and normative for an evangelical Christian culture.

The American evangelical moral worldview supports a strong social conservatism, promotes a traditional family model, attacks the gay marriage movement, and advocates against abortion. The conservative American political moral worldview promotes a laissez-faire market economy, lower taxes, and the creation of opportunities for entrepreneurs to found new markets, at home and abroad; and a government that assures national security with a strong military, and deters wrongdoers, whether at home or overseas. Finally, it favors the spread of democracy abroad for the sake of its political and economic liberty and the religious markets it opens for evangelical proselytizing (Frank 2004; Sharlet 2005). In terms of this study, the majority of evangelicals strongly supported some or parts of this political agenda; most evangelicals in the study simply took this conservative political agenda for granted.

Indeed, evangelicals in the PNW show a broad cultural and political homogeneity. They tend to be culturally conservative and identify with the Republican Party, even in a Democratic region of the nation (Killen and Silk 2004; Lunch 2003). Of the 298 evangelicals in the study, only 7 claimed to be Democrats, compared to 46 who self-identified as Republicans. Twenty-three percent of evangelicals in the study supported the Iraq War; 5 percent came out against the war; and another 6 percent were ambivalent, matching a similar rate of support for the Iraq War shown by white evangelicals in national surveys during the early stages of the Iraq War.[1] Of the twenty-four senior pastors interviewed, only two expressed ambivalence about the current conservative American political agenda. Both pastors felt that they were a minority in their community and indicated that they did not feel comfortable sharing these views with colleagues or congregants. In general, evangelicals in the PNW are predominantly Republican and conservative in their social and political views.

Voices of dissent did and do exist but they are rare particularly in the early years of the Iraq War—and they run against the grain of the evangelical subculture in the PNW.[2] The Pew Research Center reported in 2007 that approval ratings for President Bush among white evangelicals that were once nearly 90 percent had decreased to 44 percent, a precipitous decline, though not that surprising considering his overall approval of 29 percent.[3] This same decline in support for the Iraq War has occurred for white evangelicals as well. In this sense my findings come from a period when Bush and the Iraq War still enjoyed relatively high approval ratings. And while the decline has been precipitous it is remarkable that approval remains at nearly 50 percent. Changes have occurred but considering the drumbeat of bad news from Iraq, there is a base of strong support. Moreover, the moral worldview of evangelicals, as I will make clear, is not anchored around a political candidate or even a political party, much less a war, but around a central set of moral values and moral projects, addressing personal moral issues that impact political culture but are not determined by the successes and failures of political candidates and parties.

My findings on the political affiliations of evangelicals are disputed. While the most prominent American Christian political organizations, such as the Christian Coalition, are clearly both evangelically Christian and politically conservative, some scholars (Sider-Rose 2000; Wolfe 2003; Smith 2000; Greeley and Hout 2006) have challenged the notion that these special interest groups represent the political views of evangelicals as a whole.[4] However, other scholars note an association between conservative American Christianity and conservative U.S. politics (Bruce 2003; Domke 2004, 2007; Lakoff 1996; Reimer 2003; Wilcox, Debell, and Sigelman 1999; Wilcox 2000). Even as I posit a close relationship between evangelicalism and a conservative social agenda, I do not argue for a necessary correlation between evangelicalism and conservative politics; the global evangelical community does not reflect this connection (Freston 2001). Nonetheless, in this study, the relation between evangelicalism and a conservative social and political ideology was robust.[5]

What explains the elective affinity between evangelical Christianity and conservative politics in the Northwest? The primary link between PNW evangelicals and the conservative political and cultural worldviews is a powerful evangelical moral worldview that has historical and ideological roots in the Anglo American evangelical tradition (Noll 2001; Ward 1992). The nineteenth century featured a homogeneous American evangelical culture that centered on scripture. It held the gospel as the exclusive path to salvation, it sought to evangelize and Christianize the world, and believed that "civilization" and Christianization were necessary partners in the enterprise (Carpenter and Shenk 1990; Copley 1997). The rise of American fundamentalism in the 1910s captured this individualistic emphasis, totalizing scripture as "inerrant" and rejecting social reform as the liberal accommodation of the social gospel (Marsden 1982). Fundamentalism went underground, building a grassroots network, led initially by northerners but blossoming in southern soil. This southernization incorporated a conservative political agenda and began a partnership with the American military that exists today (Dochuk 2005; Loveland 1996).

This evangelical movement, grounded in its distinct civic gospel, is not shy in using the state to resist evil, spread freedom, and advocate American forms of democracy. The evangelical historian George Marsden writes:

> [Evangelicals] as compared to other Americans . . . are more likely to sanction state-sponsored warfare. Perhaps most important, despite

their sharp critiques of some aspects of modernity and their deep
suspicions of many of the pretensions of governments, they often
appear almost wholly uncritical of the immensely powerful modern
ideology of nationalism when it is manifested in their own nation.
So they seem more than willing to endorse raising the United States
to sacred status. (2006, 9)

As Marsden makes clear, evangelicals do not seek a theocracy, although
there is a minority who are political Reconstructionists. In the main, however, American evangelicals are deeply committed to religious liberty, and
are influenced by the Baptist tradition and shaped by the Enlightenment
that emphasized personal autonomy and the separation of church and state
(Smith 2000). Thus, their politics are a complex mélange of moral rectitude,
the advocacy of liberty and freedom, the expansion of economic and religious
markets here and abroad, and a commitment to security and the deterrence
of evil.

The connection between evangelicals and American conservative politics has historical roots that have combined a religious vision with a social,
economic, and political strategy that is perceived as "natural" and "normal"
by the PNW evangelicals and international missionaries that I interviewed.
This moral worldview is neither a superficial ideological instrument, nor a
passing cultural infatuation, but a deeply held moral worldview that is enormously portable and durable, as we have seen, for evangelicals in general and
for international evangelical missionaries in the midst of alien cultures in
particular.

The great transition from a dominant mainline and liberal American
Protestantism to a Protestantism dominated by evangelicals has put a new
stamp on the American Protestant voice. Liberal Protestants are rarely in the
news or on the mainstream media. This is not only a sign of their growing
weakness and influence on the culture but an aspect of the liberal moral
worldview, one that no longer has a robust desire to engage the public square
or to shape the political landscape. Liberals have internalized the postcolonial
critique and now accept and validate their marginalization as appropriate and
even theologically more faithful to the vision of their faith and, of course, their
moral worldview. Moreover, liberal congregations are politically heteroge-
neous. Liberal leaders cannot assume consensus on political or social issues, if
they ever could. They must be cautious and circumspect in their political
pronouncements. In this study there are signs that the younger liberal clergy
are becoming more interested in engaging the public square and sharing their
religion with others, but how this plays out remains to be seen.

2. Perspectives on Issues

a. Abortion

In the clash of moral worldviews, abortion is one of the key issues that drives a wedge between liberals and evangelicals. However, there is less distance between the two groups on abortion and the environment than on either gay marriage or the Iraq War. Nonetheless, evangelicals in the study were explicit and passionately expressive in their stance against abortion. Indeed, the same percentage that supported the Iraq War came out explicitly against abortion: 23 percent. For evangelicals, abortion is symbolic of the culture's moral corruption. Liberals, on the other hand, do not make as much of the issue. Indeed, no liberal spoke against it; in fact, only 6 of the 148 liberals interviewed even mentioned it. In a sense it seems to be a settled issue for liberals, tragic and difficult, but settled.

The only liberals who spoke about abortion were clergy and their perspective was deeply felt. Their opinion on abortion reflected the core of their moral worldview that the decision about abortion is an individual choice—both in terms of a civil right to make one's own choice but also a point of individual agency, given by God. That is, God gives each human the power to make responsible choices, reflecting one's moral duty as being "made in the image of God." Thus, choice on abortion is not a matter of easy tolerance, but a product of hard-fought experience and thoughtful reflection. In one case, a liberal pastor, who had experienced the trials of life for women when abortion was illegal, explained the evolution of her thought:

> When I was in college, there was no legal abortion and I saw friends
> of mine who just had terrible experiences, really terrible experi-
> ences. I don't want that to happen. And it's already happening to poor
> women because they can't get abortions. I feel that life is very im-
> portant. I gave birth to two children and I monitored every minute of
> their life from conception on through, so I have a lot of respect for
> that process. But, I don't feel that we can require anybody to do it. For
> one thing, people who have children when they're not ready to,
> whether they're on drugs, a lot of other things, the children suffer.
> Everybody suffers, but the children suffer the most. That's just wrong
> to me. What I think needs to happen is, keep abortion legal, and
> then keep educating people about how valuable children are and how
> wonderful it is to be able to conceive a child and have a child. So that
> abortions would get rarer and rarer, but they'd still be there.

This pastor's experience, sensitivity, and empathy were exemplary of liberal clergy in the discussion on abortion—and not all that different from the intentions of evangelicals—that is, abortion is a tragic choice that should be avoided. However, for liberals, context is critical. The liberal pastor's analysis looked at the terrible consequences on women when abortion was illegal and the enormous suffering to women if abortion were made illegal once again. And the pastor was particularly sensitive to poor women in the past and those today who suffer doubly because of a lack of resources. In other words, for liberals, morality is not simply of matter of a single choice that an individual makes, but involves a system of choices and effects that can create consequences that end up hurting the very people evangelicals are most concerned about: children. Evangelicals, as we will see, respond by using polemical rhetoric: abortion murders children in the womb. Nonetheless, like liberals, evangelicals argue as well that everything must be done to care for women all along the process and, as the data reflect, evangelicals do reach out to women at risk.

Liberals are *not* cheerleaders for abortion. For them, it is a tragic choice, it should be rare, but it is the mother's decision, and no one should interfere with her right to choose. Once again the great firewall for liberals is individual choice, and responsible and reflective personal decision making. As another liberal pastor argued, the choice itself reflects a core liberal theological principle:

> I have yet to meet a single person who says "I'm a crusader for abortion." I've never met such a person. I have met with countless numbers of people over the twenty-two or twenty-three years that I've been ordained, who have wanted to struggle with the choice they are facing about whether to have an abortion or not. I've never known anyone to make that choice lightly or easily. Are there people who have? I'm sure that's possible, but it's not my experience. So the question has been not one of, Does one support abortion? but Does one support the fact that God, in making us in the image of God, has given us the capacity to make moral and ethical choices in the context of our own faith? There are some people who would say that within certain faith traditions, you shouldn't dance and might hold to that tenant. We would say, If that's where your faith leads you, that's a choice you make. But we would not subscribe to that as a theological position. What we would subscribe to is the freedom to make decisions.

A woman from a lay liberal focus group and a mother of grown daughters exemplified the moral reflection of other liberals in the study: "OK. I would prefer that people not get abortions. When my daughters were young, I couldn't imagine them getting an abortion without telling me. And I guess the way I thought it out was if they would be raped, then they'd get an abortion. If it was a boyfriend that they had been dating a couple of years, I would help them to have the child." Again, the political rhetoric on both sides of the issue tends to hide the moral agony that afflicted both liberals and evangelicals when contemplating the issue of abortion. The reality of moral decision making on abortion for both of these groups is fraught with a sense of peril, principle, and compromise. Sides are taken on the rhetorical level, but on the personal level, the struggle sounded similar.

The liberal ideological foundation that guides moral thinking is the autonomous individual, critically reflective, morally serious, and theologically empowered to make up her or his own mind. In one of the liberal churches in the study, a lay couple was working closely with an orphan care group in an African country. The liberal lay couple had traveled to the country many times caring for orphans, and they wanted their church to support the mission. Indeed, through the agency their family had adopted a young African child. However, when this liberal church found out that this agency was politically active in the abortion debates their pastor said:

> That program is also heatedly anti-abortion and politically inclined and we choose not to give money to that, not because it was anti-abortion, but because we didn't want the political affiliation. And that comes back to my own influence. I think that American civic life, American political life, is so based on hate and it's based on the lines that we draw. And I hate that. So interestingly enough, I don't preach politics very much. I just preach the gospel and let people make their own decisions from there.

I saw this same avoidance of political issues in many of the interviews with liberal clergy, with most choosing not to preach on political issues from the pulpit, and nearly all staying away from supporting political parties or partisan politics. As one liberal pastor said, "I'm neither a Democrat nor a Republican; I follow the third way, the Jesus-way." This mostly means that the individual should be left on his or her own to make up his or her own mind. But more important, the way of Christ is suspicious of all political entanglements. In this sense political power by definition should be resisted and infects one with the need and even the "greed" for dominance. Moreover, by entering the political debate, as liberal clergy and laypeople said repeatedly, one enters an arena of polarization and hateful interactions. As one liberal lay leader said, "Our church fights against this kind polarized thinking—if you're not with us you're against us. We encourage inclusion and recognize and respect differences in beliefs." On the issue of abortion, government should simply stay out of the lives of women, while maintaining abortion as a legal and safe option for women to choose according to their "God-given" conscience.

As I noted above, evangelicals, unlike liberals, mention abortion on a frequent basis. For them, it is a touchstone issue, a litmus test on whether one is "for God or against him." At least on the level of public rhetoric there is little or no equivocation on the issue. This position, not unlike that of the liberals in the study, comes out of a deeply felt passion for others, for children, for those who are vulnerable. One evangelical lay leader described his own conversion from a pro-choice position of the Democrats to his present position:

> I'm registering to vote as a Democrat and also growing up believing
> as a teenager that abortion was a good answer to a bad situation.
> Until I began to grow in my faith and looked at what the Bible said
> and heard and taught, that God created a child in a mother's womb.
> And it radically changed my belief. And so my faith cannot help
> impact what I do, and that's made tremendous difference in our lives.
> That I believe in the sanctity of life from conception and the value of
> the unborn, the value of the unwanted, the disabled, the elderly,
> because life is created by God and that's affected us adopting three
> children and taking one considered hard to place, a mentally retarded
> child that we're still raising, that is twenty-five. But it has radically
> affected our lives and I don't think, if we're reading the Bible, it
> affects everything we do, although we can love and embrace people
> who don't believe like we do, we are changed by that, our beliefs.
> And hopefully they are affecting everything.

Here we note this deep commitment to the evangelical moral worldview, shaped by the absolute message of scripture, convinced that God has created all things, which trumps any one person's feeling, desires, or rights. The profound commitment to life is similar to the liberal concern, but the moral standard is a scriptural mandate to the "sanctity of life" in contrast to the liberal mandate of the individual to make up his or her own mind. I was struck by the commitment of evangelicals on the issue of abortion. If a political candidate holds all the "right" values on issues and yet deviates on abortion, evangelicals conceded that they would vote for the anti-abortion candidate.

Many liberals in the study objected to the whole notion that only the anti-abortion perspective could be called "moral." And on this matter I found the evangelical position occasionally myopic in its ability to recognize that there could be alternative views on the subject of abortion and still work within a moral worldview. But there is little doubt about the depth and consistency with which evangelicals carried the notion that abortion is wrong. In an evangelical church that was more moderate on social issues, critical of capitalism, and the Republican economic agenda, an evangelical new member was critical of evangelicals seeing the issue of abortion as their litmus test. And yet he seemed to be doing the same thing. He argued, "If you look at the Republican tax policy, it's the rich get richer and the poor get poorer. But if you look at Corinthians, it's all about giving everything you have away. I think Christianity, if you look at pure, biblical Christianity in ancient times, it was much more socialist." He then criticized the Republicans for their militarism and for straying from biblical principles on "social, economic, and environmental issues," and yet said, "I voted Republican." This decision had most to do with personal moral issues—abortion and the Republican stance against gay marriage. Once again we see the power of moral values and the evangelical moral worldview trumping economic and political principles.

Evangelicals, at least in their rhetoric, would not leave these issues in the hands of the individual conscience or make them a private matter. Laypeople, when they mentioned abortion, were most often "delighted" and "proud" that their pastor spoke up about these issues and "took a stand on them." At the same time, as I alluded to earlier in the study, a professor from a liberal arts Christian college in the region shared that at the level of everyday experience, evangelical parents made different decisions. When it came to the fact that their daughter was pregnant the evangelical family not infrequently resorted to abortion either to hide the fact that their daughter was having sex or because they did not want their daughter to carry the child to term. In other words, the public moral rhetoric may be consistent and absolute, but in the context of lived experience evangelicals resorted to a form of autonomous moral decision making not unlike what I found in the language of liberals. The struggle over the abortion issue percolates at the grassroots level of evangelical experience, not often recognized though on rare instances it was expressed. One evangelical mother shared her ambivalence:

> People have choices. I believe that people have the right to choose. I'm not the supreme dictator who tells people to do this, don't do this. But at the same time I think at the very core of who I am, believe that people are extremely important and I believe that they have a reason to be here. So I do have a hard time thinking about issues such as abortion because it makes me really sad. There are other alternatives. There are many people that can't have children and would love to give them a loving home if for some reason you weren't able to.

The issue of abortion once again exemplifies the ways liberals and evangelicals negotiate their moral worldviews. Both care deeply about life, children, and the sanctity of human life. For liberals, the responsibility of individual choice is sacrosanct; for evangelicals, the Scriptures speak to the sanctity of life, which does not begin with choice but, to use the cliché, "with conception." Human life is sacred from the fertilization of the egg. To some extent liberals and evangelicals simply begin at a different moment of human development. And while their public rhetoric differs sharply, in lived experience there is a similar struggle to come to terms with the ambiguity of the human experience of reproduction—parents, families, and individuals from each of these traditions made hard choices to have abortions. Both sides see abortion as "tragic" and in some sense a moral failure. Thus, while their public rhetoric differs dramatically, their private actions share both the agony of personal decisions and the necessity of facing that everyday life is far from being morally black and white.

b. Environment

If there is common ground for evangelicals and liberals it is around the issue of the environment, though the agreement is one that is implicit. We need to be good stewards of a beautiful region, given by God. I neither asked directly about the environment nor did the respondents volunteer much information about it. Indeed, there were only a handful of liberals and evangelicals who spoke to the issue. But when it was talked about, it was an area for concern and care and not one for disagreement. Indeed, when it was mentioned by a liberal pastor in Portland, it was suggested as one of the few issues on which "liberal and evangelical churches could get along." Two liberals in the study were quick to denigrate evangelicals and "fundamentalists" for their tendency to disregard, "exploit," and "dominate" nature, but I saw none of this kind of rhetoric among the evangelicals in the study. In fact, on a handful of occasions, evangelicals would lament how they felt that Democrats supported environmental issues, but did not support their core "moral" issues (against gay marriage and abortion) and thus a difficult choice had to made—as one evangelical lay leader lamented:

> I think myself, and maybe other people too, I think we're in a real quandary because we live in one of the most beautiful places in the country. And so I tend to support a lot of the environmental issues, which tend to go towards the Democratic. But in terms of the moral, I think the Republicans do a much more substantial job. So here I'm

faced with many times in the voters box, you get a guy who's willing to build a dam across a beautiful soaring river and tear up
the wilderness, and yet they do not support abortion. It leaves us
with a choice of OK, and I do this a lot, I'll say I go with the moral
issue. And it's tough.

In almost every case when evangelicals had to make a decision between a
Democrat, who was more environmentally friendly, and a Republican, who
was less so, but "right" on gay marriage and abortion, they said they voted
Republican. That the environment is not a "moral" issue strikes many liberals
as astonishing to say the least, but it goes to the moral worldview of evangelicals. For evangelicals, the focus of attention is the drama of the human soul.
The salvation of the individual must take paramount priority over all other
concerns. Thus, if the environment must be sacrificed for the individual and
his or her moral health, then so be it, though this is not an easy decision. I found
no evangelicals who were eager to foul the earth. Nonetheless, an evangelical
minister makes his priorities known in a pointed and in a somewhat comical
fashion:

> Well, at the core of the message on environmentalism is that God
> created the world and he commissioned us to take care of it, and
> if we're not taking care of it, then we are not honoring God. So we
> must be taking care of the environment. And we haven't done the
> best job in the past. But we are not to worship the environment, and
> we are not to put the environment or things in the environment
> above the needs of humankind. Humankind comes first. We were
> created in the vision of God and there is a hierarchy of needs and
> humans are at the top and plants are at the bottom and animals
> are somewhere in between. And if we need to let some stupid lit-
> tle brown spider go extinct that hurts us anyway, for the sake of
> mankind, we're not going to let the little brown spider take prece-
> dence over mankind. It's just foul thinking. The idea that Americans
> spend more money on dog food than they spend on missions is
> appalling to me. And now they have organic dog food. Yeah. Health
> insurance for your pet. Give me a break.

In general, when environmentalism was mentioned by evangelicals it was
in the context of being good stewards to the beauty that we have been given. In
only one evangelical church was there an active ministry intentionally related
to the environment. This was an evangelical church in an urban context with a
pastor who was at once theologically conservative, but progressive on political

issues—one of only two evangelical pastors who did not support the Iraq War. He was "eco-friendly," sponsoring a "wilderness ministry" out of the church. In the remodel of the church the pastor said that they were intentionally "green and eco-friendly in our construction materials." He supported walking and biking to church and he questioned the "model of unlimited economic expansion as a sustainable way to view the future." But the pastor's relative eco-centeredness was rare among evangelicals, although, again, no evangelical fit the stereotype that some liberals have of evangelicals as "enemies of the earth."

The liberals in the study, somewhat to my surprise, were not all that much more active in ecological ministries. The exceptions were in one urban liberal church in which the children's sermon was an engaging object lesson in wind energy, describing exactly how it worked, and suggesting to the twenty or so children that this kind of energy was the fuel of the future—to protect the land and forestall global warming. This children's sermon coincided with the coming celebration of Earth Day. In another church, to inaugurate the new building, a Native American man who was studying to be ordained in the denomination performed a ceremony from his native tradition that asked for the blessings of the earth and sky on the new building. I witnessed this event and in the middle of what was called the Eagle Ceremony, an eagle flew low over the gathering. It was coincidental to say the least and confirmed for many the blessedness of the new building. The building itself is a magnificent structure, integrating with the landscape and terrain, as well as featuring large windows above the sanctuary, giving the feel that the roof floats, while the light comes through unimpeded. This liberal church is the fastest growing of the churches in the study, and features an architecture that weds the outside and inside sensibilities of the region.

Some have suggested that nature religion is the civil religion of the region (Shibley 2004). There is little doubt that the natural world is a draw for many in the region, and a drawback for churches seeking to increase their numbers. In a sense, nature religion creates its own subculture that is in competition with other subcultures. The natural world of the PNW functions as a challenge for recruitment and evangelism for liberals and evangelicals—outdoor life in the region functions like a kind of aphrodisiac for many northwesterners. As one liberal California transplant said, "Some people I have invited said that they go hiking in the mountains and the trees are their religion and their God. And I lived in Huntington Beach and I didn't hear that there ... Here, one might say, Gortex is a religion." One liberal pastor spoke of his frustrations about the unchurched nature of the people in the region. He too, however, felt the particular pull of the natural beauty of the region: "There is something about the combination of water and mountains that's astounding. You can't live here and not have a sense that you're in the presence of something infinitely greater than anything we can imagine, whatever you choose to name that presence."

The moral worldviews of the liberals and evangelicals move in the direction of recognizing the beauty of creation in general and the region's uniqueness in particular, and both groups express an obligation to be good stewards of the environment. Each of the moral worldviews interprets the natural world as God's creation and argues the need and obligation to be its caretaker. Evangelicals are typically more cautious in this relationship, suggesting that one must not "worship the trees" and are suspicious of what they see as forms of idolatry—though they still tend to recognize the goodness of the earth and the need to care for it. Liberals are similarly eager to be good stewards of earth. Some take this obligation into their liturgies and ministries, supporting Earth Ministries, a Christian nonprofit that supports ecological responsibility, while others have become sensitive enough in their aesthetics to ponder how their buildings can integrate the environment as a part of the experience of worship. Most, however, take the beauty of the region as a given and focus on worship and ministries to the homeless and hungry. To a great extent, there is little tension between liberals and evangelicals over the environment. The common ground for them is the ecological majesty of the region; to love it takes little effort, to damage it is a self-evident mistake. But when it comes to the issue of gay marriage, passions rise and differences flourish.

c. Gay Marriage

The discourse on the issue of homosexuality is dramatically different in these two sets of churches. Nonetheless, for each group the issue creates a powerful dividing line with the other—expressing in a puissant form the underlying moral worldview of liberals and conservatives. For liberals, the issue speaks to the most profound depths of their identity. The voices often come from those who are gay. They refuse to be hidden or denigrated any longer; they demand their civil rights; and they know themselves as gay and lesbian *made in the image God*. For evangelicals, on the other hand, homosexuals do not speak, at least in the interviews for my study; homosexuality is sin; the Bible is clear about this issue; it is no more of a sin than any other sin; and, while the sin of homosexuality must be judged, homosexuals must be loved. Nonetheless, evangelicals feel defensive because they resent the media that paints their positions against homosexuality as "hateful." They are also aggressive on the issue; they argue that sin must be confronted—indeed, they are deeply critical of liberal churches that, by promoting this behavior, "cooperate in sin."

Moreover, evangelicals believe that recent gains for homosexuals in civil rights, particularly around rights for gay couples and the possibility of gay marriage, foretell a moral crisis for the culture, which not only undercuts the traditional family but threatens the evangelical ability to live as conservative Christians in a secular culture. Needless to say, the depths of these differences illumine dramatically diverse worldviews.

For liberals, the discussion over the legitimacy of gay marriage, in par-ticular, and homosexuality generally, is an internal dialogue now played out in front of the nation. One liberal gay church leader narrated his story:

> And when I first really knew that I was a gay man it was very difficult. Because we're all given all these heterosexual assumptions as we're growing up and the message "I'm bad or even evil" is some-thing that you really have to work through. And I think that what we're doing as a culture and a society at large is we are having a public conversation. When I was seventeen years old in the Midwest and realized that I was gay, there wasn't even the word *gay* for me to know, to identify with. There wasn't that word. And so now it's like front page of the newspaper. And what's happening in the public discourse isn't really any different than my personal sort of struggle. And it really was the result of something inside me, my family's love and acceptance, that allowed me to move forward in life and to be a productive and loving and caring person and to believe that I'm leading the life that God has meant for me.

The autobiographies of a number of gay liberal men and women can be summarized as a process of being "closeted" and made to feel "invisible." These stories include more nightmarish tales of emotional and physical terror. The recognition of how wrong this feels and the need to break out of their "secret lives" is paramount. One openly gay minister said, "I was in some fabulous spiritual direction with a very wise old priest, I came to realize that I couldn't share the joy of who God has made me to be and invite other people to know the joy of who God had made them to be unless I was willing to be honest about myself." In almost every case gays and lesbians (and in one case a transgendered individual) were quick to say that this was not "the defining characteristic of my personality." Moreover, gay liberals were also clear that they did not want their congregations being known as "gay churches."

Nonetheless, seven of the ten liberal churches in the study identified as reconciling, open and affirming, or More Light congregations, each having done congregational studies and having voted to designate their congregations as "officially" open and affirming to gay, lesbian, and transgendered people. As was stated before, this attracted some to these congregations and repelled others. Some evangelicals said forthrightly that liberal churches were simply doing this out of political correctness. But the fact is that the liberal churches in most cases paid a price for their positions. In one church, a congregational minister said, tongue in cheek, "It's funny how the biggest givers are the most homophobic." He reported that the Sunday his congregation voted to make the church open and affirming "Twenty thousand pledge dollars walked out the door." At the same time several of the lay liberal leaders and new members commented that they only joined their churches because of the open and affirming designation. And these were more often than not heterosexual individuals and families. In one case a mother simply said she "wanted a church where her children could come to know gay people as fellow members of her community."

Again, these congregations, and the pastors in particular, were not keen to label themselves as "gay churches" or say that this was a political action. As one pastor said when asked about the political ramifications of his support for gay men and women and the fact that he had "blessed" same-sex unions: "I would preach about the gospel and use gay rights as an example within the larger umbrella of God's love for all. I myself have performed, openly and knowingly to the community, marriages for gay couples. I do not see that as a political act. I see it as a religious act." For ministers in these churches, the support of gay and lesbian individuals and couples *comes from and is central to* what the gospel calls them to do. Gay rights is not part of an instrumental attempt to gain credit, but a deeply felt call to live into what they see as the hospitality and inclusivity of the gospel of Jesus Christ. Again, the actions of these ministers come from a deep conviction of their moral worldview, which makes it obvious for them that gay people are created as such because of God's love in Jesus Christ. They must not only be accepted but also honored, nurtured, and celebrated for their unique gifts to the community of faith.

Thus, none of the liberal ministers advocated for gay rights from the pulpit per se, but several, particularly in Oregon, were active against Measure 36—a successful referendum to define marriage as between one man and one woman. This advocacy included public education—speakers came to churches on both sides of the issue, raising awareness about the impact that the measure had on overturning marriage licenses that had been given to several thousand gay couples, including an assistant pastor in one of the churches in the study. The assistant pastor had married his longtime partner in his own church. Liberal clergy and laypeople sought to normalize these partnerships as a part of what it meant to be human—that is, nothing is unusual here, except that two people are coming together in a covenant before their God, willing to commit their lives and treasure to each other, supporting each other through the trials and tribulation of life together.

If nothing else, the mainstreaming of gay and lesbian people had occurred in these liberal congregations. Homosexuals and transgendered people were pastors, lay leaders, ministers to children and youth, trustees, leaders of the music program—and the only difference is that they were no longer closeted, but open and affirming in their full identity, no longer willing to compartmentalize their lives. And in this sense they were very much in line with the liberal moral worldview of living one's life with integrity, between mind and body, belief and behavior. For liberals, as we have seen, Jesus Christ is the fullest incarnation of the integrated and whole life; as one becomes one with oneself, integrity flows and a consciousness of God expands. This means for gay people a full acceptance and celebration of their lives in Christ.

For evangelicals, it is not only another story but another world. It is on this issue where the sectarian and fundamentalist roots of evangelicalism show themselves. For many in the evangelical community, the new rights for same-sex couples are a sign of social disorder and the triumph of sin. As one said, "Seattle is hell, we need to work within this pit before we even focus on the other pits." Another said, "He [Satan] wants us to believe in him and his ways; our society has gone to pot because the devil is taking over too many of them." Another lay leader said, "I think the Democratic Party, the ACLU, the more liberal side tends to, it feels like, tries to hush and silence people whose views are premised on biblical perspectives." One senses a conspiratorial spirit among evangelicals as well as the need to distance from what is seen as "moral chaos."

These evangelical complaints and judgments against liberalism become most potent in relation to gay marriage. There is no equivocation on this issue coming from evangelicals. A homosexual orientation is wrong and sinful, and the Bible is unequivocal about it. If one begins to question the Bible on this point it is a slippery slope and a sign of a lack of faithfulness. As one evangelical minister argued, "You know there isn't any stray passages in the Bible, you've got to believe every one of them. One little piece at a time, you can nick it away. And first it's the gays and then something else."

It is hard to exaggerate the depth of negative feelings about homosexuality coming from evangelicals. As one evangelical pastor put it when speaking directly about the issue of homosexuality, "We cannot expect Christian behavior from people who do not share the beliefs, but we should from those who claim to believe." This potent binary differentiates "Christians" from secularists who do not know any better, and further from "Christians" who should. That is, any who call themselves followers of Christ and equivocate on homosexuality are by definition outside the fold. As this same pastor goes on to explain: "Homosexuality is a distortion of the ideal of creation. God made us male and female. We were created to embrace the 'other' not the 'same.'" This ethical naturalism goes both ways. Liberal Christians argue that they were made this way by nature. Furthermore, the biblical injunctions against homosexuality are far from clear on the issue (Rogers 2005). Of course, while dueling New Testament scholars have argued that the directives against homosexuality are consistent and powerful (Gagnon 2002), there is little consensus on the issue (Wellman 1999a).

A part of this debate is rationalized by evangelicals as a necessary by-product of believing in the absolute truth of the gospel and the Bible itself. The "persecution" of evangelical faith is seen as a natural product of a relativized liberal morality. Some evangelicals see the battle as a form of spiritual warfare; the devil has a hold on some and thus evangelicals are battling "principalities and powers in high places," to quote the Romans passage. In this way, some evangelicals fear that their faith and right to speak out on issues like homosexuality might be taken away. Moreover, they resent that their disagreement with gay marriage is called "hate speech" by some. Indeed, both sides feel harassed by the media. Liberals feel that the debate over homosexuality is a constant reminder that they are second-class citizens; evangelicals feel that they are smeared by the media and muzzled by liberal bias and political correctness.

At another level, evangelicals are quick and consistent in saying that their aim on this issue is love. Indeed, from my analysis of evangelicals this is exactly what the media misses—the directed and intentional ways in which evangelicals reach out to homosexuals. For evangelicals, and this was said over and over again, we condemn the sin but not the sinner. One evangelical pastor argued this point implicitly:

> We want the best for them. And that's the crux. Our heart is love, that we want the best. And a higher truth rather than a comfort level or a lifestyle. So am I uncomfortable around them? I hope not. I hope that my heart is love. It's not like people wear a sign and you know it, but even if you knew, would I be uncomfortable and my heart would be that, no, I would not be uncomfortable. My heart is to love them. Does that mean I approve of their lifestyle? No. But does that mean I have to be in conflict with them, no. It's not my job to try to change their lifestyle; it's my job to lead them to the God who loves them more than any person can. The God who will never disappoint them and never fail them. That's my job. And I can't do that with judgment in my heart toward their lifestyle or their political beliefs or anything like that.

For liberals, this distinction between sin and sinner makes no sense; it undercuts human integrity and destroys human wholeness. For evangelicals, it is the biblical injunction that they must stand for the truth no matter their personal feelings; it is absolute and nonnegotiable. Moreover, to love the sinner and hate the sin is exactly what God does. God is righteous and holy and hates sin; the sinner can only be loved by God when covered in Christ's blood. In technical terms, the righteousness of Christ is imputed to the sinner, not because the sinner deserves it but because of Christ's mercy. In this way, evangelicals know that they too are sinners. The difference, for evangelicals, is that they recognize it and do not believe falsely that they can overcome it; they live in obedience to Christ because of grace. They are righteous in Christ because of the gift of grace; it is not their doing.

For liberals, the distinction between sin and sinner leads to double-mindedness and a lack of integrity. To be alienated from one's deepest desires makes no sense to liberals. God made these desires (in particular, to be gay and lesbian) and called humans to love who they are and who they can become. It is at this point where evangelicals simply can find no common ground with liberals. Humans cannot and should not trump the biblical witness. Where experience and scripture disagree something must give and it is not scripture. Moreover, for many evangelicals there is a sense in which God would not make humans to desire the same sex. At a fundamental level, sin, temptation, and evil have intervened. At this point, only Christ can transform the sinner. God did not make humans this way but God can and does transform the sinner.

Finally, for evangelicals, there is a deep sense that the traditional family is at the heart of what God wants for humans. Thus, evangelicals are not merely against homosexuality but are overwhelmingly for the family—the intact nuclear family. Again, it is tough to exaggerate the power of familism for evangelicals. The judicial attempts to change the definition of marriage create a real sense of anomie for evangelicals—something is wrong at the heart of the social order. Familism is an article of faith for evangelicals, as an evangelical pastor makes clear:

> I was just saying, once the definition was changed it made even
> traditional marriage between a man and a woman become less
> meaningful and people stopped bothering to get married because it
> lost its sense of sacredness or being special. And I think we want
> to preserve that. We think that a marriage is a healthy place to raise
> a family, between a husband and a wife who are committed to
> each other in a covenantal relationship.

The most common liberal comeback is How could gay marriage have any effect on heterosexual marriage? For evangelicals, the pluralism of marriage models undercuts the "plausibility structures" of the evangelical heterosexual family (Berger 1969). It may or may not be rational or empirically demonstrable, but for evangelicals, if homosexual marriage is possible, then anything is possible. A part of the dilemma for evangelicals is that biblically speaking, in reference to Romans 13:1–2 in particular, the social order is divinely ordained and thus must be obeyed: "Let every person be subject to the governing authorities; for there is no authority except from God, and those authorities that exist have been instituted by God. Therefore whoever resists authority resists what God has appointed, and those who resist will incur judgement" (New Revised Standard). Nonetheless, none of the evangelicals that I interviewed could comprehend how gay marriage could be from God, and thus, as have been mentioned several times, evangelicals could imagine that "orthodox Christianity" could at one point be "outlawed" in the United States. Moreover, and this is critical in light of the evangelical focus on the family, in light of multiple models of marriage and the family, how can evangelical parents legitimate a heterosexual marriage and family to the next generation? And this is not merely a hypothetical—public schoolchildren may now be socialized into homosexuality as one option among others for sexual relations between consenting adults further calling into question and undermining the whole structure of how to raise a family and reproduce faith.

Liberals argue that loving families—no matter their form—when they are functioning well are as good as and sometimes better than the heterosexual, intact nuclear family. But evangelicals believe that if alternative forms of marriage are normalized, a core plank of their moral worldview is undercut. For evangelicals, there is a felt sense that the moral cords that tie the culture together have frayed—confirming for many that sin and immorality corrupt the secular culture. Gay marriage is a make or break issue for many evangelical Christians; denominations have split and will split over the issue. World Christianity may experience schism over homosexuality (Jenkins 2003). Neither liberals nor evangelicals see reason for negotiation or compromise. This issue is one of the main pistons of the clash of cultures between these churches—two models of family life and worldviews that construct different norms and behaviors, each based on a powerful moral worldview that is judged sacrosanct and absolute. One might think that war—the cause for so much destruction, pain, and agony—would exercise a greater sense of passion than homosexuality. But in my study, this is not the case. The Iraq War raises emotions and the assertion of moral principles, but it is farther from the core of the moral worldviews of these two groups and thus more negotiable and open to alternative views within these churches.

d. Iraq War

The moral worldview of liberals and evangelicals is not as clear about the issue of war as it is on gay marriage. The liberal worldview of allowing each to make up her or his mind was a powerful reason why many liberal clergy were hesitant and cautious about expressing their views on the war. Moreover, the liberal congregations were far from homogenous on the issue. Liberal churches in this study have significant numbers of Republicans (economic conservatives, moral libertarians, and national security advocates) in their midst. Clergy and lay leaders know that they risk alienating many in their pews—friends *as well as* parents of men and women in the military—if they make claims about the war *for* the church. Evangelicals, on the other hand, were more demonstrative in their support for the war. Their reasons were theologically based and reflect the civic gospel of this community: the righteousness of the cause in Iraq, trust in the commander-in-chief, belief in the duty to sacrifice for the sake of an oppressed nation, potential for mission in a Muslim country, and the need to name evil and deter it at whatever price. But like the liberal churches, there was some tension in these evangelical churches, with a small minority of clergy and laypeople voicing either ambivalence or opposition to the war, for reasons not dissimilar from what I found with liberals. In general, however, the evangelical civic gospel advocates for a strong national defense, the ability and willingness to exercise state-sanctioned violence, along with forms of preemptive war as long as evil can be deterred and overcome. The differences between liberals and evangelicals are real and deep on the issue of war, and the moral worldview of each of these groups dictates distinctive reactions to the Iraq War.

There was only one liberal church that came out officially against the Iraq War. This was an urban church that voted to oppose the war and lent its support to marches in the city against the war. Several church leadership councils had discussions on the issue, led by pastors who deliberated on the just war principles of their traditions. In one case a church board did vote to endorse a stand against Measure 36, the Multnomah County initiative to define marriage as being between a man and woman, but it was unwilling to take a vote on the Iraq War. For this church board, as was the case for most liberal ruling boards in this study, a consensus could not be reached. Moreover, the leadership wanted to leave these decisions up to laypeople. One liberal pastor explained, "I just preach the gospel and let people make their own decisions from there." I heard a number of liberal leaders voice the importance of political neutrality on the issue of war, even though there was little neutrality on the gay marriage issue. The churches' unwillingness to take a stand on the war was, in part, because of their need to defend personal decision making, but also represented a strong belief in the separation of church and state. This belief goes both to a critique of evangelical encroachments on public life of the United States, and a deep sense among liberals that the mixing of religion and political power must be avoided due to the danger of religious establishment and the fear of absolutism based on religious dogmatism.

One sees the compartmentalization of liberals particularly in their reaction to war protest by several liberal pastors. Two clergy made their opposition to the Iraq War known to their churches early on. In one case a liberal clergy went on a five-day fast to protest the preemptive nature of the Iraq conflict. This was not a churchwide movement. A "few joined," he said; most did not. For this clergyman, the opposition was not partisan: "I am neither a Democrat nor a Republican; I believe in Jesus' third way." That is, he was not trying to impact a political party but to advocate for a tradition of Christian nonviolence and pacifism. Needless to say, this found little resonance with his church or with the wider liberal Protestant churches. Moreover, in this pastor's denominational tradition, there is a long tradition of Just War Theory and the need for a strong state and government to discipline and deter evil in order to keep social order. Thus, in part, the ambivalence of many within the liberal Protestant church about the war is that the Protestant tradition, in the main, supports forms of state-sanctioned violence when done for keeping social order. The nonviolent tradition is a minority movement within Protestantism, arising from the Radical Reformation and led by Anabaptists of various types, including the Mennonites, the Amish, as well as other smaller sects.

One liberal clergy came out strongly against the war without the official support of his church. He felt that the war was initiated and prosecuted in ways that compromised Just War Principles: The conflict was not a war of self-defense; noncombatants were and have been killed at alarming rates; it is questionable whether the war was declared in a legitimate fashion; and not all alternatives were used before entering into the violent conflict. This pastor said that few in his church "would be surprised by my position." As he said, "I usually handle these issues by re-creating a conversation I've had with somebody about the issue. If you put it in a story form, I think it's easier for people to listen to on all sides of the issue; I think you kind of maintain a sense of relationship. It says to people, "Even if you disagree with me on this one, we're gong to stay in a relationship." Again, liberals in general wanted to avoid dogmatism on the issue, while acknowledging their principled position on the war. They were clearly trying to be responsible to both sides of the debate, realizing that there was little or no consensus in their congregations on the issue.

The most potent objects of attack for liberals were the evangelicals who in their minds supported and even started the war. Liberals, as I will show in the next section, are not apt to create enemies, but on the issue of the Bush administration in general, and the war in particular, enemy making and blaming reached their height on the issue of war. These criticisms are consistent with the liberal moral worldview. In liberal Protestant theology God is neither a God of judgment nor wrath, and certainly not a God of war. As a liberal lay new member said, "His [Bush's] God is a God of war, my God is a God peace." That is, as I have shown, God in the liberal Protestant tradition is a God who seeks reconciliation, who includes all and is hospitable to the stranger and those left out. Thus, evangelicals are attacked by liberals precisely because of the ways in which God becomes the "head of the spear" in evangelical theology, whether God is deterring evil, judging immorality, or fighting a cosmic war against evil regimes. Liberals find this talk "primitive" at best, as one liberal pastor summed up in a sermon:

> For the fact is that in many Christian churches this morning
> worshipers are being told that this conflict [Iraq War] is part of
> God's plan to save non-Christians from themselves. That, as foretold
> in the Bible, God is waging a cosmic war on evil. And that we—
> Americans—are God's chosen instrument in defeating the powers
> of the Antichrist everywhere. And that Christ cannot come again
> until we do so. And if you think that's crazy, go to Borders after
> worship and see all the books on the supposed end-times.

For liberals, the whole idea of a "cosmic" war between good and evil has little resonance with their belief that God (or Satan for that matter) neither acts in history, nor intervenes in the details of our lives. But not only do liberals reject this evangelical worldview but they also fear that the country is moving in the direction of a "theocracy." In contrast to the "Christian Right" that claims the United States is "God's chosen nation" and was founded on a religio-moral covenant, liberals argue that it was founded in freedom *from* this kind of religion. Several liberal laypeople complained how evangelical theology and its new power "had stolen my country" primarily by undermining democracy in the United States. As another liberal layperson argued, "I think that democracy is definitely under attack in this country. And we're trying to import it overseas is such an ironic thing." The liberal moral worldview strongly supports individual rights, not only politically but religiously. For many liberals, this naturally lends itself to a strong support for keeping the state and church separate.

This separation can manifest itself in forms of privatization that discourage a strong public presence by liberal churches. And this is exactly what the study shows: a relatively quiet liberal church voice on public issues. In contrast to this liberal public quietism is a more robust evangelical public voice in which evangelicals feel the duty and the obligation to engage in the political life of the culture. This is certainly true on the issue of the Iraq War.

The civic gospel of evangelicalism coincides with and nurtures a strong national defense, the responsibility of nations to deter evil at any price, and a sacrificial ethic that permeated many of the comments of evangelicals in this study. As one evangelical pastor said, "In the evangelical world, patriotism is still a high value, sacrificial patriotism." Indeed, while many liberals spoke about the "real reasons" we went to war in Iraq as having to do with "oil and war profiteering," evangelicals in this study were certain and glad that the commander-in-chief was leading them to pay the "ultimate price" for the sake of "liberating an oppressed country from an evil dictator." Whatever liberals think about the mission, many evangelicals were dedicated to the idea that the United States has a "God-given" responsibility to "give itself" for the sake of others in the world. This sacrificial ethic comes out of the evangelical moral worldview with its core theology of a God willing to give his life for others:

> I support the freedom of the people over there. Christ died to set us
> free and in the same way I think he wants to see the freedom of
> his people. It was for freedom that he set us free and I think that our
> nation had a responsibility. There was oppression over there.
> There was a dictator who was mistreating his people and I think the
> United States, as a world power it was our responsibility to go
> over and take care of the situation. I don't know everything that's
> going on over there. There's no way, stuff is getting covered up.
> I know there's people dying over there and I don't push that aside,
> but I know that to have democracy established in the Middle East
> would be a big step in the direction of the freedom of those people.
> And also, just biblical prophecy, stuff like that area, there's going
> to be peace in the Middle East and the steps the United States are
> taking to see that over there is the fulfillment of prophecy. I'm not
> saying it's happening right now, but I think you can see it in the
> future.

This sense of a mission to liberate an oppressed people from a ruler who is said to be "evil" cooperates as well in the "fulfillment of prophecy" giving the mission in Iraq, and in the Middle East generally, a sense of destiny that God is working through world history and has a "telos" toward which all is moving. In this way, evangelicals take this mission quite seriously. In several cases parents said, "It would be selfish of me if I was not willing to send my son to liberate people for the sake of freedom." And it is not as if the evangelicals were unaware of the criticisms of the war. They were. But many rationalized these concerns, stating that whether or not WMDs had been found does not matter: "Everyone thought that they were there all along, even President Clinton." Moreover, for evangelicals, the Iraq War is put in a wider frame of good and evil. The powerful sense that the world can be divided between ultimate good and ultimate evil frames this debate for many and gives a metaphysical sense of drama to the war that brings a profound sense of urgency to it. One evangelical new member explained it this way:

> I have to differ, because I feel that the very basic dividing line is
> between good and evil and it's between what the powers of this earth
> are controlling or who they are trying to control, whether it be the
> Democratic American who calls himself Christian and may not ac-
> tually be or have anything identifying himself to Jesus Christ, other
> than what he says. So you've got forces of good and evil in America
> and Europe and in Islam and that's the very basic driving force be-
> hind these different areas that this pastor talked about and you
> could have, I'm not sure how to put this. That's basically what
> I see. We've got good and evil. You've got the spiritual powers of this
> earth that are trying to dissuade or to veil the message of the gospel.

This sense of drama of good versus evil resonates for many evangelicals. It creates a symbolic divide between good and evil, which mobilizes them to support the commander-in-chief and be willing to encourage their sons and daughters to "sacrifice" for this higher cause. On several occasions, evangelical pastors and laypeople disagreed with some of the war strategies, but were willing to give President Bush the benefit of the doubt because he "seeks a higher authority and is not trying to play God." Indeed, Bush is a man of "prayer, willing to submit to God. At least he has convictions. You know, he stands for what he believes in." The power of certainty and the proclamation about good and evil gives a sense of security for evangelicals that motivates them to accept that while mistakes might have been made, intentions have been good.

Moreover, evangelical theology is also certain that the way of Jesus is not about "pacifism." "Jesus submitted to the will of God the Father and at the time when he came to the earth the first time, it was not time for war. When he comes back the second time, it is." That is, the Second Coming of Christ is pictured not as a time of reconciliation and peace, but one of judgment and vengeance. It is not the image of Jesus the peacemaker, but the image of Jesus in the book of Revelation that evangelicals have in mind in the Second Coming: "Jesus Christ emerges from heaven in full battle array, mounted on a white steed. His eyes are as flaming fire; he wears a blood-stained vestment; and his heavenly soldiers follow him, also riding white horses. This is the warrior-king . . . avenging the world's accumulated injustices" (Boyer 1992, 41). In this sense, evangelicals have some backing from the Bible that while Jesus "prays for enemies" in the Sermon on the Mount, the book of Revelation discloses a Jesus that is full of vengeance and judges good and evil. In this way, war is not the problem, but as an evangelical layperson said, "I believe God uses war to do powerful things so I could say that I'm for the war because I believe God is. God has used war in the past." I found no evangelicals who had a theology of pacifism or nonviolence. For evangelicals in this study, as I have argued more generally about evangelicals nationally, war is normal (Wellman 2007). That is, the "end-times" are not leading the world toward peace but toward a final conflict—humans will be judged in the end by a righteous God, led by Jesus Christ; the saved will go with Jesus to heaven, the unrighteous will be damned forever. Thus, human intervention cannot stop war finally; peace will only come after God's judgment. Nevertheless, there were a handful of evangelicals in this study who took positions against the war.

The positions against the war mirrored some of the opinions held by liberals in the study. Evangelicals said that "we were lied to about WMDs." One complained that the "war had been handled poorly." Another asked, "Why did we go after Hussein when there are so many terrible rulers in the world?" One mentioned that the United States should not be the "policemen for the world." Although, after several fellow evangelicals in the focus group talked about their church's strong support for the troops and the mission, this same evangelical layperson backtracked by saying, "I'm not saying that the president is wrong to have us over in Iraq." In other words, there was a strong sense of pressure in the evangelical community to support President Bush and the Iraq War.

Perhaps the most intriguing evangelical stance against the war came from a pastor who was deft at parsing issues for his parishioners. He voiced his own principled stance against the war because it was a "preemptive attack" and therefore "against Just War Principles." As he said, quoting his own sermon, "I also said, "Oh and by the way, God favors the death penalty." One of the things I try and do, because I do feel like the kingdom of God can end up critiquing both parties, is if I'm going to speak to one issue, I'm going to speak to an issue on the other side as well." In other words, this pastor, while maintaining his own sense of a principled opposition to the war, was quick to reassure his evangelical congregants that some forms of state-sanctioned violence (the death penalty in this case) were supported by God in scripture. It was clear, particularly in urban evangelical congregations, there was division and tension over the Iraq War. Evangelicals, particularly in these urban settings, were willing to listen to other points of view on the war. Unlike gay marriage and abortion, where evangelicals were lockstep on the issue, the Iraq War created differences that had to be addressed.

The moral worldviews of liberals and evangelicals create striking differences on the issue of the Iraq War. For liberals, despite the fact that theologically it is difficult to rationalize support for state-sanctioned violence, the need to allow congregants to make up their own minds trumps any consensus on the issue. In the main, liberal clergy were generally against the Iraq War; a few made this public, most did not, and only one liberal church came out publicly in opposition to the war. The political heterogeneity of liberal congregants made agreement on the issue of the Iraq War difficult. Moreover, the moral worldview that validates personal autonomy and inclusiveness undercuts a strong public stance on most issues, with gay marriage as the notable exception. But liberal reticence tends to mitigate the influence that liberal churches have on the public square. For evangelicals, the civic gospel by definition has a public interest in creating a moral core for American public culture. Their agenda focuses on the traditional heterosexual family; it supports open economic markets, a strong military defense; and advocates for democracy and open economic *and* religious markets abroad. In this way the evangelical moral worldview creates a passionate public defense of a conservative Republican ideology supporting laissez-faire market economy and a national government willing to defend its interests, deter evil for the sake of a higher good, and spread freedom and democracy to oppressed peoples abroad. Finally, as we have seen on the issues of the Iraq War and gay marriage, the moral worldviews of liberals and evangelicals propound distinct visions of who and what is the enemy, and what to do in relation to it; I now turn to the issue of enemy creation and negotiation.

3. Relations to Enemies

My theory of religion suggests that symbolic and social boundaries in religion create individual and group identity in part by how they mark off who is in and who is out. Thus, to examine how each of these groups relates to enemies moves us farther toward understanding the core aspects of their moral worldviews. Each of these groups has enemies, though the enemies differ and are named differently. Therefore, the strategies on how to negotiate with enemies differ as well. For liberals, the enemy is the certainty and absolutism of what they call "fundamentalists." Fundamentalists are despised and in a sense pitied because of their unwillingness to allow for ambiguity and uncertainty in moral decision making. Beyond that, for liberals, enemies are far more opaque and thus more difficult to name—systems of injustice that "killed Jesus," powers that oppress the weak in general, and social mechanisms that are coercive and controlling. Moreover, liberals are reticent about naming their enemies or judging them to begin with. I noticed a self-reflexivity in liberals that made them often refuse to label others and made them occasionally confess that *they* might be the "problem." For evangelicals, there is much less resistance to naming evil, or at least what is immoral. Indeed, there is pride in knowing what is ultimately good and evil. The evil label was given to Saddam Hussein, although even here, many said his actions were evil, not the man himself. This distinction between actions and the person divided many moral judgments, such as those reserved for homosexuals, abortionists, philanderers, adulterers, and the list could go on. Evil is active in the world, not just in actions but in the spirit of evil, embodied in Satan; above all, evil is active in the human heart. This conflict between good and evil divides the world, names who is in the church and who is not, and in the end will divide humankind.

For liberals, the disparagement of "fundamentalists" became a cliché throughout the study: "We are not like them"; "Unlike fundamentalists, we are not literalists"; "We don't leave our brains at the door." These asides were frequent, signaling—without much thought or evidence—that liberals think for themselves, make up their own minds, think in complex ways about scripture, accept scientific thinking and results, and most important, liberals are not morally judgmental. And the easy response is to say, "Well, isn't this exactly what you are doing—being judgmental?" My take is that liberals at the core of their moral worldviews try very hard *not* to make judgments against people—they despise certain ideas but not people. Moreover, unlike evangelicals they do not judge actions as immoral necessarily; their moral judgments are less externally focused. If there is moral accountability it is most often a mechanism that they turn on themselves.

Liberals speak frequently about "not labeling" others and avoiding moral judgments. As various church leaders said, "We don't have an enemy list"; "We avoid naming enemies because we do not talk politics in the church"; "We let people make up their own minds." It is not as if liberals are unaware of those they despise; many spoke of "reluctantly praying for President Bush." Several churches experienced public protests by Fred Phelps, the nationally known hater of homosexuals. Indeed, several liberal churches intentionally began praying for Phelps and his followers. Every liberal church prayed for the American military *and* the Iraqi people during the war. Liberals were intentional about praying for those they knew to be "enemies" of their churches.

Theologically, liberals did not talk about or believe in a personal agent called Satan. The word *evil*, in fact, was nearly never used. The one exception, and this is critical for this study, came when liberals spoke about Jesus and the cross. For liberals, it is the "powers of evil" (political structures of social oppression) that killed Jesus—precisely because they hated his compassion and justice. One liberal pastor described the powers of evil this way:

> As the kind of overwhelming power of evil in this world that are subtle and not so subtle and the resurrection, which is what the early Christians focused mostly on, is about saying that God has the last word. That even those powers of evil, as powerful as they are, don't win in the long run. So resurrection is probably for me a source of hope more than anything else. Hope, amazement.

In this sense, for liberals, evil—embodied in forms of social and political injustice (inequality and prejudice against the socially marginal)—killed Jesus. Thus, the resurrection is not a sign that sin is overcome but that these forms of social injustice will and do not have the last word. And perhaps more important, the cross is not a confirmation of salvation for those who are saved, but actually a symbol of how the system of "in and out" is overcome. One liberal pastor made this point in a sermon:

> On the cross Jesus demonstrates the lengths to which God will go to love us. And on that cross is revealed just how radical the Christian faith really is. The former Dominican, James Alison, says that throughout history, human beings have maintained communal and tribal identity by naming and victimizing those who were not part of the community, the tribe. Israel slew the Canaanites, Rome crucified political subversives, Sunnis slaughter Shias, and liberals assassinate the character of conservatives, and on and on. "I can only be safe if you are not," has been the murderous logic of our race. And much of religion is a kind of ritual endorsement of that logic. Sacrifices have to be offered to keep God happy with us...not with them, but with us who keep the rules, who observe the regulations, who don't step on the cracks. That seems to be what's going on ridiculously in much of the church at the moment...doctrinal purity used as a means for determining who's in and who's out. Well

the cross subverts it all. In Christ there is no more in and out—the categories are meaningless.

This sermon sums up the perspective of many liberals in this study: Christianity is not a religion that creates more barriers but in fact destroys boundaries that exclude and marginalize the vulnerable "other." Moreover, and this goes to the heart of the Christian story for liberals, the cross itself not only upends the system of who is in and who is out, but it transforms the idea of grace as a "scarce resource." Grace, or unconditioned favor, is not doled out only to those who are saved. For liberals in this study, grace is an endless resource, provided ontologically to all, and it is a spigot that is always open. In this way, again as the sermon alludes to, labeling and judging "conservatives" is out of bounds and not a sign of the faith. As another liberal pastor said, "If I find that I have feelings of hatred and loathing, I ask myself What on earth is going on? What is it in myself that is perhaps being reflected from whoever or whatever group of people that makes me feel these reactions?" I found that liberals often took moments of judgment of others to ask about the state of their own moral core. Enemies, in this way, become a resource for moral reflectivity. This is not to say liberals never judged others or were innocent of labeling others; as I have shown they made generalizations about evangelicals frequently. But when asked and when I pushed them on these judgments, liberals turned the questions on themselves and how they could overcome these tendencies. For liberals, not only should forms of social and political oppression be overcome but the motive power of God is an unconditional font of grace that demands ever-expanding circles of hospitality and compassion. Judgment then leads not to exclusion but to the reverse: the demand to include all. Evangelicals pursue forms of moral reflexivity as well, but with a much different trajectory.

Indeed, in certain ways evangelicals practice forms of moral reflexiveness more than liberals. That is, for evangelicals, the moral microscope focuses on controlling their impure impulses, whether toward sexuality, food, and other addictions, or even toward hatred for others. If nothing else evangelicals are quite aware that the battle over evil takes places in the human heart—their human heart—and it is a lifelong struggle. They are quick to say before pronouncing on sin, that they are "sinners themselves." Indeed, as I have shown throughout this study, there is a sense in which evangelicals favor "tough" sermons that judge sin—their sin—and they chafe against pastors who avoid "hard" issues and "offensive" topics. Indeed, for evangelicals, there is pride in their churches over the fact that offense is taken by many when they do confront sin. As several evangelicals mentioned (with a sense of pride), "We have enemies in the community who do not like what we say here." For evangelicals, taking cues from Jesus himself, offense is exactly what Jesus brought on because he did not flinch from naming sin and marking boundaries. As one evangelical recalled from scripture, Jesus himself said that loyalty to God was more important than loyalty to kin, even to his own mother: "The level of offense would have been huge. But what he wasn't doing was diminishing their value; he was elevating that though blood is thicker than water, the spirit is thicker than blood." This was to say, for this evangelical minister, if the gospel does not cause some offense in the community (one's own and in the wider community), then one is not faithful in the preaching of the Bible.

The rationale for this evangelical offense is scripture. Scripture itself, according to evangelicals, demands cultural engagement that calls out sin and separates good and evil. This came out particularly in a conflict at one of the churches in the study. The church became the epicenter of controversy because it had sponsored a speech by General William Boynkin on the Iraq War. Boynkin came to the church dressed in his uniform expressing strong evangelical beliefs and using images from Iraq and Afghanistan to identify visual images of spiritual warfare. A reporter witnessed the event and reported on it creating a national controversy over whether the general, having expressed certain views while wearing his uniform, was representing himself or the U.S. military. The church leadership and laypeople came strongly to the general's defense. They made it clear that in no way had the general condemned Islam in particular or called it an evil religion—one of the accusations made against the general. One evangelical new member in the church came to his defense:

> His message was not to hate the Islamics, but to pray for them. It wasn't a message of condemnation between the two of them, it was a message of spiritual warfare and we have a lot of praying to do to bring these people to the knowledge of Christ and we have sent missionaries over there to do that. So it wasn't in any way a negative sermon.

In this way boundary making is a clear and present part of the evangelical moral worldview. The truth of faith comes from the authority of scripture that calls people of faith to speak this truth, no matter the offense. This kind of "truth speaking" is a part of the potent nature of faith that empowers evangelicals to say "what needs to be said," and to evangelize in places like Iraq, where faith can be planted and seeds can create the "fruits of conversion." Thus, the battle (between good and evil) is not between religions per se, or even between cultures; the "real" battle is a "spiritual one" in the human heart. It is the battle between God and Satan—a conflict first over loyalty to Jesus Christ himself, and secondarily over sinful impulses that must be overcome throughout life.

Evangelicals in the study were aware that many accuse them of being "hateful" toward Islam and, in particular, toward gay people. In one church that was involved in a petition to support Measure 36, which would define marriage between one man and one woman, an evangelical defended her church while explaining why they supported this definition of marriage: "It is not because we hate gays, because that is not the case. God loves them and he loves them as much as he loves us. We're sinners too. But we felt at that point we had a moral obligation because of what we feel scripture says about that, to address that issue. And I think we came at it very kindly, but very direct on it." The evangelical moral worldview prods and provokes evangelicals to take stands on certain issues, which from the perspective of scripture, are moral matters and make the difference between heaven and hell. And this goes to their theological core—God despises sin and cannot abide its sight. And yet God loves the sinner, and sent Christ's son to die for sin. Christ's blood, because of the atoning work of the cross, covers sin, and through what is called "imputed grace" redeems sin and reconciles sinners to God. But self-evidently, for evangelicals, this core action of grace, while typically open to all, is not received by all sinners. Indeed, some sinners remain (unrepentant) in their sin and are thus "separated" from God and must, through church discipline, be encouraged to repent and come back into the faithful fellowship of Christ (the church). In this way, boundary keeping, both in terms of sin (one's metaphysical relationship to God) and in terms of Christian fellowship (the disciplining work of the church) are critical factors in maintaining faithful Christian life in the world. Thus, grace as unconditional favor, is open to all but it is not received by all, and in this way is a scarce resource. The cross does not so much upend social injustice (although this is a consequence of the Second Coming of Christ), the cross, for evangelicals, breaks the power of sin and Satan, and opens heaven to sinners by covering sin with Christ's blood. Whereas the cross for liberals is a symbol that confronts social injustice and human self-righteousness, for evangelicals the cross is a battle for the human soul between God and Satan. God's wins, but some humans remain reluctant to the end, and not all come home to God. Nonetheless, the evangelical call and mission is to proclaim the gospel and save as many as will answer the call of Christ.

In the end then the core enemy for evangelicals is sin, not the sinner. Boundaries, however, are critical for evangelicals, and the division between God and humans is real and powerful, motivating the cross and mobilizing

Christ's followers to get their relationship to God right and to share that good news with others, before it is too late. For liberals, grace is never scarce and God hates only that which divides the human world. The good news for liberals is that in the end there are no boundaries between God and God's creation; Christ is the symbol of this absolute reconciliation. For liberals, the good news is the destruction of social systems that create social oppression. This is the "shalom" that so many liberals mentioned in the study, the peace of the world incarnated such that all are welcome and equality rules the day. For liberals, the ultimate enemy is ignorance of this unconditional favor and the sad aspect of humans creating boundaries of exclusion.

These two worldviews exercise and embody two different visions of the human problem and propose two different solutions to the dilemma; nevertheless, they use the same symbol, Jesus Christ. As one evangelical pastor said: "I don't want to rally a movement around a common enemy; I want to rally the movement around a common love. Do you love Jesus? That's why we're here. We may not agree on much else, but that's our unity." Jesus then is the central focus, but in the case of liberals, Jesus is a focus that offers compassion and hospitality to the world; in the case of evangelicals, Jesus is a source that saves them from the world by creating a new one to come. Thus, we have two worldviews, two moral visions, and two groups with sure convictions of what is ultimately good and true.

PART III

Conclusions and Explanations

12

The Spiritual Capital of Moral Worldviews

1. Preliminary Questions and Answers

I began this study with the proposition to compare vital liberal and evangelical congregations in an open religious market, explaining and understanding their strengths and how they interact and compete with each other. How do two disparate types of Christianity and moral worldviews create and respond to the PNW, to each other, and to the wider American culture and politics? I discovered that the PNW is a perfect petri dish to run this experiment. In an open cultural and religious market, with no dominant religious culture and a profoundly ambiguous political center, how do two forms of Protestant Christianity react, respond, and reproduce socially, morally, and politically? In one sense I began the project with a surprise. In a defiantly unchurched region that is noted for its political liberalism and cultural libertarianism, liberal Protestant congregations should mirror these moral values and social projects and thus thrive in the region. From my research I discovered this is not the case. Liberal churches in this study struggle to survive culturally and must work very hard to reproduce themselves religiously. A second surprise, however, was even more shocking. I found that entrepreneurial evangelicals have carved out a foothold in the region, and are fast becoming the dominant Christian religious subculture in the PNW. Whether this success will continue in the future or plateau is one of the important anticipated findings that will come in the 2010 U.S. census. But what we do know and what this study has shown is that evangelical entrepreneurial congregations can and do thrive. They use the aesthetics of the popular culture, create networks of small groups, nurture entrepreneurial leaders, appeal to young families, offer alternative forms of religiously based activities, and provide a core conservative theology that puts forward religious and moral absolutes that attract and maintain vital subcultures in both suburban and urban settings. At the same time, though with less numerical success, liberal congregations can create vital congregations. They do so by embodying a progressive liberal theology; mixing traditional liturgy and active social justice programs; facilitating adult education and worship experiences that allow for informal communities; and, with effort—shown by several congregations in this study—integrate a worship design that appeals to families and children. Liberals can appeal to younger people if they want to, but it was clear at times with the churches in this study that they did not want to. A countervailing factor to growth for liberals is the focus on individualism within their churches. Paradoxically, this emphasis on autonomy both attracts northwesterners to these churches, but also mitigates strong commitments to these groups. It is a catch-22 that every liberal congregation had to deal with in this study: How does one appeal to liberals who refuse group-think and do so in a way that stimulates their interest *and commitment to* religious institutions? As we saw, some liberal congregations are more successful than others. In particular, Episcopal churches have achieved a mix of allowing liberals to "think what they want" while at the same time offering a liturgical experience that is deeply rooted in a tradition. This balance maintains an aesthetic and ritual coherence but does not inhibit the free range of thought and action. The Episcopal churches center on the liturgy of the Eucharist—nothing could be more traditional or orthodox—and yet the members felt the greatest freedom theologically; all questions were open and opinions heard. Parishioners were rooted in a liturgical center giving tactile and sacramental form to the liminal nature of their questions and doubts. I am not sure that liberals know they want both a form of tradition and the space of free thought, but in practice this combination allowed for the most vital forms of liberal congregational life.

2. The Power of Moral Worldviews

Moral worldviews are powerful instruments of thought and action. I have shown that these two vital forms of Protestant Christianity in the PNW exhibit relatively consistent moral worldviews. That is, each maintains a moral core—I have called this a moral onion—with moral values and projects that remain relatively consistent through the five areas that I examined in this study: identity, ideology, ritual, mission, and politics. For liberals, the core value of personal autonomy in decision making and loyalty to the image of Jesus as the one who includes all and is hospitable toward all radiates through every aspect of their organizational life, including their rituals, mission projects, and political advocacy. For liberals, the power of Jesus Christ is the presence of God in one's life, which obligates one to think for one's self, to take seriously the preferences and interests of others, to reach out to those on the margin of society, and to celebrate the diversity of belief—all under the umbrella of a God who rejoices in variation and difference. For liberals, the harmony in difference is a theme that was consistently upheld, which from the outside— particularly for evangelicals—was a mark of relativism and moral lassitude. But from inside this vision, I witnessed a deep loyalty and conviction about the truth of the contingency of one's own beliefs that while relativizing its application does not undercut the conviction in these truth claims. God is the one who creates diversity, seeks harmony across differences (without subsuming them), and reaches out to those on the margins. This is a profound vision of accepting the "other" without having to make them like "us," though at the same time learning from this "otherness." Practically, it means that all the liberal congregations focused on outreach to homosexuals as equals, and churches integrated them organizationally in every way. It also means that these liberals are tentative about sharing their beliefs with others in mission, both in terms of reproducing belief in young people and in persuading outsiders to the Christian faith. Politically, there is strong advocacy for the rights of gay people—particularly on the issue of gay marriage—and some action on issues of peace, but in the larger picture there is reticence about political advocacy. Liberal congregational experience lacks ideological homogeneity, and respects individual differences and is cautious about mixing religion and politics. Liberals are most socially active in helping the poor and homeless, reaching out to but not drawing in those on the margins of the culture. In the end, liberals do not mobilize themselves by creating "out-groups"; do not seek to be hated by outsiders; and do not want to provoke strong political reactions. If liberals hate, it tends to be ideas and not people. For liberals, salvation is the presence of God leading them into a deeper sense of God's ultimate unity even as this God blesses the diversity of creation—the inherent contradictions are left undone—intentionally. Liberals are at peace with the "undoneness" of metaphysical questions and the multiplicity of ways various peoples and religions answer these questions.

The evangelical moral worldview pivots around a relationship to Jesus Christ. This relationship makes the difference for individual salvation in the world to come but also shapes congregational life in profound ways. All things, whether family life, education, missions work, ritual experience, or the moral life, start with this relationship. The question is always whether one is coming closer to Jesus Christ or is sharing Jesus Christ in words or actions with others. This center vibrates throughout the worldview of evangelicals such that the evangelical subculture shows enormous homogeneity, particularly on what are called "moral issues." Evangelicals throughout this study, whether stateside or abroad, expressed strong opposition to gay marriage and to abortion; of course, particularly in the case of abortion, this does not mean that evangelicals never had abortions. From informants in the evangelical world we know that evangelicals take advantage of the abortion option; they simply do not want to pronounce this as a live moral option for their followers. Hypocrisy in religion, whether for liberals or evangelicals, is not unusual. Nor is it something that evangelicals find earth shattering. For them, the human situation is full of sin, and so they are quite aware of their own moral failures. Sin is the currency of human life in the world; it must be confronted and evangelicals find the moral admonition from their leaders "refreshing" and necessary. Repentance of sin leads to the renewal of one's relationship to Christ—thus, again, Christ as the one who forgives and redeems. Politically, evangelicals in this study were relatively homogenous in their views on the Iraq War, supporting it as a moral cause. It liberated an oppressed people, it called for sacrifice for the sake of political freedom and democracy, and it opened up a Muslim nation for further evangelism. Some evangelicals found the Iraq War to be a mistake, but this was a minority opinion—and even these arguments were based on the evangelical moral worldview of speaking the truth and doing the right thing. For evangelicals, enemy making is biblical and validated by Christ himself; enemies tell one that sin and Satan remain powerful in the world. Moreover, one must be willing to be hated because one confronts sin, and one must hate sin wherever it is found in oneself or in others. Of course, one should not hate the sinner. In this way evangelicals believe that they follow God's path; God cannot stand the sight of sin and yet loves the sinner because the blood of God's Son covers this sin. In the end God will separate the good from the evil, and God will be vindicated in a final victory over sin and Satan. In the evangelical moral worldview, the destiny of each individual is shaped by the decision of his or her heart for Christ. In this sense, as evangelicals like to say, "Christianity is not a religion but a relationship." I would say, yes, it is a religion that has formulated a moral worldview that centers on an intimate affective connection to a personal God, symbolized by Jesus Christ; from this connection flows a coherent life of ritual, mission, and service to this moral vision.

The moral worldviews of these groups make all the difference in shaping the lives of individuals within these two subcultures. But the question that I ask is Why does one worldview seem to be more powerful (at least numerically speaking) than the other? What makes each of these worldviews vital and powerful for those in these groups? What explains the impact of these worldviews on the lives and organization of these two subcultures?

3. Explaining Vitality in Liberal and Evangelical Churches

Moral worldviews not only shape and guide values and actions but they also create organizations and build forms of social and spiritual capital that provide structures of meaning and rewards. Religions offer symbolic and social boundaries that not only answer what is true about reality but create social and subjective resources, meanings, and benefits. Thus, the question in this section focuses on What is it about these moral worldviews that followers find attractive, meaningful, and rewarding? I am not saying that religions are merely functional vehicles to meet human needs. Religions are symbolic systems that provide truth claims and social boundary-making mechanisms that shape social structures, create systems of human meaning, and offer benefits to followers. I argue that these rewards are consequences of religious truth claims; people do not follow moral and religious visions because of rewards but because they believe these visions are true.

Thus, as I have shown, the moral worldviews of liberals and evangelicals are ideologically coherent and theologically rationalized by each group. The worldviews are applied in various areas of these churches: in leadership, mission, social action, and politics. But in this section I ask, What are the rewards (the social and spiritual capital) that arise from these moral worldviews? Social and spiritual capital are real in that individuals and groups derive resources to create meaning and action from these moral worldviews. This capital is subjective to be sure, but real in its social consequences. It can be described in terms of hope (for progress in this world and the presence of God in the world to come); assurance that one's sacrifice is worth it; love, in that one senses affective feelings of being close to God—a common self-report throughout this study—which gives comfort and challenge to both liberals and evangelicals; human togetherness, as in church fellowships that support individuals in need and create networks for work, play, and social interaction; places for self-expression and the sharing of ideas and potential for new learning; and finally, outlets for social action organized for goals and projects that can make a larger impact than mere individual initiatives. All of these forms of capital, however subjective, have significant social consequences and give a sense of reward in the lives of individuals and groups. Part II of this study exemplifies in detail the variations on these themes, how meaning and action are created in individuals and groups via hope, assurance, promise, and reward—creating social, spiritual, and, in some cases, political capital used to renew, mobilize, and support individuals and groups.

These forms of capital (or rewards) are worked out in various ways in the lives and churches of liberals and evangelicals. Sometimes the rewards are obvious, at times oblique, and sometimes the rewards seem nonexistent. For liberals, rewards in terms of status in culture seem relatively nonexistent. As we have seen there is little or no pressure to attend church in the PNW. In fact, one could argue that there might be a negative status correlation for church attendance. Certainly, a part of the reason that liberals say that they do not talk openly about their faith or their church is that many of their peers may often think less of them. One runs the risk of being labeled a "fundamentalist" and thus socially rejected. I heard from liberals a consistent defense against being called a Christian in part because many would assume that they were fundamentalists, meaning for liberals intolerant or ignorant, or both.[1] At the same time, liberals in the study expressed a deep sense of reward in solidarity with other liberal believers. There were less intentional moments of organized fellowship (compared to the small group work in evangelical churches) but nonetheless, many liberals commented about informal networks in their church life that created support and fellow-feeling that they registered as critical for their lives.

Political capital of these liberal churches seemed less salient. Politics and talk about politics was largely out of bounds in liberal circles, while support for gay advocacy was strongly affirmed and the political advocacy for this cause was important. Indeed, gay people in these churches cherished how they were treated and what liberal churches did for them. In part, as a result of this fellowship and solidarity, liberal church people were active in social service. In fact, in liberal churches there were many informal and more formal organizations seeking to help not only the homeless but other groups through various social service causes. The impact and consequences of the networks that are a function of social capital are often overlooked in research. More recently, however, the impact of religious caregivers, whether liberal or conservative, has been quantified and in many ways is breathtaking in its breadth and depth (financially and in direct service) to those in need (Brooks 2006; Cnaan 2002). The social capital created in these churches has enormously positive consequences for those in need.

The most powerful type of reward in liberal churches was produced in the form of spiritual capital. Liberals in this study are men and women of the Enlightenment. That is, they believe in the power of the scientific method and its results. The motto of Kant, "Think for yourselves," is stained in their minds. They abjure most forms of what they would see as "primitive" metaphysical and theological thinking—a personal God who directs human history, or who impacts (for better or worse) the lives of individual people. At the same time, there is within liberals a deep longing for and self-reported experience of God. This God is revealed in the person and work Jesus Christ, though not exclusively so. God becomes active in their lives as a loving, inclusive, and life-transforming presence. Liberals refuse to give up this sense of something "more" in human life that comes when they hear a beautiful piece of music; witness the craggy spires of the Cascades on the horizon; feel the touch of love for someone everyone else despises; recognize the call to create equality for all humans, no matter their gender, ethnicity, or sexual orientation; catch the electricity of knowing that one's moral duty must be done regardless of an afterlife; or sense the gratitude that one is held in the midst of a life that can become a nightmare of contingency, whether in the midst of an illness, a failure (morally, vocationally, or emotionally), or in the face of one's own death. This transcendental "more" in life for liberals is neither quantified nor deconstructed; it is cherished and it gives hope by mobilizing actions toward justice, care for the poor, and celebrations of gratitude in the production of art in painting, poetry, or music. This transcendental experience of what is often called the "sacred" by liberals is spiritual capital, a resource in the form of experience that produces a sense of life's goodness and patience in times of suffering. What one notices here is that for liberals the reward is largely in the journey itself—a cliché, of course; but I never heard a liberal speak about the hope of heaven, or how one might avoid hell. In this sense, liberals seek to be good for its own sake; they make truth claims because they believe in the justice of including all; it is what they are called to do, and it is what they see modeled in Jesus Christ. Explicit rewards are less valued and, in some cases, are devalued. Liberals frequently expressed that one should not do something because of a reward but because it is right. This is a classic stance of the moral virtuoso; there is altruism among liberals that is not expressed, but implied in their criticism of those who do what is right for the sake of a reward. In this way, the liberal religionist practices a moral vision that is self-denying or at least self-forgetful. It is perhaps for this reason their churches are less immediately attractive to many; liberals do not offer many rewards; they proffer few obvious benefits that could be "sold" through marketing. Of course, this is only a problem for those who believe in another type of moral worldview. For liberals, to do what is good, true, and beautiful because of one's own internal compass confirms their worldview. It could be no other way.

The evangelical worldview has its own unique trajectory of rewards—its own forms of social, political, and spiritual capital. There is little doubt that evangelicals are in greater tension with the wider culture of the PNW. To outsiders, evangelicals are fundamentalists; most liberals with whom I spoke simply assumed that conservative Christians of whatever kind were literalists and fundamentalists—both terms of opprobrium. For evangelicals, however, this is a double-edged sword. Some evangelicals refused the term *fundamentalist*, but they often accepted that they would be "despised" for their faith, so on frequent occasions this negative labeling by outsiders became a badge of honor and a way of legitimating their faith, a kind of negative status increase. But the force of social capital comes most powerfully from within evangelical communities—their networks are truly ties that bind them together, as we saw with their small-group ministries. Indeed, evangelical fellowships seek to support one another economically, socially, and spiritually. Evangelicals take seriously their sense that they are the "body of Christ," each part of the body obligated to care for the other; no part is dispensable. This support is geared particularly toward young people in their communities, with enormous resources poured into leadership (and physical infrastructure) to improve children's and youth programs, not only for religious training but for all forms of activities. Evangelicals seek a holistic form of ministry supporting every aspect of the person and every developmental stage of the family. This social capital was also shared with others, as we saw with large social service networks in their communities and extensive short- and long-term mission work overseas. Evangelical leaders constantly reminded their followers of the need to care for the poor, to reach the unreached (the unsaved), and to nurture one another in this work. In a sense, these evangelical groups adopt a relatively seamless garment of reproduction of capital at every level. They encourage entrepreneurs in business to make more money, not so much for their own good but in order to use these resources for the purpose of helping others and sharing the gospel. Evangelicals strongly support turning their families into workshops of evangelism, encouraging family growth for the sake of spreading the gospel. One pastor put it directly, "We believe in out-reproducing the liberals." As we have seen, on this matter they have had some demographic success. Evangelicals reach out to bring people into their fellowships and they turn their fellowships into nurseries for children and for faith. Liberals reach out to serve those on the margins but they are less apt to bring people in—the liberal moral worldview does not make this necessary. Evangelicals literally produce new members at higher rates and reach out to new members with whom they share the faith—a form of social reproduction that counts spiritual capital in new members and new converts.

Political capital for evangelicals is important, though in less explicit ways. Many liberals worry that evangelicals care only about conservative politics, but from this study we know that this is not true. Evangelicals care about conservative politics that have a moral goal: a moral culture that reproduces the kind of families that they feel are desired by God and witnessed to in scripture. Politics is important but secondary; politics is not the answer, but it can nurture and shape a moral culture. Politicians are used by evangelicals for the sake of these moral aims. For evangelicals, politicians are to be used; if they do not come through on moral values they are rejected. I found many evangelicals, pastors in particular, quite willing to discard President Bush if he were to reject their moral agenda. Political capital matters to evangelicals to the extent that they can shape the moral agenda of the culture; in this way political capital is something to be used and not gained for its own sake. Politics is always a means and not an end to peace; peace can only come in the Second Coming of Jesus Christ—the penultimate reality is tension, conflict, and war (spiritual and physical) between the forces of good and evil. Politics is not the point; conversion to Jesus is. Thus, conflict and even war before the Second Coming of Christ is normal (Wellman 2007).

Just as liberals cultivate forms of spiritual capital, evangelicals seek this capital as well. For them, it is less a presence than a person—the person of Jesus Christ with whom they seek a relationship that is intimate, ongoing, and productive for salvation. It is intimate in that evangelicals treat Jesus as a kind of rosary—a relationship that they massage and obsess over. This is a relationship that is the pivot point for their lives; it is what they share with others, and in the most reduced terms is their voucher for their world to come. It is not mentioned frequently, but the "reward" of knowing Jesus is access to heaven. It would be hard to overestimate that a core of the evangelical identity is this promise. It is indeed, as Rodney Stark says, a promise that invites "an extended exchange relationship" (2000). This reward of eternal bliss cannot be verified empirically, but neither can it be disconfirmed. The sacrifice for the faith is the control of human impulses (sexual and otherwise), the willingness to go out in mission, and the renunciation of one's sin. These sacrifices are acceptable to evangelicals at least in part because of the reward that awaits those faithful to Jesus Christ. Moreover, the grace of one's salvation in Jesus Christ is a form of spiritual capital that is unconditional. That is, one can sin and fall short of the moral ideals of the evangelical faith, but there is always a second chance. This second chance comes because of Jesus' death on the cross (and the blood that covers human sin); one can always return to God. It is a form of spiritual capital in escrow, always already paid. For evangelicals, this mercy is a powerful promissory note, a form of insurance that underwrites one's life, and insures that one has eternal bliss with God in heaven.

Some liberals find this kind of unconditional acquittal a form of immorality. Some Protestant liberals believe that righteousness has to be earned, and sin must be punished in a just way by a God of perfect righteousness. Indeed, grace as unconditioned favor was considered immoral for Immanuel Kant (1960). Liberals in this study would not say this, but they would wonder why evangelicals need rewards to be obedient to God. Does not the promise of rewards undercut the nature of morality? Liberals might say so, but evangelicals simply respond that it is the nature of God to love and give benefits to those who obey God's will—the Scriptures make this plain.

Strikingly, there is within liberalism a form of grace that is not unlike the reward of heaven found in evangelical theology. In liberalism there is a belief that in Christ all are reconciled to God, no matter who they are. In this sense nothing is outside of God, not sinners, or other religionists, or anything that exists. Many liberals believe in this kind of cosmic reconciliation, which is a radical form of universalism that transcends judging moral actions. Indeed, one might say, liberalism is more absolute and unconditional than evangelical thought, since, for evangelicals, not all worship the same God and those who do not submit to Jesus Christ pay the ultimate price. Evangelicals from this point of view make heaven a place of separation between the saved and unsaved. This sharp divide in evangelical theology makes the reward of the world to come even more potent as a point of compensation for evangelical self-control, sacrifice, and submission to God's will. Thus, in the end, evangelical theology promises unconditional grace, though only for those who confess Jesus Christ.

The spiritual capital within evangelical theology is thus a scarce resource, limited to Christians and more often than not to the "right" kind of Christians: those evangelicals who call the Bible infallible and Jesus "the *only* God." Liberals, on other hand, proclaim a form of grace that is in fact an infinite resource that never stops flowing. It is a form of spiritual capital that is truly and radically unconditional. I would argue that these differences affect the "value" of these two moral worldviews. It is a truism that a scarce resource is perceived by humans as more valuable—creating a form of compensation that because it is scare is worth competing for and, perhaps, worth dying for. This economy of sacrifice creates forms of competition over these scarce benefits—indeed, engendering tension and conflict depending on the context and situation. Evangelicalism nurtures an ethic of sacrificial theology that rationalizes lose (and even death) as not the end but only the beginning. Thus, dying for

THE SPIRITUAL CAPITAL OF MORAL WORLDVIEWS 281

something bigger than the self makes sense and is rewarded. Giving one's life (in battle in the Iraq War or in mission for the sake of the poor and the "unsaved") is seen as a noble sacrifice, worthy of reward. Sacrifice, then, becomes a vehicle of one's sanctification (Wellman 2007). And for evangelicals, theologically, sacrifice as a way to overcome the distance between God and humans is at the heart of evangelical theology—the cross of Christ and the demand for the death of God's Son for the redemption of sin. Sacrifice then is the means to this end and a critical feature for the core identity of evangelicalism.

Liberalism has no metaphysical structure of sacrifice that would rationalize forms of renunciation. Indeed, it would make much less sense to die for a form of grace that is unconditional and infinite, since access to it is already always available. For liberals, the reward of grace is unlimited and unconditional; sacrifice is not necessary. Metaphysically, for liberals, peace is perennial and one achieves it not through sacrifice but by becoming peaceful and using forms of nonviolence to seek it. Of course, liberals are not all paragons of nonviolence, and not all believe in nonviolence. My point is that there is little in liberal theology that would rationalize or demand sacrifice. Moreover, there is nothing in liberal theology that one must sacrifice for; grace, as I said before, is always already available, and repentance for sin is not necessary. One must simply awaken to the fact that one is fully accepted and loved by God. The beauty of this is God's extravagant generosity. The unintended problem comes relative to the church: Why come to church for this spiritual resource? Why is the church a unique instrument of this spiritual resource? The answer is that the church is not necessary. The resource of grace and acceptance can be found everywhere; it is an infinite resource. But this creates dilemmas organizationally: What is important about the church? How is it an essential resource for this form of spiritual capital? Why should one dedicate one's life to the church? Based on their own moral worldview, liberals have a far more difficult time answering these questions than evangelicals. Of course, for liberals, one does what is good and just because it is good and just; rewards are beside the point. At the same time, the church provides, as I have shown, real connections and networks where liberals thrive and grow. The matter of saying why the church is important and faith in Christ critical remains a real dilemma for liberals, one that must be addressed more clearly in the future if liberals want to reproduce themselves and their message.

Once again these notions of spiritual capital spring from distinctive moral worldviews that create symbolic systems of meaning, social boundaries of action and distinction, and forms of capital (social, political, and spiritual) that produce unique rewards for each of these groups. In this way I have tried to excavate each of these moral worldviews and show how they create vital religious communities. Of course, not all liberals or evangelicals are covered by these data or by my observations. This study gives an in-depth view of how moral worldviews are expressed in meaning, social structure, and systems of rewards in churches in the PNW. It appears that, in general, the moral worldviews of evangelicals create greater numerical success for churches in this study. In part I think that this is true because of the uniqueness of the region. It is, as I said before, an "ungrouped" part of the country. Evangelical theology and organizational structures appeal to people in need of human connection. The PNW is a region that is entrepreneurial and respectful of a market mentality; evangelical leaders in particular resonate with this mentality of growth, expansion, and reward. In these core areas evangelicals excel and reproduce themselves. Liberals, on the other hand, appeal to the individualism of northwesterners, who value the freedom to think for themselves. Liberals, however, are less entrepreneurial, less interested in growth and expansion, and less organizationally dynamic, though they offer a religious ideology that is open and expansive, which northwesterners treasure and mirror. And yet, in this way, liberal religionists may be too much like the region in their free-thinking ways. Nonetheless, as we have seen, liberal churches can be vital in the region, expressing in a specific niche of liberal thought ideas promoting social action, inclusiveness, and spiritual creativity that many find satisfying.

4. The Protestant Future and How My Mind Has Changed

The fervency of evangelicalism was in general something that I did not expect to find until I began this research. After nearly three hundred interviews and experiencing evangelicals in many different contexts, their passion and persistence were breathtaking at times. Even against the odds, in a region where this brand of religion was thought not to work, they were neither cowed nor cautious, but indeed almost giddy with anticipation of what "God would do in the Pacific Northwest." And from my research I saw a bouquet of evangelical churches, large and small, flourishing and ambitious to grow in the future. There are few obvious signs that this will change; I do think that the growth will plateau in the near future, but only time will tell. The libertarian and liberal nature of the region is powerful and enduring; the *nature religion* of the region may not be dominant, but it is not the kind of religion that has much in common with churched evangelical Christianity. Indeed, liberal religionists in this study have much more in common with those who practice nature religion and in this way liberals are more susceptible to this form of relatively unorganized religion than are evangelicals. Nonetheless, evangelicals appeal strongly to young families who need connection and a felt sense of moral guidance, as well as to new émigrés, particularly those from the South and Midwest, who are familiar with this brand of evangelical theology.

What is most interesting, however, in terms of speculation, is to note that with a steady growth of evangelical religion in the region, to what extent will there be conflict between liberal religionists and their nature religion partners, and the growing subculture of evangelicals? More research needs to be done on this topic. Obvious tensions over gay marriage will continue, as rights for gay couples are making some headway in the region. How evangelicals react to this movement will be telling. To some extent evangelicals have acculturated to the region—but can they and will they assimilate to the reality of gay people as equal partners in the civic life of the region? Liberal Christians will find the reality of gay equality a moral victory. However, will evangelicals become more militant in this fight, or adapt by becoming more sectarian—homeschooling their children and building a separate cultural infrastructure as they have in the past? This will be worthy of further research as well.

As I have mentioned throughout this study, American evangelicals have made significant strides, nationally, in gaining a greater share of the Protestant pie. I have wondered whether they might become the next Protestant establishment. From this study I have argued that the Christian nationalism many liberals are afraid of does not have much support in the pews of the evangelical churches that I studied. Evangelicals do not seek political dominance so much as they want a "moral culture" in which to raise their children. Ironically, I heard similar thoughts and feelings from liberals. It is not as if liberals do not support a moral culture. The dream of a moral culture is different for these groups, but is real for both. For evangelicals, a moral culture means one that supports and nurtures heterosexual, intact families; for liberals, it means the support of strong, intimate bonds of love, no matter their formulation in terms of gender. Evangelicals want a culture of life where children are welcomed into the world and not aborted at whim. Although no liberals supported abortion for convenience' sake, most saw it as a tragic choice, but a necessary one that needed to remain legal and available. Evangelicals want to educate their children and young people in a context where their faith is not questioned, or at least not denigrated; liberals expect high educational levels that are open to the full panoply of questions—including the science of evolution—and see no reason to limit the reach of the scientific imagination. Evangelicals want an economy and government that opens markets, keeps the nation secure, and allows for openness to new ideas, including the sharing of the gospel. Liberals also want open markets, though they tend to be more suspicious of the "free-market" mantra and are less eager about a "strong military." Yet liberals too want a strong and secure nation and open communication across cultures, not so much to evangelize but to understand new cultures and serve others in need. In most ways these dreams are not diametrically opposed; they share many convictions and this is the point. Both of these moral worldviews are based on truth claims: evangelicals tend to hold theirs with greater certainty; liberals think their claims are true, though they are more at home with uncertainty, change, and new information. But each makes claims, and this book has sought to make clear what these claims are, how these groups understand and misunderstand each other, how each adapts to the region, and finally, what these moral claims mean culturally and politically. These are each vital religious subcultures, distinct forms of Protestant Christianity, though not ultimately foreign to each other. They are not the only religious subcultures in the region or nation, but they are two that are important, that make claims on the ambiguous middle of our cultural and political center. It should be clear that neither will finally "win" this center, but they will continue to influence it. One would hope that each comes to understand and recognize the truth claims of the other in order not to agree or fight, but to finally respect the differences— and, perhaps, to learn from each other.

This study for the author was an attempt to come to terms with these moral worldviews. I began by sharing some of the biases of liberals toward evangelicals. But through my own research I have come not to agree with evangelicals but to respect the power of their convictions and the perseverance by which they serve one another, their communities, and the world. Evangelicals, in this study, put their feet and their resources where their mouth is; they follow through on helping one another, their communities, and the world. They may not always do it in ways I or other liberals find "acceptable," but they do serve others. On the other hand, being a liberal Christian myself, perhaps because of my familiarity I found myself critical of liberals and their reticence and caution in making both theological truth claims and in their relative lack of political advocacy. But in time, I have come to understand their circumspection and deep commitment to process and negotiation. I do not always agree with their pace or their timidity in offending others (including the people in their pews), but I understand their reluctance. Both of these groups act in good faith, with good intentions. It is then for the reader to decide and reflect on what these moral visions mean for them. In this sense, this study is a moral project, mirroring and comparing moral worlds for readers to both see themselves more clearly and judge their own moral worldviews in the relative light of these worlds.

Notes

PROLOGUE

1. I elaborated on this question in "Is War Normal for American Evangelicals?" (Wellman 2007).

2. The Pacific Northwest was defined in a recent study of the areas' religion as Washington, Oregon, and Alaska (Killen and Silk 2004); for this study, I include Washington and Oregon only.

3. In 2004, based on two dozen interviews with evangelical clergy and lay leaders, I wrote a preliminary essay to make sense of evangelicals in the region: "The Churching of the Pacific Northwest: The Rise of Sectarian Entrepreneurs," in *The None Zone: Religion and Public Culture in the Pacific Northwest*, ed. Patricia O'Connell Killen and Mark Silk. Walnut Creek, Calif.: AltaMira, 2004.

CHAPTER I

1. John Green's survey (2004) confirms these trends in Protestantism. The recent Baylor Religion Survey—"American Piety in the Twenty-First Century: The New Insights to the Depth and Complexity of Religion in the U.S."—disputes these numbers, arguing that its survey shows that Protestant affiliation remains above the 60 percent mark, a figure arrived at in part because the Baylor study argues that 10 percent of religious "nones" in its survey name churches where they attend http://www.baylor.edu/content/services/document.php/33304.pdf.

2. Traditionally, the Assemblies of God have not emphasized this aspect of theology. Nonetheless, scholars are noticing this trend toward the

prosperity gospel in the United States and in the expansion of Pentecostalism in the Global South. See "Spirit and Power: A Ten-Country Survey of Pentecostals." The Pew Forum on Religion and Public Life (October 2006); http://pewforum.org/surveys/pentecostal/.

CHAPTER 2

1. George Barna found in 2006 that 45 percent of Americans in a random survey could be defined as "born-again Christians." They did not self-identify as such, but for Barna this means they are committed to Jesus Christ as Lord and that they believe that because they have repented of their sin, when they die they will go to heaven. Demographically, Barna estimates there are nearly 90 million born-again Americans, a higher percentage than the 31 percent in 1983. See http://www.barna.org/FlexPage .aspx?Page=BarnaUpdate&BarnaUpdateID=231. Baylor's recent estimate of 100 million born-again Americans adds legitimacy to Barna's numbers.

2. Information was drawn from the American Religious Identification Survey 2001 (Kosmin, Mayer, and Keysar 2001).

3. See "Spirit and Power: A 10-Country Survey of Pentecostals." The Pew Forum on Religion and Public Life, October 2006; http://pewforum.org/surveys/pentecostal/.

4. In a recent survey, most conservative Christians abjure such labels as evangelical, Pentecostal, or fundamentalist, settling most consistently on the "born-again" tag (Baylor Survey 2006).

5. Another important niche of evangelicalism, less well-known and the least represented in this study, are evangelicals who hold conservative social values but are political pacifists (Kniss 1997). They tend to reject culture, in particular governmental entanglements, but as Fred Kniss has shown, these generalizations are less accurate as these congregations have moved into the mainstream evangelical subculture.

CHAPTER 3

1. Information is taken from the Center for the Study of Global Christianity at Gordon-Conwell Theological Seminary (http://www.gordonconwell.edu/ockenga/globalchristianity/) and the Billy Graham Center at Wheaton College (http://bgc .gospelcom.net/bgcadmin/aboutus.html).

2. The 2006 Baylor Survey of American religion asked respondents about their consumption of religious media. Nearly 20 percent of Americans surveyed had read Rick Warren's *The Purpose Driven Life* (2002), and many evangelicals in my study also knew Warren's work. Jim Wallis's *God's Politics: Why the Right Gets It Wrong and the Left Doesn't Get It* (2006) was read by only 1.2 percent of Americans in the Baylor survey. And despite the fact that Wallis has tried to reach out to evangelicals, only one or two evangelicals in my study knew his work. A fifth of the liberals in my study had read Wallis, reflecting the limited reach of Wallis's work to a wider evangelical audience.

CHAPTER 4

1. I use *superempirical* rather than *supernatural* because the latter implies that the spiritual or "unseen world" is distinct from the physical world; *superempirical* includes both divine powers and/or forces that are immanent and infused in the physical world and/or transcend the empirical realm (Smith, 2003, 98).

2. Exemplary of this is that the evangelical pollster George Barna has developed a restrictive sevenfold definition of "evangelical," in which there are no criteria relating to the organized church. This definition shares seven core beliefs: that faith is very important; one should share one's faith with non-Christians; Satan is real; salvation comes by grace not works; Jesus lived a sinless life; the Bible is accurate in all ways; God, who created the world and rules it today, is all-knowing and all-perfect. For Barna, this evangelical group is a subset of "born-again Christians" and tallies only 20 million American adults. See http://www.barna.org/FlexPage.aspx?Page=Topic&TopicID=17.

3. Philip Zimbardo, the well-known social psychologist, has argued: "Most of us have a tendency both to overestimate the importance of dispositional qualities and to underestimate the importance of situational qualities when trying to understand the causes of other people's behavior" (2007, 8).

4. By conflict I mean disagreement with others, short of emotional or physical injury. Violence is thought of as relational and collective action that creates injury to others, either emotionally or physically, using words and/or actions (Bromley and Melton 2002).

5. The question of individual innovation is interesting, but it does not lessen the importance of recognizing the communal context. New religions always combine the old in new ways, perhaps adding a new twist, though commensurability between religions is always present. This is disputed philosophically, but I concur with Donald Davidson's assertion that all human knowledge has a "natural history" and therefore there is no private knowledge per se; language always has a social causation, and thus religions are natural and public phenomena, and in the end knowable (Davidson 1999).

6. In my essay with Kyoko Tokuno, "Is Religious Violence Inevitable" (2004), we show that none of the mainstream academic definitions in the twentieth century have accounted for conflict or violence as a critical aspect of religion. Hector Avalos in *Fighting Words: The Origins of Religious Violence* (2005) has taken this point further by arguing that religion by its nature as an "invented scarce resource" is inherently violent.

CHAPTER 5

1. The Southern Crossroads is made up of the region that includes Missouri, Arkansas, Louisiana, Texas, and Oklahoma; see Lindsey and Silk 2005.

CHAPTER 6

1. The significance tests are descriptive and exploratory, rather than for inferential purposes.

CHAPTER 7

1. This is in contrast to Gallagher's assertion (2003) that evangelicals use various tools of the evangelical ideology to adapt and make cultural accommodations. In my analysis, moral worldviews are not substituted easily; in fact, moral worldviews are enormously durable even in diverse cultural contexts (Wellman and Keyes 2007).

2. Analogies are never perfect and this is true of mine. There is no core in an onion. But this makes the convenient point that these moral worldviews are not ontologically given and thus I avoid an essentialist claim by using a vegetable—the onion—that has no core.

3. Brian Stanley, after a cultural critique of how Christian missionaries carry Western cultural baggage, argues in a parallel way to PNW missionaries that there are "absolute values of the kingdom of God within that particular cultural context," which must be brought to bear by missionaries (1990, 173).

4. This point was confirmed in Christian Smith's *Christian America? What Evangelicals Really Want* (2000).

5. The March 22, 2007, Pew Research Center study "Trends in Political Values and Core Attitudes: 1987–2007" leads with the line that the political landscape is more favorable to Democrats, particularly on attitudes toward gay rights. See http://people-press.org/reports/display.php3?ReportID=312.

6. The Confession of 1967 puts it this way: "The one sufficient revelation of God is Jesus Christ, the Word of God incarnate, to whom the Holy Spirit bears unique and authoritative witness through the Holy Scriptures, which are received and obeyed as the word of God written."

CHAPTER 8

1. See Lawrence Iannaccone and Jonathan Klick's "Spiritual Capital: Introduction and Literature Review." http://www.metanexus.net/spiritual_capital/pdf/review.pdf. The authors introduce the idea of spiritual capital in relation to the literature on social, human, and religious capital. Human capital is defined as resources (for individuals and groups) that evolve most fully in communal networks, and in the case of religious capital, churches. Thus, human capital has the effect of increasing civic participation and general well-being (Coleman 1988). Iannaccone and Klick relate human and religious capital and cite Robert Putnam to underscore the empirical connection: "[Faith] communities in which people worship together are arguably the single most important repository of social capital in America" (Putnam 2000).

2. I am aware that there are some religions, and perhaps some forms of religion within certain ethnic contexts, that may or may not make "universal" claims about their faith. Japanese culture generally, and their religions in particular, tend to be parochial as far as their national or religious claims go. Not all should be like the Japanese (or perhaps can be); multiple religions are validated and useful. I would argue, however, even within this more complicated cultural mix truth claims are made, even though limited in scope (Eisentadt 1996).

3. The recent report "The Spiritual Lives of College Students: A National Study of College Student's Search for Meaning and Purpose" shows extraordinary levels of interest (80 percent in each category) in spirituality, attendance at religious services, and ongoing discussions about these issues. See "Spirituality in Higher Education," Higher Education Research Institute, Graduate School of Education and Information Studies, University of California, Los Angeles, at http://www.spirituality.ucla.edu/spirituality/reports/FINAL%20REPORT.pdf.

CHAPTER 9

1. Lynne Baab (2007), using a national sample of Web sites from evangelical, liberal, and emergent Protestant congregations, came up with similar results to my sample of PNW liberal and evangelical congregations.

CHAPTER 10

1. National data back up my own findings that American religious conservatives lead in financial charity as well as volunteerism. Religious liberals are close behind, but secular liberals trail badly, underscoring the finding that religious worldviews mobilize charitable giving not only to religious groups but to secular nonprofits as well (Brooks 2006).

2. See Joel A. Carpenter and W. R. Shenk, *Earthen Vessels: American Evangelicals and Foreign Missions, 1880–1980* (1990) for the full story.

3. The Center for the Study of Global Christianity at Gordon-Conwell Theological Seminary (http://www.gordonconwell.edu/ockenga/globalchristianity/) is quite helpful in determining this figure, along with the Billy Graham Center at Wheaton College (http://bgc.gospelcom.net/bgcadmin/aboutus.html).

4. This assumption was based in part on data that indicated that the strong correspondence between evangelical Christianity and conservative politics in America is not common to evangelical movements abroad (Freston 2001). David Bebbington (1997) argues that Canadian evangelicals, while still opposing abortion, work on behalf of a number of socially progressive and liberal issues such as economic fairness and social improvement. In addition, the missionaries in the study often said that while American evangelicals tend to be politically conservative, evangelicals in other nations are not (Demerath 2003; Jenkins 2003; Reimer 2003).

5. This is not a romantic projection. David Myers (2000) shows that once basic necessities of survival are provided, there is no statistical correspondence between wealth and happiness both on a national level (comparing developed and developing nations) or on an individual level (comparing rich and poor individuals in the United States).

6. It can be said that evangelicals consistently overrate the power of personal agency in relation to systems, and underestimate the tendency of systems to shape and even determine human moral behavior (Zimbardo 2007).

7. See the Pew Survey that gives demographic evidence about the enormous success of the Pentecostal and charismatic movement in the southern hemisphere,

"Spirit and Power: A Ten-Country Survey of Pentecostals." The Pew Forum on Religion and Public Life (October 2006); http://pewforum.org/surveys/pentecostal/.

CHAPTER 11

1. A 2002 survey of 350 evangelical leaders by the Ethics and Public Policy Center found that 70 percent agreed that Islam "is a religion of violence," and that 59 percent thought the United States should use military force against Iraq; 19 percent were against the use of military force.

2. Tom Sine, an evangelical Episcopalian and a rare critic of political conservatism in this group, has written on the need to transcend the secular left and the religious right when it comes to cultural, political, and moral statements. See "Searching for Sanity in America's Culture Wars: Unpacking the Assumptions of the Politically Correct Christian Left and the Religious Right." Mustard Seed Associates, www .msainfo.org. Moreover, a recent article in the *New York Time Magazine* reported that Bill Hybels, the pastor of Willow Creek Church and the leader of the Willow Creek Association that has a membership of more than twelve thousand evangelical churches, preached a sermon on the eve of the Iraq invasion, entitled "Why War?" "Laying out three approaches to war—realism, just-war theory and pacifism—he implored members of his congregation to re-examine their own thinking and then try to square it with the Bible. In the process, he left little doubt about where he personally stood. He called himself a pacifist" ("The Evangelical Crackup," David Kirkpatrick, October 28, 2007).

3. See the Pew Research Center, June 4, 2007, http://people-press.org/reports/display.php3?ReportID=334.

4. Exemplary of this dissent are the two open letters sent by faculty, students, alumni, and friends of the evangelically oriented Calvin College to President Bush preceding his commencement address there on May 21, 2005. They criticize the president for launching the war in Iraq, for neglecting the poor to favor the rich, and for not taking care of the environment. See http://www.commondreams.org/headlines05/0523-08.htm and http://www.mediamouse.org/news/calvin_students_working_on_bush_.php.

5. A similar strong relationship is found among white evangelicals in national surveys, particularly those in the "traditionalist" camp of evangelical, mainline, and Catholic groups; all of them share the evangelical moral worldview and identify as Republicans by 70, 59, and 57 percent, respectively, representing nearly a quarter of the U.S. adult population (Green 2004, 3).

CHAPTER 12

1. It seems every group in America complains about social oppression. But in fact, through surveys it has been shown that atheists receive the lowest overall status ratings from the general U.S. populace. Indeed, it is by a large margin that atheists are rejected, for instance, as candidates for public office—by a margin nearly twice as large as homosexuals (Edgell, Gerteis, and Hartmann 2006).

Bibliography

Ammerman, Nancy T. 1997. *Congregation and Community*. New Brunswick, N.J.: Rutgers University Press.

———. 2005. *Pillars of Faith: American Congregations and Their Partners*. Berkeley and Los Angeles: University of California Press.

Asad, Talal. 1993. *Genealogies of Religion: Discipline and Reasons of Power in Christianity and Islam*. Baltimore: John Hopkins University Press.

Avalos, Hector. 2005. *Fighting Words: The Origins of Religious Violence*. Amherst, NY.: Prometheus.

Baab, Lynne. 2007. *The Future Church: Identity and Persuasion in Congregational Websites*. PhD diss., University of Washington.

Baltzell, E. Digby. 1964. *The Protestant Establishment: Aristocracy and Caste in America*. New Haven, Conn.: Yale University Press.

Baylor Religion Survey, 2006. "American Piety in the Twenty-First Century: The New Insights to the Depth and Complexity of Religion in the US." http://www.baylor.edu/content/services/document.php/33304 .pdf. Accessed October 22, 2006.

Bebbington, David. 1989. *Evangelicalism in Britain: A History from the 1730s to the 1980s*. London: Unwin Hyman.

———. 1997. "Canadian Evangelicalism: A View from Britain." In *Aspects of the Canadian Evangelical Experience*, ed. G. A. Rawlyk. Montreal: McGill-Queens University Press, 38–54.

Berger, Peter L. 1961. *The Noise of Solemn Assemblies: Christian Commitment and the Religious Establishment in America*. Garden City, N.J.: Doubleday.

———. 1969. *The Sacred Canopy: Elements of a Sociological Theory of Religion*. Garden City, N.Y.: Doubleday.

———. 1999. *The Desecularization of the World: Resurgent Religion and World Politics*. Grand Rapids, Mich.: Eerdmans.

Bonhoeffer, Dietrich. 1949. *The Cost of Discipleship.* New York: Macmillan.

Boyer, Paul. 1992. *When Time Shall Be No More: Prophecy Belief in Modern American Culture.* Cambridge: Harvard University Press.

Borg, Marcus J. 2003. *The Heart of Christianity: Rediscovering a Life of Faith.* San Francisco: HarperSanFrancisco.

Bromley, David G., and J. Gordon Melton, eds. 2002. *Cults, Religion and Violence.* Cambridge: Cambridge University Press.

Brooks, Arthur C. 2006. *Who Really Cares: America's Charity Divide: Who Gives, Who Doesn't, and Why It Matters.* New York: Basic.

Browning, Don S. 2000. *From Culture War to Common Ground.* 2nd ed. Louisville, Ky.: Westminster John Knox.

Bruce, Steve. 2003. *Politics and Religion.* Cambridge: Polity.

Bucy, E. P. 2004. Interactivity in Society: Locating an Elusive Concept. *The Information Society* 20:375–85.

Carpenter, Joel A. 1997. *Revive Us Again: The Reawakening of American Fundamentalism.* New York: Oxford University Press.

Carpenter, Joel A., and W. R. Shenk. 1990. *Earthen Vessels: American Evangelicals and Foreign Missions, 1880–1980.* Grand Rapids, Mich.: Eerdmans.

Cnaan, Ram. 2002. *The Invisible Caring Hand: American Congregations and the Provision of Welfare.* New York: NYU Press.

Coleman, James S. 1988. "Social Capital in the Creation of Human Capital." *American Journal of Sociology* 94:S95–S120.

Copley, Antony. 1997. *Religions in Conflict: Ideology, Cultural Contact, and Conversion in Late-Colonial India.* Delhi: Oxford University Press.

Coser, Lewis. 1956. *The Function of Social Conflict.* New York: Free.

Crapanzano, Vincent. 2000. *Serving the Word: Literalism in America from the Pulpit and the Bench.* New York: New.

Crossan, John Dominic. 1992. *The Historical Jesus: The Life of a Mediterranean Jewish Peasant.*San Francisco: HarperSanFrancisco.

Davidson, Donald. 1999. "The Myth of the Subjective." In *Language, Truth, and Religious Belief: Studies in Twentieth-Century Theory and Method in Religion,* ed. Nancy K. Frankenberry and Hans H. Penner. Atlanta: American Academy of Religion.

Demareth, N. J. 2003. *Crossing the Gods: Worldly Religions and Worldly Politics.* New Brunswick, N.J.: Rutgers University Press.

Dochuk, Darren. 2005. *From Bible Belt to Sunbelt: Plain Folk Religion, Grassroots Politics and the Southernization of Southern California.* PhD diss., University of Notre Dame.

Domke, David. 2004. *God Willing? Political Fundamentalism in the White House, the "War on Terror," and the Echoing Press.* London: Pluto.

Domke, David, and Kevin Coe. 2007. *The God Strategy: How Religion Became a Political Weapon in America.* New York: Oxford University Press.

Edgell, Penny, Joseph Gerteis, and Douglas Hartmann. 2006. "Atheists as "Other": Moral Boundaries and Cultural Membership in American Society." *American Sociological Review* 71 (April): 211–34.

Eisenstadt, S. N. 1996. *Japanese Civilization: A Comparative View.* Chicago: University of Chicago Press.

Ellingson, Stephen. 2007. *The Megachurch and the Mainline: Remaking Religious Tradition in the Twenty-First Century.* Chicago: University of Chicago Press.

Emerson, Michael O., and Christian Smith. 2000. *Divided by Faith: Evangelical Religion and the Problem of Race in America.* Oxford: Oxford University Press.

Evans, Christopher H. 2004. *The Kingdom Is Always But Coming: A Life of Walter Rauschenbusch.* Grand Rapids, Mich.: Eerdmans.

Finke, Roger, and Rodney Stark. 1992. *The Churching of America 1776–1990: Winners and Losers in Our Religious Economy.* New Brunswick: N.J.: Rutgers University Press.

Fleishman, Joel. 2007. *The Foundation: A Great American Secret: How Private Wealth is Changing the World.* New York: PublicAffairs.

Fogel, Robert William. 2000. *The Fourth Great Awakening and the Future of Egalitarianism.* Chicago: University of Chicago Press.

Frank, Thomas. 2004. *What's the Matter with Kansas? How Conservatives Won the Heart of America.* New York: Metropolitan.

Frankena, William K. 1973. *Ethics.* 2nd ed. Englewood Cliffs, N.J.: Prentice-Hall.

Freston, Paul. 2001. *Evangelicals and Politics in Asia, Africa and Latin America.* Cambridge: Cambridge University Press.

Gagnon, Robert A. J. 2002. *The Bible and Homosexual Practice: Texts and Hermeneutics.* Nashville: Abingdon.

Gallagher, Sally K. 2003. *Evangelical Identity and Gendered Family Life.* New Brunswick, N.J.: Rutgers University Press.

Gans, Herbert J. 1988. *Middle American Individualism: The Future of a Liberal Democracy.* New York: Free.

Geertz, Clifford. 1999. "Religion as a Cultural System." In *Language, Truth, and Religious Belief: Studies in Twentieth-Century Theory and Method in Religion,* ed. Nancy K. Frankenberry and Hans H. Penner. Atlanta: American Academy of Religion.

Goldberg, Michelle. 2006. *Kingdom Coming: The Rise of Christian Nationalism.* New York: Norton.

Greeley, Andrew, and Michael Hout. 2006. *The Truth about Conservative Christians: What They Think and What They Believe.* Chicago: University of Chicago Press.

Green, John C. 2003. "Evangelical Protestants and Civic Engagement: An Overview." In *A Public Faith: Evangelicals and Civic Engagement,* ed. Michael Cromartie. Lanham, Md.: Rowman & Littlefield.

———. 2004. "American Religious Landscape and Political Attitudes: A Baseline for 2004." American Religious Landscapes and Political Attitudes, The Pew Forum on Religion and Public Life, http://pewforum.org/docs/index.php?DocID=55.

Hadaway, C. Kirk, and David A. Roozen. 1995. *Rerouting the Protestant Mainstream.* Nashville: Abingdon.

Hadden, Jeffrey K. 1969. *The Gathering Storm in the Churches*. Garden City, N.Y.: Doubleday.

Hammond, Phillip E. 1992. *Religion and Personal Autonomy: The Third Disestablishment in America*. Columbia: University of South Carolina Press.

Handy, Robert T. 1984. *A Christian America: Protestant Hopes and Historical Realities*. New York: Oxford University Press.

Harvey, Paul. 2005. *Freedom's Coming: Religious Culture and Shaping of the South from the Civil War through the Civil Rights Era*. Chapel Hill: University of North Carolina Press.

Hatch, Nathan O. 1989. *The Democratization of American Christianity*. New Haven, Conn.: Yale University Press.

Hays, Richard B. 1996. *The Moral Vision of the New Testament: Community, Cross, New Creation, a Contemporary Introduction to New Testament Ethics*. San Francisco: HarperSanFrancisco.

Hedges, Chris. 2007. *American Fascists: The Christian Right and the War on America*. New York: Free.

Hertzke, Allen D. 2004. *Freeing God's Children: The Unlikely Alliance for Global Human Rights*. Lanham, Md.: Rowman & Littlefield.

Hoge, Dean R., Benton Johnson, and Donald A. Luidens. 1993. "Determinants of Church Involvement of Young Adults Who Grew Up in Presbyterian Churches." *Journal for the Scientific Study of Religion* 32 (September): 242–55.

———. 1994. *Vanishing Boundaries: The Religion of Mainline Protestant Baby Boomers*. Louisville, Ky.: Westminster John Knox.

Hout, Michael, Andrew Greeley, and Melissa J. Wilde. 2001. "The Demographic Imperative in Religious Change in the United States." *The American Journal of Sociology* 107 (2) (September): 468–500.

Hughes, Richard T. 2003. *Myths America Lives By*. Urbana: University of Illinois Press.

Hunter, James Davison. 1987. *Evangelicalism: The Coming Generation*. Chicago: University of Chicago Press.

Hutchison, William R. 1989. *Between the Times*. Cambridge: Cambridge University Press.

Iannaccone, Laurence R. 1994. "Why Strict Churches Are Strong." *American Journal of Sociology* 99 (5): 1180–1211.

Jacobsen, Douglas, and William Vance Trolinger Jr. 1998. *Re-forming the Center: American Protestantism, 1900 to the Present*. Grand Rapids, Mich.: Eerdmans.

James, William. 1982. *The Varieties of Religious Experience: A Study in Human Nature*, ed. Martin E. Marty. New York: Penguin.

Jenkins, Philip. 2003. *The Next Christendom: The Coming of Global Christianity*. New York: Oxford University Press.

Kant, Immanuel. 1960. *Religion Within the Limits of Reason Alone*. Trans. Theodore M. Greene and Hoyt H. Hudson. New York: Harper Torchbooks.

Kellstedt, Lyman A., and John C. Green. 2003. "The Politics of the Willow Creek Association Pastors." *Journal for the Scientific Study of Religion* 42 (4):547–61.

Killen, Patricia O'Connell, and Mark A. Shibley. 2004. "Surveying the Religious Landscape: Historical Trends and Current Patterns in Oregon, Washington, and Alaska." In *Religion and Public Life in the Pacific Northwest: The None Zone,* ed. Patricia O'ConnellKillen and Mark Silk. Walnut Creek, Calif.: AltaMira.

Killen, Patricia O'Connell, and Mark Silk, eds. 2004. *Religion and Public Life in the Pacific Northwest: The None Zone.* Walnut Creek, Calif.: AltaMira.

Kniss, Fred. 1997. "Culture Wars(?): Remapping the Battleground." In *Cultural Wars in American Politics: Critical Reviews of a Popular Myth,* ed. Rhys H. Williams. New York: Aldine de Gruyter.

Korten, David. 1995. *When Corporations Rule the World.* San Francisco: Berrett-Koehler.

Kosmin, Barry A., Egon Mayer, and Ariela Keysar. 2001. *American Religious Identification Survey.* New York: The Graduate Center of the City University of New York.

Lakoff, George. 1996. *Moral Politics: How Liberals and Conservatives Think.* Chicago: University of Chicago Press.

Lawrence, Bruce B. 1995. *Defenders of God: The Fundamentalist Revolt against the Modern Age.* Columbia: University of South Carolina Press.

Lindsay, D. Michael. 2007. *Faith in the Halls of Power: How Evangelicals Joined the American Elite.* New York: Oxford University Press.

Lindsey, William, and Mark Silk eds. 2005. *Religion & Public Life in the Southern Crossroads: Showdown States.* Walnut Creek, Calif.: AltaMira.

Lipset, Seymour M. 1960. *Political Man: The Social Bases of Politics.* New York: Doubleday.

Loveland, Anne C. 1996. *American Evangelicals and the U.S. Military, 1942–1993.* Baton Rouge: Louisiana State University Press.

Lunch, William M. 2003. "The Christian Right in the Northwest: Two Decades of Frustration in Oregon and Washington." In *Marching Toward the Millennium: The Christian Right in the States 1980–2000,* ed. by John C. Green, Mark J. Rozell, and Clyde Wilcox. Georgetown University Press.

Luckmann, Thomas. 1967. *The Invisible Religion: The Problem of Religion in Modern Society.* New York: MacMillan.

Marsden, George M. 1982. *Fundamentalism and American Culture: The Shaping of Twentieth-century Evangelicalism, 1870–1925.* Oxford: Oxford University Press.

———. 2006. "The Sword of the Lord: How 'Otherworldly' Fundamentalism Became a Political Power." *Books and Culture: A Christian Review,* http://www.christianity today.com/bc/2006/002/3.10.html.

Martin, David. 2005. *On Secularization: Towards a Revised General Theory.* London: Ashgate.

Martin, William. 1999. "The Christian Right and American Foreign Policy." *Foreign Policy* 114:66–80.

Miller, Donald E. 1997. *Reinventing American Protestantism: Christianity in the New Millennium.* Berkeley and Los Angeles: University of California Press.

Myers, David G. 2000. *The American Paradox: Spiritual Hunger in an Age of Plenty.* New Haven, Conn.: Yale University Press.

Niebuhr, H. Richard. 1951. *Christ and Culture*. New York: Harper & Row.

————. 1975. *The Social Sources of Denominationalism*. New York: Peter Smith. (Orig. pub. 1929.)

Noll, Mark A. 2001. *American Evangelical Christianity: An Introduction*. Oxford: Blackwell.

————. 2006. *The Civil War as a Theological Crisis*. Chapel Hill: University of North Carolina Press.

Putnam, Robert D. 2000. *Bowling Alone: The Collapse and Revival of American Community*. New York: Simon and Schuster.

Reimer, Sam. 2003. *Evangelicals and the Continental Divide: The Conservative Protestant Subculture in Canada and the United States*. Montreal: McGill-Queen's University Press.

Rieff, Philip. 2007. *Charisma: The Gift of Grace, and How It Has Been Taken Away from Us*. New York: Pantheon.

Riesebrodt, Martin. 1993. *Pious Passion: The Emergence of Modern Fundamentalism in the United States and Iran*. Berkeley and Los Angeles: University of California Press.

Robert, Dana L. 2002. *Gospel Bearers, Gender Barriers: Missionary Women in the Twentieth Century*. New York: Orbis.

Rogers, Jack. 2005. *Jesus, the Bible, and Homosexuality: Explode the Myths, Heal the Church*. Louisville, Ky. Westminster John Knox.

Roof, Wade Clark, and William McKinney. 1987. *American Mainline Religion: Its Changing Shape and Future*. New Brunswick, N.J.: Rutgers University Press.

Sargeant, Kimon Howland. 2000. *Seeker Churches: Promoting Traditional Religion in a Nontraditional Way*. New Brunswick, NJ.: Rutgers University Press.

Schleiermacher, Friedrich. 1988. *On Religion: Speeches to Its Cultured Despisers*. Trans. Richard Crouter. Cambridge: Cambridge University Press.

Schlesinger, Arthur. 1997. *The Vital Center: The Politics of Freedom*. New Edition. New Brunswick, N.J.: Transaction. (Orig. pub. 1949.)

Sharlet, Jeff. 2005. "Soldiers of Christ: Inside America's Most Powerful Megachurch." *Harpers Magazine*, May.

Shibley, Mark A. 2004. "Secular but Spiritual in the Pacific Northwest." In *Religion and Public Life in the Pacific Northwest: The None Zone*. Ed. Patricia O'Connell Killen and Mark Silk. Walnut Creek, Calif.: AltaMira.

————. "Sacred Nature: Earth-based Spirituality as Popular Religion in the Secular Northwest." Unpublished manuscript.

Sider-Rose, Michael J. 2000. "Through Civil Rights and the Christian Right: Moody Bible Institute and the Diversity of Evangelical Politics." *Mid-America: An Historical Review* 82 (3): 295–323.

Smith, Christian. 1998. *American Evangelicalism: Embattled and Thriving*. Chicago: University of Chicago Press.

————. 2000. *Christian America? What Evangelicals Really Want*. Berkeley and Los Angeles: University of California Press.

————. 2003. *Moral, Believing Animals: Human Personhood and Culture*. Oxford: Oxford University Press.

Smith, Christian, and Melinda Lundguist Denton. 2005. *Soul Searching: The Religious and Spiritual Lives of American Teenagers*. New York: Oxford University Press.

Smith, Tom W., and Seokho Kim. 2004. "The Vanishing Protestant Majority." National Opinion Research Center, University of Chicago. GSS Social Change Report No. 49.

Sohn, D., and B. Lee. 2005. Dimensions of Interactivity: Differential Effects of Social and Psychological Factors. *Journal of Computer Mediated Communication*, 10 (3), http://jcmc.indiana.edu.offcampus.lib.washington.edu/vol10/issue3/sohn.html.

Spong, John Shelby. 1992. *Rescuing the Bible from Fundamentalism: A Bishop Rethinks the Meaning of Scripture*. San Francisco: HarperSanFrancisco.

Stanley, Brian. 1990. *The Bible and the Flag: Protestant Missions and British Imperialism in the Nineteenth and Twentieth Centuries*. Leicester, United Kingdom: Apollos.

Stark, Rodney. 1996. *The Rise of Christianity: How the Obscure, Marginal, Jesus Movement Became the Dominant Religious Force*. Princeton, N.J.: Princeton University Press.

Stark, Rodney, and Roger Finke. 2000. *Acts of Faith: Explaining the Human Side of Religion*. Berkeley and Los Angeles: University of California Press.

Statistical Abstract of the United States, U.S. Census Bureau, Net Domestic Migration. 2000.

Stromer-Galley, J. 2004. Interactivity-as-Product and Interactivity-as-Process. *The Information Society* 20:393–96.

Stromer-Galley, J., and K. Foot. 2002. Citizen Perceptions of Online Interaction and Implications for Political Campaign Communication. *Journal of Computer Mediated Communication* 8 (1). http://jcmc.indiana.edu.offcampus.lib.washington.edu/vol8/issue1/stromerandfoot.html.

Thumma, Scott and Dave Travis. 2007. *Beyond Megachurch Myths: What We Can Learn from America's Largest Churches*. San Francisco, CA: Jossey-Bass.

Wacker, Grant. 2001. *Heaven Below: Early Pentecostals and American Culture*. Cambridge, Mass.: Harvard University Press.

Wallis, Jim. 2006. *God's Politics: Why the Right Gets It Wrong and the Left Doesn't Get It*. San Francisco: HarperSanFrancisco.

Ward, W. R. 1992. *The Protestant Evangelical Awakening*. Cambridge: Cambridge University Press.

Warner, R. Stephen. 1988. *New Wine in Old Wineskins: Evangelicals and Liberals in a Small-Town Church*. Berkeley and Los Angeles: University of California Press.

Warren, Donald I. 1976. *The Radical Center: Middle Americans and the Politics of Alienation*. Notre Dame, Ind.: University of Notre Dame Press.

Warren, Rick. 2002. *The Purpose Driven Life*. Grand Rapids, Mich.: Zondervan.

Weber, Max. 1946. "The Protestant Sects and the Spirit of Capitalism." In *From Max Weber: Essays in Sociology*, ed. H. H. Gerth and C. Wright Mills. New York: Oxford University Press.

————. 1975. *The Theory of Social and Economic Organization.* Trans. A. M. Henderson and Talcott Parsons. New York: Oxford University Press. (Orig. pub. 1947.)

Wellman, James K. Jr. 1999a. Introduction to "The Debate Over Homosexual Ordination: Subcultural Identity Theory in American Religious Organizations." *Review of Religious Research* 41:184–206.

————. 1999b. *The Gold Coast Church and the Ghetto: Christ and Culture in Mainline Protestantism.* Chicago: University of Illinois Press.

————. 2002. "Religion without a Net: Strictness in the Religious Practices of West Coast Urban Liberal Christian Congregations." *Review of Religious Research* 44 (2): 184–99.

Wellman, James K., Jr., and Kyoko Tokuno. 2004. "Is Religious Violence Inevitable?" *Journal for the Scientific Study of Religion,* 43:3, 291–96.

Wellman, James K., Jr. 2004. "The Churching of the Pacific Northwest: The Rise of Sectarian Entrepreneurs." In *The None Zone: Religion and Public Culture in the Pacific Northwest,* ed. Patricia O'Connell Killen and Mark Silk. Walnut Creek, Calif.: AltaMira.

————. 2006. "Peeling Back the Evangelical Onion: Worldviews and World Affairs." *Review of Faith and International Affairs* (September).

————. 2007. "Is War Normal for American Evangelicals?" In *Belief and Bloodshed: Religion and Violence across Time and Tradition,* ed. James K. Wellman. Lanham, Md.: Rowman & Littlefield.

Wellman, James K. Jr., and Matthew Keyes. 2007. "Portable Politics and Durable Religion: The Moral Worldviews of American Evangelical Missionaries." In *Sociology of Religion: A Quarterly Review* 68:4 383–406.

Wilcox, Clyde. 2000. *Onward Christian Soldiers? The Religious Right in American Politics.* Boulder, Colo.: Westview.

Wilcox, Clyde, Matthew Debell, and Lee Sigelman. 1999. "The Second Coming of the New Christian Right: Patterns of Popular Support in 1984 and 1996." *Social Science Quarterly* 80 (1): 181–93.

Williams, Rhys H. 1996. "Religion as Political Resource: Culture and Ideology." *Journal of the Scientific of Religion* 35 (4): 368–78.

————, ed. 1997. *Culture Wars in American Politics: Critical Reviews of a Popular Myth.* New York: Aldine De Gruyter.

Winter, Gibson. 1961. *The Suburban Captivity of the Churches: An Analysis of Protestant Responsibility.* Garden City, N.Y.: Doubleday.

Wolfe, Alan. 2003. *The Transformation of American Religion.* New York: Free.

Wuthnow, Robert. 1988. *The Restructuring of American Religion: Society and Faith Since World War II.* Princeton, N.J.: Princeton University Press.

————. 1989. *The Struggle for America's Soul: Evangelical, Liberal, and Secularism.* Grand Rapids, Mich.: Eerdmans.

————, ed. 1996. *I Come Away Stronger: How Small Groups Are Shaping American Religion.* Grand Rapids, Mich.: Eerdmans.

————. 2003. *All in Sync: How Music and Art Are Revitalizing American Religion.* Berkeley and Los Angeles: University of California Press.

Wallis, Jim. 2006. *God's Politics: Why the Right Gets It Wrong and the Left Doesn't Get It*. San Francisco: Harpersanfrancisco.

Zimbardo, Philip. 2007. *The Lucifer Effect: Understanding How Good People Turn Evil*. New York: Random House.

Zuckerman, Alan S. 2005. *The Social Logics of Politics: Personal Networks as Contexts for Political Behavior*. Philadelphia: Temple University Press.

Index